D0718785

700040917952

Colin S. Gray is Professor of International Politics and Strategic Studies at the University of Reading. A dual UK/US citizen, he has been an adviser to the US and British governments for twenty-five years and has contributed to policy and to strategic ideas in such areas as nuclear strategy, arms control, maritime strategy, space forces and special operations forces. Dr Gray worked closely with the US ICBM, BMD and military space programmes for many years. From 1982 to 1987 he served on the President's General Advisory Committee on Arms Control and Disarmament. The author of twenty books, he has recently published a study of America's role in the world, *The Sheriff: America's Defense of the New World Order* (2003). His other books include *Modern Strategy* (1999), *The Second Nuclear Age* (1999), *Strategy for Chaos: Revolutions in Military Affairs and the Evidence of History* (2002) and *Strategy and History: Essays on Theory and Practice* (2006). *Another Bloody Century* was shortlisted for the Duke of Westminster Medal for Military Literature 2006, which is awarded by the Royal United Services Institute for Defence Studies.

ANOTHER BLOODY CENTURY

Future Warfare

COLIN S. GRAY

PHOENIX

To my daughter, Tonia. May she live in a peaceful
world, contrary to her father's expectations!

A PHOENIX PAPERBACK

First published in Great Britain in 2005
by Weidenfeld & Nicolson
This paperback edition published in 2006
by Phoenix,
an imprint of Orion Books Ltd,
Orion House, 5 Upper St Martin's Lane,
London WC2H 9EA

An Hachette UK company

10 9 8 7 6

A CIP catalogue record for this book is available from the British Library.

ISBN 978-0-3043-6734-4

Printed and bound by CPI Group (UK) Ltd, Croydon, CR0 4YY

The Orion Publishing Group's policy is to use papers that are natural,
renewable and recyclable products and made from wood grown in
sustainable forests. The logging and manufacturing processes are expected
to conform to the environmental regulations of the country of origin.

www.orionbooks.co.uk

Contents

List of Tables and Figures

List of Illustrations

Preface

Historical perspective is the only protection we have against undue capture by the concerns and fashionable ideas of today. These concerns and ideas may be valid and important for now, but they are inadequate as a basis for understanding future warfare. In this book I strive to take a long-term view of the subject, and to distinguish between its changing and unchanging features. The Cold War is barely fifteen years gone, yet already it is orthodox among both liberals and many conservatives to claim that major war between states is obsolescent or obsolete. If history is any guide, this popular view is almost certainly fallacious.

Another Bloody Century does not argue that nothing changes, only that little if anything of profound importance does. This is not exactly a majority position to hold, even among those who identify themselves as defence professionals. To illustrate my claim, I will quote from the 'Summary of the Discussion' of a conference at which I spoke in May 2004, in Washington, DC. The summarizer reported, faithfully, that

> Only one panellist, Colin Gray from the U.K., was willing to speculate about a re-emergence of great power rivalry by 2020. Thinking specifically about Russia and China, he challenged the prevalent notion of most panellists that 'decisive war between major states is rapidly moving towards history's dustbin'.

No one can know which competing view of the future of major inter-state war is the more correct. But what I do know for certain, is that today there is a near consensus among those widely held to be expert in strategic matters that war of that kind is now all but infinitely remote. I cannot disprove that speculative belief, but I hope that I provide some persuasive logical and historical grounds for promoting mental unease among its adherents.

It has been a novel challenge to write a book on future warfare. I am grateful to Penny Gardiner of Weidenfeld & Nicolson for issuing that challenge, but I will confess that on many occasions I questioned the wisdom of my acceptance. Insofar as there is a debate about future warfare, we find antagonism between culturalists and materialists, which is to say between those who emphasize ideas and those who lay stress upon machines. In one vital respect, however, most theorists and other commentators share a common world view. They see the future as the logical, linear continua-tion of today's trends. That is an error which derives both from a lack of historical perspective, and from an assumption that humankind can improve its performance in the provision of peace with security.

This book conveys an unpopular and unglamorous message. I argue that the future of warfare will be very much like its past. Future warfare will be strategic history much as usual. Of course, some periods have been bloodier than others, with the short twentieth century of 1914–91 being the bloodiest of all, both in actuality and even more in its nuclear possibil-ities. It is exceedingly difficult to write a book about a subject utterly bereft of facts. The future has not happened. No measure of skill in scenario invention, or indeed in any other methodology, can alter the reality of our ignorance. The challenge is to write a book that says worthwhile things about the future, all the while accepting the inescapable limits of our knowledge.

My approach has been to argue that although most of war's contexts are constantly changing, albeit not at constant rates, much of what is most important about war and warfare does not change at all. It so happens that although we know nothing in detail about warfare in the 2020s or 2050s, we do know an enormous amount about war and warfare per se. After all, we have access to nearly three millennia of strategic history! And it is improbable that there will be a traumatic breakpoint in history's continuities, including the continuity of its discontinuities, in the near future.

Readers will find this work holistic, strongly opinionated, but not pessimistic. I do not believe in progress in security affairs, as my principal title, *Another Bloody Century*, declares up front. I am impressed, however, by our ability to muddle through. The book has no axe to grind, beyond a commitment to advance forceful argument in praise of history as the best available, actually the only, source of education on the future. I argue some unfashionable theses on terrorism and insurgency, as well as on major interstate warfare and the limited strategic value of high technology. Similarly, to return to the claim for holism, I am at some pains to insist that there is more to war than warfare, that war is about the peace that follows, and that the succeeding peace is the breeding ground for future conflict.

I am grateful to the School of Sociology, Politics and International Relations at the University of Reading for granting me the study leave necessary to complete most of the writing of this study. In particular I would like to thank the School's Head, Dr Robert McKeever, for providing vital financial support. Two friends served nobly as honest critics. James Kiras and David Lonsdale were able both to save me from myself and achieve some vengeance for past doctoral pains. I am much in their debt. Also, I am grateful to my long-time friend, now my colleague again, Ron Barston, who made an important contribution to my argument at a vital moment. Needless to say, he is not responsible for the use that I made of his wisdom.

I must thank my very good friend and colleague, Dr Keith B. Payne of the National Institute for Public Policy in Fairfax, Virginia, for his permission to borrow the superb shortlist of fallacious scientific predictions from his 1986 book on *Strategic Defense*. Also, I wish to record my gratitude to Dr Everett C. Dolman of the Air University at Maxwell Air Force Base, Alabama, for the generosity with which he has allowed me to deploy his diagrams explaining, at least illustrating, some of the mysteries of 'orbitology'.

The arguments in the book were field-tested in a seminar held at

Oxford by Professors Hew Strachan and Adam Roberts, in a conference in Washington organized by the Center for Naval Analyses for the National Intelligence Council, and in a presentation to the Principles of War Seminar, also in Washington. I benefited from those outings; I only hope that the others attending felt the same way about my presentations.

After thirty-five years of self-indulgent, extensive and discursive foot-noting, *Another Bloody Century* is a bold experiment in parsimony. The text is supported strictly by references, with no footnotes. This is a dramatic departure for the author, who had long been in the bad habit of all but con-ducting a dialogue, even a debate, between text and footnote. As it is, the text carries the full burden of explanation.

I am tempted to provide a list of acronyms, but have decided against it for two reasons, one minor, one major. The minor reason is that the book contains few of them; the major one is that provision of such a list could give a false impression of the character of the work. On the one hand, I believe that the book is technically accurate and that it reads, as it should, as the product of a defence professional. On the other hand, *Another Bloody Century* is not a technical treatise and, on balance, is sceptical and even disrespectful of some of the ideas behind the more fashionable of contemporary acronyms.

Closer to home, I am deeply grateful to my friendly and most competent word-processing person, Barbara Watts, who, yet again, has triumphed over confusion. Even closer to home, as always I cannot express adequately my gratitude to my long-suffering family, to Valerie and Tonia, for their support and generally cheerful toleration of my bad habit of writing books.

Colin S. Gray
Wokingham, UK
March 2005

It is impossible to predict the future, and all attempts to do so in any detail appear ludicrous within a few years.

ARTHUR C. CLARKE (1962)

The past is an uncertain guide to the future, but it is the only one we have.

MAX BOOT (2002)

We judge the unknown to be unlikely.

S. DOUGLAS SMITH (2004)

Technologies come and go, but the primitive endures.

RALPH PETERS (1999)

The history of ideas obeys a law of irony. Ideas have consequences; but rarely those their authors expect or desire, and never only those. Quite often they are the opposite.

JOHN GRAY (2003)

Introduction

The Plot

Writing twenty-four hundred years ago, Plato offered the grimly cynical opinion that 'only the dead have seen the end of war'. Our bright and shiny new twenty-first century had barely begun before expert commentators were proclaiming, credibly, the appearance of the century's first war and, with some hyperbole, possibly even the eruption of the Third World War.[1] Osama bin Laden and his friends and allies plainly are determined to deny us grounds for optimism that humankind might be outgrowing its erstwhile war-prone condition. One may question whether or not the war against terror, terrorists, and terrorism, proclaimed by the United States and its friends, allies, and fellow travellers, warrants labelling as the Third World War. However, there is no doubt that the new century opened strategically with several dramatic bangs on 11 September 2001. But what did that mean? Was it a harbinger of the leading character of future strife, perhaps a signal that an era of intercivilizational, intercultural conflict had dawned?[2] Or was it merely the latest manifestation of the revolutionary phenomenon that, off and on, has plagued the modern structure of order since at least the 1870s? In 1878, Narodnaya Volya (People's Will) was founded to undertake propaganda by terroristic deed in tsarist Russia. More to the point, perhaps, even if 11 September should prove to be an accurate sign of times to come, how important is war between terrorist and counter-terrorist likely to be when viewed in the full context of future strategic history? Nearly 3,000 people were killed on 11 September, but the Third World War that was widely anticipated for forty years from 1949–89 might well have resulted in fatalities numbering in the hundreds of millions. Is the prospect of such a holocaust now safely behind us, or has it just been resting while the major players shake down and recover from the Cold War that was?

Truly it is said that nothing dates so rapidly as yesterday's tomorrow. This book can rely upon no strategic historical narrative. Since, by definition, future warfare has yet to happen, what can be said about it that will be important, interesting, and unlikely to be invalidated by tomorrow's headlines? I may be criticized by some for assuming that war has a healthy future. I address this fundamental matter in Chapter One. It is probably important to register the fact here and now that far from simply assuming that there will be future warfare, I have thought and written critically for more than thirty years about the causes of conflict, and the causes of peace also. The argument here does not proceed from an unexamined assumption that the future must resemble the past, albeit with somewhat different technology. It is not unfair to comment that although many historical developments are possible, some are far more probable than others. Future warfare has yet to occur, of course, but it is reasonable to require a substantial burden of proof-by-argument if we are to take seriously the proposition that humankind is in the process of curing itself of the habit of war. Such a transformation has not occurred in the nearly three millennia of history variably accessible to our inspection: why should it happen now?

Another transformational fallacy, though of a less fundamental kind, is that which sees not merely the character but even the nature of war radically altered by technological, social, or cultural advance. That perspective insists that new technologies, when interpreted by innovative military ideas, and when organized in the necessary mass in tailored military units, allow for transformation in the nature of war. Also, there is a view that social, even cultural, attitudes towards war, its legitimacy and its conduct, already have had a transformative impact upon its occurrence and character. Again, such a focus upon discontinuity in experience must place at a severe discount what we thought we knew from the evidence of strategic history.

Another Bloody Century is not casually dismissive of the claims, either, that warfare has no future, or, even less, that its character can alter dramatically. However, powerful evidence suggests both that warfare will long continue to be a much favoured human activity, and that that which seems new in its conduct will be balanced by the importance of features that are timeless. For example, new 'toys' will excite journalistic comment, but novel weaponry can be effective only in the right context and only in the hands of troops both well trained in its use and adequately imbued with the will to fight. It is a besetting sin of unimaginative theorists to envisage a future that really is just like today 'only more so'; in other words, a thoroughly familiar tomorrow. But it is a parallel error to predict a future for warfare that bears few hallmarks of conflict as we have known it. As a general rule, the further into the future we peer, the less confident must be our predictions. Guesses about the character and conduct of war from today to, say, 2025, should be markedly superior to our predictions for the years 2025 to 2050, let alone for the second half of the century.

The political fuel propelling societies to war over the next few years should be discernible today. Similarly, the weapons and civilian support technologies which will enable societies to fight tomorrow, either exist now or are, at least in principle, common knowledge among those who follow such things. Armed forces cannot be remade overnight. Warships and transport and combat aircraft, for example, are all expected to remain in service – barring attrition through combat and accident – for thirty or forty years or even longer. Mid-life refits and periodic modernization of the electronics for navigation, targeting, sensing and communications, mean that major combat vessels designed today and procured over, say, the next ten years, could well still be with the fleet in 2050. Designing ships with 'open architecture' means that new suites of weapons and electronics can be plugged in to replace the old. This is not to claim that future warfare is pre-programmed by yesterday's purchases of military hardware. History shows that although weapons must have a major influence on tactics, they do not mechanistically drive operations, strategy or policy. The course and outcome of war is shaped by many factors, not least the human, the cultural, and the political, in addition to the possibilities opened by machines. Indeed, recent scholarship has shown how, historically, common technology is apt to promote uncommon tactics, for reasons of differences of culture.[3]

From today's vantage point, where the inter-war period ushered in by the demise of the Soviet imperium has now come to a close, alas it seems all too safe to predict that this new century will be strategically un-remarkable. In other words, it promises to be yet another bloody era. This book treats future warfare as a continuation of the strategic historical narrative from the past, through the present, to the future. Unfortunately for orderly story-telling and analysis, however, future warfare will not be the neatly predictable linear consequence of what is visible today. History, including strategic history, is often non-linear. Trends come in bunches, interact unpredictably, and may produce a future which, though necessar-ily built on familiar material from the past, is so qualitatively different from what went before as to frustrate prediction. The huge changes in society, politics, industry, and technology of the inter-war period of 1871–1914 were well appreciated by thoughtful soldiers, especially in Germany.[4] But what did all of those changes, all of the trends, considered holistically, mean for the probable character and course of the next Great War? The soldiers of 1914 were not, as a general rule, idle or stupid. Rather, their ability to under-stand modern war was overwhelmed by too many profound developments, all acting together for a unified outcome which defied prior understand-ing. It is to the credit of at least a handful of military leaders, Helmuth von Moltke the Younger, Herbert H. Kitchener, and Joseph Joffre, for leading examples, that they anticipated a long war.[5]

Another Bloody Century treats both the likely incidence and the plausibly possible character of its subject. This breadth of concern is necessary if the book is to avoid the pornography of studying war and battle in ways innocent of political and other contexts.[6] Like Caesar's *Gaul*, the work is divided into three parts, though in this case those parts are of distinctly unequal length.

The chapters in Part One, entitled 'Basics': discuss what we do and do not know about the future, and warn of the perils in prediction; explain the vital driving, certainly shaping, influence of the political and social contexts, which addresses the point about the pornography of battle stories; explore the role of technology in war, and are at some pains to argue that the history of warfare is not synonymous with the history of technology.

The Massif Central of *Another Bloody Century* is a Part Two that ranges promiscuously, and admittedly pessimistically, over 'Warfare in the Twenty-First Century'. Its chapters present alternative as well as complementary versions of the strategic history of 1800–2100, according to different perspectives; examine the two dominant contrasting styles in warfare, regular and irregular (including terroristic), also classified by some today as symmetrical and asymmetrical; and consider the challenges posed by the sundry horrors encapsulated in the now familiar acronym, WMD, or Weapons of Mass Destruction. The final chapter in Part Two discusses the new frontiers of warfare opened up by the expanding geography of combat; most especially it considers war in outer space and cyberspace.

Last, but by no means least in significance, Part Three, the shortest of the book's divisions, confronts the pressing issues of the control of politically motivated organized violence and the challenge of providing peace with security. The discussion divides conveniently into a review of those approaches to control that are almost always exercises in futility, as contrasted with approaches which sometimes work.

The inescapable opacity of future warfare is assaulted here by five themes which bind together what could be a hopelessly disparate subject, as well as by a historically rooted master argument. The discussion has near constant reference to these themes: continuity and discontinuity in strategic history; the roles of politics and technology in shaping the character of warfare; symmetrical versus asymmetrical styles in conflict; shifting relations among the expanding range of geographically specialized forms of military power; and, last but not least, the enduring pre-eminence of the human dimension: people matter most. The several industrial and scientific revolutions of 1800 to the present (coal and iron; electricity, oil, and steel; plastics, electronics, and atomic energy; and now nanotechnology, directed energy, biotechnology and artificial intelligence) did not sideline the human being. There is no good reason to believe that technological changes in the twenty-first century will be any more potent in that regard.

This could be said to be a book with attitude. Certainly it is one with an unambiguous master argument. The five themes, and indeed everything else in these pages, provide a tough work-out for the robustness of that argument. Although some of its elements have been mentioned already, it is useful to present the full story at this early juncture, albeit in barest outline. What follows is simply the tersest of summaries. All parts of the argument are explained and debated in the appropriate places in the text, and the whole edifice of assumptions and beliefs is revisited in the concluding chapter. So, what is the master argument, including the attitude to its subject, that shapes the whole of this analysis and its conclusions?

1. War and warfare will always be with us: war is a permanent feature of the human condition.
2. War, and warfare, has an enduring, unchanging nature, but a highly variable character. It follows that history is our best, albeit incomplete, guide to the future.
3. Irregular warfare between states and non-state foes may well be the dominant form of belligerency for some years to come, but interstate war, including great power conflict, is very much alive and well. In fact, today, while most eyes are fixed on irregular forms of conflict as the supposed wave of the future, the next round in strategic history's cycle of great power antagonism is already taking shape. A possible Sino-Russian axis may be emerging that in time would pose a formidable challenge to the American notion of a desirable unipolar world order.
4. The political context is the principal, though far from sole, driver of

war's incidence and character. Above all else, warfare is political behaviour.

5. Warfare is social and cultural, as well as political and strategic, behaviour. As such it must reflect the characteristics of the communities that wage it.

6. War and warfare do not always change in an evolutionary linear fashion. Surprise is not merely possible, or even probable, it is certain.

7. Efforts to control, limit, and regulate war, and therefore warfare, by international political, legal, and normative–ethical measures and attitudes are well worth pursuing. However, the benefits from such endeavours will always be fragile, vulnerable to overturn by the commands of perceived belligerent necessity.

Each piece of the puzzle that is our framework of working assumptions requires explanation and the noting of caveats. Nonetheless, the argument and attitude of this analysis do lend themselves to concise clear statement with a lack of ambiguity. When the chapters that follow seem to muddy the water, readers may be comforted to know that the book has a powerful, overarching and binding structure of consistent argument. It is even possible that this early, pre-emptive, statement might help readers stay the course as the analysis unfolds.

PART ONE Basics

Chapter one

Back to the Future

ON WAR AND WARFARE

The social institution known as war survived the agrarian revolution of
c. 6,000 BC, and the industrial and scientific revolutions of the nineteenth
and twentieth centuries. It should be a safe prediction to expect war to
adapt, or be adapted, to whatever changes technology, economies, and
social and political mores will lay up for us in the future.

In the immediate aftermath of the Great War of 1914–18 (the one that
was intended to end all wars, we might recall sadly), both scholars and more
practical people, appalled by recent events, set out to discover why wars
happen and how they could be prevented in the future. Unfortunately, moral
outrage, sincerity of intention, and even excellence in research design could
none of them evade the authority of the rule that the impossible truly is
impossible. War is not a general problem, akin to some global disease, that
should surrender to cure by a powerful general theory. Books and other
studies on the causes of war, and wars, continue to proliferate. Many are
persuasive as far as they go, while some employ sophisticated methodologies.
It would be unjust and ungenerous to suggest that the literature on the
causes of war is entirely useless, but such a judgement does have much to
recommend it. Suffice it to say that more than eighty years of fairly intense
study have yet to offer any unambiguous advance in our understanding over

that provided by Thucydides in *c.* 400 BC. He had the Athenian delegates to Sparta in 432 explain the motives for empire with reference to the potent trinity of 'fear, honor, and interest'.[1] We shall return to that deadly trio.

If an apparently convincing general solution to the problem of war were achievable, it is probable that someone would have discovered it by now. The fact that none such has yet been promoted suggests that the scholarly campaign against war may have been thoroughly misconceived. The disease analogy is useful. Whereas individual maladies can be explored for their causes, and many can be treated and even cured, disease per se does not lend itself to direct scientific assault. So it is with wars and war.[2] Individual wars, possibly even clusters of wars that erupt in like contexts at roughly the same time, certainly have determinable origins, causes, and precipitating events. But war in general does not lend itself to useful scholarly attention. It is simply too rich a subject to be captured, let alone prospectively controlled, by the conclusions of general theory. Approached as a vital issue of public policy, war as a problem is beyond our skill to retire from political and social behaviour. So much for the bad news. The much better news is that particular wars sometimes can be prevented, while the actual conduct of warfare is almost invariably influenced by factors that limit the damage that is wrought. Of course, one has to be careful in making claims for success in the prevention of particular possible wars. Nothing can be certain until it occurs.

Some confused theorists would have us believe that war can change its nature. Let us stamp on such nonsense immediately. War is organized violence threatened or waged for political purposes. That is its nature. If the behaviour under scrutiny is other than that just defined, it is not war. The activities of terrorists can be identical to those of criminals; what distinguishes the two is the dominant motive. Over the centuries, and in different circumstances, violence has been variably organized, and what today we understand as political purposes, generally meaning the policy goals of states, have certainly shown wide cultural variety. Nonetheless, the definition of war offered here, somewhat rough and ready though it may be, when applied with common sense is fully adequate to capture all of our subject in every period, past, present, and future. As usual, Carl von Clausewitz penetrates to the heart of the matter. On the very first page of *On War*, he advises that 'war is nothing but a duel on a larger scale'. He proceeds to insist that '*war is thus an act of force to compel our enemy to do our will*'. He reminds us that 'force – that is, physical force, for moral force has no existence save as expressed in the state and the law – is thus the *means* of war; to impose our will on the enemy is its object'.[3]

Unlike many defence theorists, officials, and commentators today, who talk loosely about either military transformation or the transformation of war itself, usually without recognizing the night and day difference between the two concepts, Clausewitz was crystal clear both on the nature of war and on warfare's potential for change. Lest some readers suspect that this discussion is in danger of straying into arid academic territory, they should be reassured, if possibly surprised, to learn that what the master had to say about the nature and character of war and warfare was resoundingly correct for all time, and indeed has never been stated and explained more clearly. Clausewitz argued that war has two natures, objective and subjective.[4] The former consists of the universal elements that distinguish war from all other activities. In other words, war is war, in all periods, of all kinds, between all manner of belligerents, and regardless of the contemporary weaponry and tactics. He insisted that war was an instrument of policy (or politics); that, as noted already, it was always a duel conducted for the purpose of imposing one's will on the enemy by force; and that perennially it had a distinctive 'climate' made up of four elements: danger; exertion; uncertainty; and chance.[5] Clausewitz found war, all war that is, to be a 'remarkable trinity', composed of violence and hatred, chance and probability, and reason or policy.[6]

On the offchance that inadvertently I may have obscured what is clear in the pages of *On War*, it is useful to quote Clausewitz's summary claim on war's permanent 'objective' nature.[7] We are told that 'all wars are things of the *same* nature'. It would be difficult to misunderstand or misrepresent that statement. One might disagree with it, but that is another matter entirely. The continuing authority of Clausewitz's argument that the 'objective' nature of war does not change with technology, or indeed with anything else, is usefully underlined by the potent support it has received from Britain's leading military historian, Michael Howard – a translator of *On War*, one must hasten to add. Howard explains that:

> After all allowances have been made for historical differences, wars still resemble each other more than they resemble any other human activity. All are fought, as Clausewitz insisted, in a special element of danger and fear and confusion. In all, large bodies of men are trying to impose their will on one another by violence; and in all, events occur which are inconceivable in any other field of experience. Of course the differences brought about between one war and another by social or technological changes are immense, and an unintelligent study of military history which does not take adequate account of these changes may quite easily be more dangerous than no study at all.[8]

By way of contrast to the eternal universal realities of war (its first nature), war's subjective (or second) nature is always changing, albeit at different rates at different times. In the eighteenth century the pace of change was slow. Strategic history accelerated with the cumulative effects of the French and Industrial Revolutions. Those convulsions posed problems of comprehension for governments and their professional military advisers probably more severe than those that press upon us today. For example, what did the coming of the railway mean for defence planning and the conduct of war? Or the advent of the electric telegraph? Or the availability of canning for rations? Or the revolution in range and lethality of infantry small arms, and of artillery, the arrival of new explosives, and the perfecting of reliable machine-gun technologies? Clausewitz's theory is completely unfazed by the permanence of the impermanence of the character of war. He writes that 'we wanted to show how every age had its own kind of war, its own limiting conditions, and its own peculiar preconceptions. Each period, therefore, would have held to its own theory of war'.[9]

Why, one might ask, does all this theory about the nature, in contrast to the character, of war matter? The answer is twofold. First, despite what this chapter argues below about the awesome perils of prediction, it transpires, if Clausewitz, Howard, and this author, among many others, are correct, that we know a great deal *for certain* about future warfare. If, truly, 'all wars are things of the *same* nature', not least because of the continuity of the human dimension, then the past should have much to tell us. In fact it may be that what changes about war and warfare, although it can be very obvious and can seem even dramatic, is actually overmatched by the eternal features of war's nature. At war's sharp end, revolutionary changes in material or political conditions lose most of their meaning as candidate-defining elements. Whether one served in the front ranks of an ancient Greek phalanx, or whether one served in the US Army's First Air Cavalry division and was helicoptered into the Ia Drang Valley in November 1965, one was in acute peril of one's life. The difference between an enemy with long pikes and one with AK-47 assault rifles is a secondary matter of detail. What mattered most was the essential unity of the two experiences guaranteed by the extremity of personal danger. It may be felt to be depressing to make much of the key continuities of warfare through the centuries, indeed the millennia. However, we cannot claim that we have not been warned. Historical experience is a goldmine for the understanding of future war and warfare. This can be so because of war's unchanging nature.

The second reason why it is important to risk readers' patience and goodwill with this disquisition on war's permanent nature but changing character, is to combat a dangerous but attractive illusion. Not for the first time in modern history, and almost certainly not for the last, the seductive notion that war, major interstate war at least, is obsolete to the point of near impossibility, has gained many adherents. This view typically is not extended to cover all forms of warfare, as that would be empirically challenging in the extreme, given the mayhem in the rather extensive 'zone of turmoil' that includes much of Africa, the Middle East, Caucasia, and South Asia, *inter alia*.[10] More often than not, the unsound belief that major war is obsolete, or at least obsolescent, rests on nothing more solid than superficial trend spotting. It is scarcely a triumph of perceptive scholarship to notice that major interstate wars, even just interstate wars per se, have taken a back seat to domestic and transnational forms of conflict. As usual, the challenge lies not so much in gathering the facts, but in their

interpretation. Provided one can agree on what is meant by a *major* interstate war – a war of totally mobilized societies? nuclear war? – does its
current absence from the world scene betoken anything of huge significance for the future of warfare? After all, major interstate war appeared
almost infinitely remote in the 1920s. The all-too-Great War of 1914–18
had delegitimized the enterprise for a while. Even more to the point, by
far the most probable instigator of a possible 'Round Two' was temporarily
hors de combat, though its much reduced professional military establishment (limited to 100,000 at Versailles) was busy preparing, intelligently and
energetically, to perform better next time.[11]

Optimism and pessimism can be perilous as attitudes that undergird
policy. But of the two, optimism is apt to kill with greater certainty. Whereas
pessimism may inspire a grand strategy, and especially defence preparation, that triggers responsive countermoves abroad, optimism has the
potential to risk national safety and even international order more generally.
A security policy that rests on a pessimistic view of international behaviour
admittedly is liable to be self-confirming, as foreign powers take precau-
tionary measures in self-defence. But a policy that amounts to an investment of hope either that humankind has forsworn most forms of warfare,
or, more likely, that someone else will be on call to bear the security burden,
is in danger of functioning as a self-denying delusion. Inadequate preparation for national security may well encourage countries or movements
with roguish intentions to believe that optimists, or the 'useful idiots' (as
Lenin characterized foreigners who failed to grasp the nature and purpose
of Bolshevik power), can be bullied or worse.

Clausewitz did not argue that war is an eternal feature of the human
condition. Such a task would have exceeded his self-imposed mandate to
provide a theory of war, as well as contradicted his strong distaste for
prophecy. He believed that war and its several behaviours, including its
military conduct, or warfare, required no special justification. In Clausewitz's day, indeed for almost another hundred years, war was regarded
simply as an inescapable and presumably permanent dimension of the
human social condition. Bear in mind that war has to be a social activity;

it is activity that can only be performed in and by societies. Although there is a long and distinguished tradition of dissenting commentators on behalf of peace, there is an even longer and rather more distinguished offsetting, principally religious, tradition of theoretical and doctrinal writing in defence of the concept of the just war. In the just war canon, war is treated as an occasional regrettable necessity, sanctioned by the need for we humans to survive, and defend the right so to do, in a decidedly imperfect world.

We have been greatly chastened by the ghastly events of the century recently concluded. That century witnessed two hot world wars and a cold one (that, had it turned hot, most probably would have terminated what we know as civilization), to cite only the high (or low) points in one of history's strategically more busy periods. Now it is commonplace, not to say fashionable, to hear generic condemnation of war and no less generic praise of peace. It is inconceivable that the most senior soldier of a Western country today would say, or even think, what Field Marshal Helmuth Graf von Moltke, the victor in the wars of German unification, said in 1880:

> Eternal peace is a dream, and not even a pleasant one. War is a part of God's world order. War develops man's noblest virtues, which otherwise would slumber and die out; courage, self-denial, devotion to duty, and willingness to make sacrifices. A man never forgets his experiences in war. They increase his capability for all time to come.[12]

How times have changed. The passage of a bloody century and a quarter, and the uneven emergence of the modern and post-modern somewhat globalized world, give Moltke's all too sincere words the misleading appearance of self-parody. It is easy to forget just how recent in human history is an explicit commitment to peace. Michael Howard quotes the nineteenth-century jurist Sir Henry Maine, who observed that 'war appears to be as old as mankind, but peace is a modern invention'.[13] Howard himself advises that 'archaeological, anthropological, as well as all surviving documentary evidence indicates that war, armed conflict between organized political groups, has been the universal norm in human history'![14] That this is true can hardly be doubted. Why it should be so is a question of live interest since it must have some bearing on the likelihood of humankind turning its back on war. This author is agnostic on the issue of whether or not the human race will ever forswear war. The question is paradoxically both important yet thoroughly uninteresting.

Admittedly, some kinds of war and styles in warfare are currently out of fashion, but they may well be resting rather than declining in an irreversible obsolescence. Major interstate war, including nuclear war, indeed interstate war of any kind, fortunately is not much in favour at present. However, the conditions that have produced those facts are certain to change. When they do, the current literature which proclaims the obsolescence of 'old (regular) wars' between states, or which finds large-scale war obsolete because of the slowly growing likelihood of it having a nuclear dimension, or proclaims the mature arrival of war's largely extra-statist 'Fourth Generation', will look more than a little foolish.[15] Alas, it is the fate of optimistic prophets to be perpetually disappointed.

Many people fail to understand that one cannot sensibly have a 'peace' policy, at least not directly. Peace is not achievable as a direct object of purposeful behaviour. Instead, peace is the product of the circumstances that enable it to thrive. In common with love and happiness, peace is the result of much enabling and promoting behaviour. One must add that just as peace per se cannot be pursued intelligently, nor can war be assaulted directly, no matter how sincere and intense the motives. War is not a problem. Rather is war a hundred, perhaps a thousand, problems. Moreover, all historical experience tells us as plainly as can be that war, or war-proneness, is a condition of human society. Its popularity ebbs and flows, and ebbs again, but there is no convincing evidence extant to suggest that we are marching in virtuous lock-step towards a war-free world, at least not in any timeframe of interest to readers of this book. More optimistic views are not hard to find, however. Readers in quest of hope could do worse than sample the 'communitarian' theory advanced by the distinguished sociologist, Amitai Etzioni.[16] I believe that his grand notion of a truly global community is a forlorn hope, but I would be thrilled to be proved wrong.

We have inherited a belief in progress, a belief which our material

BACK TO THE FUTURE

triumphs appear to confirm, certainly encourage. As we explain in the next chapter, there is no doubt that, in the Western world at least, attitudes towards the acceptability and legitimacy of war most certainly have altered dramatically over the course of the past century. Snake-bitten (as the American saying goes) on the Somme, at Verdun, and by the Götter-dammerung of 1945, the powers of West–Central Europe have been convincingly debellicized. It is improbable, though, that the peaceful example of interstate relations provided by the polities of the European Union can be a practical model for other regions, notwithstanding the potency of economic globalization.

Definitions can be a blight. They are invitations to scholarly pedantry. Nonetheless, they are necessary. In the absence of definitions, we may, quite literally, not know exactly what is being talked about. It is necessary that the difference between war and warfare be flagged. War is a relation-ship between belligerents, not necessarily states. Warfare is the conduct of war, primarily, though not exclusively, by military means. The two concepts are not synonymous. There is more to war than warfare.[17] Because this book is mainly concerned with strategic topics, which is to say with matters bearing directly or indirectly on the use of force, it addresses the future of warfare rather than war. However, as must be obvious from the discussion already, the concepts of war and warfare necessarily overlap hugely. In truth, this discussion is about the future of both war and warfare. But because war in its many grisly guises is judged by the author to be a permanent blot on, and contributor to, the course of human history, warfare is deemed the more profitable subject to pursue. We know with a sad certainty that war has a healthy future. What we do not know with confidence are the forms that warfare will take.

PERILS OF PREDICTION

It is a general rule that the more detailed a prediction the more useful it should be. Unfortunately, degree of detail correlates closely with like-lihood of error. Beware of experts who have grown fond of the comforting, but highly misleading, phrase, 'the foreseeable future'. The future is not foreseeable. No one has unique access to a trustworthy crystal ball. That granted, fortunately it so happens that we are in possession of information that should yield guidance for understanding a great deal about the future, including the future of warfare. But, making sense of that information is no simple matter. In its report on the *Quadrennial Defense Review* of 2001, the US Department of Defense ventured the modest, but safe-sounding, opinion that 'we can be clear about trends, but uncertain about events'.[18] Alas, even that ambition is likely to prove unduly heroic. History is not reliably linear. The trends about which American officials are 'clear' may prove self-negating, because their recognition could spur investment in countervailing trends by others. Alternatively, those trends might meld to produce some super trend not discernible from examination of individual trends. For the future, as in the past, we cannot be confident of understanding what trends mean when they interact, as they must in matters to do with warfare. The First World War, the Second, and the virtual struggle of the East–West Cold World War, were none of them well comprehended in advance. That was the repeated case despite the clear visibility of relevant trends and, in the case of 1914–18, the pessimism of thoughtful soldiers in Germany, France, and Britain, who did not subscribe to the 'short war' illusion. Why should we expect to fare better in the twenty-first century? There is always a prophet or two who, considered in long retrospect, did 'get it right enough'. The trouble is that there is no way of knowing at the time which among the contending voices has genuine insight into the future.

Trend spotting is easy. It is the guessing as to the probable meaning and especially the consequences of trends that is the real challenge. For some examples, one can cite three civilian technologies in the nineteenth century and three in the twentieth that have had profound consequences for the conduct of war. In each case a notable leap of the imagination was needed to perceive the implications of invention. As cited already, in the nineteenth century the first appearance of railway, electric telegraph and food-canning technologies had profound consequences for the practicability of waging war on a very large scale over great distances, all the while maintaining the effective coordination and control of separate armies. In the twentieth century, the availability of easily portable radio, of television, and of the personal computer, singly and eventually in combination have helped transform both the actual conduct of war and, perhaps scarcely of lesser significance, war's social context. As recently as the 1970s, IBM, among others, did not anticipate much of a future for the personal computer. What use would it be to people? Fifty years earlier it was not uncommon to find people believing that the radio would prove to be just a passing fad. It is usually much easier to predict technological change, even to understand how it should work, than it is to comprehend what it will mean. This is as true in military as in civilian fields, to the limited degree to which the two are distinguishable.

The future of warfare is not simply a given, a course to be played out with the hands that history deals to belligerents. We make much of our own future; our beliefs about it and hopes for it can shape that future. We do not just discover the truth about future warfare as time passes. In addition, we construct that truth through the decisions we make. Future warfare can be approached in the light of the vital distinction drawn by Clausewitz, between war's 'grammar' and its policy 'logic'.[19] Both avenues must be travelled here. Future warfare viewed as grammar requires us to probe probable and possible developments in military science, with reference to how war actually could be waged. From the perspective of policy logic we need to explore official motivations to fight, though the richness of that subject has to discourage the well-meaning optimist. Violence without political context can be many things (crime, banditry, sport), cultural expression even, but it cannot be war as we have known it and chosen to define it. Future warfare cannot be discussed intelligently when innocent of political, social, and cultural contexts. But neither can it be considered prudently as an option for policy undisciplined by recognition of military constraints. War's grammar and its policy logic must be approached as mutual dependents. Strategy is a practical business. If the troops cannot do it, policy is mere vanity.

This book cannot be a work of history, not even history of the perilously misleading genre known as 'virtual'. Virtual history, like virtual love or virtual wealth, is an illusion. It is almost trivially easy to show how fine minds, steeped in experience, can make the most appalling political, strategic, and technological misjudgements about the future. For example, speaking in the House of Commons on 17 February 1792, barely a year before Britain was obliged to embark on twenty-two years of near continuous war with France, Prime Minister William Pitt (the Younger) observed, without contradiction from the floor, that 'unquestionably there never was a time in the history of this country when, from the situation in Europe, we might more reasonably expect fifteen years of peace, than we may at the present moment'.[20]

The future is full of surprises. Even statesmen who appear to have some usefully personal armlock on the course of history can be embarrassed by the non-linear flow of events. Field Marshal Paul von Hindenburg famously declaimed in 1932 that 'I have no intention whatever of making that Austrian Corporal either Minister of Defence or Chancellor of the Reich'. In his Mansion House speech in 1942, Winston Churchill shared with his audience the painfully sincere, but injudicious and ultimately despairing atavistic determination, that 'I have not become the King's First Minister in order to preside over the liquidation of the British Empire'. Pitt, Hindenburg, and Churchill, to cite but a representative smattering from a vast array of political predictions and solemnly declared intentions, were all unfortunate rather than stupid. If political prediction can be hazardous, so too can be the venturing of supposedly expert scientific predictions.

The now global media has an insatiable appetite for knowing the unknowable. Experts are invited, sometimes bullied, into offering opinions that they should not. The market for knowledge of the future is always a healthy one. Books such as this on 'future warfare' all but tempt the author to exceed his or her expertise. Although we know a great deal about the future, because of its continuities with the past (the certainty of some non-linearities duly expected) and because it has to be made from the diverse material we can observe today, we cannot predict what will happen. Many a reputation has been dented when vanity seduced its owner to venture a guess too far. To underline the importance of the point that prediction is perilous, and that as a consequence many of the popular beliefs of today needed to be regarded sceptically, I will now offer some examples of unwise prophecy from the history of science and technology. These are amusing, but they are provided because they carry a serious security warning. I am indebted to my colleague Keith B. Payne for assembling such a glittering shortlist:[21]

> Rail travel at high speed is not possible because passengers, unable to breathe, would die of asphyxia.
>
> Dr Dionysus Lardner (1793–1859)
>
> Professor of Natural Philosophy and Astronomy, University College, London

> Heavier than air flying machines are impossible.
>
> Lord Kelvin
>
> Mathematician, Physicist President of the Royal Society, c. 1895

> It is apparent to me that the possibilities of the aeroplane, which two or three years ago were thought to hold the solution to the [flying machine] problem, have been exhausted, and that we must turn elsewhere.
>
> Thomas Alva Edison, 1895

> To affirm that the aeroplane is going to 'revolutionize' naval warfare of the future is to be guilty of the wildest exaggeration.
>
> *Scientific American*, 16 July 1910

> I can accept the theory of relativity as little as I can accept the existence of atoms and other such dogmas.
>
> Ernst Mach
>
> Professor of Physics, University of Vienna, 1913

> This is the biggest fool thing we have ever done … The bomb will never go off, and I speak as an expert in explosives.
>
> Admiral William Leahy,
>
> Advising President Truman on the impracticality of the atomic bomb, 1945

Many readers will have their own favourite examples of the genre just illustrated. The point is not that it is foolish to predict. Prediction is essential. Rather the point is simply that because there is no technology or method-ology available that can negate the fact that the future has yet to happen, many predictions will prove to be wrong. The pressing challenge is for us to anticipate the future as best as we are able in ways that reduce, hopefully minimize, the risk of our committing errors in prediction that are likely to have catastrophic consequences. The necessary skill is to pursue a strategy of minimum regret. But in order to do that, first one needs to be alert to the probability that some of today's confident assumptions about the future will not survive the test of experience yet to come. In the tech-nological realm in particular, there is a popular tendency to assume that the future will be like today, only more so. Ironically, this unimaginative bias is encouraged even by so prescient a dictum as 'Moore's law' (after Gordon Moore, co-founder of Intel Corporation), which in 1979 predicted astonishingly an indefinite doubling in computing power every eighteen months. There is a universal law of diminishing returns to effort which should make one sceptical even of Moore's law. Paul Hirst has given us a most timely, not to say historically well-founded, warning against the comforting assumption of a surprise-free tomorrow. The subject of his scepticism is of particularly high relevance for the argument of this book. Hirst speculates as follows:

> It may thus be possible that after a period of rapid and major change in the next half-century military technology will begin to come up against basic limitations of information and engineering technologies. A burst of radical change followed by stasis is thus perfectly possible.[22]

To many people in the US defence community, Hirst's warning will seem absurd. However, history and common sense, resting on the law of diminishing marginal returns to effort, suggest that his words should be treated with respect. The fact that Hirst, and we here, are considering future warfare, an activity that we know must be a duel, should encourage open minds in the prediction game.

All warfare is a race between belligerents to correct the consequences of the mistaken beliefs with which they entered combat. Though subject to the astrategic discipline of budgets and social values, military preparation, particularly in a lengthy inter-war period, also expresses what a security community believes, or would like to believe, about its future. History books can offer fresh interpretations of French colonialism, or of British general-ship in the Great War, but this work locks author and reader into the same room as the responsible policymaker of today. Historians know what did not work well for the Third Reich, or for the United States in Vietnam: they have an inalienable advantage over their historical subjects. The 'culminat-ing point of victory', to borrow from Clausewitz yet again, tends to be clear only in the light of grim experience.[23] In this exploration all commentaries start equal. Historians can be expert on what went right and what went wrong on the Western Front from 1916 to 1918. But no one, repeat no one, today is expert on the remainder of the twenty-first century.

Efforts to understand and hence prepare for future warfare have to be undertaken by someone on our behalf. To cite the difficulty of peering into the future is no excuse for not trying. Our society and the global community of societies, most of them with states, have no choice other than to be interested in the future of warfare. To quote the old saying, you may not be interested in the future of warfare, but the future of warfare assuredly will be interested in you. The study of war is not simply an optional extra, even for thoroughly debellicized Europeans. Contrary to the argument of American military historian Russell F. Weigley, in his book, *The Age of Battles*, war retains a unique power of decision. He asserts that 'if its power of decision was the "one virtue" that war had ever had, then war never had any virtue'.[24] It may be true to claim that wars are won, and lost, more at the peace table than on the battlefield, but the players in the nego-tiations and political manoeuvring depend vitally upon the worth of the military hands that they hold. It is necessary to remember that 'success in battle, according to one military maxim, may not, on its own, assure the achievement of national security goals, but defeat will guarantee failure'.[25] That is a general, though not strictly universal, truth. The politicians and officials who mind the store of defence for us have to make particular decisions based only on a general knowledge, or more often, guesswork. What will warfare be like in the 2020s, 2030s, 2040s and beyond? Beyond the miniscule ranks of science fiction writers, how many people in the early 1900s could envision the air fleets and panzer divisions of the early 1940s? Most probably there are people writing today who have a clear and accurate vision of future warfare *c.* 2040, but we do not know who they are, and nor do they.

One of the several reasons why defence analysis and strategic theory mocks the 'science' in social science is because investigator and subject matter are vitally linked in a most unscientific manner. Rather like the O. J. Simpson contaminated crime scene, future warfare is in good part what we choose to make it, or elect to allow others to make it, rather than sitting out there in the decades to come just waiting for History to tap it on the shoulder. Defence decisions are taken today in order, one hopes, to reduce others' options tomorrow; it is called dissuasion and deterrence. However, to say that we help shape our own future is not to claim that we make that future. Readers are invited to select countries of especial personal interest and, as an exercise in strategic judgement, decide how much of their strategic history over the past one hundred years was truly self-guided and self-propelled. Even when we locate an extreme and persuasive case of a country that sought to make its history according to the beat of its own drummer, the typical consequence has been armed conflict shaped significantly by the efforts of other countries who resist the roles they are assigned, most especially that of compliant victim. In a complex world wherein many polities play the game of nations, personal and national will rarely triumph for long over the weight of contrary interests: witness the Third Reich for an admittedly extreme illustration.

All things are possible, though not equally probable, but there are no pressing reasons today to believe that the future of warfare is likely to register sharp discontinuities with its past. Given the fact that history has registered non-linearities, only limited confidence can be placed in that claim. Of course, contexts will change. Political, social–cultural, and technological circumstances will alter, but war will remain recognizably what it has always been; the application of organized violence for political ends. This is not to seek to minimize the influence of technological or other kinds of change. But it is to suggest that much of the future of strategic history is likely to resemble its past. Just how close that resemblance will be must depend upon our level of analysis. For example, although the tools of war have evolved radically over the centuries, for the individual combat soldier the essence of the matter is unchanged and unchanging. The military profession is unique in requiring its members to be prepared to act in the most literal peril of their lives. Similarly, the core competence of a fighting force is its skill in killing and injuring people and damaging things.[26] It was ever so. In speculating about future warfare, we have to be at least as respectful of the noun as we are of the adjective. We do not know much in detail about the future, but we know a great deal about warfare. How can that be true?

CONTINUITIES AND DISCONTINUITIES

Future strategic history, which is to say the history of the threat and use of force and its consequences for the course of events, can legitimately be viewed as a glass half empty or half full. Nearly three millennia of such history provides us with a treasure trove of strategic information, lore, and an abundance of horrors. And yet, every period is different. History cannot tell us what will happen, but in reminding us of what has occurred it must help shape our expectations, certainly the confidence with which we are armed when we peer into the future. Rather against the grain of the argument, which has been emphasizing the impact of historical non-linearities, it is necessary to recognize that strategic continuity and evolution are remarkably resilient in the face of apparent breakpoints and even revolutions. As an exercise in history and strategic imagination, we might try to fast-forward a century to guess what the twenty-first century will have produced by way of future warfare. If that is too much of a stretch, there is much to recommend a terse retrospective on the century recently concluded. Futurologists know not to aspire to anticipate the detail of the time, place, belligerents and technology of future warfare, but they should harbour the ambition to get many of the really big things right enough. Official defence planners are in exactly the same situation. They cannot know what will happen unless they plan to do it themselves. Even then, well-plotted and cunning plans may go wrong on the night, not least because war is a duel and the enemy may prove uncooperative. Defence establishments know that they cannot help but make many mistakes in their planning, but they can aspire to make mainly small, rather than large, errors.

For example, for reasons of cost, politics, and current doctrine, Britain's Royal Navy may acquire two 55,000-ton aircraft carriers after 2012 which fall some distance short of the ideal. But it is most likely that the Navy will have got a very big thing right enough. Playing deputy to the American sheriff in this new century requires the ability to conduct maritime expeditionary warfare, if needs be against coastal states that would deny access forcibly were they able. Seaborne air power is vital for the projection of force ashore as well as for the protection of the fleet. The details of provision of that maritime air will be eminently debatable, but the principle in question is persuasive beyond plausible challenge. Global strategy for a world the surface of which is 72 per cent water, and a large percentage of the population of which lives within 200 miles of the sea, mandates a strategy of sea control to enable power projection from the sea against the land. The international sheriff and its deputy must maintain a fleet balanced among its several duties, the cutting edge of which will be the ability to reach out and touch friends and foes far beyond the shoreline. The futurologist and the official defence planner inevitably will make some mistakes over the detail of desirable naval capabilities, twenty and more years into the future. Such errors are routine and to be expected. However, the kind of errors for which strategic history would not be forgiving would include, for example, a decision to abandon sea-based air power altogether.

Flexibility and adaptability are military virtues, not least because history shows that forces frequently are used for duties for which they were not originally designed. In the twentieth century, submarines intended to serve as adjuncts to the battlefleet made their truly historic mark conducting independent, and typically illegal, warfare against trade. As large fleet carriers became the new capital ships after 1942, so battleships and battle cruisers – yesterday's capital ships – found that their duties shifted from ship-to-ship surface combat to shore bombardment and fleet air defence. The principle that there is military security in diversity and in sheer quantity of assets can be hard to explain to narrow and economy-minded budgeteers who do not relate to a strategic context.[27] In military affairs it is rare for there to be only one solution to a challenge. Soldiers do not have to perform impeccably to win; they simply have to outperform a foe who is certain to fall short of military excellence in several regards. Similarly, defence policy and plans and the equipment and forces they generate do not need to be in some absolute sense correct. Instead, they need only be correct enough, bearing in mind that enemies in the future, as in the past, will have their weaknesses too.

The real or apparent discontinuities in strategic history stare at us from flickering newsreels, and now from video feeds to space vehicles servicing the global media. We have knowledge of the twentieth century that futuro-logists a century ago would dearly liked to have had. Of course, many of their predictions, based on such privileged esoteric knowledge, would not have been believed. Many a professional reputation has failed to blossom because it was constructed upon predictions and advice which, though accurate and prudent, were unfashionable, carried unacceptable implica-tions for needed action, or seemed unduly implausible to contemporaries. One can venture the perilous thought that there may be strategic, or other relevant, developments in the twenty-first century which would, so to speak, upset the game board of future warfare. This possibility brings us face to face with the somewhat imperial thesis that strategic history advances irregularly by great convulsive irregularities, or discontinuities, even non-linearities, to resort again to the popular jargon.

Scholars have labelled these breakpoints Revolutions in Military Affairs (RMAs). The argument is that from time to time a radical change occurs in the way in which war is conducted. People in the 1790s who expected the next war with France to be a replay of previous contests were to be overrun by the military consequences of the changes in French society triggered by the Revolution. Or the leaders of the somewhat Napoleonic armies of 1914 – with horse, foot, and guns – were obliged to learn the trade of modern warfare in real time under fire, as by 1918 war assumed structural aspects of combined arms combat that persisted into the 1990s and beyond. This possibility of radical discontinuity is treated in some detail in Chapter Three. Suffice it for our purpose here simply to record the basis for concern.

Strategic history does not move at a constant pace, or at least does not appear to do so. In practice, though, military evolution tends to be fairly steady. Dramatic change is highlighted only when society commands that the key be turned to set the military machine in motion, and the machine actually works. Long years of peace can incline soldiers, their political masters, and society at large, to forget that an army is maintained for the pre-eminent purpose of waging war, an activity that must entail killing people and breaking things. We are at liberty to be amazed at what changes in the activity we know collectively as warfare, and/or at what does not. Consider the bloody twentieth century. Deliberately to mix military technical with political and social contexts, future warfare for the strategic theorist and defence planner of a hundred years ago contained the following interesting items for eventual professional digestion:

- A military domain that expanded from just two geographical dimensions, the land and the surface of the sea, to include the depths of the sea, the air, space (Earth orbit, at least), and now cyberspace. So warfare became much more complicated for those who had to try to manage and execute strategic history.

- The occurrence and recurrence of no fewer than three great wars, two hot, one cold, with an ideological dimension becoming more prominent from war to war, and each progressively more total in its involvement of whole societies than was the last.

- The variably painful demise of the European colonial empires which had expanded to colour all the vacant map space available. Colonization and decolonization were not significant contributory causes of any of the three *grandes guerres,* but their course and consequences made major donations to the column of future warfare.

- The incorporation of additional geographies into the strategic realm meant that new technologies threatened established military beliefs and practices. In the twentieth century, people had to learn how to run a war economy and armed forces on oil rather than coal and horsepower. Also, mechanization, flight, submarines, electronics (radio, radar, computers), ballistic and cruise missiles, and spacecraft all had to be tamed and exploited. The development of atomic weapons in the early 1940s appeared almost as a wild card, of uncertain meaning for all forms of military power, traditional and new.

- Finally, towards the close of the twentieth century a radical change in social values affected those Western societies that earlier had compliantly and repeatedly delivered generations of infantrymen for strategic disposal by the statecraft and generalship of the day. By the 1990s they appeared unwilling to tolerate casualties on any scale even faintly reminiscent of the recent experience of total war. This is the common wisdom of our day. It is somewhat true, hence its listing here. Nonetheless, it is necessary to note that our apparently debellicized societies have not actually been asked to bear a heavy burden of casualties in defence of ultimate values. Nuclear strategy in the Cold War may seem to contradict this point. But a quite unjustifiable confidence in the reliability of mutual deterrence rendered the prospect of nuclear warfare and its staggering potential to break all historical records for casualties almost wholly unreal.

This new century will show its equivalents to the listing specified immediately above. There will be political surprises on the grand scale. For speculative examples, we can imagine – actually we observe today – a new international alignment that will pit China and Russia against the United States, while systems for space warfare are bound to come of age. By space warfare we mean warfare for the control of space, warfare in space, and warfare from space. At present, space is only militarized. Long before this century draws to a close, space will see weapons deployed also. The strategic logic is inescapable. It should not be forgotten that future warfare will comprise both the novelties of the new century and a massive carry-over from past warfare. Strategic innovations from the seventeenth, eighteenth, nineteenth and twentieth centuries are all to be found in the military institutions of today, and prospectively tomorrow. The nuclear revolution of 1945 and the nuclear era that it ushered in remain militarily authoritative today, though nuclear weapons have ceased to be the preferred instrument of the strong. In common with terrorism, with which it has a troubling synergistic relationship, the nuclear weapon has become a tool of the weak. Usable military power is non-nuclear for the most powerful of states. The point of note is that future warfare will contain many elements with which we have become long familiar. Recall, for example, that aircraft, ballistic and cruise missiles, nuclear weapons, space systems, and computers in all their military applications, have been layered on to military preparation and the conduct of war as usual. The hardware of war is constantly changing – and that is important – but it shrinks in significance when set against the continuities that bind the future to the past and present of warfare. Those continuities are made of such resilient material as politics, culture, and human nature, at least of human nature functioning in society, as it must.

Before considering briefly the continuities in strategic history that allow us to write with some confidence about future warfare, if not about future wars, a caveat about focus and point of view is all too necessary. Because of its wealth, strategic significance and cultural dynamism, the United States is wont to scoop the pool of attention when its scholars and officials contemplate future warfare. In technology, ideas, organization, and recent military experience as the sheriff for the current international order, the United States is, of course, in a class of its own.[28] There is general agreement today that the United States will not face a peer competitor in the near future. Some people identify that near future as 2015-plus, others as 2025-plus. But if we relax our understanding of what it would take to be a peer competitor militarily, and instead think grand strategically, it will not be long before a hostile bloc led by China and Russia would be more than capable of thwarting most US initiatives on behalf of global order. If by future warfare we mean the future grammar of warfare, military science, especially in its technological dimension, then there is no doubt that ours is a thoroughly American subject. The United States, at present almost uniquely, is advancing the frontier of regular military capability. This is a product of wealth and the investment of that wealth, of geopolitical responsibility willingly assumed, and of sheer momentum in innovation. However, the temporary absence of worthy 'regular' foes does pose something of a historically unusual challenge. Past surges in military effectiveness usually have been triggered by specific fears and their authors had definite, identified, enemies in mind. The military revolution currently under way in the United States, keyed technologically to the exploitation of the computer, is designed to succeed against both regular and irregular enemies. The United States today is at war with terrorism. In the words of a US Army publication, 'the most salient aspect of the current security environment is that we are a Nation and an army at war – a war unlike any we have experienced in our history'.[29] This rather indeterminate political contextual reality places a premium on flexibility and adaptability. The past century witnessed a reduction in the number of great powers from possibly five or six before the Great War (France, Germany, Russia, Britain, Austria, perhaps Italy), to two in the Cold War, down to only one today. The number of great powers was demonstrated by the Suez fiasco of 1956 to have shrunk to two, as British and French pretensions to be significant independent players were exposed beyond repair. But throughout the Cold War the major NATO allies of the United States could each field forces in all geographical environments able to stand in the line of battle with their US counterparts and perform competently, if not quite seamlessly. What has happened since the 1980s is that the enormous disparity in resources committed to military research and development between the United States and, literally, everyone else, has resulted in the superpower writing a new chapter in the ever-continuing history of military capability and effectiveness. However, a study of future warfare cannot sensibly focus only on the country that in some obvious ways is the market leader.

To present an emerging American way of war as the exemplar of future warfare would be to commit the same mistake as to confuse a new Ferrari with the future of motoring. Most people will not drive Ferraris, and most soldiers and other warriors will not pursue their deadly quarrels in ways prescribed by an American way of war. Future warfare is a catch-all net for the organized violence undertaken in the name of politics or religion; it does not necessarily refer neatly only to what appears to be the finest flowering of the military art and science of the period. A great American strategic theorist, Bernard Brodie, once wrote that 'strategic thinking ... is nothing if not pragmatic. Strategy is a "how to do it" study, a guide to accomplishing something and doing it efficiently. As in many other branches of politics, the question that matters most in strategy is: Will the idea work?'[30] Today an American style in warfare is undoubtedly the cutting edge of the future, much as Spanish, French, and German military prowess successively over nearly four hundred years set the pace for what was modern in their periods.

But most of the fighting, certainly most of the dying, in future warfare will not be done by Americans. Enemies of America who cannot afford to emulate US investment in, say, space systems, long-range air power, or networked communications, will be obliged to pursue Brodie's logic and seek strategic behaviour that works well enough, be it ever so inelegant and probably decidedly irregular. A handful of martyrs armed with box-cutters who can hijack and then command large passenger aircraft full of fuel comprise a weapon system that works. When we discuss the most modern of military capabilities, we must remember that a dominant US mode in warfare must motivate materially challenged belligerents to hunt for asymmetrical and hopefully equalizing tactics, operations and strat-egies. Furthermore, most of the military mayhem in the world of the future will be caused by organizations and people who are militarily modern only in a few respects (e.g., they may use automatic assault rifles and mobile phones). The American superpower guardian of the international order is the very embodiment of an unfolding excellence in the prospective conduct of future warfare, understood as regular battle. It is not so reliable in the conduct of war as a whole, and especially is it weak in relating its military performance to political purpose even when the performance is first-rate.[31] Furthermore, America could be strategically thwarted by regional enemies who had invested intelligently and highly selectively in tools and tactics intended to reduce the effectiveness of US military power. For example, smart mines, diesel submarines and cruise missiles, probably with some handfuls of weapons of mass destruction of modest range in the background, should not suffice to deny US military power access to a region of interest, but they just might.[32] At the very least such offsetting weapons and methods must raise the stakes for an American polity that by definition is less interested in an issue (e.g., breaking a mainland Chinese blockade of Taiwan) than is the regional foe.

It follows that the subject of future warfare must include both new developments and the adaptation of traditional military skills to new circumstances. Because this author is Anglo-American, the text may well suffer from lack of empathy for the concerns and probable experience of those from other backgrounds. If the United States could conduct air and ground operations in Central Asia in 2001–2002, an area of no previous interest to Americans, one must hesitate before asserting a limited geopolitical writ for an American way in future warfare. Nonetheless, even if we grant that for the next several decades warfare will be conducted in the shadow of the possibility of US intervention, still it is certain that most combat around the world will be waged by security communities for reasons of little interest to Americans. Future warfare is not synonymous with future American warfare.

MILITARY, LET ALONE STRATEGIC, competence cannot be gauged with high confidence without reference to the strategic context in which it is to be applied. Furthermore, if the world's outstanding military machine is sufficiently fortunate as to be exercised repeatedly only against enemies who approximate a rabble in arms, flaws in the appearance of excellence are likely to pass unnoticed. The next chapter addresses the vital matter of the political, social, and cultural contexts of future warfare. The US military unquestionably is, and should long remain, the world leader in the conduct of a regular style of warfare. That style is characterized above all else by the ability to deliver devastating firepower. There is an aspiration to excel also at decisive manoeuvre, but US ground forces lack the numbers and, to date at least, the swift mobility for true operational dexterity to become a reality. The US military machine, even when further down its impressive transformation road could be frustrated in strategic contexts wherein firepower, agile manoeuvre, and the warrior spirit are not at a premium. Contemporary events in Iraq provide textbook illustration of this caveat. As we must keep insisting, war is a duel. For reasons of policy, geography, or enemy cunning, an American military power excellent in its way, which is to say on its own preferred terms, but which is inflexible and non-adaptive to unexpected circumstances, could fail miserably. Remember Vietnam? The US Army recognizes this problem, and is taking far-reaching steps to change its doctrine and organization so as to provide a range of ways in war. Today it is an open verdict on how successful it will be.[33]

It is only prudent to assume that some future belligerents will be skilled, and perhaps lucky, in exploiting their limited strengths, even though they lack the general technical and tactical excellence of a 'transforming' American military machine. America's easy battlefield successes and victories of the 1990s and early 2000s cannot be taken as an authoritative predictor of future triumphs. The 'war after the war' in Iraq has been a sobering educator to many American analysts who were showing signs of that familiar malady, 'victory disease'. The US Army War College stated revealingly in a conference report in 2003 that America's future wars would, by and large, be conducted against 'Indians' (of native American genus!).[34] That dismissive characterization, even if not intended as such, revealed a confidence bordering on hubris that should alert us to the probability of history delivering some unpleasant surprises.

Time and again in this opening chapter, context has been claimed to be of the utmost importance. The discussion now moves on to explain and justify that claim.

Chapter two

Context, Context, Context

A WAR-PRONE FUTURE

Three sets of mutually supporting reasons ensure that warfare has a healthy future. They comprise the persisting, familiar workings of world and domestic politics; the varied and substantial attractions of war to political leaders; and some enduring features of human nature functioning in society, including its potential for exhibiting a popular belligerency. We cannot know who in the future will fight whom, when, with what, and over exactly which issues. Fortunately, though, this analysis does not stand or fall on the plausibility of speculation over second-order matters such as those. What we can provide is some robust grip upon the probable character of future warfare, in all – or at least in much – of its rich variety of possibilities. As 'location, location, location' is the central truth which unlocks the mysteries of property valuation, so 'context, context, context' decodes the origins, meaning, character and consequences of warfare. If we are broadly correct in our grasp of the contexts that comprise the relevant future, then it should follow that our expectations about future warfare, as about so much else, should also be tolerably well founded. This is not to detract from the scepticism displayed thus far towards trend analysis: trends can be reversed, indeed may be self-negating as people recognize them and strive to change them. Also, the power of contingency, even of just rank accident and incompetence, can never be dismissed entirely. Nonetheless, treatment of the contexts of future warfare, especially those referred to at the beginning of this paragraph – the political, the policy instrumental, and the human – enables the remainder of the book to proceed without the necessity of conducting constant rearguard actions against the theories of sundry well-meaning but erroneous idealists.

The rationale for this discussion was expressed with exemplary clarity by Clausewitz. 'It should be clear that war should never be thought of as *something autonomous* but always as an instrument of policy; otherwise the entire history of war would contradict us'.[1] That statement holds as firm for the twenty-first century as it did for all previous periods. Unless we recognize and accommodate in our analysis 'the multiple contexts of war', discussion of future warfare must lack all meaning.[2] Since, following Clausewitz, war cannot be approached as an autonomous activity, if it is considered bereft of context it becomes literally senseless. Unless one subscribes to the eccentric view that warfare is a form of collective madness, most suitable for study and treatment by social psychologists, it needs to be explained with reference to contexts largely external to itself. This is not to ignore the fact that the relationship between warfare and the contexts explored here is one of reciprocal influence. It is probably no exaggeration to claim that warfare, in all its dimensions, has had more influence on the course of history – ancient, mediaeval, and modern – than has any other collective human behaviour. I take no satisfaction in registering that point, or in quoting classical historian Victor Davis Hanson in its support: 'Yet battles at least alter history for centuries in a way that other events cannot.'[3]

The analysis here strives to avoid a conceptual confusion that can threaten to destroy the value of contextual discussion. Context has two meanings: it refers to that which is 'out there' and surrounds the subject of interest; but also (from the Latin root, *contextere*) it means that which weaves together.[4] In much plainer English, it is necessary to think of warfare as having political, social–cultural, technological, historical, and strategic contexts which give it meaning and character. However, in vital addition, warfare has to be thought of as an integral part of, at the least as a major shaping influence upon, those contexts. We can be sure that this new century will witness a great deal of warfare which invariably will be explicable with reference to the dynamic political context. We can also be certain that future history will be impacted to a greater or lesser degree by the anticipation and reality of warfare.

So important is war's political context that it is examined in pole position as the next section. At this early juncture in the treatment of warfare's contexts, the story confines itself simply to the registration of its magisterial significance.

The trajectory of this part of the discourse begins with the broadest of contextual perspectives, recognizing the nature of world politics, the attractions of war as an instrument of policy, and the crucially important, yet hard to corral, human factor. Subsequent sections examine in some detail warfare's political and social–cultural contexts. Exploration of the technological context for future warfare is deferred to Chapter Three, where it is considered critically and at length. It may be important to highlight a potential problem that frequently is the inadvertent and unanticipated consequence of the workings of an unduly tidy mind. It is analytically convenient to dissect our subject for distinctive political, cultural, technological, and other, examination. But the truth is that the phenomenon under study, warfare, contains and expresses all those dimensions, or contexts, all the time, and they each influence all the others. We must never lose sight of the holistic reality of future warfare, just because it is convenient to abstract particular aspects and distinguishable forms of belligerency for separate study.

War retains its unique value as an instrument of policy for regular and irregular players alike. The old saying that the resort to war is the final argument of kings remains true. For more than two hundred years war as an institution has been widely criticized on both ethical and pragmatic grounds. In the twentieth century in particular, the opinion that war does not pay was as unremarkable as it was generally unarguably true. This opinion was in sharp contrast to the attitude that helped launch the armies of Revolutionary and then Imperial France on their repeated rampages across Europe at the close of the eighteenth and beginning of the nine-teenth centuries. The costs of each war were recouped by the spoils from the next, or such at least was the intention. Few wars are launched because cost-benefit calculations indicate the strong likelihood of achievement of a large net profit. The anticipated benefits of war tend to register in the coin of such intangibles as honour, reputation, feelings of security, and simply fear of a worse future if force is not employed.

Warfare lends itself to many descriptions, but above all else it is political behaviour. Other points of view are not hard to find; they are, however, mistaken. A serious challenge to the argument advanced here, my claim that warfare is effectively a permanent dimension of human existence, has been launched by one of Britain's most gifted and popular military his-torians, John Keegan. Apparently in contradiction to a strictly Clausewitzian perspective, with its insistence upon the primacy of the political, Keegan argues that war is a cultural phenomenon. In a withering, though in my opinion thoroughly misguided, attack on Clausewitz, he offers the inter-esting thought that

> Had his [Clausewitz's] mind been furnished with just one extra intellectual
> dimension – and it was already a very sophisticated mind indeed – he might
> have been able to perceive that war embraces much more than politics: that it is
> always an expression of culture, often a determinant of cultural forms, in some
> societies the culture itself.[5]

The appropriate response to Keegan's assault on Clausewitz is, surprisingly perhaps, 'of course'. We agree strongly that warfare is an expression of culture. We happen to believe, however, that warfare, cul-turally influenced though it must be, is also, primarily, conducted for political reasons. War's cultural dimension has been greatly under-appreciated. Keegan has performed a valuable service in elevating it to high prominence for attention. But, as with many sound ideas, it is easy to take it too far. Culture is notoriously difficult to define, but we can all agree, at a minimum, that it refers to acquired or learned characteristics. Keegan is moved to suggest, misleadingly, that 'all that we need to accept is that, over the course of 4,000 years of experiment and repetition, war making has become a habit'.⁶ It has to follow that if war is basically a bad habit, albeit one of the utmost antiquity, it should yield to a change in attitude that would delegitimize it as newly unacceptable behaviour. The incentive is presented by Keegan in predictably apocalyptic terms: 'Unless we unlearn the habits we have taught ourselves, we shall not survive.'⁷

As the next section makes abundantly clear, warfare always serves purposes that can plainly, at least plausibly, be called political. Furthermore, politics, which ultimately is about power, seems certain to continue to carry warfare among its arsenal of threat and action options. The important fact that war is cultural does not diminish the logical and historical authority of the argument that war primarily is political. To describe war merely as a habit, one which needs to be given up for all our welfare, is a serious misrepresentation of the subject. Moreover, that misrepresentation might encourage fantasies of dramatic progress that would not be helpful as we try to control warfare in the future. We agree with Clausewitz that 'war is not a mere act of policy but a true political instrument, a continuation of political activity by other means. What remains peculiar to war is simply the peculiar nature of its means'.⁸ Brutal? Yes. Somewhat out of step with liberal optimism? Yes, again. Unfortunately, the great man was correct; for his day, for ours, and on the evidence of history for the future as well.

Historian Donald Kagan, on the basis of studies of wars both ancient and modern, offers an important judgement that many people will find almost counter-intuitive.

> The reader may be surprised by how small a role in the instances studied here [Peloponnesian War, Second Punic War, First and Second World Wars, Cuban Missile Crisis], and, I believe, in many other cases, considerations of practical utility and material gain, and even ambition for power itself, play in bringing on wars and how often some aspect of honour is decisive.⁹

Bearing in mind the crucial importance of people, including individuals, to our analysis, we dare not forget the personal satisfactions that can flow from organized violence. Nothing excuses terrorism, but the current fashion in self-sacrificial acts of terrorism has political, cultural–religious, and economic contexts in which it breeds.

As an act of violence involving self-sacrifice can give meaning, albeit briefly, to an otherwise apparently empty life, so organized violence, the conduct of war, remains an essential instrument of policy all but universally. Most popular criticisms of the social institution of war are thoroughly justified, save only for the regrettable fact that the option of war remains a necessity for national security and international order. This book has no brief for warfare. But there are occasions, fortunately rare for most communities, when war is judged the least bad of a short list of unattractive policy choices. Some dangerous ideas, possibly inhabiting disturbed personalities, cannot usefully be met strictly with the 'soft power' of better ideas; instead their authors and carriers need to meet the 'hard power' of the iron fist: they have to be shot. Would that this were not so, but such is the real historical context that assuredly will generate a great deal of future warfare.

Public attitudes towards war certainly have changed hugely over the course of the past century. However, the relevant cultural context for future warfare, in the Atlantic West, if not so clearly in the West European continental West, is, and is likely to remain, one that deems the use of force legitimate and in some circumstances essential. It is true that the resort to war requires a degree of public justification, and preferably international legal approval also, that is historically novel, but there is no question of war fading away through disuse as a social institution. The prospect of war being formally abolished in some foolish replay of the nonsense of the Kellogg–Briand Pact of 1928 is precisely zero. The agents of international order must be capable of imposing discipline on the agents of disorder. Sometimes, war is necessary.

The human context for our subject is as richly varied as it is basically unchanging. We should have no truck with simplistic essentialist assertions about the human race. Humans are not essentially warlike, or peace-loving, or probably anything else except security-seeking. Contrary to the academic fashion which privileges the study of security over strategy, it is the opinion of this author that the former is a notably unhelpful concept.[10] As Richard K. Betts has observed, security studies are deficient in focus and, indeed, are 'potentially boundless'.[11] Given that security can be pursued along a multitude of incompatible, as well as complementary paths, not to mention its apparent conflict with the quest for adventure and excitement, preferably vicarious, to note its authority is not to register anything very useful. The history of war is not primarily the history of weaponry; rather is it the history of the person who wields the weapon. In the sage words of Ralph Peters, 'In this age of technological miracles, our military needs to study mankind'.[12] Where optimists see hope in our humanity, pessimists, realists perhaps, judge humanity to be the root of the problem of warfare. The human context for future warfare is, alas, entirely permissive.

The human race, affiliated by state-tribe as its members like to be, universally, has shown itself capable of anything and everything. In the century just concluded it waged three great interstate wars, and the third of those – the virtual conflict that was the Cold War – could well have terminated in a bloodbath unprecedented in all historical experience. And that possibility faded only as recently as 1991 with the demise of the Soviet Union; it did not, however, fade away entirely. Nuclear wars, large and small, have joined the club of permanent horrific possibilities. If Man's inhumanity to Man is not sufficiently indicated by the argument thus far, one need only cite the repeated exercises in genocide, quasi-genocide, or, at the least, in crimes on a massive scale against helpless civilian populations. Consider the Armenian massacres of the First World War at the hands of the Turks, the Holocaust committed by Nazi Germany that surely set the standard for beastliness for the ages, the Balkan and Central African atrocities of the 1990s, and the Sudanese mass murders of the 2000s. Human beings have shown that local culture leads ethics when it comes to the politics of security.

The point is not that the human race is inherently murderous or warlike. The fact appears to be rather that we humans, given the appropriate stimuli – which is to say in the right context of politics and culture –

are capable of anything. Nothing that we know today about humanity in the future affords much, if any, confidence that evolving beliefs and values will serve as an impermeable barrier against war. We must hasten to add the caveat that the recent emergence of a global electronic mass media, especially in its visual aspects, may prove to have some cultural and political influence hostile to the exercise of organized violence. Alternatively, and more likely, the global media may transpire to be only a complication for policy and strategy, one which can be exploited as well as feared by those with deeds to hide. As a scholar has noted, the global visual media is rendering warfare a worldwide 'spectator sport', a source of vicarious excitement and even pleasure.[13]

THE POLITICAL DRIVER

The political context which has sparked and given meaning to modern war – interstate and civil, regular and irregular – is not obviously in the process of benign transformation. As today's (and tomorrow's) problems for strategy would be generically comprehensible to military leaders throughout history, so the lore of statecraft has altered remarkably little over the centuries. Religious and dynastic principles and motives have been superseded by calculations of state interest, but that is a matter only of detail. The exercise is approximately the same, as are its most vital components. It is true, as good historians and anthropologists remind us, that different cultures have somewhat different understandings of what constitutes war, winning strategies, and decisive victory, as well as who is licensed to fight. However, we need to be restrained in our enthusiasm for relativist analysis and judgement. In a series of forcefully argued books, the classical scholar, Victor Davis Hanson, has sought to demonstrate that 'the Western way of war', invented in ancient Greece, has long been the high road to military success.[14] It is important not to be unduly dazzled by Hanson's argument. After all, history records more than a handful of lethal ambushes for over-confident representatives of the Western way. Moreover, as John A. Lynn reminds us in his path-breaking cultural study of *Battle*, when assessed over two millennia and more, the Western military record is not overwhelmingly impressive.[15] Hanson's is one of those powerful theories that reads as if it ought to be true, but, on closer inspection, proves to be fatally flawed. History does not really support it. It is worth recalling the quotation from Bernard Brodie provided earlier. Strategy is a pragmatic business. Quaint culture-specific ways in warfare, and the political authority dependent upon them, do not survive in an interconnected world when they meet 'the Western way' in the unforgiving brutal shock of battle – or so the story goes. However, that Western way, with its emphasis on regular direct combat, is a standing challenge to enemies of Western powers to find modes of warfare that evade some Western strengths. Warfare inherently is competitive behaviour.

Admittedly, the political context for future warfare is constantly evolving. It is always possible, if exceedingly unlikely, that some political revolution of global domain and potency will entirely change the game of world politics as it has been played for centuries. To date, novel would-be universal religions, exciting new political ideologies, and startling techno-logical innovations have all signally failed to compel the human race to pursue its security in ways that make a sharp break with the past. If 'the war that will end war', in the words crafted by H. G. Wells on 14 August 1914, its even greater successor twenty years later, and then the atomic discovery, did not suffice to oblige humankind to change its political habits, it is difficult to see what could do so in the future. Even a threat from outer space or abrupt global climate change would not conclude our strategic history. Either would simply redirect the focus of belligerency. Some readers probably would be disinclined to engage with the discussion of future warfare were they not first convinced that the political context for such behaviour will persist. Lest there be any residual ambiguity, this author expects the context of world politics dominant over future warfare to have the following principal features:

- The world will remain one of states. The demise of the state through the corrosive influence of globalization has been much over-anticipated. The decline in the occurrence of interstate warfare does not speak to any alleged growing irrelevance of state affiliation. Those who discern in the European Union (EU) a new kind of political entity, one enabled by a decline in atavistic national affiliation, will have to temper their idealism in recognition of the growth of the EU's statelike characteristics.

- Ultimately, each state is the ward of its own court. Assistance from the institutions and procedures for global governance for peace and security, to mix platitudes, can be unreliable, or at least slow, in arriving.

- States seek to improve their security by influencing the outside world in their favour. At one extreme this rule may be seen in action with a country that has only some slight ability to motivate its neighbours to care about its well-being; it will be a marginal player in the game of nations. While at the other extreme there is the US superpower which aspires quite openly to dissuade other states from developing competitive challenges to its global influence.

War is about politics, and politics is about relative power. That statement, together with the three points listed immediately above, is so basic, and should be so familiar, as to verge on the banal. Nonetheless, no study of future warfare can be worth reading if it neglects the fundamentals of the future political context. It is only a grasp of that context that enables us to say anything of value about the warfare to come. Warfare is political behaviour, as Clausewitz taught, while in addition it is social and cultural behaviour, and it is certainly an expression of a society's level of economic, especially technological, development. However, war and warfare is only about politics. War is not *about* culture, or social organization, or technology, or indeed anything else. Similarly, the human dimension to warfare is critically significant, both with reference to particular individuals, who do make an historical difference, and to the general characteristics that we recognize as integral to our humanity. But war and its conduct is only endemic in the human condition through the filter, or mediation, of politics.

This part of the discussion risks trying readers' patience with its insistence upon some essentially simple fundamentals, because it is the most important element in the whole argument about future warfare. The claim advanced here for the primacy of politics is not merely a dutiful nod towards the classics of scholarship on statecraft. Rival schools of thought, belligerent legions of convinced commentators, let alone sharply divergent university courses and hugely distinctive book-length treatises, rest upon assumptions about the future political context. If those assumptions are ill founded, manufacture of the books that proceed on their basis is a crime against the natural environment.

Future warfare is as important a subject as it is deeply unsatisfactory. How can we study that which has yet to occur and perhaps may never happen? As we develop in the chapter on regular warfare, this seemingly philosophical question is all too real to those people in every security community who are charged with devising defence policy and conducting defence planning. Since future warfare is literally meaningless if considered outside a political framework, the challenge is to specify the framework of assumptions most likely to be proof against the surprises, and effects of such surprises, that the twenty-first century assuredly will throw our way. My answer to this challenge is to argue, with very high confidence, for the continuing authority of the basic working of politics, domestic and international. It is necessary to be obedient to the principle that one must strive to get the biggest of things right enough, so that one's errors should be confined largely to second-order matters. In that spirit, this chapter has claimed that future warfare will be the varied expression of a political context characterized by: the persistency of states as the dominant form of political organization; the enduring condition of a semi-anarchic condition to world politics, wherein self-help is the practical reality of national security; and the fact that states will seek to improve their security by shaping their international circumstances as best they are able. We have claimed, in addition, that war, and therefore warfare, will continue to have a unique utility as an instrument of policy. Furthermore, we argue that humanity is at least as much a part of the problem of war as it is of any possible solution. If pressed, and as noted already, this text also would argue that it is a grave mistake to approach war as though it were a single problem that can be solved or cured.

The focus here is on the international political context of warfare. However, it is scarcely less important to appreciate the influence of the domestic political context. Some countries need war and seek it for reasons almost wholly explicable in domestic terms. To broaden the point, a great deal of politically motivated organized violence, or warfare, is entirely, or almost entirely, domestic in origin, purposes, and activity. We consider the future of domestic warfare in the section below on the social–cultural context. Reacting against recent chaos, the founders of the Westphalian world required warfare to be a behaviour monopolized by states. International law, including the laws of war, reflects that principle. But times have changed. While interstate warfare remains a serious prospect, a considerable diffusion, even privatization, of military capability has occurred. We are nowhere near returning to the free-for-all context of much of early-modern Europe, but plainly states have lost some measure of the near monopoly on the use of force they enjoyed for more than three centuries.

Between the apparent banality of truly fundamental, if actually controversial, great assumptions about the workings of the future political context, and the impossibility of predicting specific political events, there lies a hazardous zone that tempts the bold theorist. As one such, wisely or not, though with all due humility, I will now provide at least some broad detail about the future. The necessary purpose of this exercise is to suggest some not implausible shape to the course of future history.

Five major items serve to summarize what this book judges both likely and unlikely to happen. The intention here is to outline the future political context positively, as well as to dispose of a few fashionable illusions. I do not forget that what follows could legitimately be labelled mere guesswork. But it is the view of a classical realist who, though alert to the possibility of history's discontinuities, also is deeply respectful of long-standing patterns in statecraft and strategy. Above all else, this analysis does not forget the most potent of all sources of continuity, the human.

First, the current US hegemony, which is most manifest in the military sphere, rather less so in the political, economic, and cultural, is likely to persist for many years, though fewer than complacent American hegemonists assume. The American lead in military power, resting as it does upon an unequalled research base and unmatchable continuing investment, may increase, or appear to do so, even as the international political context alters to the US disadvantage. By hegemony we mean simply leadership and a dominant position. Historically, different hegemons have behaved in ways both individual to their culture and in a manner fitting the norms and expectations of the period. Nonetheless, for all their differences, hegemons through the ages have shared some characteristics. Imperial Athens and the contemporary United States, for example, though markedly distinct in the style with which they exercised their preponderant position, share a common view of the rights, if not the duties, of hegemony. In 416 BC, Thucydides tells us that the Athenians sent an expedition to the Spartan colony on the island of Melos. On thirty-eight ships the Athenians carried 1,600 hoplites (heavy infantry), 300 archers, 20 mounted archers and an additional 1,500 hoplites from the allies. This was no mere demonstration of potential force. It was an entirely credible threat. In words that echo down the ages, in their meaning if not quite in the brutal honesty with which they are expressed, the Athenians had this to say about the realities of relative power:

> For ourselves, we shall not trouble you with specious pretenses – either of how we have a right to our empire because we overthrew the Mede, or are now attacking you because of wrong that you have done us – and make a long speech which would not be believed; and in return we hope that you, instead of thinking to influence us by saying that you did not join the Spartans, although their colonists, or that you have done us no wrong, will aim at what is feasible, holding in view the real sentiments of us both; since *you know as well as we do that right, as the world goes, is only in question between equals in power while the strong do what they can and the weak suffer what they must.*[16]

The Athenians proceed to drive home the point that power is self-legitimizing.

> Of the gods we believe, and of men we know, that by a necessary law of their nature they rule wherever they can. And it is not as if we were the first to make this law, or to act upon it when made: we found it existing before us, and shall leave it to exist forever after us; all we do is to make use of it, knowing that you and everybody else, having the same power as we have, would do the same as we do.[17]

The 'Melian dialogue', from which we have just quoted at some length, is of course notorious for its blunt statement of the morality of superior power. It is highly relevant to our analysis of future warfare, because it speaks eloquently to key features of the current and future political context. Imperial Athens and hegemonic, not imperial, America claim international leadership, ultimately, because of their unmatched military strength.[18] In addition, both could claim some authority deriving from the soft power of their civilizations, of the political ideas and practices they represent. Fundamentally, however, hegemony, though containing economic and cultural dimensions, has to be strategic or it will not be long for this world. Military power trumps economic power as well as the power of ideas. It is necessary to be clear on this point. Unlike the Athenians, contemporary and future Americans will not threaten to kill all the men and enslave their dependents in troublesome weak, failed, or roguish states, but they will insist that their will be done. There is no need to invent scenarios of future statecraft to illustrate this point. In 2002–2003, the United States was determined to bring Saddam Hussein to book for his many sins, real and imagined. The rights and wrongs of that controversial venture are not of interest to this discussion. But what is of interest is that the United States, in common with Athens and other hegemons, could and did insist that it would do as it wished.[19]

The Melians argued, correctly if to no avail, that Athenian aggression against them would create problems for the future. They warned the spokesmen for the hegemon as follows: 'How can you avoid making enemies of all existing neutrals who shall look at our case and conclude from it that one day or another you will attack them?'[20] I am not suggesting that the liberal, democratic, belligerent, and somewhat globalized America of the twenty-first century will succumb to the hubris of hegemonic power as did Imperial Athens, though the possibility should not be dismissed out of hand. Rather is the point that American military hegemony, with its political implications, is not and will not be regarded as a benign development in much of the world. As the global guardian of international order – the sheriff, if you will – the United States is shaping a political context wherein from time to time it is obliged to coerce 'rogue' states, discipline ambitious regional powers, and generally play bully on behalf of its own standards of good international conduct. The historical reality of the US exercise of its military power may be occasional and careful, but a substantial fraction of the attentive world audience will be inclined to fear the worst. America's deeds might be limited and eminently justifiable, not simply the expedient flexing of muscles, but such unbalanced power fuels envy, anxiety, and hostility abroad.

My second point is that major interstate war may be out of style these days, but old-fashioned interstate rivalry is not. The historically most unusual phenomenon of a single superpower, a condition which is barely fifteen years old, may seem to be hewn out of granite. Of course, it is nothing of the sort. This political context, marked by just one superpower, no real great powers worthy of the name, and a short list of lapsed, aspiring and potential, as well as probably declining, states of some notable strength, will not last. The questions of most interest are: how long can a political context endure that may be described fairly as the United States and the rest? For how long will the United States be able to prolong its strategic moment of apparently unassailable hegemony? And, as this now familiar political context changes, as change it must, what will take its place?

My second prediction, less politely my guess, about the future political context, derives inexorably from the first item above, which simply stated the obvious – that America is Number One, especially in strategic matters. Specifically, it is as close to a certainty as anything can be in the dangerous jungles of political prediction, that American hegemony will erode and come to be viewed by most sensible people in what we call the West as an all too brief golden era.[21]

President George W. Bush seeks understandably to prolong America's hegemonic moment as the sheriff of world order. He has been artlessly, even undiplomatically, agreeably explicit.

> It is time to reaffirm the essential role of American military strength. We must build and maintain our defenses beyond challenge.[22]

In case the message is not clear enough, he offers the emphatic clarification that 'our military must dissuade future military competition'. This is not a reasonable objective, though the long American lead in military effectiveness should be good for decades to come. Ultimately, however, it is doomed to fail. The reason why it is doomed to fail is, alas, all too central to the argument of this book. The political context is always evolving, while occasionally it is even transformed. But statecraft, or security politics for an eponymously more neutral designation, does not change in its essentials. What has changed over the past two decades is not world politics, but simply the distribution of power. One should not be confused by the obvious features of globalization, and the prolonged relative rarity of inter-state warfare, into believing that the future political context is going to be vastly different from the past, again, in its essentials.

It is true that, with the minor and probably temporary exception of some aberrant fanatical brands of Islam, ideology has ceased to be a factor in interstate relations. The poisonous and genocidal nonsense of Communism and Nazism lent a quality of totality to the great struggles of the twentieth century that had not been witnessed since the early years of the Thirty Years War in the seventeenth century. It cannot be prudent to proclaim 'the end of history', meaning the historical conclusion of ideological struggle, with the definitive victory of liberal democracy, free trade, and capitalism.[23] However, it is unlikely in the extreme that future warfare, beyond the challenge posed by some Islamic insurgents, will be driven or even influenced by ideology. And for that we can be grateful.

The story of the future political context for warfare in the twenty-first century is going to be dominated by, or at the very least have as a major theme, America's efforts to retain its hegemony, and the endeavours of its rivals to hasten America's relative decline. To recognize the inevitability of this is scarcely an exercise in 'rocket science', as the popular phrase has it. George W. Bush affirms with confidence that 'our forces will be strong enough to dissuade potential adversaries from pursuing a military build-up in hopes of surpassing, or equalling, the power of the United States'.[24] The future may not witness competitive military build-ups of quite the kind characteristic of the age of industrial mass warfare, an age that is past for some of the world at least. But the aspiration behind the President's policy is best describable as a forlorn hope. Rather more realistically, President Bush confides that:

> We are attentive to the possible renewal of old patterns of great power competition. Several potential great powers are now in the midst of internal transition – most importantly Russia, India, and China. In all three cases, recent developments have encouraged our hope that a truly global consensus about basic principles is slowly taking shape.[25]

Unfortunately, the consensus about basic principles that is firmly in place, not merely slowly taking shape, is one of a return to the kind of balance of power politics that dominate in eras when ideology is not in contention. To make my argument suitably direct, I am claiming that it is all but inconceivable that the rest of the world will be content to acquiesce in, and enjoy the benefits of, a world order policed by American hegemony. The new century is barely begun, the ink is scarcely dry on the new American policy commitment to an explicit hegemonism, yet already the declarations of opposition have been legion. The usual suspects, most notably China, Russia, and France, with many fellow travellers of convenience, have let it be known, unsurprisingly, that they are not content that the twenty-first should be an American century. What is at issue is not whether the US hegemony can be exercised in so benign a way for the general good as to be indefinitely acceptable to all – well, most. Rather is there uncertainty over how rapidly and how effectively will the would-be makers and shakers of the course of history be able to mount serious opposition to the American hegemon. Even at this time of writing, evidence is mounting for the recent tentative, certainly careful, creation of an anti-hegemonic bloc led by a Sino-Russian axis. These are early days. The bloc may fail to cohere, or, probably more likely, the bloc will develop eventually to the point where world order again has as its centrepiece a bipolar balance of power. Given the deep historical cultural and geopolitical antipathies between China and Russia, a Sino-Russian alliance would not exactly be a marriage made in heaven. Moscow might well decide that a distant America, with whom it has few specific disputes, would be a more comfortable ally than would a China that is all too close.

The 'war on terror' is the obsession of the hour, maybe of the decade or even longer. However, the political context most likely to drive the occurrence and character of future warfare is not one organized around religious fanatics, with or without a few weapons of mass destruction. Instead, future warfare on the larger scale, and regular in character if most likely asymmetrical in mode, will be about what past warfare was about, though absent the ideological dimension, *relative power and influence*. The alliance ties and some of the informal alignments familiar today cannot be assumed to be eternal. Alliance is not made in heaven and forged with faith. Rather is it constructed for reasons of state and it is always liable to reassessment as the political context alters. The twenty-first century may well register dramatic shifts in international alignments. As a rising China and a recovering Russia, most probably in alliance, at least for a while, challenge US hegemony, as noted above, other state players will have to calculate where their best interests lie. We return to this issue below in the discussion of NATO's roles in the future.

My third prediction is that the political context for future warfare is not going to be shaped significantly by multinational institutions, at least not for many decades to come. The qualification is added not because the prediction is shaky, but simply to acknowledge the theoretical merit in the principle that one should never say never. Of recent years the United States has been much criticized for demonstrating a unilateralist preference. This tendency is an inevitable consequence of hegemony. It is also the inevitable consequence of the ineffectiveness of multinational organizations, and sometimes the plain obstructionism of their members. Needless to say, perhaps, that is a pejorative way of describing what many other commentators regard as necessary efforts to try to rein in the hegemon. It is probably essential that from time to time this text should remind readers that the subject under scrutiny is future warfare, not the wisdom or otherwise in recent US policy and strategy. American matters cannot fail to figure prominently in this analysis. It could hardly be otherwise, given America's current and future hegemonic role and its cutting edge prowess in the conduct of most forms of warfare. Nonetheless, our subject is not the United States, save insofar as American issues are significant for the future of warfare. In case there is any residual doubt, the author does not and will not shy away from expressing his personal view which is strongly supportive of an American role as principal guardian of international order. The book, however, is not designed as a defence of that role.

Trend analysis is notoriously difficult, as we have argued already. However, to venture where even angels might fear to tread, in the strategic realm history appears to be moving towards the sidelining of the multinational institutions that we have inherited from the twentieth century. This is scarcely surprising, since such inventions as the United Nations and NATO were created on the basis of political assumptions that are almost wholly irrelevant today and in the near-term future, at least. Both organizations perform some useful functions, though it is debatable whether or not their potential for harm renders them a net liability for international *strategic* security. The problem is that the political context has changed, but those organizations have not, indeed, in most respects, cannot. The UN, particularly its Security Council, illustrates graphically everything that is wrong with the fallacious theory of collective security. The villains, the policemen, and the largely disinterested, are all permitted to play on the same security team. Self-regarding statecraft is what is practised through the UN. Membership in the organization does not cause countries miraculously, indeed irresponsibly, to transcend the selfish habits mandated by the nature of world politics.

The UN cannot possibly prosper in the twenty-first century as an important contributor to international security, because it is thoroughly inappropriate to support the world-ordering mechanism of the period. Rephrased, the Security Council, and especially its five Permanent Members, cannot function de facto as a substitute for a missing world government. One of its members is too powerful and, as a consequence, some of the others generally are more interested in controlling the hegemon than they are in addressing other problems of global strategic security. It is only just to observe that my claim for the strategic irrelevance, or worse, of the United Nations is not really a criticism of that institution. The UN and the behaviour that is staged there on the East River in New York, reflects the way of the world. We have the UN that we deserve. It cannot be otherwise. In a rather less deterministic vein, we need to be careful lest an ill-advised and undue respect for UN rules and procedures is permitted fatally to obstruct the forces of order, which is to say principally the United States. To adapt the old saying, if the UN is unable to help, at least it should not be allowed to hinder.

This discussion, probably contrary to appearances, is not framed as a wholesale assault upon the UN. My argument is only that the political context for future warfare will not provide a significant role for the organization. Moreover, on balance, the UN offers more potential to harm than to help the mission of international strategic security. Whether or not, and how often, this proves to be the case must depend upon the courage, good sense, and relative strategic power of the forces for order and other civilized values. This discussion should not be necessary, so obvious does it seem to the author. However, first-hand experience of public debate, and the continuance of much fuzzy warmth of feeling towards the UN as somehow a 'good thing', compels this delivery of the bad news that the normal practices and malpractices of world politics are not checked in the cloakroom on the East River. I am not pointing a finger of blame. The United States, we must hope, will perform as it should as hegemonic guardian of order. That endeavour will be opposed, more or less effectively, from issue to issue by the countries who see advantage in so doing. Eventually, US hegemonic dominance will decline and the UN, inevitably, will provide a stage for the expression and conduct of old-fashioned balance of power politics.

If the UN is not destined to play a noteworthy role in the political context of future warfare, what can be said of the prospects for NATO? The organization has several signal virtues. Against the historical backcloth of an ever troubled, but overall most successful, past, NATO has lost its way. At least it has lost its way as a collective defence organization. Of NATO's three classic purposes, 'to keep the Russians out, the Germans down, and the Americans in', only the third is actively relevant today. Will NATO survive its loss of binding purpose, to serve as a barrier to Soviet expansion by functioning, in minor key, as a US continental bridgehead and, in major key, as a guarantee organization that engages a distant super-power in European security? It would be easy to write off NATO as yesterday's solution to yesterday's (Soviet) problem. That would be a mistake, though an understandable one. At present, certainly, the Russians do not need to be kept out of West–Central Europe, though the same cannot be said for the now detached marchlands of the old imperium in Caucasia and Central Asia. NATO's eastward enlargement is viewed in the West almost wholly in political and cultural terms. It is regarded as a long overdue reconnection of truly European societies to the European whole. NATO membership is linked to some domestic political and administrative reform and, quite reasonably, is seen as an important factor helping to reintegrate the former satrapies of the Soviet imperium into the mainstream of European history.

So much for the dominant Western European and American perspective. The newly liberated countries of Eastern Europe endorse the arguments just cited. But their appalling experience over the past two centuries, squeezed between the competing monstrosities of rival Russian, German, and even Austrian and Turkish, power, has made them very clear sighted about national security. They know the truth in the old saying that 'geography is destiny'.[26] Poles, Lithuanians, Czechs, and others, have learnt that geopolitics and geostrategy are apt to be cyclically menacing when your national territory lies in, indeed comprises, the gateway into and out of continental Europe. You lie between the European 'Rimland', as Dutch-American geopolitican Nicholas J. Spykman put it, and the 'Heartland' of Eurasia, to quote the greatest of all geopolitical theorists, Sir Halford J. Mackinder.[27] The 'Old Europe' of the continental core members of the European Union, as US Defence Secretary Donald H. Rumsfeld dismissively described them, may be in a happy post-military condition, but the 'New Europe' to the East, the most recent adherents to the EU, is not thoroughly convinced that bad security times are gone forever. Many local motives lie behind the accession of NATO's new members in the East, but by far the most important is to secure a guarantee of national security from the American superpower. The future is unpredictable. NATO membership, which means, or is believed to mean, a US underwriting of the basic values of one's security, seems to the whole of Eastern Europe to be a prudent insurance policy. Germany, of course, is now debellicized and integrated into the EU project, and yes, Russia is weak and largely unmenacing, Westwards at least. However, times could change, and indeed are changing. Recall that earlier in this chapter we argued that the political context, the most potent driver of the likelihood and character of future warfare, is most probably going to be shaped significantly by a return of fairly explicit balance of power rivalries. The US hegemony will be opposed ever more vigorously. Alliance ties will alter. The weak polities of Eastern Europe know that their geopolitical location between 'Europe' and Russia, even when they are members of the former, renders them ever vulnerable when there is a sharp deterioration in international civility among the greater powers. From the Russian point of view, NATO's eastward enlargement is not especially menacing in geostrategic terms, but politically it can have a deeply destabilizing effect. Especially is this true with respect to developments in a democratic Ukraine.

Few people today are thinking of the future of NATO in the terms advanced here. Now the emphasis is all on the alliance as peacekeeper, with evidentiary reference to Bosnia, Kosovo, Macedonia, and Afghanistan. NATO can and does complement American efforts. The United States performs the strategic heavy lifting, while some of its allies, utilizing NATO assets and preferably with UN blessing as well, undertake to contribute non-trivially to stabilizing the peace that the American military has made or enabled. This is a necessary and valuable task. So much for the good news. The less good news is that NATO is failing to complement or replace the efforts of the US sheriff and its British deputy on a really useful scale in Afghanistan. As for Iraq, the Atlantic Alliance has scarcely functioned as such. If one were attracted to the practice of making 'surprise-free' predictions, one would be bound to assert that NATO has little future. Looking to the longer term, however, on a more positive note, and returning our focus to the political context of international rivalry, NATO could play a crucial role in war prevention. Recalling the argument made earlier that the twenty-first century will witness an anti-hegemonic struggle on the part of rising, or returning, great powers, there will be a lengthy and probably rather messy and uncertain process of picking up sides for the conflict. A NATO that is still alive, if not necessarily very well, offers several huge advantages for the prospects for order.

NATO is the only international institution that keeps the United States more or less actively involved in security in Europe, at a time when Europe is likely to be well down the list of US strategic priorities. Moreover, it provides a proven alternative to the hazards of an independent European security course. By spanning the Atlantic, the alliance reflects the geo-political and geostrategic truth that 'the West', as a security community does, and should, embrace both Europe and North America. It would be agreeable to be able to predict with high confidence that a tolerably vibrant NATO will survive the perils that beset it. The charge of irrelevance is levelled by those ignorant of the cyclical nature of political and strategic history. Then there is the pressure from 'Old Europe', led by France, of course, to construct a distinctive European foreign and defence policy on the back of a new political foundation. At present, the European project of the EU, certainly in federalist mode, looks to be in major disarray, seemingly its enduring condition. But the future is a long time. The fact that today the EU is not prospering as a prospectively unified political community, means very little. EU-Europe will remain a permanent threat to that workable unity of 'the West' that NATO both expresses and forwards. By its very existence, NATO offers a security home alternative to the EU, and by virtue of that fact it must discourage the emergence of a federal European superstate.

As my fourth prediction, no enquiry into the mysteries of future warfare can be complete in the absence of some speculative commentary on the meaning of globalization. A superior textbook on the subject offers a sensibly minimalist definition. 'By globalization we simply mean the process of increasing interconnectedness between societies such that events in one part of the world more and more have effects on peoples and societies far away.'[28] Globalization means many things to many people. To Americans it tends to mean the global spread of American values and behaviour. In that view, a globalizing world is one benefiting from the spread of liberal democracy, fairly free trade, and capitalist economic practices. To its more severe critics, from many nations, globalization means the exploitation of human and natural resources for the profit of giant multinational companies. While of particular interest to this analysis is the opinion that the processes of globalization are transforming the political context of future warfare.

I am not especially sceptical of the phenomena of globalization, but in two regards I am moved to ask, 'so what?' Despite the more exciting claims advanced by commentators who are sailing with the flow of intellectual fashion, humankind is not suddenly entering a globalized world, if such an absurd-sounding concept has any real meaning, that is. The first 'so what' stems from recognition of the historical antiquity of the phenomenon. Climate change in Central Asia almost certainly set the Huns in motion westwards in the late fourth century AD, a movement which had ultimately dramatic knock-on effects on other nations, leading finally to the barbarians mounting intolerable pressure on the Rhenish and Danubian frontiers of both the Western and Eastern fronts of the Roman Empire by the beginning of the fifth century. It is true that the histories of China, Japan, and India, for prominent examples, were more or less wholly unknown to Europeans in ancient times. That can be asserted notwithstanding some trading connections and, for Central Asia and North-West India, the two-way impact of the Hellenism brought by Alexander the Great to some Asiatic societies. But close examination shows not how isolated were societies and their polities in ancient and mediaeval times, but rather how well they tended to be connected, despite the uncertainties of geographical knowledge and the slowness of communications relative to today. The known world of the Romans and Byzantines, for example, was highly interconnected.

The more we look, historically, the more interaction we discover or recognize. Of course, there were exceptions. For example, the civilizations of the Americas were not connected with the forces of globalization until small numbers of murderous Spanish adventurers introduced the local cultures of Mexico and Peru to the cutting edge of European civilization. The conquistadors brought steel weapons, gunpowder, horses, new diseases, Christianity, and an alien way in warfare, to a previously isolated continent.[29] However, such an exception to a history of globalization does not suffice to undermine the validity of the claim that globalization is old news. Europeans waged a global conflict between 1756 and 1763, the Seven Years' War, while the succession of European colonial empires were increasingly global in their domain from the late fifteenth until the mid twentieth centuries. In terms of finance and trade, the world was virtually as interconnected in the years preceding the First World War as it is today. Globalization is a fact, but it always has been. Those among us who are entranced by the allegedly transformative potential of the internet revolution, indeed who view it as close to a panacea for the world's troubles, would do well to remember there has already been an internet revolution, *in the nineteenth century*. Tom Standage's outstanding study of *The Victorian Internet*,[30] which is to say the electric telegraph, shows that we humans are prone to use new technology, in this case almost literally the wiring or cabling of much of the world, in order to do more efficiently what we were doing already. If anything, the electric telegraph, beginning in the 1840s and paralleling the growth of railways, was more revolutionary in its impact on interconnectedness than is the IT revolution of today. The telegraph and the undersea cabling that came to girdle the globe, effected a greater change in the speed of information flows than has the internet. Sad to say, it is hard to imagine the conduct of modern, industrial age warfare without the benefit of the electric telegraph.

My second 'so what?' follows directly from the discussion above, as does the most plausible answer. So what does globalization mean for future warfare, its incidence and its character? One has to be careful to avoid inadvertently setting up a straw target. We can all agree on the essentials of what is occurring. Courtesy of such technological achievements as the invention of the semiconductor, realized as the transistor in 1948, the integrated circuit in 1958, and the microprocessor in 1971, the computer, or IT, revolution is a significant fact for much, though not all, of the world. But the historian and the strategic analyst must ask, 'so what?' New technologies, or major improvements in old ones, are almost bound to lead to new styles in, perhaps new forms of, warfare. If your primary interest lies in the important field of how we fight, and with what, then the IT revolution, and the many military–technical revolutions that preceded it, are topics of burning concern. We must hasten to note that although the IT revolution obviously has a military–technical dimension, it has nearly always been a civilian project – which is not to deny that the internet had its origins as a US military venture. The same point can be made about the telegraph and the railways in the nineteenth century.

The problem with an IT-led globalization is not so much to establish the probable facts concerning ever greater interconnectedness among peoples, societies, and governments. Rather is the challenge to understand what it means, in our case for future warfare. Different aspects of the IT-led revolution in communications are analysed in later chapters. At this relatively early juncture, what needs to be registered with the utmost clarity is the historically founded judgement that the computer and everything that it enables will make little difference to the incidence of warfare. IT is merely a tool, the latest in a very long line of tools. Nothing, repeat nothing, in the past or the present, has cured humankind of its willingness to fight for whatever political reasons are deemed sufficient in local contemporary assessment. Some people harbour the optimistic notion that the internet will, or might, eventually promote near universal peace because of its facility in connecting people and institutions instantaneously, viruses and other perils permitting. The assumption is that war is born out of misunderstanding and ignorance. It has to follow, pursuing that logic, that any development that erases the effects of barriers between peoples, must be good news for a more peaceful future. I am not entirely dismissive of that idea, but, overall, it has to be discarded as nonsense. In their time, the electric telegraph and the railway were both touted as panaceas for international conflict.

Perhaps the internet can achieve what the machine gun and nuclear weapons manifestly failed to accomplish, and effect a technical deconstruction of the case for war in the future. But I doubt it. What will happen in the future, as today, is that the scientific and technical engine of globalization will be harnessed to change some of the ways in which war is waged. When a political phenomenon like war is falsely conceptualized as a challenge to be met by technology, or law, or education, for some examples, disappointment is assured. However, war is by no means only a political phenomenon. It is a social institution, it can engage whole societies, and to some degree its conduct must express the cultures of the belligerents.

The single most important consequence alleged to follow from globalization is the decline in the sovereign autonomy of the state. This would mean a decline in the state itself as the dominant form of political organization.[31] If true, the implications for future warfare would be far reaching, though probably less so than one might judge initially. There is no doubt that states, even the greater among them, are unable by their individual, autonomous efforts, to manage their economies as they might prefer; incapable, if unaided, of protecting their citizens from strategic harm; not able, alone, to fight the spread of infectious diseases, which now can travel around the world at the speed of a 747; and are quite incapable of devising strictly national measures that would be at all effective in an attempt to alleviate the harmful consequences of climate change. These and similar arguments are valid beyond question. In some truly key respects, the state today, and presumably even more the state tomorrow, apparently is in decline as it fails to meet the needs of its society. More and more of our problems – terrorism, health, climate, economic stability – are essentially global and can only be addressed usefully on a multinational, preferably global, basis – so the argument proceeds.

There is a killer difficulty with the sound-looking thesis that the state is in decline. Notwithstanding the many good arguments made in its cause, the declinist claim is empirically false, at least insofar as the matter can be assessed. One might think that a failing organization, like the state, would lose legitimacy and loyalty as an inevitable consequence of its evident debility. Is it likely that the political context for future warfare will cease to be dominated by polities of the kind that have run human affairs since the seventeenth century? Perhaps the modern state has had its day. If this is so, what would it mean for warfare? Obviously, interstate war would continue to decline as a historical phenomenon. But, would warfare itself decline? One is also moved to ask whether the most probable alternative to a world of fairly sovereign states would not be some global variant of the current post-military EU, but instead might be an international realignment into a number of superstates.

As my fifth and final prediction, I suspect strongly that the political context for future warfare is going to be impacted massively, perhaps dominated, by the multidimensional negative consequences of climate change. It is because this possibility is so uncertain that it has been relegated to the rearguard in our list of major items shaping the future political context. Deliberately, climate change is treated after US hegemony, anti-hegemonic balance of power struggles, multinational institutions, and globalization. At present there is a convincing scientific consensus to the effect that: global warming is happening; it is the result of human activity; and that it is far too late to arrest, let alone reverse, the process. But there is no consensus on the details or the consequences. Will climate change be gradual or will it be abrupt?[12] If it should be abrupt, the political consequences almost beggar the imagination. Recent studies show that even modest changes in average annual temperatures, up or down, across large parts of the world, would almost certainly create economic, social, and hence human and political chaos. Natural resources of many kinds would be at a premium, and would need to be fought for against polities that could no longer sustain their levels of population. This is far too speculative a matter to warrant elevation to the leading political contextual argument anticipated to drive the incidence and character of future warfare. However, global warming is a fact. A fairly sudden acute shortage of arable land and fresh water would, I predict, show up many of the optimistic liberal assumptions and expectations of today for the illusions that they are. The resort to war is highly contextual. Political decisions to fight are taken not because it is in our human nature to be belligerent, but rather because some vital interest is at stake. And vital interests can be survival interests that have to be defended by any and every means available, if society is to persist.

This fifth item is included because it refers to a potential influence on the changing political context of such magnitude as to overshadow all else. But it is only a possibility. Climate change may be gradual, essentially linear, recording no abrupt and catastrophic consequences for human life on a large scale. We just do not know. However, when, as here, one considers major influences upon the political context that must drive the occurrence of future war, there is no way that the consequences of abrupt climate change can responsibly be ignored. It is far too uncertain to be allowed to dominate this enquiry, while in an important respect it does not matter overmuch for our story whether the ecological disaster theory is or is not well founded. Our subject, after all, is future warfare, not so much the ever variable causes of war. Nonetheless, we will return to this disturbing topic in the Conclusions.

Now we must pursue the contexts of future warfare beyond the explicitly political, into the fundamental regions of society and culture.

SOCIETY AND CULTURE

War is a social institution and to some extent an expression of a society's culture. The latter claim had to be qualified, because war, as a duel, imposes its own discipline, and does not permit culturally driven but militarily ineffective ideas and practices to prosper. As we have noted already, Clausewitz wrote of the military grammar as contrasted to the policy logic of war. It is essential to respect war's grammar, that is to say the actualities of contemporary warfare, which may or may not permit achievement of the goals of policy. But style in warfare, including the attitudes of soldiers, is not universally uniform, even if the material culture of war is well nigh common. In this section, and indeed throughout this text, I will argue that war is a social and therefore necessarily a cultural activity. Furthermore, the argument extends to embrace the claim that the social and cultural context of future warfare is more important than the technological. This is not to be dismissive of technology. It is a judgement of relative importance, not the registration of a choice between alternatives. A fine comprehensive statement of the relationships among war's principal contexts has been offered by Jeremy Black.

> In its fundamentals, war changes far less frequently and significantly than most people appreciate. This is not simply because it involves a contrast – the willingness of organized groups to kill and, in particular, to risk death – but also because *the material culture of war, which tends to be the focus of attention,* is less important than its *social, cultural and political contexts and enablers.* These contexts explain the purposes of military action, the nature of the relationship between the military and the rest of society, and the internal structures and ethos of the military. Having 'high-tech', the focus of much discussion about the future of war, is not the same as winning particular wars, and, anyway, does not delimit the nature of conflict.[33]

One must add, 'Amen', to Black's well-chosen words. Readers are advised that the argument here is intended to be digested together with the discussion in the next chapter of war's changing technological context. Properly addressed, as I hope here, future warfare must be considered holistically, which is to say with all of its principal contexts and dimensions allowed their due. War is political behaviour above all else, but it is also social and cultural behaviour, and it always has a technological dimension or context.

Studies of future warfare are apt to slight the social and cultural contexts of their subject,[34] the working, and I believe, false, assumption being that future warfare will be conducted by Universal Soldiers following a Universal Grammar of war. The currently fashionable adoption of the notion of asymmetrical forms of warfare does not necessarily imply a sophisticated and empathetic grasp of the diversity in war's social and cultural contexts. It should be easy to see why this discussion is of the utmost importance for our mission. The next chapter examines the military transformation that is under way in the US Armed Forces in particular, and elsewhere in much lesser measure. That discussion focuses especially upon the IT-led revolution that is the tip of the spear of innovation in this era. However, the official American obsession with technology, even when treated sensibly in the round, in the context of organization and doctrine, has a way of diverting attention from a more important transformation. The American defence community and its foreign admirers, both friends and potential foes, spent the 1990s and beyond conducting seemingly endless existentialist debates about the reality or otherwise of an information-led Revolution in Military Affairs (RMA), now known as transformation. What that community substantially missed, though, was the possibility, maybe even the probability, that military transformation was being dwarfed in significance by a transformation of war itself.[35] More particularly, some people outside the ranks of professional defence analysts are suggesting that the social and cultural context of war has changed, is continuing to change, and probably has profound implications for future warfare. After all, war is not only, or even primarily, a technical military exercise. It is also, indeed more basically, a political, social, cultural, and distinctly human undertaking.

Several notable disagreements that bear on this tale lurk close to the discussion of society and culture. We will pose the question, where will future warfare come from? We could just as well ask where will future peace come from? All theories of war must be theories of peace also. If they are not they are fatally flawed. Of recent years, there has been an interesting, though, in the opinion of this author, misconceived, debate between so called neo-realists and culturalists.[36] Some scholars, self-styled realists, believe that political behaviour is fully explicable with reference to inter-state power relations. Statesmen act rationally to advance the interests of their security community, usually a state, defined in terms of relative power. It may be needless to add that power is a slippery concept if ever there was one. An alternative view holds that state and other political bodies' behaviour is, or might often be, understood better as an expression of its culture. A controversy is still running between scholars who identify themselves, not without some ambiguity, as classical realists, and those who follow the banner of the American theorist, Kenneth N. Waltz, and proudly champion the cause of neo-realism. The latter take the view that high policy, certainly decisions for peace or war, can be explained satisfactorily, strictly with reference to the distribution of power.[37] The domestic, social context of statecraft matters not at all, say the adherents to this approach. All political actors behave in the same way. What differs is their situation, defined in terms of relative power. By contrast, although classical realists agree that statecraft, indeed politics, is about the power that should enhance security, they reject the thesis that states, or other players, can and should be regarded as closed black boxes or billiard balls, albeit balls of different sizes. The classical realist insists that the domestic context for, including the human agents of, policy making can be crucially important.

I apologize for the brief venture into the generally unrewarding woods of International Relations theory. Alas, it is inescapable in a book on future warfare. In point of fact it should be regarded as inescapable in any book on warfare in any period, past, present, or future. To be blunt, does the domestic social and cultural context matter, or matter much, in explanation of behaviour bearing on war? Since this section addresses the social and cultural context of future warfare, no prizes will be awarded to those who assume that the author sails under a culturalist banner, at least to a modest degree.

A major debate that I spared readers in the paragraphs immediately above, though passing mention of it has been made earlier, is that between realists of several kinds, with all adjectival modifiers, and liberal optimists.

The former, including yours truly, believe that warfare in pursuit of power in its sundry forms will be with us always. The latter, the liberal optimists, argue that humankind can either unlearn the ways of war, or so reorganize itself that war becomes obsolete. Strictly speaking, of course, this debate is beyond resolution, except by the verdict of future history. All debaters have a severe evidence problem about the future, though one would think that clear realist conclusions deriving from several millennia of historical experience should carry superior weight.

Academic, if not a little arcane, as this discussion may appear to be, it bears in the most direct and significant of ways upon our mission. To repeat, where will future warfare come from? If we strive to reduce the incidence of future warfare, whither should our efforts be directed? How important is the domestic context? I have grappled with these questions for more than thirty years. Initially, I worked on theories of arms race dynamics.[38] The dominant Western explanation of how the strategic nuclear arms race worked seemed to be empirically unsound, as well as improbable in the light of the history of other arms races. Beliefs about arms race dynamics played a significant role in shaping US arms control policy (remember the ABM Treaty of 1972) and weapon deployment choices.

In the 1960s and 1970s it was orthodox to believe that the Soviet–American arms race was a spiral of futility, governed by the iron logic of a tight pattern of action and reaction. Such a neat theory had no role for domestic factors on either side. Like much of modern strategic theory, this explanation of how the arms race worked was an exercise in pure logic. It did not rest upon careful historical study and it owed nothing to sociology. The domestic politics of weapon acquisition are always significant in the United States, as the administration of the day bargains among its agencies and then with Congress. On Moscow's side, post-Soviet era testimony has revealed that a great deal of the detail of Soviet strategic arms procurement had little if anything to do with an action–reaction mechanism of interstate competition, but reflected rather the interests of party-industrial empires in maintaining continuous production.[39] Popular arms race theory underlines the merit in a maxim coined by Charles E. Callwell a hundred years ago. 'Theory cannot be accepted as conclusive when practice points the other way.'[40] Empirical enquiry can be lethal to a popular thesis.

As a sometime student of social anthropology, I joined a few others who conceived the radical thought that it might be an intelligent idea were we to try to understand our Soviet adversary on its own terms. After all, it was US policy and strategy, firstly, to try to deter the USSR from going to war, or even behaving dangerously. Secondly, should war occur anyway, the ever-growing flexibility in the US nuclear war plans were supposed to maximize the prospects for success with so-called intra-war deterrence. But the United States simply assumed that one size of strategic theory must fit all countries. Domestic, including cultural, variations were deemed irrelevant. This belief was as convenient as it was absurd and moreover, highly dangerous in its absurdity. Enough of ancient history. Suffice it to say that I, and of course this analysis, have a clear position on the significance of the social and domestic context for future warfare. As just illustrated, this position has been hard won and much tested over many years and through several 'eras' – Cold War, post-war / inter-war shakedown decade, and explicit American hegemony after 11 September 2001.

A dedication to definition rarely adds to a book's sparkle. Occasionally, though, definition is unavoidable, if all interested parties need to be sure that they are discussing the same thing. Culture is an example of what scholars mean by a contested concept; in fact that description must be one of the more monumental understatements of modern times. Obviously the understanding we ascribe to it has to matter, because if we fail to specify what it is, and is not, any discussion of its relative importance for future warfare would be literally meaningless. In this book, culture refers to ideals, attitudes, ideas, habits of mind, and, somewhat controversially, behaviour.[41] The essential feature of culture, its nature if you like, is that it is learned and not genetically inherited. So, culture can change. But if we describe a prominent feature of national or tribal behaviour as cultural, we mean that it is deep rooted and does not express merely the passing fancy of the moment. It is commonplace, and unchallenged, to claim that Afghans are warlike and that a penchant for local raiding is an integral part of Afghan culture. Similarly, the American romance with machinery is understood to be cultural. Americans like machines and for the better part of two centuries, really since the 1840s, have sought to substitute technology for human effort whenever they could. Every country, perhaps we should say every tribe, expansively understood, has a more or less distinctive style in its thought and behaviour. That is culture. It is needless to emphasize that culture, manifested in action as style, must influence how security communities, states and others, prepare for and wage war. A necessary caveat is the reminder of Clausewitz's insistence that war is a duel. Because statecraft and warfare inherently is directly competitive behaviour, necessity can drive a country to act in a way that is contrary to its political and strategic culture. For example, in the First World War, by August 1915 specifically, Britain committed itself to fielding an army on the largest of continental scales. That decision ran contrary to its long traditional strategic and cultural preference for a maritime way of war with only a limited continental commitment.[42]

If war is cultural, which it certainly is, surely it can be unlearnt? Perhaps the liberals are right in their belief in the possibility of a much less war-prone, if not quite war-free, world? Unfortunately, it is not at all probable that they are correct. They are wrong for the same reason that it is unsound to consider the 'zone of stability' that today is North America and most of Europe, and see in it a model for universal peace, despite the extent of the current 'zone of turmoil' in the Islamic lands (the Dar ul Islam), Africa, and some of non-Islamic Asia. Both culture and reason of state are not practical targets for measures other than those that might alleviate the fuel of conflict. As war is not a single problem that can be solved by some genius aiming at a Nobel Peace Prize, so culture, though ever changing, is not liable to dramatic shifts. Moreover, it comes, of course, in many more varieties even than does Heinz's soups. Culture is about our identity and our loyalties. It is what we have learned about ourselves, our society and state, and the world, and it is about *how* we have learned to approach those vital matters.

We can reconcile the various schools of thought on why and how world politics works as it does, and indeed as it long has done and is likely to continue to do in the future. At least such reconciliation is possible provided one discards the extremes of neo-realism that treat all states as if they were alike, and a constructivist culturalism that would have us try to build a peaceful world by acts of (good)will. Scholars can be too clever as well as emotionally, dare I say culturally, biased, to understand their subject. The obvious is not infrequently rejected because it is inelegant as an explanation or, more often, does not accord with the world in which they wish to believe. To bring this rather diffuse topic into some useful order, the following paragraphs summarize the reasons why, and ways in which, the cultural context is important for an understanding of future warfare.

All policy and strategy is made at home. It will be influenced, perhaps triggered, sometimes dominated, by external considerations, but the making, administration, and execution of policy and strategy is a process embedded in the culture of a domestic context.

Foreign and defence policy must succeed in domestic politics before they can be exercised against outsiders. Future warfare is, of course, a story of potential strife among different security communities. It is also a story of certain strife among the contending interests within the polity. The domestic political, social, and cultural context is the playing field on which policy struggles, personality clashes, and budgetary battles are waged .

Not only must foreign and defence policy be made at home, but not infrequently decisions for war or peace are taken primarily with domestic considerations uppermost in mind. The Iran–Iraq War of 1980–88 yields a particularly clear example of this domestic referent for war. Once the new Islamic Republic of Iran (IRI) had weathered the initial, highly incompetently conducted, Iraqi military storm, and restored a close approximation to the strategic status quo, it made the classic mistake of seeking to advance beyond what Clausewitz timelessly termed its 'culminating point of victory'. But, to be fair, you cannot be sure until you try. After five or six years of inconclusive, desultory, but occasionally extremely bloody warfare, it was unmistakably apparent that decisive victory was not on the cards for either side. However, Iran's Supreme Leader, the Ayatollah

Ruhollah Khomeini, was less interested in liberating Iraq's oppressed Shi'ite majority, or in holding a victory parade through Baghdad, than he was in consolidating his revolution at home. In practice, few of Iraq's Shi'ites welcomed the Iranians as liberators: apparently they felt more Iraqi than Shi'ite. Despite the fact that this eight-year war of attrition ended in a draw, and caused 1.067 million casualties (367,000 dead and 700,000 wounded), and cost an estimated $1.188 trillion, both regimes emerged strengthened by the long trial of arms. It was credible reports of serious war weariness, in the context of a grim economic and strategic situation, that persuaded Khomeini that enough was enough.[43] War is often a cohesive force, particularly for regimes that are none too well established. The prospects for the incidence and duration of future warfare will not depend strictly upon rational calculations about the distribution of power in the international arena. All warfare has a domestic hinterland, usually several such.

If the theorists of 'new wars' are correct, most future conflicts will be waged between, probably among, groups within the territorially specified states that are recognized in international law. This view discerns some return to the confused situation prior to the 1648 Peace of Westphalia, when there was no very convincing and unambiguous distinction between domestic and foreign affairs. The thesis that the state, let alone the nation state, is in decline as the sole form of legitimate political organization for a security community, is only a limited truth with modest implications. In most of the world, today and predictably for a long time in the future, the state appears certain to retain first claim upon the loyalties of most of its citizens. But, there are some exceptions. These are weak states, failed states, and some strong-seeming states whose enemies are almost wholly domestic. My claim for the importance of the social and cultural context of future warfare is no less, indeed it is more, potent, if the prophets of globaliza-tion in its several rather vague meanings are right. On one side at least, war begins at home, while in uncivil civil strife it is conducted entirely in, and about, the domestic context. Sweeping predictions concerning the future of warfare cannot afford to neglect the social and cultural context from which warfare springs. Whether or not the state is in decline, the domestic context is always important.

In time of crisis, particularly of war, political leaders like to add the legitimacy provided by such symbolic military trappings as are available, notwithstanding the risk of inviting ridicule. Some politicians perform well as statesmen, while a few even have superior gifts in the difficult field of strategy. But it must not be forgotten that all statesmen are domestic politicians. If they are not, or cease to be, successful in domestic politics, then they must lose their executive influence over foreign affairs. Not only is warfare waged between rival social and cultural contexts, however organized, though generally as states, it is led on all sides by people who are distinctively encultured. Those war leaders may or may not score high marks for competence in the ever-dynamic grand assay of historians' judgements. What matters is that they satisfy, or otherwise control, their own social and cultural context. Victory in war is highly desirable, but many a political leader has survived limited defeat.

Culture is pervasive. Recall the Latin *contextere*: the cultural context weaves it all together. Future warfare, as with warfare in all periods, will in a sense be cultural, certainly it will be waged by inescapably distinctively encultured people. However, it is almost certainly a great error to argue that future warfare will be about culture. There is always an exception. Although Hitler's attempt at European dominion was a bid for hegemonic power, in addition it was a war conducted to realize an idea. *Mein Kampf*, written in Landsberg Prison in 1924, was all too deadly serious as a statement of faith and intention. Napoleon's claim when in exile on St Helena, that his grand purpose had been to liberate, modernize, and unite Europe – a forcible precursor to the EU – is rather less persuasive than is the case of Hitler. Nazi Germany was the bearer of an ideology, really a quasi-religion, that shaped its policy and strategy.[44] Culture is so pervasive that, to a greater or lesser extent, greater for Germany in the 1930s and 1940s, it is all but indistinguishable from policy, and much else besides. In 1993, the dean of American political scientists, Professor Samuel P. Huntington of Harvard University, advanced the startling grand theory that the future would see a 'clash of civilizations'.[45] Instead of states jostling for power and profit as usual, the principal fault lines of future conflict would be those that separated the world's civilizations. This fascinating notion found a ready niche in the market for big ideas. It was eagerly debated by the professional scribblers and media 'talking heads' who, with the demise of the Soviet Union, were feeling the loss of a truly big idea to order their view of the future. Huntington's theory, which suggests that culture will be the major villain as a cause of future war, is thoroughly unsound. Those who interpret al Qaeda's depredations as vindication of Huntington's nightmare vision of *kulturkampf*, should take a deep breath and remind themselves of how miniscule among Muslims is the army of willing martyrs, notwithstanding its capacity for mayhem.

The social, especially cultural, context is of quite extraordinary importance in helping explain, or predict, human behaviour. But, culture is not determinative. If considered as a contributing element, there is everything to recommend the study of the cultural context as a factor in peace and war. Inevitably, some culturalists, or constructivists, would have us believe that future warfare, particularly its avoidance, can be controlled by the potency of ideas. For example, there is a substantial literature on the subject of an alleged nuclear taboo. There are many adherents to the worthy, if rather naïve and Western-centric theory that a useful barrier against nuclear proliferation, and certainly against nuclear use in anger, is the delegitimization of these horrific weapons by what amounts to a universal taboo.[46] The theory is simply wrong. Such a taboo does indeed exist. But, unsurprisingly, it holds sway only in the debellicized societies of EU-Europe, and in a US hegemon whose superior usable military power is conventional. The game of nations, as international politics has long been known, is rarely *about* culture, but it is always conducted by people who are the products of their local cultural context. That context will influence how they think about war and peace. Jeremy Black, a historian already familiar in these pages, advises convincingly that there are 'differing understandings of victory, defeat, loss and suffering' between societies. He proceeds to claim that 'war and success in war are cultural constructs'.[47] By way of illustration of Black's point, it can be a shock for Westerners to realize that Saddam Hussein was genuinely convinced that he was victorious in the Gulf War of 1991. How could this be so? In his own mind, and to many Arabs, he was victorious, and justly celebrated the victory with the construction of a gigantic 'victory arch', because he stood up to the American bully, indeed to the great coalition assembled to humble him, and he and his regime survived. Washington had no comprehension of this unhelpful cultural fact. The misunderstanding had some tragic consequences as the political outcome in Iraq of the hundred-hours' war proved acutely disappointing to US policymakers. Realists, meaning classical realists, not the neo-realists who view states as black boxes, should have no difficulty employing cultural analysis in their political strategic analysis. At least, this classical realist has no trouble doing so. States, and other politically organized units, compete for power and influence, most typically in non-violent ways. State behaviour, including the waging of war, must be conducted by representatives of specific cultures, and their choices cannot help but be coloured by perceptions, attitudes, and habits of mind, that should be termed cultural. To say that, however, is not to argue that cultural impulses frequently will be permitted to override calculations of interest. Politics, and war as an instrument of policy, fundamentally and permanently is about power and is conducted according to the lore of reason of state. Each political culture pursues its reason of state after its own cultural fashion, but generally subject to acute recognition of the discipline provided by balancing power.

Culture changes, albeit usually slowly. Attitudes towards war alter with demographics, particularly when single-child families become normal rather than exceptional. Add to demographics the slow but inexorable effect of the revolution in women's rights, and society is on course to regard war somewhat differently than it did even in the recent past. To the factors of demography and gender we must blend in the emergence of a highly individualistic, hedonistic, popular culture. As if those elements were not sufficient to trigger cultural change, we need to take account of the influence of a globalized mass media that reveals some of the seamier side of high policy and strategic behaviour. Elements such as those just cited plainly are effecting a change, even a radical change, in the social and cultural context of war, in the West at least. The demographic factor of smaller families is highly significant in both Russia and China, but its causes there are different from those in the West. In Russia population decline is an unwelcome result of poor health provision, bad diet, and loss of territory; while in China it is official policy to slow or reverse demographic growth with a draconian insistence upon the one-child family. A Western Europe cured of much enthusiasm for warfare by the events of 1914–18 and 1939–45, then subsequently accorded strategic security as a gift from America, enters the future as an all but post-military zone. Warfare would play little or no role in our future, were the whole world blessed with the social features and cultural attitudes of Western Europe. Unfortunately, the rest of the world, not excluding the United States, is not on the road to being debellicized, European-style. Culture does change as society evolves, or is shocked into a reversal of some attitudes, but it does not change uniformly around the world. Furthermore, cultural change is not irreversible. Trends can be reversed as conditions alter. There is a non-trivial danger that fat, happy, fun-loving, rich, and peaceable Westerners might fail to recognize the rise of strategic challenges from less irenic cultures. History and common sense both tell us that it takes two, or in this case many more than two, for true political peace to break out and become supposedly irreversible. Most Europeans, even most Germans, wanted peace in 1939: they were rewarded with the most devastating war in history. Our debellicized West is an island of calm in a sea of troubles. Whether one views that fact as a beacon of hope for the world, or as a perilous source of self-delusion, is a matter for individual choice.

INEVITABLY, IF UNHELPFULLY, our knowledge of the future, which has to rest upon our understanding of the past, the only evidence available, is beset with many questions. We know, for example, that a military transformation keyed to information technology is well under way, led by the United States. But is a parallel and much more important transformation of war also underway, a transformation driven by a changing social and cultural context? Scholars claim that in Western societies there has been a Revolution in Attitudes toward the Military (RAM), which has rather more profound implications for future warfare than does the military–technical RMA which has been the focus of so much attention for the past decade.[48] Scholars have also investigated the alleged reality of a 'civil–military gap', especially in the United States.[49] That gap describes the somewhat contrasting realms of the military culture of professional armed forces, and the distinctly unmilitary values of the society they are charged to defend. If the gap is real, does it much matter and will it persist? Also, what dare we read into the future of warfare from what we believe we understand about our Western culture(s)? A recent major study of the diffusion of military technology and ideas emphasizes the diversity and significance of cultural differences. The editors warn that 'software [referring principally to organization and doctrine] generally does not travel as well as hardware'.[50] They offer telling illustrations of the difficulties that other countries found in attempting to emulate Napoleonic military art, and later in copying the believed excellence of the Prussian–German military system. They flag an opinion that is thought-provoking indeed, and which speaks to the current interest in the asymmetrical possibilities in warfare.

> Culture will continue to shape the development and diffusion of military
> knowledge, producing indigenous adaptations that will be difficult to predict.
> True emulation is rare, implying that others will probably not leverage the IT–RMA
> the same way as the United States.[51]

Social–cultural factors are not clearly distinguishable from the political, which is why this discussion has bracketed the political, social, and cultural contexts for examination together. Social attitudes, which can be termed cultural if they are more than the opinion of the moment, must impact political choice. All regimes, of all political stripes, are attentive to public opinion. It is appropriate to close this segment of our journey by citing a few of the major questions that bear on future warfare that have heavy social–cultural context. Will American society be content to serve as sheriff

of global order, accepting the casualties and resentment inevitably consequential from that role? Will other countries be content to allow the United
States to perform as global hegemon? If so, for how long? In the context
of globalization, for how long will the United States be able to sustain its
hegemonic position, and hence its policing role? Finally, are the pressures of
globalization fatally undermining the national and tribal loyalties that have
been so prominent a feature in the record of major war for the past two
centuries? If political loyalties are being subverted, a development with
profound implications for the willingness of people to fight, or even pay
for war, how widespread is the phenomenon? If it is very uneven across
the globe, how perilous might that be for Western societies and cultures
that are notably post-military?

Chapter three

Technology and War

TECHNOPHILES AND TECHNOPHOBES

Future warfare is not synonymous with future technology, even though war must always have a technological dimension. Because military vehicles for all geographical environments typically are photogenic, it is an all too common practice for videoed strategic narrative to equate war with the use of equipment. Such a mechanical orientation is characteristic not only of the Fourth Estate. Especially machine-minded armed forces, like the American, have long been inclined to seek to reduce the conduct of war to mechanical mobility and the application of firepower. A fundamental error in understanding is signalled unambiguously by programmes that present 'the weapons which won the war', rather than 'the weapons with which the war was won'. A problem is that military technology, particularly in the form of such combat platforms as long-range bombers, major surface vessels, and main battle tanks, are far easier to count and assess in prospective action, than are such intangibles as training, morale, organization, doctrine, and quality of leadership. In the new information age of warfare, although numbers, mass, will probably be useful, the old habit of 'bean count' comparisons of soldiers under arms, divisions, combat vehicles of several kinds, and so forth, will be of greatly reduced relevance. Such metrics were significant in war's industrial age, a period that died after

1991. The Gulf War of that year was its last hurrah. Needless to add, perhaps, the more advanced the technological prowess of the armed forces under scrutiny, the more true this argument must be. By the same logic, regular war between states or communities that are still in warfare's industrial age, must continue to rely on large numbers of the traditional elements of military power, soldiers and vehicles.

It is far from a simple matter to make sense of future military–technical options (when in the future? against which enemies? for what goals in war?). It cannot be denied that commentators can evade treating a great deal of warfare's rich complexity and uncertainty, if they are able to reduce future strategic history to predictions about military technology and its estimated effectiveness. Some readers may well believe that this book should reflect the conviction expressed in January 1919 by the British military theorist, Major-General J. F. C. Fuller.

> Tools, or weapons, if only the right ones can be discovered, form 99 per cent of victory ... Strategy, command, leadership, courage, discipline, supply, organization and all the moral and physical paraphernalia of war are nothing to a high superiority of weapons – at most they go to form the one per cent which makes the whole possible.
>
> In war, especially in modern wars, wars in which weapons change rapidly, one thing is certain: no army of 50 years ago before any date selected would stand a 'dog's chance' against the army existing at that date...[1]

Fuller was, and remains, monumentally wrong. However, he was certainly right to draw attention, if it was needed, to the pace and significance of change in the technical character of warfare. If Fuller were correct, then this book should be organized around more or less confident predictions about future military, and relevant civilian, technology. That would be most convenient for an author such as myself who would find his task very much simplified if war could be reduced to hardware and, increasingly, to electronic software. Fuller is not at all persuasive in his devotion to machines, for reasons that the argument in this chapter explains in some detail, but his technical emphasis cannot be dismissed or ignored.

The course of warfare in the twenty-first century, if we knew it, could be narrated in its technological elements. But, given that warfare is going to be waged hundreds of times in this century by dozens of communities – some with states, some without – it is obvious that much of the military kit would not be familiar to the American warriors who hone their skills at the National Training Center (NTC), Fort Irwin, California. Moreover, given the diversity of strategic and military cultures around the world, and given the powerful incentives that weaker belligerents have in finding and executing asymmetrical tactics, operations, and strategy, even military equipment (and civilian, recall 9/11) with which one is familiar may well be used in surprising ways. Even if we could settle confidently upon the probable trends in military technology, there remains the inconvenient fact that Fuller and his latter-day disciples have lost the plot about war. He forgot that in *On War* Clausewitz made distinctive reference both to the material and to the moral strengths of a belligerent.[2] Strategic history tells us that people matter more than machines. In the timeless words of Admiral Alfred Thayer Mahan: 'Historically, good men with poor ships are better than poor men with good ships.'[3] History also tells us that relative technical prowess in weaponry is rarely more than just one among many reasons why combatants win and lose. Lest I be accused of exaggeration, let it be noted that none of the major wars of the past two hundred years were won and lost because of an imbalance in technical competence in weaponry. Even the US resort to the atomic bomb in 1945 is not an exception to this judgement. Japan had lost the war long before Hiroshima and Nagasaki. Of course, we can find wars between tribal levies and modern colonial powers, or more recently between American superpower and the hapless and hopeless holy warriors of the Taleban in Afghanistan and the overmatched and demoralized defenders of Ba'athist Iraq, wherein the contest is technically so uneven that its outcome is a foregone conclusion. Such, however, is not generally the case in strategic history. War and strategy are so multidimensional that a technical shortfall, even a major one, often can be made good in the coin of other strategic qualities or quantities. The winning of battles, even to the point where military events seem to be concluded victoriously, is not the same as winning a war, though it is certainly a helpful enabler. War is a political, social, and cultural phenomenon, not only a military one.

Contrary to appearances, perhaps, this discussion bears directly upon our theme of future warfare. For reasons of the laws of physics we do not, and cannot, know very much that is definite and specific about future warfare. But we do know a great deal about past and present warfare. Moreover, our strategic reach into the past is historically so extensive and tolerably well researched that we need not be shy in endorsing a few ambitiously robust generalizations about the future roles and relative significance of weaponry in war. This chapter concludes with just such.

The American strategic theorist, Eliot Cohen, speculates persuasively that there are 'technophiles and technophobes'.[4] The former love every new machine, and fantasize that it may be so advanced, so modern, and so superior, that it offers at last the reliable prospect of waging brief and highly successful war at next to no pain to ourselves. Whether or not the particular marvellous device of the hour is plausible as the recipient of such star billing, the true technophile knows, really knows, that yet more wonderful mechanical and electronic devices are sure to appear before long. The technophile worships at the altar of technical progress. The genuinely novel combination in Afghanistan in 2001–2002 of special operations forces (SOF), cued by unmanned aerial vehicles (UAVs), communicating via space systems to strike aircraft, was hailed by excited journalists as if they had witnessed the Second Coming. It is easy to forget that means and methods of warfare are always liable to change, which is not to deny that history has witnessed lengthy periods of near stasis in military technology. Today's military solution should be sold at a discount because usually there will be an enemy motivated and able to hamper performance. For example, NATO's air campaign against Serbia (over Kosovo) in 1999 was so poorly waged for reasons of politics, inadequate technology, and the weather, that the effort was only saved by a combination of Russian pressure upon Belgrade, a threat of invasion on the ground, and economic blockade. Technophiles look to new technologies to solve military challenges of the kind that have frustrated the military profession through all of history. In his 2000 book, *Lifting the Fog of War*, Admiral Bill Owens promised that

> The technology that is available to the US military today and now in development can revolutionize the way we conduct military operations. That technology can give us the ability to see a 'battlefield' as large as Iraq or Korea – an area 200 miles on a side – with unprecedented fidelity, comprehension, and timeliness; by night or day, in any kind of weather, all the time.[5]

While technophiles enthuse about the promise in tomorrow's technology, technophobes seize every opportunity to demote machines down the hierarchy of factors contributing to strategic and military effectiveness. A similar contrast was evident in naval debate a hundred years ago. A 'material' school argued, indeed assumed, that almost everything worth knowing about warfare had to be rewritten so as to keep pace with the opportunities and perils of new technology. By way of contrast, a 'historical' school, the precursor of today's technophobes, maintained that even though material conditions changed radically, the human, cultural, and organizational qualities that produced fighting sailors and victorious fleets did not alter through the centuries.[6] The relevance of this debate to our text could hardly be more stark. Both schools have some merit. Science and technology will march on through the twenty-first century, sometimes at an apparently slower pace, sometimes at a speedier. Also we know that the engines of war can perform no better than the people who must direct them.

At some risk of sounding complacent, there is merit in the historically well-grounded view that technology never – well, hardly ever! – drives the course and outcome of warfare, because it contributes merely on one dimension of strategic effectiveness. Few states have been equally all conquering in every geographical environment. Security communities today may not be as specialized in their excellence as were ancient maritime Athens and continentalist Sparta, but still history, geography, culture, and economics, shape the armed forces of every country so that their air forces, navies, and armies are rank-ordered in priority for investment. In the 1930s, Britain favoured the RAF, the Navy, and the Army, in descending order for rearmament. That ranking showed unmistakably when prime time arrived in May 1940. Admittedly, times are changing. Future warfare may be conducted more by combat vehicles or weapon platforms, which just happen to be ships, or aircraft, or all-terrain machines. In principle, future combat may be prosecuted from alternative geographies, with their specialized vehicles, without traditional organizations any longer owning roles and missions that henceforth can be performed, as convenient, in different ways. This idea of the homogenization, the literal unity, of military power is little more than common sense, up to a point, at least. Although modern technology enables us to overfly both land and sea, that geographical distinction remains basic. It is useful to provide some forward-looking historical perspective upon the significance of technology in future warfare. This section concludes with three propositions, each of which has far reaching implications.

First, technological change has long been routinized and rendered transnational by the complex processes of diffusion. Innovation happens, it is countered by emulation, adaptation by other cultures, or evasion, and there is no final move. This matters for our story because it means that we are not obliged to hunt for Pooh Bear's non-existent Woozle.[7] We are not committed to a futile quest to identify *the* great winning technology (military, civil, or both) for future warfare. Why? Because all of strategic history tells us that belligerents will compete in their own ways – culture and geopolitics matter, as this tale keeps insisting – and that the technological element will be only one strand contributing to their performance. In the sensible words of Mary Kaldor, not an author usually favoured in these pages, 'every society has its own characteristic form of war'.[8]

Second, it is likely that this new century will produce scientific surprises of the same order of awesomeness as were heavier-than-air flight, ballistic missiles, space flight, nuclear weapons, and the invention and development of the computer. Futurologists, including those with military interests, speculate that biology and chemistry comprise as yet relatively virgin territory. Already we know, for example, that nanotechnology and genetic engineering have profound, if uncertain and disturbing, implications for military effectiveness. Most of us will be reluctant, though, to endorse the creation of people genetically engineered to be super-warriors. What matters most for this text is simply to grasp the facts that technology is up and running; that scientific knowledge, if not always manufacturing know-how, potentially is universal through diffusion as well as parallel discovery; and that there is no end to this process. It is not particularly helpful to try and play the game of 'spot the coming technologies'. Industry and government does just that, and rightly so. But it suffices for the strategic historian and the theorist looking forward to know that assuredly there will be new technologies, and that in due course they will be countered, evaded, or offset. It is always so. The reason why we should choose to be relaxed about the awesome 'maybes' of future history, is that we have seen their kind time and time again. Of course, anything is possible. However, if statecraft and warfare by states and others could survive the twentieth century essentially unimpaired as modes of behaviour, albeit noticeably shaken and somewhat humbled, only a heroically bold theorist would dare predict a breakpoint imposed by some technological wizardry in the near strategic future.

Third, we should expect future warfare, its incidence and severity, to be driven far more by political and social–cultural developments than by the new weapon technologies. At present, a Revolution in Military Affairs (RMA), keyed to the exploitation of information, is under way in the United States. Such a process of military transformation, however, is close to trivial in significance when its impact is compared with that of the political revolution which rewrote the league table for world politics in 1989–91. To unlock the secrets of future warfare we have to look into the hearts of people, not examine the glossy brochures of arms manufacturers. New forms of warfare, space and cyberwarfare, for example, and novel technologies, sooner or later will be matched in kind, borrowed or stolen and adapted, or will be evaded by asymmetric design. The strategic history of this century assuredly will not be written pre-eminently by military technology. Rather will that history be shaped and prodded erratically by political and social forces employing whatever agencies of grand strategy are to hand and, one hopes, can be employed prudently. The military–technological does intrude pervasively into the political and social realms. Appreciation of the salience of Clausewitz's grammar of war influences war's policy logic, at least probably it should do so rather more than often is the case. The great theorist insisted that 'a certain grasp of military affairs is vital for those in charge of general policy'.[9] The future of warfare will be driven by Thucydides' 'fear, honor, and interest', not by the opportunities apparently on offer from exciting new ventures across the technological frontier.

FROM RMA TO TRANSFORMATION

With some support from historians, theorists speculate that strategic history accelerates irregularly as it is driven forward by what have been called Revolutions in Military Affairs (RMAs). More is definitely less when it comes to definitions. An RMA is defined most usefully as a radical change in the character or conduct of war. This Very Big Idea of RMA can organize our understanding of a whole century, even the better part of an entire millennium, if we let it. With good reason, historian Jeremy Black warns us 'to be wary of meta-narratives (overarching interpretations)'.[10] The revolution in RMA requires noteworthy discontinuity. To understand future warfare, it might be thought that the task could be reduced to one of predicting forthcoming RMAs. However, predicting what is largely unpredictable cannot be a high confidence enterprise. For a little historical guidance, it can be claimed that the twentieth century witnessed RMAs: in naval warfare (1900s); in combined arms warfare with predicted artillery fire the key (1916–18); in mechanized warfare (1920s and 1930s); in atomic (1940s) and nuclear warfare (1950s); in guided missile warfare (1950s); in the military use of space (1960s and 1970s); in information-led warfare (1970s to the present); and in cyberwar. The mechanized RMA of the inter-war decades can be disaggregated usefully so as to focus distinctly on aircraft and on armoured fighting vehicles.[11] What the tank and half-tracked armoured personnel carrier meant for the horse cavalry, the aircraft carrier implied for the battleship and battlecruiser. Japan's temporary removal from the active list of all but one of the American battleships in the Pacific on 7 December, 1941 at Pearl Harbour, accelerated precipitately US acceptance of a naval RMA keyed to the aircraft carrier as the new capital ship. Necessity is a persuasive educator.

However one chooses to do the labelling, it is a fact that the last century saw several radical changes in the character and conduct of war. In principle at least, this new century also could be shaped in its strategic history by major discontinuities in the grammar of warfare. The twentieth century saw the novel commitment of whole societies to repeated rounds of total war, and registered war in and from the air, beneath the sea, and potentially in nuclear mode. There are no especially good reasons why the twenty-first century will break the mould. This new century, as with the last, and indeed as with the one before that, can be approached as an RMA proving ground. Thinking along those lines, we could strive to spot probable revolutionary changes in warfare, the twenty-first century's successors to aircraft, nuclear weapons, ballistic missiles, spacecraft, and electronics. It is not too fanciful to suggest that this century will witness: warfare in space; cyberwar; war wherein weapons of mass destruction (WMD) are used bilaterally; the systematic application of nanotechnologies (as, for example, in the piezoelectric fan for the cooling of electronic equipment at a fraction of the previous power demand); the harnessing of biotechnology to produce physically and psychologically genetically engineered soldiers; and a proliferation of non-lethal weapons.[12] But, as we keep insisting, future technology is no more synonymous with future warfare than past technology carried the complete story of war's history.

The history of the RMA concept illustrates the significance of the dialogue between theory and practice for the practical subject of strategy. The intellectual history of RMA has been very much a Soviet story. During the inter-war years, V. K. Triandafillov and Mikhail N. Tukhachevskiy pioneered the theory and would-be practice of 'deep operations' by fast moving mechanized forces:[13] the former died in a plane crash in 1931, the latter was murdered by Stalin in 1937. In the 1950s and early 1960s, following Stalin's death in March 1953, previously mandatory faith in the strategic authority of 'permanently operating factors' in war, which had been his strategic mantra, was overtaken by enthusiastic endorsement of a nuclear and missile-led revolution in military affairs. The 1970s and early 1980s witnessed Soviet speculation about a new RMA keyed to 'advances in microelectronics, automated decision-support systems, telecommunications, satellite and other advanced sensors, lasers, and, especially, non-nuclear munitions so accurate and lethal that they could wreak levels of military damage comparable to those attainable with tactical nuclear weapons'.[14] There was a double historical irony. First, the revolutionary Soviet notion of mechanized deep battle was aborted by Stalin's purge of the Red Army in 1937–9, but the practice of that very notion had to be survived when it was applied by the German foe in 1941–2. 'Deep battle' was rediscovered and adapted brilliantly in real time in the later course of the Great Patriotic War. The second irony was that the third surge in Soviet military enthusiasm for deep-thrusting mechanized campaigning, in the late 1970s and early 1980s, following two decades of nuclear-missile enthusiasm, was thwarted by the acceleration of the American computer-led RMA. The Soviet concept of deep mechanized operations thus was negated by politics in the 1930s, when it was probably militarily sound. It re-emerged briefly in the 1970s as an arguably effective answer to NATO's nuclear firepower and doctrine of flexible response, only to become instantly obsolescent in the face of Western emerging technologies (ET). The Soviet General Staff realized that NATO's conventional ET, most particularly the US 'Assault Breaker' technology development programme, was rendering obsolete their entire strategy for the rapid conquest of Europe by the pile-driver effect of deeply echeloned armoured forces. The concept of operations driving 'Assault Breaker' was for smart conventional munitions and sub-munitions, delivered by missiles, to be cued by advanced sensors (especially large synthetic aperture radars) on to Soviet targets as small as a tank platoon a couple of hundred miles behind the front line.

Eliot Cohen, Director of the US Air Force's (USAF's) *Gulf War Air Power Survey* (1993), makes plain the relative tardiness of American adoption of RMA concepts.

> Soviet conceptions of a military-technical revolution seeped into the West, chiefly through the US Department of Defense and its Office of Net Assessment. It gradually became clear that the Soviets had portrayed the Revolution too narrowly. They had focused on one type of warfare in a single theater – armoured conflict in Central Europe – and concentrated almost exclusively, as befitted the materialism of Marxist–Leninist thought, on technology and weapons rather than the organizational dimension of warfare. With the groundwork laid for an American assessment, the 1991 war with Iraq crystallized awareness among military planners in the United States on this momentous issue.[15]

As the saying goes, the rest is history. Whether or not RMA truly is a superior idea, its US popularity in the 1990s probably bore only tangential relation to its inherent merit. To put the matter in comparative context for maximum clarification, Americans in the 1990s found RMA theory as irresistible as did Russians the theory of geopolitics, and for approximately the same set of reasons.

Russian strategic thinkers, newly adrift from the comforting certainties of a military science guided and legitimized by the organizing tool of Marxism–Leninism, shifted credo to a new faith in geopolitics. American thinkers whose strategic compass no longer had a true north of 'dominant threat' (in the USSR), could reorient their attention to the usefully master idea of RMA. This is not to suggest that geopolitics and RMA are without value as large organizing ideas. Far from it. It is to suggest, though, that each of the two new credos was chosen because it promised to fill a strategic void in ways characteristically attractive to Russians and Americans.

Where Russians tend to be polychronic and attracted to political driving forces, so Americans are wont to be monochronic and to latch on to technical motors of change. RMA, though a complex notion when viewed properly as strategic behaviour, lends itself to simple monochronic explanation.[16] What could be more American than to believe that 'technology rules!' The conceptually imperial notion of strategic change propelled by the engine of RMAs driven by technology, was just the idea needed to fill the vacuum created by the self-retirement of the Soviet threat. In its Soviet phase, the RMA concept, though keyed to technology, was cocooned in the embrace of the all-encompassing explanatory power of Marxism–Leninism. In its subsequent American phase, RMA for many years was free-floating, bereft of the political or strategic context which yields a pressing purpose. Historical case studies of RMAs reveal unambiguously that they have been effected in response to real contemporary strategic need. In their conclusions to a book of outstanding scholarly essays on historical RMAs, the editors offer a firm judgement on the importance of pressure from the strategic context.

> Revolutions in military affairs have emerged from evolutionary problem-solving directed at specific operational and tactical issues in a specific theatre of war against a specific enemy. Successful innovators have always thought in terms of fighting wars against *actual* rather than *hypothetical* opponents, with *actual* capabilities, in pursuit of *actual* strategic and political objectives.[17]

The contrast with the United States in the 1990s could hardly be more stark. Even today the United States is earnestly pursuing what now is termed military transformation, but to what end? The answer appears to be for the general purpose of ensuring that the country will be so powerful that potential or actual rivals should be dissuaded from competing. It is probably a sound maxim to hold that a hegemonic state cannot be too powerful militarily. If it slackens its commitment to military primacy, it is likely not so much to reassure anxious potential foes, but rather to give them hope that they might catch up. This is something of a rationalization on my part. It would be both unfair and a gross exaggeration to argue that the process of military transformation is being pursued in all its high-tech glory simply because it can (perhaps) be done, but that judgement does contain more than a grain of truth.

The US Army, at least, is committed to a process of transformation that does not appear to overvalue the material culture of war. In a 2004 publication it insisted, unexceptionably, that

> As the ultimate combination of sensor and shooter, the American soldier is
> irrefutable proof that people are more important than hardware and quality
> more important than quantity.... However much the tools of war may improve,
> only Soldiers willing and able to endure war's hardships can exploit them.[18]

There is no doubt that the Army is undertaking the most radical
reorganization in more than half a century. It is shifting from a division-
based, to a brigade-based force, and is striving to focus on an expeditionary
style of war that could include protracted and even indecisive operations
against irregular enemies. In short, the US Army is undertaking a com-
mendable effort to remake itself for a strategic context wherein its foes
will not be significantly symmetrical to itself. The US Army understands
that for many years to come American policy will require it to control
territory and people in what may be long wars with no decisive engagements, a classic feature of irregular warfare. At the same time, that Army
must be able to take down hostile regimes, as well as remain on the cutting
edge of competence in regular warfare vis-à-vis some major rival intent
on challenging US hegemony. These are demanding requirements.

As a friendly critic, this author is impressed by the US Army's approach
to transformation, and its plainly sincere endeavours to learn from its
mistakes, and successes, in Afghanistan and Iraq. Whether or not the Army
will prove able to shed, or soften, a traditional national 'way of war' which
is all too apt to privilege firepower unduly, remains to be seen. Also, it is
far from certain that the new recognition of a prevalence of irregular and
otherwise highly asymmetrical enemies, in practice will promote a style
in warfare that is effective in counter-insurgency. Moreover, there is, and
long has been, a problem in American strategic and military culture which
stems from the sharp distinction drawn between war and peace. Americans
have demonstrated notable incompetence in translating the effort and
sacrifice of their soldiers into the political reward that they merit. If words
alone mean anything, this weakness is being addressed. The same Army
document from which I quoted above, opens with a statement by the Chief
of Staff and the Secretary which proclaims that 'whereas for most of our

lives the default condition has been peace, now our default expectation must be conflict'.[19]

US armed forces, transformed to be more net-centric, lighter and therefore more agile, and better able to conduct so-called Effects Based Operations (EBO), will be capable of performing even better in a style of warfare at which they excel already.[20] That style is focused upon the delivery of overwhelming firepower. US forces will be more flexible, better informed, and more able to fight with precision. However, as a friendly sceptic, this author must register a few caveats. High technology forces have characteristic problems. They require a large maintenance 'tail'. They are severely subject to 'friction'. They may be vulnerable to relatively low technology offsetting tactics (e.g., electromagnectic pulse [EMP] from a nuclear explosion, cyber attack). And, the high technology forces may well be ill fitted to cope with many of the strategic missions of the next several decades. While the United States must keep its lead in regular warfare, particularly in its ability to command the 'commons' of the sea, air, and space, most of its warfare in the 'contested zone' on land will not be concluded by firepower, no matter how precise, or by decisive manoeuvring enabled by firepower.[21] Competent irregular enemies, in particular, are reluctant to present themselves as lucrative target sets to be pulverized from the air, or to be outmanoeuvred for annihilation. The US Army knows this, and is doing its best to change its culture to adjust to the new strategic context. It is far from certain to what degree it will succeed. As I have argued at length elsewhere, the dominant American strategic problem today lies not in a lack of net-centricity, but much rather in a persisting inability to wage war in a manner that serves the country's political goals effectively.[22] The contemporary long-term process of military transformation, whatever its technical virtues, will be devalued by a persistent and debilitating political deficit in the American way of war. All too often there is a black hole where American strategy ought to reside.

Is strategic history propelled predominantly by an irregular series of great discontinuities in the grammar of warfare? Have we lurched from upheaval to upheaval? The proposition that from time to time there are radical changes in the character or conduct of war, the RMA hypothesis, is entirely reasonable. The plausibility of such a minimalist statement of the RMA argument is, however, easily shaken by more ambitious efforts at definition.

In 1994, Andrew F. Krepinevich wrote what came to be widely accepted as the founding definition for the American RMA debate: 'What is a military revolution? It is what occurs when the application of new technologies into a significant number of military systems combines with innovative operational concepts and organizational adaptations in a way that fundamentally alters the character and conduct of conflict.'[23]

Can there be radical, even transformational, change in the conduct of war without the application of new technologies? Even when new technologies are present, as usually will be the case, how important are they relative to other factors? It is hard to locate new technology in the Napoleonic RMA, for example. The new machines in the mechanized RMA(s) of the 1930s, and the IT behind the information-led RMA which arguably laid down a historical marker in the sand in 1991, were both dwarfed in relative significance by training, discipline, staff work, and tactical combat skills, not to mention the stupidity of the enemy. This is not to claim that the technology of *Blitzkrieg* in 1939–41, or of parallel air operations in 1991,[24] did not matter. Nonetheless, the defeat of France (and the BEF) in 1940 was enabled by the modern machines which granted the possibility of an operational mobility that was simply mechanically unavailable to the soldiers of 1918. But it was secured because the Germans were better trained, better led, enjoyed higher morale, had the sounder tactical and operational doctrine, *and were extremely lucky* to face a Franco-British enemy whose incompetence at the operational level of war was truly extraordinary.

Some of the dazzle of RMA dissipates when the concept is removed from theoretical discourse as well as from the context of current defence issues, and instead is introduced to the full complexity of historical narrative. Even though history can be non-linear, 'nothing comes from nothing, nothing ever could', as the song from *The Sound of Music* affirms persuasively. Obviously, radical changes occur in the character and conduct of war. But is it defensible to argue that there has been an irregular series of succeeding, sometimes overlaying additional, historical RMAs? Furthermore, even if there have been such historically demonstrable events, have they been of decisive importance, given the multidimensional complexity of strategic history? In other words, have well attestable RMAs shaped the course of history?

A trouble with RMA theory is that, in English parlance, it over-eggs the pudding, and it tends to do so at the expense of ingredients more mundane than obviously different technologies. The better among RMA commentaries are at pains to point out that 'technology alone has rarely driven them; it has functioned above all as a catalyst'.[25] No one should dispute the facts of change in the character and conduct of war, even of radical change, and occasionally perhaps radical change effected swiftly. But, do those non-controversial facts, which we may choose to equate with historical RMAs, help to explain very much? On close examination, it transpires that although the RMA label can be applied plausibly to particular changes in warfare, those changes are far from functioning independently in their influence on the course of events. It is true that a lead in military prowess should have strategic consequences with practical, including political, benefits. However, no prizes are awarded for the less than brilliant insight that better armies tend to beat worse armies. Unfortunately for neatness of analysis, only rarely is modern war usefully reducible to an austere contest between carbon-copy armed forces. If warfare has become a spectator sport hosted by the globalized media, do *our* relatively few professional warrior-gladiators fight *their* relatively few warrior-gladiators, while the rest of us watch the entertainment in detached comfort on television from the comfort of our sofas? States, coalitions of states, and above all else, *societies*, make war. This remains true, despite the global trend towards wholly professional armies. The better army, at least in terms of net body counts, the German, lost both World Wars.[26] Moving on, the nuclear revolution has only modest explanatory power to help solve the mystery of why the USSR lost the plot in the 1980s and crumbled so precipitately. It may well be true that it was the emerging and anticipated IT revolution that proved fatal to the Soviet system.[27] But the reason why this should be so has politics, society, and culture, at its core and technology only as a dependent factor.

RMA theory is a glass half-full, or half-empty, as the commentator prefers. But, the more useful we find the RMA concept the more aware we need to be of its systemic bias in favour of discontinuity. RMA theory asserts a break with the past. Even if a candidate RMA poses novel-looking challenges, many of the ingredients that produce military effectiveness either do not change at all, or change only slowly. Earl H. Tilford reminds us that 'in the final analysis, war is about people, not systems. Armies, air forces, and navies function with people who use and employ machines and weapons'.[28] And, as General Sir Ian Hamilton once wrote, 'the soul of an army' is fighting spirit, or morale, not its most favoured items of weaponry.[29] The need for the sound military organization, the discipline, the comradeship, pride, and realistic training that fosters fighting spirit and channels it for maximum effect, and the self-belief that flows from a tradition of victory, has been a constant from Greek hoplite warfare to the NTC and Top Gun. There is a danger that enthusiastic endorsement of the RMA postulate dulls recognition of the 'permanently operating factors' which are prominent among the eternal basics making for military effectiveness: morale, leadership, discipline. In addition, RMA theory can undermine appreciation of the importance of much of yesterday's wisdom about military science, not excluding the much maligned 'Principles of War'.[30]

To illustrate the last point, the skilful use of artillery in combined arms warfare was perfected in 1918: technologies have improved since then, but not comprehension of the challenge of warfare in the third dimension or the methods needed to wage it effectively. The British artilleryman– historian, Major General Jonathan Bailey, has written that 'today [1996] it is said that we are experiencing a new RMA, but in truth the fundamentals look like echoes of the First World War and hardly revolutionary by comparison'.[31] More recently, however, Bailey gives evidence of being rather more impressed than he appeared to be in 1996 with the promise in the

technologies of military transformation. In the conclusion to his definitive history of artillery in modern war, he sounds a note of technical
optimism.

> A new phenomenon is, however, emerging that will reshape battlespace geometry
> and the style of warfare, probably as radically as they were reshaped by indirect
> fire at the beginning of the twentieth century. The technologies at the heart of
> the US Army's 'Transformation' and the so-called revolution in military affairs,
> are primarily those that will deliver precision almost irrespective of range. They
> will restore the underlying 'logic' and 'geometry' of fire relative to the battle-
> space that obtained in the first half of the twentieth century, even though the
> appearance of combat and military organizations might appear radically different
> in the future. The new technologies of precision will also expand the land
> component's battlespace still further into the third dimension, making the 'above'
> as vital as 'close', 'deep', and 'rear'.[32]

The mechanized warfare and aviation RMAs of the inter-war decades
persuaded all major powers, save only for the USSR (and to a lesser degree
the United States), to abandon the bloodily learnt lessons of 1914–18
concerning good artillery practices. Only by 1944 did the British Army, and
arguably the American, recover the lost art of the proper centralized
management of artillery. The German Army in the Second World War,
over-impressed with the potential of mechanized firepower on the ground
and especially from the air, never came close to recovering the combat
power of its lost artillery skills of 1918. The Israel Defence Forces of 1973
similarly were over-persuaded that tanks and air power had largely
overtaken apparently old-fashioned artillery. When they ceased to rule the
skies, Germans and Israelis rediscovered the necessity for a powerful artillery
arm, albeit too late in the German case.[33]

Critics of Admiral Owens' variant of RMA theory – a 'system of
systems' to lift the fog of war and exploit the novel totality of information
– have not been slow to note that he and his close followers have developed
a techno-centric story about future war that is almost wholly lacking a
human dimension, not to mention an intelligent enemy. After all, Man, as
combatant, victim, influential bystander, taxpayer, parent, and so forth, is

the most constant of constants both across the entire spectrum of possible forms of war and throughout all of strategic history. For a vital example, the human dimension of war and strategy always plays, in that a self-willed enemy must be motivated, and may be able, to craft terms and conditions of conflict that pose an awkward challenge to our preferred style of fighting. The current fascination with asymmetric threats shows all the weaknesses characteristic of intellectual fashion.[14] However, this rather obvious idea is no less important just because it is not exactly an earth-shattering discovery deriving from penetrating strategic thought. It helps keep alive understanding of the permanently competitive *nature* of war and strategy. No RMA, of any character, can overturn the order of the nature of war. That nature is the struggle for advantage between the independent, and interdependent, wills and mobilizable capabilities of rival security communities.

Intrepid readers of RMA literature may be puzzled, possibly repelled, by the swamp of jargon that theorists have created over the past decade. This book ruthlessly collectivizes the contending terms under the simple, if admittedly reductionist, rubrics of RMA and transformation. But because of its importance for our theme of technology and war, as well as because of the confusing diversity of usage, let us pause briefly to itemize an intellectual survival guide to the key ideas, of which there are no fewer than the rather forbidding seeming total of eight.[15] However, although it is necessary to understand the distinctions flagged here, we shall try not to allow scholasticism to override common sense. Wherever possible in this analysis, we will refer simply to RMA or transformation. Only if radical change of a particular kind is important to the argument at issue will we draw upon the finer distinctions in the list.

1. *Military Revolution.* These are very rare events, effectively beyond prediction or guidance, and have been likened to geological tectonic shifts. They are tied to deep, sweeping, unavoidable, and irreversible political, social, and usually, though not invariably, technological trends. The emergence of the modern state in the sixteenth and seventeenth

centuries, the French and Industrial Revolutions, and the upheaval of the First World War – all are associated with Military Revolutions. The nuclear, and now the information (computer-based) revolutions, also merit classification as history-reshaping Military Revolutions.

2. *Revolution in Military Affairs (RMA).* Military Revolutions are preceded, implemented, and succeeded by RMAs. RMA refers to a radical change in the character of war. The engines of such change include, but are by no means limited to, technological innovation. Scholars note that most historically plausible RMAs have not obviously been led by new technologies.

3. *Military–Technical Revolution (MTR).* Those RMAs wherein the spur to, and agent for, radical change is overwhelmingly technological, are called Military–Technical Revolutions. Some theorists allege, for example, that today's 'information revolution' for warfare (and much else besides) is merely yet another such revolution.

4. *Revolution in Strategic Affairs.* This idea directs attention to broad and profound changes in the utility of the threat or use of force. Lawrence Freedman has written the most perceptive analysis of this vital perspective on the topic.[36]

5. *Revolution in Security Affairs.* Whereas a Revolution in Strategic Affairs looks primarily to sharp shifts in the relative effectiveness of military power, a Revolution in Security Affairs points up notable discontinuities in the relevance of military power altogether. The premise is that defence and security are not synonyms. A globalized world community will have, or has already, a new security agenda that is not dominated by traditional strategic issues. This idea has been advanced most consistently by Barry Buzan.[37]

6. *Revolution in Attitudes toward the Military (RAM).* A revolution has occurred in the way the military profession, and indeed all things military, are viewed in Western societies. Contemporary lifestyles, demographic trends, and the gendering of political life, to cite just three potent influences, have created a social and cultural context that is not permissive of military action that may incur heavy

casualties. Moreover, Western societies are sensitive to the imposition, as well as the suffering, of casualties, especially if the victims are non-combatants.

The final two ideas, taken together, comprise a rough cut alternative to the scholar's paradise presented thus far as items 1–6. The magic word now is transformation. Like globalization, transformation is gloriously imprecise. Nonetheless, two broad deployments of the term are in common currency and have important meanings, residual ambiguities notwithstanding.

7. *Military Transformation.* This term of art has replaced RMA in officialese, but its meaning is the same. It refers to a radical change in the character and conduct of warfare. Krepinevich's popular definition of RMA, quoted earlier, could serve just as well to define a military transformation. It may be helpful to suggest that RMA can lead to transformation.

8. *Transformation of War.* This is a concept with a distinguished lineage. Commandant Jean Colin of the French École de Guerre wrote an excellent treatise on *The Transformations of War* in 1912.[18] The concept is truly ecumenical. Its broad church welcomes everything not reserved for the narrowly military matters covered by the idea of military transformation. Debate about the possible transformation of war includes, at a minimum, the subjects embraced by the ideas of revolutions in strategic and security affairs. The common thread binding theorists who write about the transformation of war, is the conviction that war and warfare cannot intelligently be treated strictly as a military–technical enterprise.

Since societies prepare for war, and fight, according to their distinctive characters, at least insofar as enemies permit, we should not be surprised to discover that future warfare will contain familiar trends and attitudes. Given the proclivity of events to ambush the complacent, identification of what is happening today can only have educational merit, it cannot serve as the raw material for prediction. Even if our grasp of the character of future warfare is secure and persuasive, that is not the same as knowing about future wars. Still, it is necessary to understand the subject as best we are able, even though that understanding cannot yield a predictive wisdom. We are confident, indeed we observe, that information-age societies plan to fight as they conduct their other vital activities, which is to say making maximum use of information technologies. Their predecessors, industrial-age societies, illustrated this necessary truth with their human and material mass mobilizations for the total wars of the twentieth century. Today's broad and deep Military Revolution, driven by IT, the expression of an information age, may or may not be made manifest in a RMA which literally transforms armed forces. Whether or not transformation happens should depend on the vision, energy, and resources applied by policy, if policy judges radical change essential. At least, that is how things ought to be. In practice, transformation may be pursued more because it can be done than because policy sees any great strategic and political value in it. Whether the current military transformation underway in the United States is propelled more by technology push than policy pull is an open and important question. It would be an error to assume that the US defence establishment has a single military culture or a single view of military transformation. The very different characters of war on land, at sea, and in the air, necessarily produce distinctive world views. Whereas the Navy and the Air Force inhabit military environments literally dominated by technology, the Marine Corps and the Army inhabit a universe that is far more complex and human. While there are technophiles aplenty in the Office of the Secretary of Defence, and in the Navy and Air Force, as one would expect there are relatively few in the Army. All US forces may be unduly committed to firepower solutions to problems of an apparently military nature, but the Army, at least, is driven in its current drive for transformation at least as much by the 'lessons learnt' from recent warfare, as by the promise of IT.[39]

Since our topic is future warfare considered globally, different security communities will modernize their military power distinctively, as they believe they must and, no less, as they can afford. The ideas of Revolutions in Strategic and Security Affairs, or their conflation into the transformation of war, suggest the value of keeping in mind the political, social, and cultural contexts that give military power most of its meaning. Perhaps there will be ever fewer circumstances wherein the threat or use of force would be judged legitimate. As a consequence, our security anxieties may have less and less of a military dimension. If that proves to be the case, then a technically focused analysis of future warfare would misunderstand the relevance of its subject comprehensively.

It is only sixty-six years ago, on 3 September 1939, that a British government solemnly chose to go to war over an issue of convenience, Poland's frontiers, even though it had no plausible theory of eventual victory. The decision to fight over Poland looks almost frivolous by the standards of today, though of course the determination to resist further German aggression was entirely sound in principle. As for 1914, the assumptions and attitudes which fed the interacting decisions to fight appear more irresponsible than prudential.[40] Obviously, the statesmen of 1914 did not expect the war that they launched, but they did know that they were signing on for a general European conflict, the first such in a hundred years. Also, some at least among them knew that the war would be a long and unprecedentedly bloody affair. Attitudes to war have changed and continue to do so. The information technologies that lie at the heart of the American process of military transformation are generically the same as those that enable the contemporary global media market. If future strategic history will be dominated by spectator-sport warfare, it is unlikely to be warfare as we have known it in modern times. The conduct of war can be driven not only by technological prowess, but also by public acceptability, which is to say by the values prominent in a belligerent's culture, and indeed in other cultures important for a war's political context. There is a trialogue among what technology permits, what politics requires, and what society allows. It is necessary to note that political requirements are liable to change in the course of a war, while society's tolerance of war's brutalities generally expands under the pressure of events.

A military transformation which privileges some of the leading political, social, and cultural concerns of a transformation of war, is always liable to be ambushed by one or two of history's nastier surprises. The casualty sensitive, variably debellicized societies of EU-Europe, faint but pursuing in the wake of the American-led military transformation, have the culture of complacency.[41] Societies that feel comfortable and secure can afford to be casualty-shy. They can insist that their military guardians must wage their states' wars of discretion while paying great respect to the decent opinion of mankind. Culture, and the values it embodies, is, however, very much the product of political and strategic context. A military transformation shaped by a culture that anticipates no serious strategic threat to its security, might not produce the kind of armed forces that would be needed for more testing times. An army that parades prettily could be acutely short of warriors, a deficiency that probably would escape notice in a long period of peace.

What follows are six historically well-attested conclusions about the significance of technology relative to warfare's other dimensions. These should be no less valid as guides to thought about future warfare, as they are persuasive summaries of historical experience.

First, relations of technological advantage and disadvantage are dominated by the political, strategic, and operational contexts within which they play. For example, RAF Fighter Command won the Battle of Britain in August–September 1940 even though it had marginally inferior equipment to the Luftwaffe and, particularly at the outset, notably less skilful pilots and inferior tactics. But the battle was waged by a British *air defence system,* the world's first such; guided by sound operational concepts; directed by intelligent strategy; with good enough equipment and combat skills at the sharp end; over friendly geography. Though arguably superior unit-by-unit in combat, the Luftwaffe lacked consistent sound operational direction; pursued an ambiguous strategy; was logistically overextended; and was obliged to fight over unfriendly geography with aircraft critically limited in range. The RAF needed neither clearly superior technology, nor the bloody rout of the foe. What it needed was equipment that was simply good enough, which is to say combat competitive. Victory could be achieved by not losing. The Germans had to achieve air superiority over the Channel and most of Kent and Sussex; the RAF did not. So long as RAF Fighter Command could continue the fight over the prospective invasion beaches and beachhead hinterlands, the Germans could not invade. In Vietnam, the North Vietnamese Army (NVA) did not have to defeat USMACV (US Military Advisory Command, Vietnam) in battle. Instead, it only had to stay in the fight. To that end it needed equipment good enough to sustain itself and to enable it to outlast US political determination at home. The NVA was confident that eventually it would have an unblocked run at the Army of the Republic of Vietnam (ARVN).

The demands made upon technology, and the benefits and disadvantages of technical superiority or inferiority, depend critically upon the contexts within which military competition and war is conducted.

Second, the use made of technology typically is more important than is the technology itself. Early in the Pacific War, in 1942, Japanese military aviation enjoyed a distinct lead over American. But this temporary advantage in equipment was more than offset by an American response keyed to training in new aerial dog-fighting tactics that derived from painful combat experience. In France and Belgium in 1940, French and British land forces on balance were marginally superior to German in quantity and quality of equipment, as well as in numbers of men. The Germans, however, characteristically handled their forces with a tactical and operational skill of which their enemies could only dream. By 1918, the RMA of the First World War, 'the modern style of warfare' as Jonathan Bailey has called it, had matured on both sides of the Western Front.[42] The evolution of that style had required some new technologies (e.g., tanks, light machine guns, asphyxiating and poison gases, more robust aircraft, better communications, and so on). But the distinguishing feature of warfare in 1918, as contrasted with 1914–16, was the skill with which the Germans, British, and French could wage genuinely combined arms combat.

Third, the person behind the gun matters more than the gun itself. Cliché or not, it is true that people, not weapons, kill people and wage war. People, not weapons, also deter and keep the peace. Of course, people perform those functions with weapons. However, if a military unit, even an army, does not fight well, it will not much matter whether it fights poorly with equipment superior or inferior to that of the enemy. There are many reasons why the fighting power and military effectiveness of a force can be unimpressive and uncompetitive. Provided its kit is good enough, which is to say is within the compensatable range, war can be won. The necessary compensation may be provided by superior training, discipline, morale, leadership, numbers, intelligence, logistics, and use of terrain, among a long list of possibilities. History does reveal, though, that technological inferiority in weapons and other equipment is rarely the dominant cause of poor military performance. By analogy, the technically marginally superior Formula One racing car does not necessarily win every race. The car's driver is vitally important, albeit not all-important. He will not win regardless of his measure of technical disadvantage.

The relative importance of technology varies with the geographical environment, as I have indicated above. Navies are technology intensive. They always have been. Airmen have to ride their technology into harm's way. The history of sea and air warfare shows that the human element and his military skills and qualities of character can be decisively significant. Nonetheless, in sea and air warfare the warrior is totally dependent upon technology for survival. Machines are required to carry the warriors into battle. It is only because of technology that humans can function at all in the unfriendly environments of the sea and the air. In the more complex geography of the land, the soldier is relatively less dependent upon the reliability and combat performance of the technology at his disposal. In the space environment, warfare eventually will be conducted in orbit among unmanned spacecraft, while unmanned satellites will bombard terrestrial targets. Nonetheless, human skills will remain vitally important. Even space warfare will not approximate automated, robotic combat. However, it will be a form of warfare with only the minimum of human participation. Cyberwarfare may appear to be an exercise in technological combat. But in reality it resembles gladiatorial fighting, with each belligerent's cyber champions relying as much, if not more, on their skill, experience, cunning, and luck, than on the sophistication of their IT weaponry. The human part of the weapon system always matters, indeed typically matters most. But technology is relatively more significant in warfare at sea, in the air, in space and in cyberspace, than it is on land. Land warfare will long remain manpower intensive, while warfare in all other geographies has to be technology intensive.

Fourth, in principle though not always in practice, it is relatively easy to compensate for technological disadvantage. When we consider the contribution of technology among the many dimensions of war and strategy,[43] it is all but self-evident that this realm of relative advantage and disadvantage should be among the easiest to manage. After all, the technologies behind military and usefully supportive civilian systems are the artefacts of social, political, industrial, and military procurement processes and decisions. Those technologies are influenced by strategic and military cultures and they express particular geographical circumstances and orientation. The technology in weapons and support systems is highly derivative. It would be vastly more difficult to alter the contexts from which weapons technology emerges, than to improve the machines themselves. Even if the pertinent contexts place a belligerent at a comparative technical disadvantage, in principle it is possible for choices to be made in policy, strategy, operations, and tactics which should offset technological deficiency. If our tanks are markedly technically inferior, as was the case in 1944–5, then we need to wage a style of combined arms warfare which has tanks amply supported by close-support aircraft (weather permitting), towed and self-propelled artillery, and – of course – infantry well armed with personal anti-tank weapons. In the last resort, we have to find compensation both in numbers and in tank-fighting tactics which prescribe manoeuvre to secure advantageous firing positions on the flank and to the rear of enemy armour. But available compensation for technological disadvantage is never guaranteed. The Luftwaffe was defeated in the air Battle of Germany in the late winter and early spring of 1944. Had that not been achieved, had the Luftwaffe instead been available to contest the skies over northern France, the Allied armies would have paid a possibly fatal price for their errors in tank design. The dominant American tank model, the *Sherman*, was designed for mobility and mechanical reliability, not for survivability or lethal striking power in combat. It was a matter of culture. Germans designed fighting vehicles around the gun. Americans designed them around the chassis and engine.[44]

Fifth, true technological shortfalls happen. Although ways usually can be identified to work around technological deficiencies, the impression should not be given that such improvised offsets are always practicable. Some forms of non-technical compensation can be prohibitively expensive. For an extreme example, an enemy with superior firepower (e.g., the United States in Vietnam) might be overwhelmed by a vastly superior number of bodies. In this case, the bodies were generally well equipped with small arms, were tactically adept, adequately led, tightly disciplined, and enjoyed high enough morale. Similarly, if one lacks the artillery, specialized vehicles, and engineers to clear minefields in a properly professional manner, and if time is of the essence, one can send bodies to find the mines. There is, of course, a generic problem with the principle of human compensation for technical deficiency. Heroic and desperate personal achievement is likely to be required of the chosen agents of compensation. If ballistic missile defence (BMD) and air defence does not work well to achieve defensive counterforce, then the offensive forces need to be extraordinarily competent or lucky, since they alone will have to perform the whole counterforce mission. If the enemy's tank armour is all but impenetrable to our anti-tank guns, and if poor weather deprives us of close air support, then we may look to the individual infantryman to earn the tank destroyer medal by highly personal endeavour. It can be done, but not reliably and not for long, at least not by the same heroic warriors.

Systemic technological limitations can have profound operational, strategic, and hence political consequences. For example, Napoleon's Grande Armée was always likely to fail in Russia in 1812, because it suffered from a technological weakness that impeded its mobility. The Emperor's animal-powered logistical train could not support the pace of advance required to support his operational ambitions. Time and time again, Russian armies escaped Napoleon's traps because the invader could not move with sufficient speed. In Western Europe French armies could live off the land, but not in Russia.[45]

For another case, the most modern and militarily potent armies in 1918, the British and German, lacked the technical means of transportation to transform a break-in, and then a breakthrough into an operational level breakout. This was strictly a technological–industrial problem. For technical reasons the generals of 1918 could not exploit battlefield success. The German problem was worse than the British, because they had failed to develop and mass-produce the tank. At the end of the war Germany had a mere twenty tanks compared with the Allies' eight hundred. This meant that the Germans had to waste men's lives, artillery ammunition, and precious time, overcoming the tactical challenge of barbed wire barrier zones. The crushing of extensive barbed wire entanglements was the one challenge that the primitive tracked fighting vehicles of 1918 could meet successfully. As the doyen of historians of the First World War, John Terraine, has explained persuasively, the generals of 1914–18 were uniquely doubly disadvantaged among the generals of all periods.[46] Such was the technological context of that war that military leaders lacked the means of reliable real-time communication with forces once they were committed to battle. This meant that the classic way in which a general could shape a combat to influence the outcome, by choosing the time and place to commit reserves, was not available to him, save as a matter of rank guesswork. As just noted, the other unique technological disadvantage under which the generals of 1914–18 suffered was the absence of means for rapid tactical, then operational, mobility. In a previous era, the cavalry could exploit infantry success. In a later period, armoured fighting vehicles could traverse and break out of the battle zone. But the generals of 1914–18 on the Western Front were caught in a fatal hiatus by the demise of the cavalry as an offensive arm, and the immaturity of mechanized mobility.

There is no shortage of cases of the true technological shortfall; the vital machine that either is absent or, worse, is present and does not work reliably or well enough. An especially painful historical example is provided by the bug-ridden history of the torpedo. Both Germany and the United States began operations in the Second World War with a submarine force whose principal weapon was, at best, highly unreliable. It is extraordinarily difficult for a submarine fleet to find tactical, or other, compensation for torpedoes that fail to explode when they should. For another case, scarcely less perilous to unfortunates, British soldiers facing the Zulu Army in the late 1870s discovered that the metal cartridges for use in their newly issued Martini-Henry breech-loading rifles expanded as the weapon grew hotter in action. The result was a cartridge case which could not be ejected, therefore a jammed rifle, and a consequent need to demonstrate prowess with the bayonet.[47] The defenders of Rorke's Drift were obliged to rely heavily upon cold steel, a fact plainly revealed on the bodies of fallen Zulu warriors.

Sixth, and for my final conclusion, technological advantage tends to be fleeting. If a technological lead is rarely decisive, also it is bound to be temporary. So varied are the machines both of war and relevant to war, yet so globally common in modern times is scientific, technological, and even industrial expertise, that expectations of enduring technological advantage should be retired. Such advantage is restrained from exercising militarily decisive effect for two reasons. First, it comprises only one element in the total brew which produces military and strategic effectiveness. Second, it cannot be sustained in the context of a globally technological civilization. The diffusion of knowledge is the historical norm, never more so than now. Although technical diffusion self-evidently is correct for today, it happens also to be true for the entire strategic history of competition among peer belligerents. The great struggles in history, from Ancient Greece to, and including, those of the twentieth century, were not decided by technological advantage. Perhaps one should never say never. Nonetheless, the historical record of technological advantage proving partial, fleeting, and strictly only contributory to strategic success, is impressive indeed.

THE STRATEGIC CULTURE of a defence community is revealed in the style of its strategic behaviour. As a machine-minded culture on the cutting edge of a largely information-led military transformation, the American is inclined to seek advantage through the exploitation of technology. In and of itself, a quest for technical improvement is strategically innocent, indeed is only common sense. But if reliance on the benefits believed to be conferred by better military tools becomes an article of faith in the power of machines, great harm can be done. Better golf clubs help the game only of good golfers. To contextualize technology is certainly not to dismiss it. Technology and human performance are interdependent. A weapon system comprises a material device and a human operator. If soldiers, sailors, and airmen lack confidence in the reliability or performance of their equipment, morale suffers, with catastrophic consequences. Compensation may be sought, and found, in triumphs of asymmetrical ingenuity. Or, the fighting men may be demoralized. The quality and quantity of weapons matters. Technology is only one of strategy's dimensions, but it is always relevant. The last word in this part of the book is granted to the ever quotable Ralph Peters. With characteristic realistic pessimism, he reminds us that 'technologies come and go, but the primitive endures'.[48]

PART TWO

Warfare in the Twenty-first Century

Chapter four

Grand Narratives of War, 1800–2100

The history of warfare is complex, sometimes seemingly non-linear, and even chaotic. Undaunted by that empirical reality, scholars strive to impose some order on the course of events. In a noble quest for understanding, we offer the discipline of a story arc. A besetting sin of a great deal of the more technical literature on future warfare is the neglect of context. In particular, possibilities are outlined, quite bereft of plausible political meaning. Warfare is abstracted from its purposes, from consideration of social and cultural influences, and not infrequently from recognition of the choices that an adaptive adversary may be able to exercise. It is possible, however, to be too helpful in explaining the contexts of war. One can offer too big a big picture. The admittedly immodest intention here is to outline generally complementary explanations of the changing historical context of war over a 300-year period. This multi-pronged approach opens different windows on the past, present, and future of warfare. Readers are not invited to pick their preference, though they are more than welcome to do so should the idea appeal.

As the economist, F. A. Hayek, has written, 'without a theory, the facts are silent'.[1] Future warfare has historical and strategic contexts. Moreover, as we explained earlier, context has two meanings. For this discussion it means both that warfare can make sense only with reference to its multifaceted circumstances – political, social, cultural, and so forth – and that it is itself a part of those circumstances. We suspect that history is a seamless web of awesome complexity, governed as much, if not more, by contingency as by inexorable and largely impersonal forces (e.g., technological progress, globalization). But still we are wont to insist upon the creation of an orderly narrative. When prosecuted with appropriate caution, and with due respect for those features of behaviour that are historically constant, there is everything to be said in favour of the quest for context. Problems arise, however, when the constructed histories of scholars tell us more about their theories, and probably about themselves, than they do about the course of events. Treatment of the future, an exercise necessarily deprived of empirical referents, is especially liable to imaginative manipulation in aid of theorists' beliefs. That granted, future warfare must have historical and strategic contexts that should be revealed, albeit speculatively, in the light of what we do know. We have to acknowledge the likelihood, even the certainty, of some great surprises, apparent or actual non-linearities. Despite that necessity, it is my contention that we know a great deal about future warfare. The future has to flow from, is made by, the past and the present. That is what is meant by historical context.

The already large, and still growing, literature on future warfare supports a variety of what may be called grand, or meta-, narratives. That is to say, theorists have signed on to a dominant idea which they employ to explain the basic structure and trajectory of events. Instead of history being just 'one damned thing after another', a pattern, even a direction, is discerned, if not invented. This irresistible urge by scholars to seek large causes for large events has much to recommend it. Plainly it has huge, indeed potentially directive, relevance to our enquiry. After all, the somewhat complementary and somewhat competitive grand narratives now available in the marketplace of big ideas could, perhaps should, provide the keys to unlock the mysteries of future warfare. The future has to be unknowable in detail. But the veil of ignorance has to be significantly lifted if we can show how future strategic history should follow a pattern already well established and demonstrated persuasively by events. Some of the analysis below has a rather critical, certainly sceptical, tone. That tends to reflect only dissatisfaction with exclusivity implied by, or claimed for, the theories on offer. Each of the candidate grand narratives presented here tells an important story about the past and future history of warfare, and has to be accommodated, even if it is rejected in its grander form. This author is as strongly drawn to grand narrative as is the next person, and believes that a dominant idea about future warfare is, or would be, an excellent explanatory, even – dare I say it – predictive, tool. It would be agreeable to be able to argue convincingly that the issue in dispute is not grand narrative or dominant idea per se. Rather is it which grand narrative or narratives, expressing which dominant idea(s)? Unfortunately, there is a systemic problem with the truly grand narrative.

Notwithstanding its popularity and potential utility, the quest for a dominant narrative is a mistake. It is an error identical in kind to the hunt for a general theory of the causes of war. Neither strategic history writ large, nor the occurrence of particular wars specifically lend themselves to explanation by general theory. It is no secret why this should be so. Both are too complex, too variable in historical detail, to succumb to the discipline of a single grand narrative of comprehension. It must follow that efforts to devise grand narratives of reasonably tidy explanation are a waste of endeavour.

It is important to note that several of the candidate dominant ideas examined below have the unfortunate effect of encouraging the fallacious belief in progress. They carry the message that warfare not only changes, but has changed and is changing on a historical trajectory towards its marginalization, effective control, and perhaps its elimination altogether. A perennial problem with grand narratives is that they are wont to seduce their authors into constructing a story that not merely moves on, but moves on apparently purposefully. Alas, history is not like that.

The literature of strategic and international studies, past and present, is littered with candidate dominant or grand narratives of war. Most defence professionals, let alone those they serve, are not strategic theorists. It follows that the few bold intellects who do seek the Holy Grail of the master narrative, the intellectual formula that explains why, how, and when, strategic history moves, usually can gather a body of supporters before interest wanes, circumstances alter, or the next big idea comes along. By way of example, the theory of so-called Fourth Generation Warfare (4GW), which I discuss in detail later in this chapter, currently is staging a revival; it surfaced first in the late 1980s.[2] This very big idea conveniently organizes the strategic history of the past two centuries into four eras, called generations. 4GW theory has something to recommend it, but then it always did. All but invariably, and certainly in this case, one discovers on close inspection that enterprising theorists have reinvented the wheel, given it a fancy name, and sold it as the answer to our strategic dilemmas. Each big idea is retailed as providing the golden key that unlocks the mysteries of strategic history, past and future. Or so it is claimed. In fact, especially when they are targeted upon a defence community largely innocent of historical knowledge, the more imperial of would-be dominant narratives on balance tend to be a menace. Their merit in providing valuable perspectives is offset, usually more than offset, by their habit of proceeding well beyond their 'culminating point of victory'. Each of the grand narratives discussed below contributes some important insights about strategic history. But none, save the final one, which in truth is more of an *anti*-grand narrative, should be trusted to provide the magical elixir that turns the base metal of a confusion of events into strategic gold. Despite the reservations expressed about grand theories with their dominant ideas, it is necessary to take what value we can from them.

From the catalogue of somewhat alternative master ideas, the selection of twelve should suffice to capture most of the content of, and attitudes in, the current debate about future warfare. The choice of 1800 as a historical book end is less arbitrary than is 2100. The 1790s and 1800s were extraordinarily important years for the changing character of war,[3] while the selection of 2100, or any similar prominent date in the future, has to be no more than a convenience. Each grand narrative has some merit, otherwise it would not be represented here, though I will not pretend to apply a wholly judicial even-handedness. The argument of this book endorses and in its argument reflects the perspective of the twelfth option. That said, the others most definitely are not presented simply as straw targets. Indeed, to repeat, I find some value in each of them. As soon will be evident, these alternative master narratives differ markedly in their historical reach and focus. In summary form, to be elaborated and discussed later, the following are the twelve dominant, organizing ideas:

1. The rise and fall of total war.

2. The obsolescence, perhaps demise, of major interstate warfare.

3. The decline and fall of 'old (interstate) wars', deemed, inaccurately, to have been of a Clausewitzian 'trinitarian' character, and the rise of 'new wars' of an allegedly post-Clausewitzian, post-modern, and 'fourth generation' kind.

4. The emergence of a new security agenda that, some believe, has little by way of a strategic dimension.

5. The recurrent struggle to dominate, and resist domination of, the Eurasian landmass by a single power or coalition: the grandest narrative of geopolitics.

6. The successive occurrence of Revolutions in Military Affairs (RMAs), and, less often, of the more profound phenomena of Military Revolutions (MRs).

7. The history of technology as the history of warfare.

8. The expanding geography of war, from two to five dimensions.

9. The relatively sudden appearance of the new 'apocalyptic', religiously inspired terrorism, as the defining threat of the twenty-first century.[4]

10. The slow but inexorable proliferation of weapons of mass destruction (WMD), in this Second Nuclear Age as the leading security threat for the new century.[5]

11. The gradual limitation or taming of warfare through its widespread, though not yet quite universal, delegitimization, as a result of cultural change.

12. Warfare of many kinds are possible, indeed probable. In its political, social, cultural, and strategic essentials, the past history of warfare is the best guide to its future. The historical study of warfare provides invaluable education on what is likely to come.

Each of these dominant ideas provides a fairly clear answer to the question, what is the dominant context for warfare in the twenty-first century? These twelve all have important and variably convincing stories to tell. Directly or indirectly, each carries a message that we could choose to endorse as the organizer of our view of future strategic history. Although the twelve options are of course associated with particular theorists, the presentation and analysis here is strictly my own. The discussion does not purport to explain the opinions of individual commentators. The options are presented at this juncture because each in its way offers notable insights into the possible and probable character of future warfare. Moreover, the popularity of several of these candidate organizing ideas could well have a significant, including dire, impact upon the course of future history. As the analysis will make abundantly clear, this text is not at all neutral and even-handed between what it regards as truth as opposed to error. Each of my choices from the menu of 'very big ideas' could be permitted to serve as our guiding light as we strive to answer Marshal Ferdinand Foch's timeless question, 'de quoi s'agit-il?' What is it all about?

THE RISE AND FALL OF TOTAL WAR

Many historians have found the thesis of the rise, decline, and finally the fall, of what has been called, rather ambiguously, 'total war', quite irresistible. For those among us who try to teach the strategic history of modern times, total war is the master narrative from a Harrod's catalogue. Armed with this huge idea, we can organize and interpret nearly two hundred years of blood-soaked history. Moreover, when we social scientists enter the lists as seers on the strategic future, the decline and fall of total war is a grand tale that has potent implications, one is tempted to say momentum, for the understanding of the future of warfare.

Lest I be accused of exaggerating the popularity of the story of total war, I appeal for support to historian Roger Chickering. He claims that 'the [master] narrative [keyed to the idea of total war] informs all the standard histories of modern warfare'.[6] Chickering explains that: 'The master narrative of total war has had enormous appeal to military historians in the second half of the twentieth century, for it has provided a coherent structure and a compelling heuristic framework to address aspects of warfare that have left an enduring imprint on our own world.'[7]

Before the celebration of conceptual victory runs to excess, he proceeds to dampen enthusiasm in ringing tones. 'It [the master narrative of total war] also has inspired enough bombast, confusion, misinterpretation, and historical myopia to invite the question whether it ought to be rethought and its central element, the concept of total war, be jettisoned.'[8]

Such can be the lot of unduly imperial concepts. The first half of the twentieth century recorded the apogée of total war. Such conflict was the malignant product of the mutual enablement and reinforcement of three historical factors: the appearance, or eruption, of truly national feeling, first occasioned by the American and French Revolutions; industrialization; and the revolution in communications effected by the electric telegraph, the railways, and then the telephone and the internal combustion engine. When rival ideologies are mixed into the brew as a high octane fuel of motivation, additional to traditional reason of state, then total war can approximate a literal description of behaviour. The German–Soviet war within the Second World War was the exemplar of just such a conflict. It was waged on both sides as a war of political and physical extermination. The second half of the twentieth century registered the virtual, though still real, conflict of the great Cold War. That war had its origins in both ideology and realpolitik. Once the superpowers had equipped their striking forces with hydrogen bombs, which is to say after 1954, the rather loose concept of total war acquired a whole and grim new meaning.

The theorist is able to show and explain the emergence of fairly total war in the pre-industrial Europe of the very early nineteenth century as a grand narrative. That development contrasted sharply with the practice of waging wars of *raison d'état,* which had been the non-ideological norm from the second half of the Thirty Years War (1618–48) until revolutionary France broke the mould in 1792. The hypothesis of total war lends itself to expedient service as a packaging agent that binds the course of strategic history from the late eighteenth century to either the middle or near the close of the twentieth. Nuclear weapons may be regarded as the apotheosis of war's potential for totality, as well as the technological development that rendered the concept of total war an absurdity.

Although it is plausible to end the total war saga either in 1945 or 1991 (with the demise of the Soviet Union), this particular historical grand narrative almost begs to be extended into this new century. If the rise and fall of total war is regarded as the main event, or process, in modern strategic history, it can be shown in clearer focus when it is contrasted with the dominant forms of warfare that both preceded its emergence and prospectively succeeded it. The theory of the rise, decline, and fall of total war, invites, almost requires dramatically, a sharply contrasting period to follow. If the eighteenth century was the perfect prologue to the tale of total war, so the twenty-first, many commentators insist, will provide a fitting epilogue.

THE OBSOLESCENCE OF MAJOR INTERSTATE WAR

The rise and fall of total war can be augmented by the theory that major interstate warfare is either obsolescent or obsolete. In the blunt words of two scholars from the US Army War College: 'Decisive war between major states is rapidly moving towards history's dustbin.'[9] Such adjectives as major and decisive conceal as much as they reveal. One knows what the authors mean. Large-scale warfare between powerful states, concluding with a clear victory for one side, is now passé. This thesis can be employed as an extension into future strategic history of the grand narrative. What is on offer is a most important negative judgement, employed to shape expectations of the entire character of future war. This theory claims that the time of major interstate wars has passed. There is no denying that this candidate dominant idea has profound implications for national and international security as well as for defence planning. It implies that states need no longer invest in the kind of armaments most appropriate for waging war against other states. But, despite its high popularity at present, the proposition that major interstate war, in common with its close relative, total war, is now a matter only for historians to debate, is neither true nor plausible. Notwithstanding the number of its adherents, the theory of the demise of such warfare is not a fact, it is only a theory that rests upon a recent trend. The reasons advanced most often to support the theory do not fare well under close interrogation. The key word, 'major', is desperately ambiguous, while, more seriously, none of the explanations for the death of major interstate war are even persuasive, let alone conclusively so. The principal weaknesses of this particular grand narrative are: the unsound assumption that states, even the greatest among them, are in decline as significant players in international security politics; an unduly narrow view of the reasons why states have fought each other, and may well do so in the future; and, finally, an unwise belief that a current trend, even if accurately interpreted, represents history's last move. In short, the theory, or grand narrative, which holds that the dominant story of modern and future warfare is about, first, the rise and fall of total war, and, second, the decline and demise of major interstate war, is not to be trusted.

'OLD WARS' AND 'NEW WARS', INTO THE FOURTH GENERATION

The corollary to the hypothesis just criticized is the fashionable thesis that strategic history is imposing upon us a period, irreversibly many would allege, to be dominated by new kinds of warfare that do not fit what some scholars mistakenly hold to be the Clausewitzian paradigm.[10] Our second grand narrative was negative. It told of the decline, further decline, and all but complete obsolescence of major interstate war, or wars between major states, which is not quite the same. This third narrative is positive, albeit certainly not in any normative sense, in that it asserts the rise and dominance of warfare within states and with or between non-state entities. If the theory of 'new wars' is to be believed, the state is in terminal decline as principal provider of security and as the object, perhaps icon, of primary public loyalty. In this view, the time is approaching when we should talk of a post-modern, certainly post-Clausewitzian, context. States with armies, indeed states as the only legitimate, and legal, war-making entities, somewhat propelled by popular passions, are no longer the main agents in warfare. Or, if that is too robust a statement for today, at least it is the unmistakable story of future warfare.

The degree to which this view is now commonplace is well illustrated in the *Collins Atlas of Military History*, published in 2004. The two-page spread on 'future war' in this generally excellent work, opens with the following claims: 'Future war will be shaped by a range of post-modern changes in politics, culture and society as well as by technology. Non-state actors have become as powerful on the world stage today as they were in the pre-industrial age.'[11]

The first claim is somewhat true, while the second is both confused and distinctly arguable. The authors mean early modern, not pre-industrial. The claims quoted do indicate plainly, however, how strongly the tide of opinion is running against anxiety about future interstate warfare.

This grand narrative holds that we are participant observers of a transformation of war away from the dominance of interstate conflict. A superior variant holds the more realistic view that the grand narrative of future warfare will be the tale of states waging warfare against highly asymmetrical non-state enemies. The same Army War College authors quoted already provide interesting detail on what they regard as the character of the new warfare of the future.

> As states themselves are constrained from overt military aggression, the armed forces of all nations will be involved in promoting internal stability and confronting internal enemies, whether separatists, militias, insurgents, terrorists, armed criminal cartels, or something similar. The first two decades of the 21st century will be dominated by protracted, complex, ambiguous armed conflicts rather than short, politically and ethically clear ones leading to decisive outcomes.[12]

There is much sense in that. But is that vision, carefully limited by the authors to the next twenty years, plausible as the dominant narrative for future warfare? One can endorse much of the argument advanced by Steven Metz and Raymond Millen, the War College authors, without buying it on an exclusive basis. There is merit in the claim that many, even most, of the wars of today, and probably tomorrow, will take the form suggested by Metz and Millen. However, that measure of agreement does not oblige one to sign on for belief in the demise of interstate, even major interstate, warfare.

Many scholars have argued in favour of this third candidate grand narrative. Indeed, currently this is the most fashionable view of future warfare. Martin van Creveld, an Israeli professor of military history with a canon of brilliant writings to his name, is probably the most influential prophet of the allegedly new warfare.[13] His 1991 book, *The Transformation of War,* truly was both a landmark and a signpost work. Whether his analysis was correct, or correct enough, as well as brilliant, is another matter. At approximately the same time that van Creveld was preparing his study, the same theory was advanced by the outstanding and bold American theorist, William S. Lind.[14] Lind's very grand narrative of future warfare was supported by an architecture of past generations of warfare, three to be precise. In nutshell form, Lind argued that warfare from the seventeenth century until now has passed through: a first generation dominated by the smooth bore musket, and its consequent tactics; a second generation of industrial age warfare keyed to fire and movement, increasingly the former, especially artillery; and a third generation ruled by the quest to restore freedom of operational manoeuvre from the tyranny of attrition by dominant firepower. Fourth generation, or future, warfare will be conflict among, or certainly with, many belligerents by and large other than states. Recall that states have been the only legally legitimate war-making agents since the mid seventeenth century. This view of the future is keyed to the assumption that processes of globalization, *inter alia*, have set the state on the path of irreversible decline. It carries the rather grim prediction that the wars of Yugoslav succession, and the genocidal conflicts in Africa in the 1990s and today, comprise the future of warfare – at least until the fifth generation appears and is recognized and celebrated as such by the tidy-minded theorist.

The theory of Fourth Generation Warfare, or 4GW, merits extended critical attention here for several reasons. It appears to be a very big idea indeed. Its author and his followers profess to be able to explain how and why warfare has evolved both over the past 350 years, and on into the future. In a recent publication, Lind tells us that the First Generation 'runs roughly from 1648 to 1860', while the new firepower of rifles, automatic weapons, and recoilless artillery, effectively banished the old 'line and column tactics' and mandated a new, modern, style in warfare.[15] Lind attributes the development of Second Generation Warfare (2GW) to the French Army 'during and after World War I, when it sought a solution to the problem of tactical mobility in mass firepower, most of which was indirect artillery fire'. He is correct to flag artillery as the key to success in the First World War. It was that firepower which enabled infantry movement. Lind proceeds to date Third Generation Warfare (3GW) also from the First World War, as intelligent soldiers on both sides sought ways to restore manoeuvrability to armies. German storm trooper infiltration tactics of 1917 at Caporetto in Italy, and on the Western Front in the great offensives of 1918, were characterized by 'speed, surprise and mental as well as physical dislocation' of the enemy. This was Blitzkrieg without mechanization.[16] It was also a formula for the taking of casualties among élite formations that Germany could not afford in 1918. By 1939–41, the machines were available for the new form of 'manoeuvre warfare' to have its brief heyday as mature 3GW.

The object of our contemporary interest, 4GW, is not precisely dated, but is tied umbilically to the perceived decline in the authority and competence of the state. 'The state loses its monopoly on war ... and Fourth Generation war is also marked by a return to a world of cultures, not merely states, in conflict.'[17] We are told, to repeat. That 'at its [4GW] core lies a universal crisis of legitimacy of the state'. Lind claims that 4GW 'is not novel but a return, specifically a return to the way war worked before the rise of the state'.[18]

Talented and intellectually brave strategic theorists are in such short supply that I hesitate before drawing a bead on Lind and his grand narrative of succeeding generations of warfare. Nonetheless, there is no avoiding the judgement that 4GW is a rediscovery of the obvious and the familiar. For reasons that sociologists and accountants may be able to explain, defence professionals, military and civilian, have a record of rallying to the latest slogans and buzz words that masquerade as profound thought. Some of these buzz words secure official endorsement and decorate plans and doctrine for a few years. Readers of this book have met a few of these totemic acronyms and concepts already. For example, there is network-centric warfare (NCW), at the heart of the current US military transformation; nor should we forget the idea of transformation itself. In addition, we find Effects Based Operations (EBO), asymmetric threats and strategy, and last but not least, 4GW. What these ideas have in common is that they all repackage the obvious in ways that mislead the credulous. It is not quite the case that they are vacuous, but rather that they contribute nothing new to the intellectual tools available to help us understand the dynamism of strategic history.

There is nothing new about NCW, except that the IT revolution married to space systems should allow all, or many, combatant units to fight from the same page of hopefully dominant information. NCW is fine when it works and if the people at the sharp end have time to digest and use the data flow. NCW has long been a military aspiration. In and of itself, even if it functions effectively, it does not address the real problems with the preferred US way of war. Those problems mainly have to do with an over-dependence on technology in general, and massive firepower in particular, as well as difficulty in using force effectively for the kind of peace desired. EBO is an oversold rediscovery of what military forces have always been about in action. Surely, all applications of military power are intended to achieve particular effects? The probable fact that new technology permits forces to be more precise in their behaviour is simply an improvement upon what they have always striven to achieve. Indeed, how could military power be employed except as directed in EBO? The concept is essentially void of meaning. Even the current master talisman of 'transformation' is less informative than might be assumed. Today, transformation is so official in the United States that every element in the armed forces is obliged to demonstrate its fidelity to the notion by devising transformation plans. Given the cumulatively radical changes that the US Armed Forces have absorbed over the course of the past century, it is hard to resist the conclusion that the contemporary transformation is less extraordinary historically than the concept promises. Of course this is not to deny that 'the Army is pursuing the most comprehensive transformation of its forces since the early years of World War II'.[19]

To its prophets, 4GW *is* future warfare, pending, as we have noted, the arrival of war's Fifth and then Sixth Generations. Paradoxically, the main problem with 4GW as master narrative lies not so much with what is false or at least dubious about the theory, but much more with what is correct about it. William S. Lind and Thomas X. Hammes, the most prominent among 4GW theorists, tend to write persuasively for the excellent reason that 4GW in good part is an empirical reality: it is substantially true. But, for a killer caveat, it is not true enough. In fact, on close examination the identification of four generations of war to date, though in the main accurate, is a gross over-simplification of historical reality. From the gospel according to Hammes, future warfare, which is to say

> Fourth-generation warfare (4GW) uses all available networks – political, economic, social, and military – to convince the enemy's political decision makers that their strategic goals are either unachievable or too costly for the perceived benefit. It is an evolved form of insurgency. Still rooted in the fundamental precept that superior political will, when properly employed, can defeat greater economic and military power, 4GW makes use of society's networks to carry on its fight. Unlike previous generations of warfare, it does not attempt to win by defeating the enemy's military forces. Instead, via the networks, it directly attacks the minds of enemy decision makers to destroy the enemy's political will. Fourth-generation wars are lengthy – measured in decades rather than months or years.[20]

We may be forgiven if we observe that Hammes describes not merely an alleged 4GW, but the nature of war in all periods. War is, and has always been a contest of wills. As for the claimed novelty of not seeking victory 'by defeating the enemy's military forces', that is simply a restatement of the structure of irregular warfare. The irregular belligerent generally aspires not to win on the battlefield, where he is fatally disadvantaged in contrast to the regular enemy, but rather in the minds of the regular foe's leaders and populace. Victory is secured when the latter can be encouraged to decide that the further prosecution of a conflict is not worth the effort. This is an eternal mode of warfare, not warfare's Fourth Generation. It is worth recalling that Clausewitz defines war as an act of force to compel our enemy to do our will.[21] Ideally, in his view, the enemy would be rendered physically powerless to offer further resistance, but in practice most wars, regular and irregular, are concluded when one belligerent decides that it has had enough. For a historically distant, but telling, example, a leading historian of the Roman way of war informs us that 'in a very real sense any war in this period [100BC – AD200] was a conflict between the respective wills to fight on of the peoples involved. A war was decided when one of the participants admitted defeat and was no longer prepared to continue the fight'.[22] That sounds familiar.

We are bound to conclude that 4GW has discovered nothing in particular beyond a vital aspect of the permanent nature of war. In addition, it is hugely vulnerable to the strong probability that its faith in the decline and fall of the state is lethally premature. Sad to say, there are good reasons to believe that regular warfare, as well as irregular, is destined to enjoy a long life yet. This argument is developed in the next chapter.

A NEW SECURITY AGENDA

The next grand narrative to note is the plausible claim for the rise of a new security agenda. This argument comes in two main variants, one of which this text substantially endorses, while the other is rejected. The thoroughly unpersuasive variant is the assertion that by far the most serious problems of security in the twenty-first century have no connection with strategic issues. Whereas national security traditionally has been virtually a synonym for national military defence, it is popular today to argue that the threats to the nation's security now lie overwhelmingly in the realms of environmental degradation, health, economic stability, and cultural identity. Even the menace of terrorism is defined largely in non-strategic terms. It is regarded as a challenge primarily to Arab and other Muslim countries to change the domestic conditions that allegedly breed the mindsets that al Qaeda can exploit. Without denying the necessity for physical protection against terrorists, the new security agenda school insists that the task is not primarily, if at all, a military problem. Rather is it a job for the intelligence services and the police, in a context of intimate international cooperation. The storyline of this narrative thus is that the prospect of warfare in the future, certainly warfare on the larger scale, should fade away. Warfare simply will not be relevant to the great problems of security in the future. Global warming, floods of illegal migrants, possible disease pandemics, and economic and financial instabilities, can none of them be addressed by military means. War will not be waged because it would serve no useful purpose.

Up to a point, but only up to a point, the view just presented is thoroughly plausible. The typically global, at least transnational, issues that preoccupy those fixated on the new security agenda, are indeed serious problems. It is necessary to take a broad approach to security, one that transcends narrowly strategic concerns. Unfortunately, however, the new security agenda although apparently non-strategic, has a frightening potential to provide ample fuel for some exceedingly major wars in the future. The grand narrative of the new security agenda does not really explain what happens to old-fashioned interstate rivalries. Geopolitics and the balance of power presumably fade into insignificance in the face of the rising perils posed by the new security threats. But a more holistic, and convincing, analysis suggests that the new danger of global warming, for the leading menace, is likely to trigger violent competition for scarce resources. Paul Hirst is all too credible when he writes:

> What happens if the advanced countries [as well as the poorer] are facing massive environmental degradation and pressures for population movement within and between themselves? The scope for war between nations and civil wars will increase greatly, particularly as the climate changes may be too rapid for orderly adaptation.
>
> The state of the international economy in these circumstances is difficult to predict. One thing is fairly certain and that is that basic natural resources will become more salient than they are in the current economic system and certainly more than they are predicted to be by the prophets of the New Economy [IT-led globalized commerce]. Oil, gas, water and farmland are likely to become scarce resources.[23]

If Hirst is right with his powerful argument, 'we may see a greater emphasis on territoriality...'.[24] This could be rephrased as geopolitics meets the information age. Those who claim that wealth and human well-being generally increasingly are created and sustained by the mastery of information technologies, may be in for a rude and violent surprise. In a stable and orderly twenty-first century, one with a fairly open international trading system keyed to global communication networks, the threat or reality of large-scale warfare would have to appear atavistic. But if the resources essential for the sustainment of life, and hence political order, become increasingly scarce, then the fragility of information-based prosperity is starkly revealed. Information superiority is highly desirable, but in and of itself it grows no food, waters no crops, and does not provide living space for growing populations. It is ironic that even as many among us wax lyrical about the benefits of computer technologies, we are moving into a century where irreversible climate change may well place a premium on such real assets as land for food, oil, and water. It is plain to see that even if this century witnesses the rise of a new extra-geopolitical security agenda, the old reasons for conflict have not disappeared, while the new agenda items are themselves all but certain to spark future warfare.

GEOPOLITICS

In Anglo-American perspective, the pre-eminent strategic narrative of 1800–1991 was the recurring necessity to prevent the domination of Europe, then of Eurasia, and then, prospectively, of the whole world, by a single state or coalition. In a supremely bold argument delivered in 1904, the British geographer and occasional geopolitical theorist, Sir Halford Mackinder, warned that control of the landmass of Eurasia could well lead to control of the world.[25] A recent biographer of Mackinder, Brian Blouet, offered this notably grand narrative: 'From a geopolitical perspective the twentieth century with the First and Second World Wars, and the Cold War, was a struggle to prevent Mackinder's prediction coming true.'[26]

Mackinder was not quite a geopolitical determinist, but he did predict that the unification of great contiguous continental territories by railways would mean that the future belonged to land power rather than sea power, strategically at least. He argued that the sea powers of Atlantic Europe had dominated global commerce and been strategically pre-eminent for approximately four hundred years, from 1500–1900, the 'Columbian Era' as he called it. The most pre-eminent of those sea powers, indeed the exemplar of the breed, was of course the polity fears for whose future security gave Mackinder cause for the gravest concern, the British Empire.

Mackinder's geopolitical grand narrative of history, with a temporal reach of 1,500 years, not the mere 300 of my analysis, postulated a see-sawing of strategic advantage between continental and maritime power. 'For a thousand years, a series of horse-riding peoples emerged from Asia through the broad interval between the Ural Mountains and the Caspian Sea, rode through the open spaces of southern Russia and struck home into Hungary in the very heart of the European peninsula....'[27] In the Columbian Era, peripheral Europe deployed its new maritime and military technologies to forge global trading empires. The theory Mackinder first advanced in 1904, and then refined and amended in 1919 and 1943, offered a plausible grand narrative, despite the arrival of air power, and then of nuclear weapons, ballistic missiles, and space systems.

Mackinder's first great conceptual invention was what in 1904 he called 'the geographical pivot of history' (his second was in 1943 with the 'Midland Ocean', which translated well to mean eventually the Atlantic-oriented community of NATO).[28]

> Is not the pivot region of the world's politics that vast area of Euro-Asia which is inaccessible to ships, but in antiquity lay open to the horse-riding nomads, and is to-day about to be covered with a network of railways? There have been and are here the conditions of a mobility of military and economic power of a far-reaching and yet limited character. Russia replaces the Mongol Empire.[29]

He warned that the polity that controlled, or was, the Pivot (1904) or Heartland (1919, 1943) area of Eurasia, a concept that evolved from a strictly physical geographical conception to a strategic one, would be in a position to stage a credible bid for domination of Eurasia. It would enjoy the interior lines of communication attendant upon central location and abundant resources. From its geographically contiguous continental fortress, and if untroubled by major diversions on land, the Heartland state or coalition would be able to acquire the maritime and other assets necessary to challenge for world hegemony. It could compete with the sea power of the states of what he termed, geopolitically, the 'Outer Crescent', especially Britain and the United States.

Mackinder was open-minded regarding the identity of the continental foe. In 1904 it was Russia; in 1919 and 1943, Germany. Had he survived to witness the beginning of the Cold War, he would undoubtedly have transferred his strategic anxiety back to Russia. In addition, he considered China a distant possibility to succeed as the Heartland polity. The identity of the foe is not important for the cogency of the theory. In common with a long tradition in the rationale behind British foreign policy, the Heartland theory identified a permanent interest and postulated a permanent policy solution. Britain needed to encourage or create the second strongest state or coalition, so as to deny continental hegemony to the threat of the day.

Geopolitical theory continues to be unfashionable. It is deemed simplistic, deterministic, irrelevant in an anti-territorial globalized information age, and still tainted by association with the German theorists of *Geopolitik* who allowed themselves to be employed as a tool of Nazi propaganda.[30] All save the last charge cited are incorrect. Mackinder wrote of risks, dangers, and trends, not of certainties. During its four hundred years of strategic ascendancy, the sea power of Atlantic Europe never dominated, let alone conquered, the Eurasian Heartland. Similarly, the thousand-year strategic superiority of Asian horse armies never succeeded in conquering all of peninsular Europe. So, Mackinder's theory was not deterministic. It was certainly simple, but it was so in a way that added greatly to the persuasiveness and utility of the central notion. What his geopolitics offered was nothing less than a master framework, and explanation of the key dynamic, to explain the course of strategic history. Moreover, his grand design does fit the facts of 1800 to the present, and bids fair to fit the century to come also. The basic reason is the inescapable reality of the way in which the world's continental masses have been arranged, or rather clustered, by nature. Like it or not, it is a fact that most of the world's assets of all kinds are gathered together in what Mackinder called the 'World-Island' of Eurasia and Africa. Later in life he came to recognize more and more the potential of North America as a possible continental scale rival to the Eurasian Heartland. But even then, he realized that Eurasia was the principal, really the only, power house from which credible bids for world domination and conquest could be launched. Geography could be destiny.

Of course, there is far more to world politics and strategic history than was flagged by Mackinder. That granted, it is hard to deny that in essentials he was correct.[31] The greater wars of the past two hundred years can all be explained geopolitically with a fair measure of satisfaction. The Great War against France from 1792 to 1815 was precisely a struggle to deny France the continental imperium on the basis of which it could build a navy adequate to defeat maritime Britain at sea. From 1854 to 1856 Britain and France waged a balance of power war to discipline a Russia that was becoming unduly assertive. The twentieth century, as interpreted persuasively by Blouet in words quoted already, seems almost to have been crafted by some unseen hand of history to demonstrate the truth in Mackinder's geopolitics. The great hot and cold wars were waged to deny continental domination to the actual (Soviet Union) or aspiring (Germany, twice) Heartland power of the day. Given the global distribution of land and sea, it is undeniable that super threats to international order really can only come from Eurasia.

If we fast-forward through the twenty-first century the geopolitical tale does not change. It is plausible to the point of being compelling, to argue that the principal story of war will be yet further endeavours by the powers of the 'Midland Ocean', pre-eminently the United States, to deny Eurasian domination to the menace of the era. Most probably, that menace will be China and Russia in alliance, though it could be an axis of China and EU-Europe. Japan and India would find themselves compelled to align with a new US-led maritime coalition, albeit perhaps with a vulnerable

Russian continental partner. For a different perspective on this geopolitical narrative, one could argue that the greater continental powers of Eurasia one day will forge a strategic alliance for the purpose of humbling a hegemonic America. In either variant, Mackinder's theory still holds. The larger examples of future warfare, in common with past experience, will be struggles to achieve or deny the continental domination of Eurasia which could be the launch pad for a truly global imperium of unbalanced power. Today, at the beginning of the twenty-first century, it is all too easy to predict the rise of a new menace from the Heartland of continental Eurasia, a Sino-Russian axis. Already, it is beginning to appear likely that the geopolitical pattern of the twentieth century will repeat itself. The maritime world led by the United States will be locked in a protracted struggle, probably a new Cold War, with a Eurasian continental coalition. The only major uncertainty lies in the identity of China's strategic partners: Russia? Russia and EU-Europe? EU-Europe alone?

Some people will judge geopolitical narrative to be yesterday's storyline, if that. Surely, in an emerging period of globalized commerce, information-led military capabilities, wealth creation preponderantly by the electronic manipulation of data and ideas, and less and less territorially sovereign states, geopolitics belongs in the dustbin of history? Particularly should this be true if major interstate war is believed to have no future. One uninhibited critic of Mackinderesque geopolitics, Christopher J. Fettweis, recently went so far as to register the double claim that *'at the upper levels of international relations geopolitical analysis is already as obsolete as major war itself'*.[32] Would that he were right. I disagree profoundly with both his claims.

REVOLUTIONS IN MILITARY AFFAIRS (RMAs)

An unquestionably grand narrative that can organize the centuries from 1800 to 2100 conveniently for us, is the notion that strategic history is propelled irregularly by a succession of great changes in the character of warfare. Because this idea has been discussed already in Chapter Two, it will be treated only briefly here. As a guiding light for speculation about future warfare, the RMA key unlocks a twenty-first century dominated by cumulatively radical changes. Whether or not those military changes have radical political and strategic consequences, though, is quite another, and more important, matter.

The RMA narrative rests upon some impressive, if sometimes arguable, historical evidence.[33] To simplify, I choose not to distinguish here between RMAs and the much greater Military Revolutions.[34] The past two hundred years recorded RMAs that, successively and additively, produced warfare the dominant characteristic of which was: mass participation by the nation in arms (1792–1991); exploitation of the tools provided by the industrial revolution (1861 to the present); the perfection of warfare in the third (overhead) dimension, in the form of excellence in the use of artillery (1917 to the present); mechanization (1918 to the present); and the development of nuclear weapons (1945 to the present). Future warfare, in this narrative, will be dominated initially by the use of information both as a multi-pronged weapon in its own right, and as an enabler for ever more lethal armed forces, not only for weapons per se. This information-led RMA is now under way all around the globe, simply because an information-led style of combat is where Clausewitz's grammar of war happens to be in this period. Bruce Berkowitz offers the potentially ethnocentric insight that 'everyone is adopting similar methods, because that is what works'.[35] Most of the IT technology useful for warfare is commercially available. Berkowitz argues fairly convincingly that because of the logic of IT, even such extreme opposites as al Qaeda and the US superpower are operating in some significantly similar ways. Overall, competent terrorist organizations and forward-looking states are both committed to fighting with a networked, rather than hierarchical, form of warfare, a style made feasible by mastery of IT.

Beyond the information-led RMA, there is speculation that future warfare may be dominated by an RMA driven by biotechnologies. The stuff of dreams and nightmares, certainly of science fiction, might be the outstanding feature of contemporary warfare. Artificial intelligence, man-machine cyborgs, and genetically engineered warriors, for examples, may belong to the next RMA, once the information age has matured and probably slowed.

What should be an important element in the RMA narrative is the argument that future, in common with past, warfare can usefully be interpreted as a succession of great changes in society and its prevailing attitudes and values. Such changes are not unrelated to technological developments, but they should also be considered apart from machines. Recall that in previous discussions we have noted the appearance of claims for a broad gauged transformation of war, in addition to, some would say more significant than, a narrowly military transformation or RMA dependent upon IT.

The RMA narrative does offer insight into strategic history. But to this author it suffers from an inalienable privileging of novelty, and an equally biasing tendency to undervalue those aspects of warfare that either do not alter or which alter only slowly. Furthermore, for all its exciting promise, the RMA concept explains too little of the rich and complex multidimensionality of war and strategy.

TECHNOLOGY

The past, present, and future of warfare is sometimes treated as if it were synonymous with the history of technology, particularly weapons technology. The material culture of war is confused with war itself. Means and ends are reversed. There is nothing wrong with telling the story of the evolution of weapons technology.[36] Problems arise only if war's technological dimension pushes other, no less important, dimensions aside. Because weapons, certainly machines, tend to be photogenic, dramatic even, and with their human handlers are the actual agents of destruction, they attract a degree of attention that more often than not exceeds their true relative significance. The crucial significance of such perennials as time, friction, chance, danger, fear, leadership and so forth, even of strategy, operations, and tactics, can be under-appreciated because of their abstraction. The engines of war are both easy to visualize and are subject to change. They lend themselves to being miscast for the leading role in a grand historical narrative. Looking to the future, we find an abundance of discussion of biological warfare, chemical warfare, and, of course, information warfare. Moving backwards, there is a huge library of (mercifully data-free) studies of bilateral nuclear warfare. Back still further, we discover armoured warfare, railway warfare, machine-age warfare, and gunpowder warfare, to cite only some of the more prominent features in a crowded historical landscape. There are two serious problems with this elevation of technology to central place in a historical roll of honour. First, such a focus cannot help but demote by implication other, more important, dimensions of war. The troops may be well armed with the machines that we allow to give their name to the period, but will those soldiers fight with determination? Are they well led?

Second, weapons and their support systems are only the tools of war. They are, or should be, the servants of strategy and high policy. If we talk carelessly of nuclear, biological, or information warfare, we risk conveying the absurd idea that the subject with integrity and meaning is the adjective rather than the noun. This error is by no means confined to amateur students of warfare. Defence professionals, people steeped in expertise on nuclear or information warfare, are entirely capable of treating nuclear and information-led operations as ends in themselves. Technology, weaponry, is not strategy. Bruce Berkowitz tells the revealing story that the United States and NATO wished to employ its new cyberwar capabilities to strategic effect in the 1999 war with Yugoslavia over Kosovo. Alas, 'no one had responsibility for designing information operations aimed at a strategic objective, like overthrowing a government'.[37] The future history of warfare can be told, speculatively, as a story of technological evolution and revolution. But it is a certainty that such an approach must mislead more than it can enlighten. War's other contexts, the political, social, cultural, and strategic, will be as, or more, important than the technological.

THE EXPANDING GEOGRAPHY OF WAR

The geography of war, or as it is called today by the cognoscenti, the battlespace, is one of the grander, if arguably dominant, narratives of modern warfare. Few facts so convincingly demonstrate the unity of past, present, and future warfare as does the expansion of its geography. From 1800 to 2100, the geographical dimensions of warfare will have expanded from two to five. Warfare on land and sea predates recorded history. Our accessible, if often unreliable, historical knowledge of such warfare extends backwards for two and a half millennia. Land and sea warfare were very different enterprises. For reasons best summarized as geopolitical, polities typically were stronger either on land or at sea; very few were pre-eminent in both domains. History reveals the recurring strategic problem of how superior land power and superior sea power struggled to find ways to translate their geographically specialized excellence into a war-winning advantage. From Athens and Sparta, through Rome and Carthage, Macedonia and Persia, Byzantium and the Arabs, all the way to Britain and Napoleonic France, there was a pattern of struggle between land-bound tigers and sea-confined sharks.

Until December 1903 technically, and 1916 in reality, combined, what today is known as 'joint' (following American usage) operations could only mean cooperation between navy and army. But the twentieth century, for the first time since humans used boats in war, well before there were historians to celebrate such an epochal event, saw the expansion of exploitable battlespace into the sky. So familiar have we become with air power in all its shapes, sizes, promises, and some performances, that sheer familiarity has tended to dull our appreciation of the monumental change in warfare it introduced.[18] How often in history has a previously closed geographical dimension suddenly been opened for use? The answer is not once, prior to the twentieth century.

Those inclined to the grander form of historical narrative, can argue with some plausibility that the principal strategic challenge of the twentieth century was the necessity to understand, exploit, and perfect the novel air weapon. Indeed the strategic history of the last century lends itself, in my view unsatisfactorily, to interpretation as the rise, further rise, and ultimately the near perfection, of air power. From quaint and fragile toys in the 1900s, aircraft evolved by the 1990s at the latest to the status of the 'leading edge' or 'key force' in warfare.[19] By century's end, so the story went, even if air power could not win wars on its own and unaided directly by land and sea forces, assuredly it had the power to decide which belligerent would win.

This book is not particularly interested in retelling for its own sake the familiar, albeit fascinating, history of air power in war from Italy in Libya in 1911, to the United States and Britain in Iraq in 2003. But we are interested in seeing if the near century-long experience with air power in war has much of significance to reveal about warfare in this new century.

As just noted, a popular thesis holds that the twentieth was a century dominated strategically by the promise and performance of air power, to ignore the nuclear complication for the moment. On the apparent evidence available, it would seem to follow that the twenty-first, in its turn, will be the century of cyber power and space power. What air power meant for warfare in the last century, cyber power and space power will mean for the future. We will interrogate the grammar of these new modes of combat in a later chapter. The purpose here is to ensure that the new geographies of warfare, cyberspace and outer space, are approached and understood correctly. Nearly all the detail of how cyber power and space power will influence future warfare can be only a matter for speculation. Fortunately, though, we know a great deal about warfare per se, and that knowledge is of priceless value as we try to unlock the mysteries of such novel phenomena as cyberwar and space war.

It so happens that what we do not, and cannot, know about those forms of future combat, or about their contributions as enabling agents in joint warfare, is dwarfed in significance by the pertinent strategic lore that the classical theorists have hewed out of historical experience for our education. In the sage words of the Prussian grand master: 'Theory exists so that one need not start afresh each time sorting out the material and ploughing through it, but will find it ready to hand and in good order.'[40] Our experience of cyberwar and space war is non-existent or trivial, but our experience of war on land, at sea, and in the air, unfortunately is almost superabundant. Strategically viewed, the future is the past. No doubt some readers will recoil in horror from so conservative, even pessimistic, an assertion. So be it. We must beg to differ. Warfare is distinctively warfare, and strategy is no less distinctively strategy, regardless of the geographical environment at issue.

What do we know for certain about warfare in cyberspace and outer space?

They must both be obedient to the unchanging nature of war, particularly as it was explained by Carl von Clausewitz. His theory of war applies to each and every geographical environment.

Neither offer panacea solutions to the timeless challenges of war. Cyber power and space power are not wonder weapons, capable independently of reducing enemies to the status of helpless victims.

Both cyber power and space power must serve strategic ends. It is not sufficient to note the impressive performance of space and information systems. A strategic story is essential. Enemies will certainly adjust to the distinctive threats posed by cyber power and space power. Over time, ways will be found to evade, as well as emulate and counter, such forms of power. In this respect, behaviour in, and bearing upon, cyberspace and outer space will obey the general logic of war, which is the logic of the duel.

Cyber power and space power will be layered on to, and integrated with, land power, sea power, and air power. They may well transform the character of some warfare, but they will not revolutionize war itself into a zone where one could begin to talk about a possible alteration in war's very nature. That would literally be an impossibility, as I have explained already. However, a popular school of thought is advancing the fallacy that cyber power and cyberwar will change the nature of war.

As cyberspace and outer space assume ever greater importance in the twenty-first century, they will make warfare an activity of yet greater complexity. Although in theory instant communications, the feasibility of truly networked forces, and exploitation of the ultimate high ground, will solve many age-old problems in the conduct of war, the reality is likely to be rather different. The principal reason is because warfare, even in and through cyberspace and outer space, is not a game against nature. Rather is it a deadly contest, or duel, against an adaptive enemy.

Many people today believe that the information age and the associated exploitation of space systems is in the process of civilizing warfare. Casualty-low, if not quite casualty-free, warfare, is held to be an important theme in the grand narrative of the future. Ever more precise weapons, ever better targeting intelligence, real-time monitoring by the global visual media, are all combining to render warfare less and less of a bloody melée. I am thoroughly sceptical of this view, even though it has some validity in its separate tactical parts. If we consider the scope of possible future warfare, not excluding the certainty of countermeasures to the proclaimed 'new American way of war' as unleashed in Kosovo (1999), Afghanistan (2001), and Iraq (2003), confidence in a casualty-light future recedes abruptly.[41] History shows that new technologies do not always reduce casualties, though they do alter some of the ways in which military power delivers death and destruction.

If you select your enemies with great care it is possible to wage all but casualty-free warfare. General Kitchener managed it in the Sudan in 1898, as did the United States in Kosovo in 1999, as well as in the more regular phases of the wars in Afghanistan in 2001 and Iraq in 2003. Those famous victories were not, however, quite the end of the relevant strategic stories. It is always desirable to suffer few casualties, but contrary to the liberal and humane spirit of this age, it is not always strategically desirable to inflict relatively few casualties on the enemy. Since war is about, and only about, the subsequent peace, the stability of that peace not infrequently depends upon the enemy understanding that he has been defeated. Truly surgical bombardment and daring ground force manoeuvre is apt to contribute too few enemy bodies to lend emotional conviction to the military fact of defeat.[42] If there is no societal tradition of popular armed insurgency, the infliction of an unmistakably definitive military defeat of the enemy's regular forces offers at least a good prospect of diminishing the likelihood of continuing, irregular, resistance. With this principle in mind, the victorious power or coalition, while it may be generous in its success, should not be generous in de-emphasizing the scale and scope of its victory. If the war is not to continue in an irregular mode, or is not to be renewed in regular mode before long, it is essential for the defeated belligerent to accept its defeat as a fact, and to be willing to negotiate a lasting peace on that basis.

Finally, networkable cyber power and space power for certain will not banish what Clausewitz referred to as the friction and fog of war. New technologies will help us communicate more effectively. Also they will remove some of the potential for the growth of a fog that can paralyse decision making. But no technical panacea can eliminate uncertainty altogether. Technology cannot revoke war's very nature, which has risk, uncertainty, chance, and friction, as permanent constituent elements. As Barry D. Watts has written: 'Human limitations, informational uncertainties, and non-linearity are not pesky difficulties better technology and engineering can eliminate, but *built-in* or *structural* features of the violent interaction between opposing groups we call war.'[43]

TERRORISM

It is popular today to proclaim that the struggle against global terrorism is the grand narrative of the twenty-first century. Countering terrorism is the Third World War, or so many believe. This item on my menu of historical grand narratives claims that terrorism and the struggle to contain and defeat it will be the dominant form of, the paradigm for, future warfare. The significance of a grand narrative is that it should answer the most important questions of concern. In particular, it must provide a clear *and dominant* storyline. In only one sentence it has to penetrate to the heart of our subject. In this case, the story is that future warfare will be mainly about the struggle against terrorism. To many readers that may seem to be an utterly unremarkable claim. It is, however, deeply controversial, as we shall see. We defer discussion of the likely significance of terrorism in future warfare to Chapter Six, where it is treated in its proper context, which is to say as a mode of irregular warfare.

WEAPONS OF MASS DESTRUCTION (WMD)

It is fashionable to see the threat, and some actuality, of future warfare dominated by the struggle to acquire, and resist acquisition, of weapons of mass destruction (WMD). This fashion inadvertently provides a convincing example of the reversal of means and ends. The nuclear variety of these weapons is, of course, especially troubling. Understandably enough,

WMD are judged to be a 'bad thing', as Sellar and Yeatman would have put it in *1066 and All That*.[44] By way of qualification, if the WMD are ours, or belong to our close allies and friends – to ignore the fact that states do not have friends, they have interests – they are not quite such a 'bad thing'. At worst, we may concede they are a 'bad thing' that is regrettably necessary for the purposes of maintaining order. Countries acquire or seek nuclear weapons for a variety of external and domestic reasons. One size in explanation does not fit all cases. Nonetheless, the fundamental security function of a nuclear arsenal is to protect the basic political and territorial integrity and values of the state and its society. A nuclear armed power ought to be secure against catastrophic defeat, always provided it has protected its arsenal suitably against surprise attack. No enemy with a home address (i.e., to exclude most terrorists) would dare make the leaders of a nuclear adversary truly desperate.[45] At least, that is the theory. Today, the American superpower, on behalf of international order and, naturally, its own vital interests, is scarcely less committed to opposing the further proliferation of nuclear weapons than it is to waging war on terrorists, worldwide.[46]

No great insight is needed in order to perceive that the struggle against further proliferation, though sensible, is profoundly hypocritical. The current nuclear weapon states – the United States, Russia, China, Britain, France, Israel, India, Pakistan, and North Korea – have no intention whatsoever of abandoning their nuclear armaments. The truth is that nuclear weapons are useful both diplomatically and prospectively strategically. It is for that blindingly obvious reason that some states seek to acquire such weapons. Inevitably, the states that pursue nuclear capabilities with the greatest energy and ingenuity are precisely those that the West trusts the least with their custody. Those among us who have persuaded themselves that there is a potent nuclear taboo are, alas, deluding themselves. It is true that most states are not interested in nuclear weapon status and are appalled by the thought of conducting nuclear diplomacy, let alone nuclear war. But, as always, it is not most states that are the problem for international order, peace, and security. A nuclear taboo is culturally authoritative only in a permissive security context. In cases of perceived dire national necessity, all talk of a taboo would be shown to be no more than hot air.

As the candidate grandest of grand narratives for future warfare, the struggle to contain, slow, and perhaps reverse the proliferation of WMD, is not persuasive. Certainly it is *a* narrative, and it is an important activity rendered all the more so by the probability that terrorist entities eventually will succeed in joining the ranks of those armed with WMD. But there is a fatal weakness in the claim that the campaign against proliferation is going to be the defining struggle of the twenty-first century. Specifically, no country, including the United States, really has the countering of WMD proliferation as its top, *and overriding* policy objective. Some theorists may confuse means with ends, but states usually do not. Nuclear weapons are generally deemed to be a 'bad thing', except, of course, when in the hands of responsible polities committed to a tolerable vision of international order. But, opposing the spread of those weapons as an end in itself has only limited political appeal. The pace of proliferation can and should be slowed, but to pursue an anti-proliferation policy vigorously would be to chase an illusion. In common with terrorists, WMD are here to stay. In practice, the American sheriff of international order will tolerate some proliferation in the future, as it has in the past, because it will have no prudent choice but to do so. America will really care about the rise of China, the emergence of an antagonistic European Union, the possible recovery of Russia, access to oil, and the potential for abrupt climate change, to pick just five matters of vital concern. Compared with such issues, the proliferation of WMD is strictly of secondary moment. As a grand narrative to explain an important thread in future strategic history, opposition to the proliferation of WMD has much to recommend it. However, proposed as the grand narrative which most persuasively should provide order to our expectations of future strategic history, it is a non-starter.

THE DECLINE OF WAR

Despite appalling contemporary evidence of human savagery, it is argued by many people that the dominant narrative for future warfare is its slow, but hopefully inexorable, decline. Allegedly, more and more of the typical brutalities of war are ceasing to be culturally acceptable. There is some hope that one day the institution of war itself will be so discredited, so socially then politically illegitimate, that it will cease to blemish our history. The belated demise of slavery is often cited as an allegedly relevant example of the potency of a social taboo. From the mid nineteenth century, when the International Red Cross was founded (1864) and the first Geneva Convention was signed (1864), to the present day and prospectively on into the future, a coherent narrative can be traced showing the growth of international legal rules for the limitation of warfare. Leslie C. Green's exemplary study of *The Contemporary Law of Armed Conflict*, shows in great detail just what has, and has not, been achieved to date by way of the establishment of a legal framework for warfare of all kinds.[47] Unfortunately, the cumulative success in amassing a body of international law has not been matched by a coherent parallel narrative in the actual conduct of war. It is easy to succumb to cynicism. We can set against the impressive body of international conventions on the laws of war the dreadful evidence of some notable steps backwards in actual behaviour. Adam Roberts hits the target when he concludes that

> Following the Hague Conventions of 1899 and 1907, there was indeed an advance to barbarism in two world wars in this century. This is a sad conclusion for any who believe that treaty law alone can civilize or limit warfare. It suggests that much else is involved in the limitation of war.[48]

As so often with our subject, the truth is far from simple. This eleventh of my chosen dominant narratives warrants inclusion because it is quite widely believed, because it contains some merit, and because it rests upon an illusion that may have dangerous implications for international security. On the positive side, there is no contesting the fact that the past century and a half has registered a most impressive body of laws, rules, and customs, what Michael Walzer terms the 'war convention',[49] all intended to civilize the conduct of warfare. Furthermore, there is no doubt that public attitudes to military behaviour and to war itself changed significantly in the course of the twentieth century. One can speak fairly plausibly of there having been a revolution in attitudes towards war and warfare, at least in the Western world. There is abundant evidence of Western cultural change.

Military forces today are schooled to be obedient to distinctly constraining 'rules of engagement'. Not only are Western publics intolerant of casualties, they are not prepared to excuse much by way of the imposition of 'collateral damage' in the form of unintended harm to innocent enemy civilians. Even enemy soldiers can be dispatched only in the lowest numbers compatible with military necessity. Western theorists tell us that we are in an era of post-modern warfare, wherein our more and more precise weaponry allows the ever more discriminate application of violence. The age of surgical warfare is with us, and it is a trend that will long continue for both technological and cultural reasons. But this techno-cultural development does not come totally cost-free in strategic terms, however. As noted already, the irrepressibly politically incorrect Ralph Peters reminds us that some enemies are notably unimpressed by targeting restraint and precision in weapon delivery.[50] On occasions a high body count, not entirely excluding the innocent, is the pathway to strategic effectiveness. Western societies have specialist professionals to do their dirty work for them; the days of the nation in arms are definitely past. Instead of participating personally in national defence, Western, and increasingly some Eastern also, publics have become spectators of warfare. Combat already is presented very much as a sport, a visually compelling entertainment delivered directly, even live, into the home. When there is a pause in the military action, impatient news anchorpersons tend to be critical, and speak as if they and their audience are owed continuous visual excitement.

The decline of the social institution of war is a high-calorie thesis. Moreover, it contains some truth. However, it is not the whole truth, and for a study like this of future warfare it is grievously flawed. There are several reasons why we must reject the attractive proposition that warfare is becoming ever more controlled, or civilized, perhaps to the point of its ultimate demise.

Modern history reveals a sharply non-linear course in attitudes towards warfare. When the social and political contexts altered, so, inevitably, did the conduct of war. The extreme savagery of the wars of religion of the sixteenth and early seventeenth centuries was succeeded, in good part in reaction, by a century and a half characterized generally by great restraint in the conduct of wars for reasons of state that were modest in ambition. The limited wars of the eighteenth century were followed, initially briefly, by warfare driven significantly by newly discovered, or invented, national passions. The short French Revolutionary and Napoleonic period was regarded as an atrocious episode, and Europe sought to put the clock back to more civilized times wherein public feeling was not required to play a vital role in national defence. From the 1860s onwards, however, and as Clausewitz had predicted, it was evident that the genie of national passions could not be put back in its box.[51] Equipped, fed, and transported by the surplus wealth created by the Industrial and Agricultural Revolutions, war became ever more total in its scale and, in part as a consequence, in its brutality.

The last hurrah for total warfare was the contingent willingness of many states to wage, at least participate in, a nuclear outcome to the Cold War of 1947–89. This is not to deny that most people regarded their country's nuclear arsenal as a shaky guarantee against war, not as a useful instrument for war's actual conduct. Until the end of the 1980s, our societies were prepared to wage the most total of wars imaginable, yet today we are held to favour only 'post-heroic' forms of war, conducted by a relatively few military champions on our behalf.[52] But what if the social attitudes of the 1990s and early 2000s do not anticipate the future? And what if those squeamish or, less pejoratively, humane views are not widely shared beyond the supposedly crumbling borders of our post-military Western polities? The course of modern history has registered some dramatic shifts *in both directions* in attitudes towards the acceptability of forms of conduct in warfare, even towards the legitimacy of war itself. It would be a brave and foolish theorist who would dare predict that the attitudes towards war and warfare, war's cultural context, extant today, will continue and deepen in linear fashion into the indefinite future.

It is a besetting sin of Western theorists to equate their cultural realities with everyone else's. As Jeremy Black, in particular, has argued tirelessly and persuasively, the history of Western warfare is not the history of warfare.[53] Never has this caveat been more true than it is now. American enthusiasts for a new American way of war, keyed to the country's lead in the exploitation of IT, should be sobered by reading the rather startling 1999 study, *Unrestricted Warfare,* written by two of China's most innovative strategic thinkers.[54] Even in a somewhat globalized era, warfare does not have a single cultural context.

Great perception is not required in order to discern a shift in contemporary Western public attitudes towards organized violence, a change triggered by the brutalities of the new terrorism. Societies generally adopt attitudes that suit their strategic context. This eleventh dominant narrative, which postulates a steady growth in war-aversion, is refuted both by historical experience and by the logic of human and political survival. States do, and their societies tolerate and probably applaud, whatever is necessary to ensure their security. The ethics of statecraft and strategy are shaped by perceived necessity. Culture is not free-floating as an influence upon war and warfare. Rather is it a variable body of beliefs that is ever liable to shift as the context moves. If we fail to grasp the truth in this reality, nurturing instead the agreeably optimistic fallacy that humankind is bound inexorably on a generally linear and irreversible journey towards war's demise, a rude awakening will ruin our twenty-first century.

HISTORY: OUR PAST IS OUR FUTURE

The final approach to a dominant narrative presented here is the one that this author prefers. While not quite an anti-narrative, it reflects the view that all of the candidates for dominant story discussed thus far are insufficiently inclusive. This final, preferred, approach holds that warfare of many kinds are possible, indeed probable, in the future. It argues that in its political, social, cultural, and strategic essentials, the past history of warfare is the best guide available to the future. Rephrased, future warfare will be much like past warfare, albeit with some different machines and in somewhat different political, social, and cultural contexts. The important continuities will far outreach the discontinuities. The strategic surprises, the discontinuities or non-linearities, assuredly will alter the contemporary grammar of war. But a historical grasp of war's variety and dynamics provides the best protection against being fatally ambushed by the effects of surprise. After all, although popular literature may imply to the contrary, there is not very much that twenty-first century war can throw our way generically, that we, or our ancestors, have not had to cope with already. Even the more novel-sounding of developments in the field of military transformation, network-centric warfare for a leading example, have ample partial precedents in historical experience. Moreover, the conduct of war is about far more than the efficient application of precise stand-off firepower or the efficient coordination of disparate units. It is important not to permit enthusiasm for the latest technology-dependent dominant idea blind us to that eternal fact. Pre-eminently, the conduct of war should be about the generation of the strategic effectiveness that will promote a subsequent peace with the character we desire. The on-going transnational debate on RMA and transformation has a pronounced tendency to neglect the point that 'the object in war is to obtain a better peace'; it is not victory per se.[55] Military victory by some definition is usually necessary, but it cannot be an end in and of itself. War is about politics, as we have said.

My dominant narrative of future warfare, to risk exaggeration, is not in any degree teleological. Humankind is not on the road to the abolition of war, not even just of major war, whatever that ambiguous concept may mean. We do not know what the dominant narrative will prove to be, or indeed, if there will be one at all. Anticipated grandly in its horrific entirety, future warfare probably will show evidence in plenty of each of the narratives advanced above. But will any of them merit coronation as the dominant story of the future? I very much doubt it. The reason is simple, though paradoxically it privileges complexity. So many are the contexts, factors, dimensions, or elements, that comprise the activity of warfare, that no would-be dominant narrative with a restricted causal focus is likely to capture adequately the engine that will move future strategic history.

Unsatisfactory though it may appear, this book sees the essentials of future warfare as, historically speaking, more of the same, or the mixture as before. The character of warfare must alter with changes in society, culture, politics, and technology. But future warfare is not the mystery that one might imagine. In matters of detail, surprise is a certainty. However, if we study warfare in historical perspective, as we should, little if anything of great significance about the future will occur to amaze us.

THIS CHAPTER HAS provided ample illustration of the thesis that there are many ways in which the history of warfare may be understood. We chose twelve among the cohort of possibilities, including the one we judge the most enlightening. Unfortunately, perhaps, the favoured option is the almost anti-grand narrative which has as its central tenet the conviction that historical experience is the best guide to the future. Some of the other candidates to be the master organizing proposition would be much simpler to employ, were they only adequate to the task. Jeremy Black offers persuasive words of warning, some of which we quoted already: 'It is important to be wary about meta-narratives (overarching interpretations), and to be cautious about paradigms, mono-causal explanations and much of the explanatory culture of long-term military history.'[56]

Whatever one may prefer by way of a dominant narrative, the analysis just concluded should encourage the belief that the past, present, and future of warfare comprise a unity. Despite the occurrence of surprises or discontinuities, great and small, future warfare will resemble past warfare in its basic nature and broad purposes. In the title to the first chapter of his scintillating book, *Warrior Politics*, Robert D. Kaplan asserts that 'There is no "Modern" World'.[57] I will close this part of our analytical journey by adapting Kaplan's formula to read 'There is No Future Warfare'. In nearly all the ways that matter deeply, future warfare will simply be warfare. And that, as we know all too well, is behaviour with which humankind is nothing if not familiar.

Chapter five

Regular Warfare

VARIETIES OF WARFARE

As an act of bold, perhaps reckless, division and conflation, this enquiry treats future warfare as coming either in a regular or an irregular mode. The former refers to combat between the regular armed forces of states. The latter targets combat between the armed forces of states and other belligerent entities. To clarify: the irregular combatant may be foreign or domestic, and may have no fixed abode. Although this neat division covers most cases of interest, as always there are complicating exceptions. States or proto-states (e.g., Palestine), may elect to wage a wholly irregular style of warfare. Such a choice could reflect either a great asymmetry in regular military strength, or it might express recognition of the undesired dangers of escalation that would attend the conduct of a regular form of warfare. For a further complication, regular and irregular styles in warfare are frequently, indeed almost routinely, mixed, ideally combined within a belligerent's total military effort. According to Mao Tse-tung, protracted warfare should move through three stages, with the third being the conduct of conventional operations, following stages characterized primarily by political mobilization and terrorism, and then by a mixture of guerrilla and mobile combat.[1] For a balancing point, even in the case of large-scale regular warfare, military activities of a highly irregular variety also are likely to be prosecuted. The agents of such irregularity may be civilian amateurs in arms (e.g., partisans), or highly professional regular soldiers waging warfare in an unconventional style (e.g., special operations forces).

It is important to be aware of the complications just noted, but we will not permit them to drive the organization of this discussion. For many years and through several books this author has insisted upon the holistic study of war and strategy.[2] In historical reality wars do not often accord with the clear categories that we analysts find so convenient. Future warfare is certain to exhibit examples of land, sea, air, cyber and space warfare. Each environmentally specific variety will attract its own literature, as well as its own theory and doctrine. Some of that analysis will be technically, tactically, and operationally first-rate. But the military and strategic integrity of such writings must always be questionable because of the self-imposed limits of their subjects. States do not wage land, sea, air, cyber and space wars. Instead, they wage war. In principle, at least, this fact is well recognized today. The US Armed Forces in particular are moving from paying obeisance to the deity of 'jointness' – which is to say each service working smoothly with the others – to worshipping at the altar of true functional integration of effort in military operations, joint interdependence as it is now called, an integration enabled by networked communications.[3]

Despite the declining semi-autonomy of warfare in distinctive environments, there is no evading the raw facts of physical geography. Newly networked forces of different kinds are able to cooperate with an ease unimaginable in years past, but each environment still imposes its own conditions upon combat possibilities. The final section of this chapter discusses the grammar of future regular warfare. That analysis is careful to pay due attention to the unique terms of engagement mandated by the different physical geographies, even in an age of networked joint or integrated forces.

The principle embodied in William of Occam's Razor is that one should pare away all inessential matters, leaving only the minimum necessary to explain the subject. This chapter and the next attempt to follow William's good advice. The extensive range of ways in which future warfare could be categorized is reduced simply to two, regular and irregular. This is by far the most useful, as well as economical, organization of a hugely messy prospective reality.

YESTERDAY'S PROBLEM?

As we reported and discussed briefly in Chapter Four, increasingly it is claimed that large-scale warfare between the regular armed forces of states is as obsolescent as are supposedly sovereign states themselves. The technological, economic, and social pressures of globalization allegedly are eroding the authority of governments and the real independence of countries, and those pressures must radically change war's political context and character.[4] The future political world will see violent strife, but certainly not on the pattern of yesterday, so the popular story maintains. The political and technological dimensions of our subject interact, with the former, as usual and properly, in the driver's seat. This part of our discussion addresses a subject that many forward-looking thinkers have come to regard as yesterday's problem. War between states, the only kind of belligerency sanctioned by international law from the mid seventeenth century until the third quarter of the twentieth (1977 to be precise, in Protocol II to the 1949 Geneva Convention)[5] purportedly has died or is dying, a significant distinction.[6] If that is a little too bold for comfort, one can amend the proposition to hold that major war between states is now plainly obsolescent.

It is a problem that obsolescent does not mean impossible. A further problem lurks in the prudent suspicion that the belief that major war has had its too-long day may not be true; at least it may not be true enough. Commentators playing theorist have proceeded inductively. They have noticed, fairly accurately, that few recent wars have been waged between states. While broadly agreeing with the claim that interstate warfare has been overtaken in frequency by internal and transnational irregular combat, it is far too early to write the obituary for the former. They may not have been major wars, but Kosovo in 1999, Afghanistan in 2001, and Iraq in 2003, were all three of them cases of interstate conflict. If we grant, with some reservations, that there is a trend away from interstate warfare, there hovers in the background the thought that it is a trend that might be reversed abruptly. No country that is a significant player in international security today, not least the United States, has yet reorganized and transformed its regular military establishment to reflect the apparent demise of 'old (interstate) wars' and the rise of new ones. To date, the process of military transformation exploiting the information-led RMA is geared overwhelmingly to advance prowess in regular warfare. A paradigm shift may be needed from the regular combat of like against fairly like that was viewed as proper war from 1648 until the end of the Cold War, to the several forms of asymmetrical conflict that combat can assume between seriously unlike belligerents. All of this is highly speculative, of course, and military institutions are apt to be conservative when it comes to reforming themselves in the face of pressures from fashionable ideas sparked by the threat of the day or decade.[7] Furthermore, the claim that 1648–1991 was a Clausewitzian period characterized by the kind of interstate conflicts recognized by international law, is a grotesque oversimplification. Wars of empire were almost continuous through those centuries. Moreover, the bloodiest wars of the nineteenth century after the fall of Napoleon I were the domestic wars in China known to history as the Taiping Rebellion (c. 1850–64, 20 million dead), and the American Civil War (1861–65). The latter was the bloodiest conflict by far in the whole American historical experience. An authoritative study of American military history, that by Allan R. Millett and Peter Maslowski, records that American deaths in the First World War, the Second World War, and Korea totalled 564,000, but still do not reach the Civil War total of 620,000.[8] Federals and Confederates waged almost wholly symmetrical forms of regular war. Whether or not that conflict was an interstate war was, perhaps needless to say, what the struggle was all about.

Argument over alternative visions of future war has profound implications for defence planning and programming. Armed forces optimal to engage other armed forces, and then to seize and hold ground, are unlikely to be armed forces optimal for hunting down irregular enemies in dense jungle, mountainous terrain, or in mega-cities. Similarly, the high-technology killing machine that IT-transformed forces may approximate is likely to be short of infantry numbers and unskilled in the art of friendly public interface that the civic protection and peace enforcement aspects of irregular warfare demand. It is most unlikely that future war has a single dominant character, even for just one country alone. It follows that enthusiastic endorsement of a new paradigm of warfare is as likely to lead a country astray, as it is to promote strategic effectiveness. People confident in their intellectual and policy grasp of the needs of future war should be given pause by this judgement from the pen of Field Marshal Sir Nigel Bagnall, a British Chief of the General Staff: 'Over the centuries identifying a nation's future strategic priorities has proved to be a very imprecise art, and as a result peacetime force structures have seldom proved relevant when put to the test of war.'[9]

If by major war we mean the all but total industrial age conflicts of 1914–18 and 1939–45, then indeed they are yesterday's problem. But major war in the twenty-first century cannot resemble closely its antecedents in the twentieth. As we keep insisting, the character of war is driven by its contexts, political, social, and technological, pre-eminently. The American historian, Eliot Cohen, explains that 'the age of the mass army is over … the emergence of quality as the dominant feature in military power has rendered obsolete, if not absurd, today's systems of calculating relative military power'.[10] Future regular warfare, major or minor in scale, will be conflict wherein quality, including quality of thought, trumps quantity, at least in those cases where quality is present. Since 1991, Western states have become used to wars wherein their military prowess has been flattered by a signal advantage in such key military qualities as technology, doctrine, training, and sheer professionalism. What happens when Western regular military quality meets Eastern regular military quality we may well discover before this new century is more than a decade or two old. That unhappy possibility, even probability, is most likely to occur as the People's Republic of China (PRC) declines to be contained by the long-standing American security system for East Asia. Also, we must emphasize again that future warfare is not the exclusive preserve of American superpower. Even if 'the age of the mass army is over' for NATO countries, it is far from over for, say, India and Pakistan, or Iran and a future Iraq. Future warfare between powerful regional belligerents may well have a character of massification given by the threat and use of weapons of mass destruction, as well as by massive quantities of soldiers and military material.

It is nearly always difficult to know why anticipated events did not happen. This is a classic difficulty with deterrence. Western theorists and policymakers like to flatter themselves that they prevented the East–West Cold War of 1947–89 turning hot by the excellence of their ideas on, and practice of, deterrence. But they do not and cannot know for certain. Recognition of the indeterminacy of historical evidence on war causation is of great importance for our understanding of the future. It is distinctly possible that the popular belief that interstate war, certainly major interstate war, is obsolete, rests on a significant misreading of recent history. Among the many reasons that can be advanced to explain the comparative rarity of regular interstate warfare today, five in particular merit special notice.

First, such warfare is believed to be unattractive because it would be unprofitable. In an information age, wherein wealth accrues principally from the quality added by skilled people in an ever more globalized economy, it is hard to conceive of advantage being secured by war. While there will always be an exception to any such generalization, still the commentators of an optimistic stripe remind us of the sound axiom that war does not pay. This wise, if somewhat banal, proposition would be a source of greater comfort than it is, had it not been true for the whole of the twentieth century. Moreover, the fact that large-scale regular war would not turn an economic profit was common knowledge at the time; it did not come as a rude surprise. There was an exception. The United States enjoyed huge economic benefits from both world wars. History reveals that we humans are not, at least not only, economically rational, profit-maximizing creatures. To believe that major interstate war is obsolete because it is unprofitable, is to be captured by a view of public behaviour that is blind to the true range of motivations to fight. Recall that Thucydides points to the authority of 'fear, honor, and interest', as principal reasons for war.

Second, major war between states allegedly is obsolete because fewer and fewer societies will tolerate it. The theory of the democratic peace holds that since democracies do not fight each other – at least, they have not recently – the global diffusion of liberal democratic practices should translate as a severe shrinkage in the war-prone zone. The anticipated universal ideological triumph of the values of capitalism and liberal democracy thus may mean that fewer and fewer governments will be free of the domestic constraints which should favour policies other than war. Among the legion of difficulties with democratic peace theory is the inconvenient point that thus far it is supported only by the 'Scotch verdict' of 'not proven'. Rather more damning is the fact that no one has yet managed to explain satisfactorily just why it is that democracies are supposed not to go to war with each other, if indeed they do not. Are publics in democracies less bellicose than authoritarian governments? The political complexion of a rival state can be a matter of some propaganda interest, but it is next to impossible to find recent historical examples of wars conducted in any real sense because one country was democratic and the other was not. Strategic history suggests that there is no correlation between authoritarian government and a proclivity to fight. Dictators typically are careful of their lives and property and, as prudent people, know that war is much too risky a business to undertake save in cases of perceived dire necessity or anticipated walkover.

Third, perhaps with better reason, major war between states is widely held to be yesterday's problem because of the powder trail of escalatory danger to nuclear use. States with nuclear weapons have to be assumed to be willing to use them rather than tolerate defeat in conventional war. Alternatively, if a country, Japan say, were humiliated by a nuclear armed adversary, perhaps China or North Korea, it is a safe prediction that such a victim would seek to acquire a balancing nuclear capability of its own as rapidly as should prove feasible. In the Japanese case, that would be very rapidly indeed. It is not safe to draw far-reaching conclusions about the meaning of nuclear weapons for future warfare from the strategic history of the roles of those weapons in the great East–West Cold War. Both

American and then Soviet officials realized that inadvertently they had created nuclear arsenals of such magnitude (peaking at approximately 32,000 weapons for the United States in the mid 1960s, and perhaps 45,000 for the Soviet Union in the mid 1980s) that these Death Machines really only had 'utility in non-use', in a famous phrase of the period.[11] But, Indian, Pakistani, Israeli, and one day probably Iranian and other governments may believe, with some good reason, that nuclear weapons are military weapons as well as devices with which to terrorize, short of war, on behalf of national security. Both the restricted ownership of nuclear weapons, and a possibly disturbingly conventional view of their utility, has to dampen hopes that future major warfare between states is likely to be disciplined rigorously by general appreciation of the extraordinary quality of nuclear peril.[12] The world's first bilateral nuclear war, perhaps between India and Pakistan, may change the politics of nuclear proliferation and counter-proliferation, but I doubt it. Once the radioactive dust has settled, strategic minds around the world will consider what benefits, if any, accrued to the nuclear combatants. The honest answer may not be helpful for the cause of non-proliferation.

Fourth, major war between states could be impracticable given the historically unusual measure of the contemporary American strategic dominance. Whether or not the United States elects to thrust itself into regional disputes, say in East Asia, the Gulf, or Palestine, let alone intervene militarily, it would have the ability to render victory either impossible or unprofitable for the belligerents. Politically and economically, if not militarily, any state that launched a major cross-border war in the face of American opposition could be riding for a heavy fall. The United States is not officially the world's sheriff, but it is the closest to such that we shall see for several decades.[13] Only American military power can reach anywhere on earth to defeat military adventures, or at the least it can ensure that any unwelcome military success does not stand as a source of profit and prestige to the victor. It would be difficult to exaggerate the importance of American hegemony as a global influence against major war. Some states may well choose to ignore US displeasure, India and Pakistan spring to mind, while others may not realize fully that in our contemporary hegemonic, unipolar system they need to 'square' the Americans before they move. In short, the logic of this argument against major interstate war falls well short of the status of a guarantee. Unlike all other periods in modern history, a state considering large-scale military action today against another state will search in vain for a friend or ally able to neutralize American displeasure. Such a would-be belligerent will understand, as Libyan and Indian officials have commented, that there is no reliable alternative to a national nuclear arsenal to discourage US intervention. Alas for that candidate nugget of sound realpolitical advice, the highly official shift in US policy and strategy in 2002 towards pre-emption could well mean that nuclear-weapon status would attract violent disarming action.[14] In 2004 Libya saw the error of its ways and opted to join the ranks of virtuous non-proliferants. That well-calculated conversion will be the exception that proves the rule that WMD are politically useful, if not essential, for some states. It is worth noting that the pre-emptive alleviation of proliferant menace is by no means strictly an American option. Iraq in the past, and perhaps Iran in the future, can attest to the seriousness of Israeli counter-proliferation policy and strategy.

Fifth, the social context hostile to interstate war supposedly has evolved to the point of being so non-permissive that even the idea of going to war appears close to absurd. Exceptions may be cases where the motive is humanitarian, the cause is blessed by the UN Security Council, and the casualties and financial cost are anticipated to be exceedingly low. Modern, hedonistic, allegedly globalized societies, have no interest in the risks or even the putative benefits of war. The global media feeds a global market with vicarious thrills because it presents warfare – more or less organized violence, at least – as entertainment. For the peoples of EU-Europe in particular, war is not merely old fashioned, indeed obsolete, it is wholly uninteresting, except as a non-participatory recreational diversion. The societies of peninsular Europe today face no security problems of a kind that demand a military response, at least not as they choose to define their problems. When a US administration seeks to persuade its European allies to cooperate actively in the latest scheme for ballistic missile defence (BMD), for example, it fails to recognize the degree to which its friends have become thoroughly debellicized. The European aversion to military solutions is not simply an opinion of the moment, but instead is now sufficiently deeply rooted as to warrant description as cultural; it is an attitude.[15] On the one hand this is extremely good news for those worthy reformers and people of goodwill who have campaigned noisily for peace for many decades. On the other hand, though, it is less good news for the cause of international peace with security if a profound aversion to military issues is concentrated overwhelmingly in the societies of the globalized West. The intra-NATO quarrel about war with Iraq, both before and after the event in 2003, illustrates this phenomenon precisely. Beneath the explicit and acceptable reasons to question the wisdom of US and British policy is a cultural distaste for warfare by societies that have, in effect, become post-military.

One of the firmest of eternal rules in world politics is that the peace has to be kept, which means order must be maintained, by someone. As the United States contemplates the prospects for, and implications of, future warfare, already it finds that it is unmistakably short of friends and allies who have not written off major war as yesterday's problem.

WARS BETWEEN STATES

Future warfare between states requires a political context that finds organized violence useful and legitimate. Unfortunately, contemporary history has not witnessed a thoroughly convincing benign revolution in attitudes towards the utility of the use of force in most of the world, albeit with Europe, minus the Balkans, excepted. We can predict with confidence that the future will register war of many kinds between states. Moreover, we can be sure that the reasons for hostilities will be entirely familiar from the whole course of strategic history. It seems that war is integral to the human social and political condition. This is not to deny that societies can lose their appetite, certainly their prudent opportunity, for organized violence. The great wars of the twentieth century undoubtedly had that effect in much of Europe. Alas, war, past and prospectively future, is not a manifestation of insanity by political leaders, and neither is it an aberration from normal statecraft. Future war, as with past war, will be about what Thucydides' Athenian delegates asserted in 432 BC, and what we are obliged to keep quoting: fear, honour, and interest.

We cannot know whether or not major interstate wars will scar the twenty-first century. Wherever we look in the world, though, with the notable exceptions of North America and NATO–EU Europe, the prospect of interstate war is more than a mere theoretical possibility. There will be wars between states, 'old wars' in the dismissive words of post-modern commentary, because they will have a great deal about which to fight. For example, an acceleration in deleterious climate change is likely to spur a renewed focus on territorial issues, as states compete violently to control scarce resources in a context of demographic expansion. Would that we could dismiss interstate warfare as yesterday's problem. Unfortunately, we cannot. More to the point, many among the world's defence planners are obliged to assume that they may need to deter, and possibly fight, the regular armed forces of state adversaries. Today, it is fashionable to approach future warfare in terms of meeting terrorism and insurgency as the dominant threat. That granted, thus far no country has chosen to reshape its military establishment comprehensively so as to focus exclusively upon the radically asymmetrical menaces posed by irregular foes.

The reasons why regular war between the military machines of states will long remain possible are all too familiar. Rising powers will seek more influence in their regions, a process that must promote concern, if not alarm, abroad. China, India, and Iran, for some cases in point, can be expected to bid for more respect as their relative national standing on the international hierarchy improves. States bound on regional promotion will risk military action at the hands both of local rivals and also on the part of the global ordering power, which for the time being can only be the United States.

It is neither feasible nor particularly helpful to try to predict particular future wars between states. But it is essential to remain alert to the possibility of such events. What follows are a few hypothetical examples of the regular warfare that could trouble this new century. The intention here is not to try and spot tomorrow's wars, rather is it simply to register resoundingly the claim that regular warfare between states will long remain a feature of world politics. It is worth noting that all but one among these illustrative examples include a greater or lesser measure of nuclear danger. Here are some hypothetical regular wars of the future.

- *A Sino-Russian Axis versus the United States.* The first example, though hypothetical with respect to war, is becoming ever closer to a reality today as an emerging interstate conflict. China and Russia, together with Iran and other states hostile to an American-policed Western-style world order, are beginning to forge what could become a continental bloc to challenge American hegemony. Sir Halford Mackinder's nightmare vision of the 'Heartland' power or axis dominating Eurasia and posing a first-class menace to the maritime realm, may be in the early stages of realization. Those who argue that irregular warfare is the leading paradigm for twenty-first-century warfare, need to reconsider their position with reference to the possibility, even probability, of a new long-term conflict between the United States and a Sino-Russian alliance. This is not to ignore the many deep sources of Sino-Russian antagonism. However, in international politics the enemy of my enemy is my friend (for a while). Should that antagonism prove fatal for alliance cohesion, we can be sure that China will strive energetically to find other partners in its quest to become the other pole in a new bipolar international system.
- *China versus the United States,* ostensibly over Taiwan, though fundamentally over which country is to be the leading organizer and guardian of security in East Asia. The logic of international politics, certainly the logic of geopolitics, points to Sino-American rivalry and conflict with as much confidence as it did to the enmity between Athens and Sparta, Rome and Carthage, and rather more recently, the United States and the Soviet Union. The Chinese and American defence establishments agree that the other poses what will probably be the defining threat for its national security in the future. It is improbable

that terrorism will be allowed to dominate the official American vision of future warfare and the architecture of its national security policy.

- *Russia versus China,* as in the Sino-American example, ostensibly would be about particular Chinese grievances. The principal item of long-standing Chinese discontent is Beijing's unhappiness with what it regards as the inequity in the exact location of its exceedingly long continental border with Russia, especially in the Far East. At root, though, warfare between these neighbours would be about the changing terms of their political relationship, as China rises and the Russian Federation continues to decline. Also, it would be about Thucydidean honour, as China sought to correct past affronts. If Sino-Russian relations should deteriorate so that they hover around the brink of war, which is where they were in 1969–70, then both would seek urgently for friends of expedience, if not quite allies. An EU-Europe, floating diplomatically and detached from what used to be the Atlantic Alliance, would be geopolitically as interesting a partner for China as the United States would be for Russia. These may appear as wild and woolly speculative thoughts today, but the strategic history that produces future warfare has delivered many diplomatic revolutions in the past. For example, within ten years of defeat in the greatest of total wars, the three leading Axis powers were all firm partners of the Western Alliance in what had become the Cold War.

- *Russia versus Ukraine* would be intended not as a war, but rather as a vital step in the restoration of the Russian empire. After all, with 22 per cent of the Ukrainian population ethnically Russian, the separation remains as uneasy in human terms as it is historically, geopolitically, and economically. Russian reabsorption of Ukraine would speak to each of Thucydides' famous motives for war. It would answer the *fear* that Ukraine might join an aggressive new European superstate. It would restore Russia's *honour* lost in its rejection by Ukraine in 1991. It would serve Russia's geopolitical *interest* by both protecting its southern flank in Europe and restoring direct access to the Black Sea and hence the Balkans. Should Ukraine succeed in its expressed desire to join NATO, conflict between Moscow and Kiev would have the potential to trigger a very wide war indeed.

- *Russia versus Latvia and Estonia* would be another case of a war of imperial restoration. With no less than 39 per cent of the Latvian people being of Russian and Belorussian descent, excuses for intervention on the part of a Russia determined to restore much of its geopolitical position on the Baltic would not be difficult to arrange. Estonia, with a public that is 28 per cent Russian, occupies a uniquely sensitive strategic geography vis-à-vis St Petersburg and, again, is viewed very much as unfinished business in Russia. Of course, for a major complication, 'the Baltics' are now all in NATO, and the EU also. But how much that would matter for the discouragement of Russian revanchism can only be a matter for speculation. The political and strategic contexts would be all important. What will EU-Europe mean, politically and strategically, over the next several decades? No less to the point, will NATO survive as a living enterprise long into this century?

- *India versus Pakistan* is a popular favourite among predictions of future war. This long-running contest is all about honour, has nothing much worth mentioning to do with interest, but has acquired a potent additional dose of bilateral fear, deriving from the demonstrated nuclear prowess of each party. Were it not for the healthy effect of mutual nuclear deterrence, it is more likely than not that a fourth interstate conflict in the subcontinent would not still repose strictly in the future war column.

- *The United States and/or Israel versus Iran* could be a very serious enterprise. The guardian superstate and its principal regional ally might feel obliged for their own security, at a minimum, forcefully to retard the Iranian programme to develop nuclear weapons. Alternatively, as the maximum aspiration, they could attempt to trigger domestic developments that might produce a benign regime change in Teheran. It is probable that American enthusiasm for regime change as a war aim will be dampened for some years to come by its recent experience in

Iraq. The United States was reminded that '*combat* is characterized by breaking things and killing people; *war* is about much more than that'.[16] The author of that basic truth, Frederick W. Kagan, advises also that 'it is much easier to destroy a sitting regime than to establish a legitimate and stable new one'.[17] Nonetheless, a US–Iranian conflict is yet another plausible example of interstate conflict, potentially on a major scale.

- *Greece versus Turkey* is a malign nexus we can trace for a millennium. Greeks and Turks have an intertwined history packed with poisonous memories. Those memories include the 'dreadful day' of the Battle of Manzikert in 1071, when not entirely sound history has it that the (Greek) Byzantine Empire lost its Anatolian heartland irretrievably,[18] to the Ottoman capture of Constantinople in 1453, through the subsequent all but four centuries of Turkish oppression. Though nominally partners and allies in NATO for fifty years, Greece and Turkey were always more interested in fighting each other than in serving as a barrier to Soviet penetration of the Eastern Mediterranean. Future war between these two countries would not want for geopolitical and ethnographic excuses, but in reality it would be about honour, identity, and serving the flame of ethnic and cultural hatred for yet another era and generation.

- *North Korea versus South Korea and the United States.* The Korean peninsula is an armed camp on both sides of the 1953 truce line. It is not difficult to invent scenarios of cross-border warfare; defence planners have been doing just that for decades. An economically ever-desperate North Korea, seemingly its perpetual condition, might seek to use its well-placed artillery to turn greater Seoul into a 'sea of fire', as it has often threatened. It could hope to withhold securely its small but nuclear-armed missile force, as a guarantee against effective US military intervention (beyond the 2004–2005 scale of American garrison which totals 34,500 military personnel).

- *The United States versus rogue states* that earn that descriptor either because they support international terrorism, or because they have active WMD and missile delivery programmes. The American policy document, *National Strategy to Combat Weapons of Mass Destruction* (December 2002), proclaims a willingness to conduct regular inter-state war. With a clarity unusual in such productions, that presidential statement warns that 'we will not permit the world's most dangerous régimes and terrorists to threaten us with the world's most destructive weapons'.[19] Rather than specify a mainly speculative rogues' gallery of states for the future, readers are encouraged to fill in the blank spaces for themselves, and pick their future rogues-of-choice.

- *A superpower Europe, possibly in alliance with Russia or China, versus a strategically still hegemonic United States and its allies.* On the one side this would be an anti-hegemonic interstate struggle, while on the other it would be a contest to maintain a US-preferred international order against those who would destroy its architecture, and its architect, of global strategic security. However, the strong probability of US–EU-European conflict is likely to be mitigated notably by two structural elements on the European side. First, Britain would not sign up to a European policy of general opposition to the US superpower. Second, most of the new members of the EU in Eastern Europe will be far more worried about possible future Russian menaces than they will be about American hegemony. To those new members, the United States is the solution, not the problem. The former satellites of the Soviet Empire regard close association with the US superpower as a guarantee against both a Russian return, or its functional replacement by a Franco-German-Italian hegemonic triad. These factors inhibiting transatlantic antagonism are unlikely to suffice, though, to prevent the EU from adopting a general policy intended to balance US influence. It is plausibly predictable, therefore, that European opposition to US hegemony must promote both hostility in the United States and a crisis within EU-Europe itself.

- *Strategic surprise.* It is only prudent to cite interstate wars in an *unknown unknowns* category as mystery guests on the long-running show that is the history of warfare. Some of these wars will include those which follow historically downstream as a consequence of wars that we can anticipate, if not quite expect. Also, they include wars that are utterly unpredictable today. There are probably some wars in the future whose eruption will show the limitations, even the vanity, of the assumptions behind all current schools of thoughts on future conflict.

The future history discussed immediately above has the potential to mislead the unwary. It is unfortunately unavoidable that in seeking to stimulate the imagination, and illustrate the claim that there will be inter-state wars in the future, notwithstanding denials, inadvertently one might convey the message that *these* are the wars that are coming. Furthermore, one invites a critical response along the lines of 'those are not the wars that I believe to be most probable'. However, by far the greatest risk in the speculative illustrations just outlined, is the possibility that they will provide a dangerously confining focus to strategic imagination that needs to be maximally open to possibilities. The best that I could do to offset the peril of the accidental constriction of the imagination, was to cite, as my final entry, the strategic surprise of the 'unknowns'. I am claiming that the future of warfare will contain interstate conflicts that no one today who carries weight as a supposed expert on the future is imagining. Even if there is a theorist somewhere who is making accurate predictions about the wars of, say, the 2030s and 2040s, short of the events themselves how can we know that he or she is correct? Of course, it is always possible that the game of strategic prediction can produce a self-denying prophecy. A fearsome credible prediction of war might just galvanize serious official endeavour to prevent the catastrophe. In that happy case, in retrospect the gifted, or lucky, futurist would appear to have made a faulty prediction. This possibility is akin to the difficulty of knowing how well one is per-forming with a strategy of deterrence. It is hard to document the wars that do not happen.

Respect for what we should allow historical experience to teach drives this author to look kindly on the suggestion that the greater among future strategic dangers will be those that were not anticipated long in advance. By analogy, it will be the asteroid that we did not see coming that may well end our strategic, and every other kind of history once and for all. In other words, the unknown unknowns, history's jokers almost, are as certain to occur as they must prove uniquely testing of the ability to cope adaptively. There are perennial hindrances to preparation for, let alone the taking of action to prevent, a strategic catastrophe. Few will be convinced that an outlandish peril is sufficiently probable as to merit serious attention. Even if some influential people suspect that the great, if strange, danger really is quite likely, the predicted peril may be so great that the necessary antici- patory response would be socially unacceptable. After all, it may never happen. Cross your fingers and pray.

The examples offered above highlight the probable, I claim the certain, longevity of an interstate form of warfare which, alas, is not at all old fashioned. They are not predictions, a mission in which I have no interest, but rather simply are illustrations of the history-based assertion that we must assume that there is interstate warfare in our future. That is exactly the point. This is not to deny that the need to assume the continuing relevance of that which is apparently old fashioned does stir controversy. To argue for a future marred by interstate wars is a denial of what many people see as the consequences of the globalizing trends of our age in eroding the authority of states. The concept of interstate warfare is now deeply unpopular among many of the strategic cognoscenti. The sharpest edge of contemporary Western, certainly American, strategic thought, is not risking blunting itself on the kind of warfare – of a major kind between states – that political intellectual fashion now decrees is as dead as the horse cavalry. In 2001, the United States did wage an interstate war, against Taleban Afghanistan. In 2002 the somewhat misnamed statesmen of India and Pakistan strove mightily to prove that interstate warfare between the regular armed forces of countries had yet to run its full historical course as a serious possibility. And then, in 2003, America waged war upon Ba'athist Iraq. But the American episodes just cited have not shaken the fashionable conviction that wars between states belong to the strategic history of yes- teryear. The new orthodoxy is that *major* interstate warfare is improbable, while the outbreak of such atavistic misbehaviour by the greater states, certainly those of the G8 club, is now close to inconceivable. We must hasten to point out that the current intellectual dominance of the challenge of all forms of irregular warfare is not exactly reflected closely in the 'transformative' behaviour of the US Armed Forces. The Army's impressive plans for transformation, including their frank and sophisticated recognition of the irregularity and asymmetry of their most probable enemies, are less than compelling in their counter-insurgency dimension – to this theorist, at least.[20]

It may seem odd that it can be controversial, as here, to claim that a study of future warfare must take more than passing notice of the prospects for interstate conflict which engages regular armed forces. The forward edge of contemporary theory does not look with much favour on belligerents of a similar kind conducting war along lines both generally recognized in the laws of war and which dominates in staff college teaching around the world. The next chapter gives irregular warfare its due, perhaps more, and casts a particularly critical eye over the conflict between regulars and irregulars; what British theorists, and the US Marine Corps, quaintly used to call 'small wars'.[21]

The regular military forces of states are designed, equipped, and trained pre-eminently to fight their own kind. Admittedly with some latitude and variation in actual performance, those regular forces are obliged to fight only in lawful ways. There are rules of war aplenty, and the armed forces of states are expected to follow them.[22] The greatest challenge to the colonial soldier a century ago, as indeed to the American warrior for democracy, or international order today, is to bring the irregular enemy to battle. The Iraqis in 1991 and the Taleban in 2001 committed the fatal error of presenting themselves as armies (admittedly, only loosely speaking in the Afghan case) in the field, where they could be located and duly pulverized. In 2003, the Iraqis allowed the US Armed Forces to demonstrate just how easily a grossly inferior regular enemy can be defeated decisively. Sophisticated modern armed forces are critically dependent upon the delivery of firepower from altitude; they need targets. The US Army and Marine Corps have talked a lot about so-called manoeuvre warfare, sometimes giving the impression that this ancient concept is a profound contemporary discovery.[23] But much, if not most of what is celebrated today as evidence of military transformation owes more to an attritional, than it does to a manoeuvrist, vision of future warfare. This is not to deny that American military power as applied in Bosnia in 1995, Yugoslavia / Kosovo in 1999, Afghanistan in 2001–2002, and Iraq in 2003–2004, has been restrained, precise, and likely to meet reasonable application of canonical Just War criteria. Anyone who doubts this claim is invited to contrast US military performance with the appalling Russian campaigns in Chechnya, especially the actions taken against Grozny in 1994–6 and 1999–2000. The Russian approach to a recalcitrant enemy bears more than a casual resemblance to the Roman. The Russians have yet to sow salt in the fields of Chechnya, but perhaps only because they have not thought of it.

DILEMMAS OF A DEFENCE PLANNER

The world's defence planners and their political masters face the same dilemma as does this author. The strategic *Zeitgeist* of our age screams 'irregular' and 'asymmetrical,' while leading politicians identify terrorism, the ultimate in irregularity and asymmetry, as the defining threat for insecurity in our times. But how much of that searchlight on terrorism is a passing fad? Terrorism will neither vanish nor be comprehensively defeated (technically an impossibility, since it is a mode of warfare), but it may resume its more usual position as a permanent background danger, typically of much lesser gravity than interstate war. Not being academic theorists of International Relations, defence planners must ask not 'do we believe there is interstate war in our future,' but rather 'can we afford to assume that there is no such war in our future'. Armed forces, tailor-made for agility in the chase after terrorist-rats in their urban and other natural habitats, will not be ideal to deter or defeat the regular military power of states. Sad to note, the worlds of the terrorist and his or her opportunistic state-fellow traveller frequently overlap, both conveniently and otherwise. As a surrogate target for the all-too-elusive irregular and transnational terrorist foe, it is expedient to have the coordinates of a state with an army, a capital city, and the rest of the trimmings of sovereign statehood. But it is inexpedient in that mighty military effort can be expended to little real effect in draining a swamp or two wherein irregulars sometimes are known to lurk.

Are we witnessing either what is, or as some claim what should be seen as, a paradigm shift in warfare? If warfare against irregular enemies employing highly asymmetrical methods is the dominant mode of future warfare, should not the principal military establishments of the world wake up and transform themselves so as to become agile terrorist rat-catchers? Could it be that a US military transformation, or RMA, with its centre-piece the leverage of information for the delivery of precise firepower and the agile execution of decisive manoeuvre on the ground, would be, by and large, the wrong transformation for a changing strategic context? Needless to add, perhaps, the US Army promises to transform itself so that it can cope with any and all challenges, regular and irregular. Perhaps what states require is not the ability to replay the folly displayed during much of America's experience in its Indian Wars, wherein an army schooled in 'civilized' European warfare blundered about vast Western territories in pursuit of enemies who would rarely stand and fight, save when they had no choice.[24] Instead, states need a security strategy, with a strong military element, able to reach and defeat irregulars on their own terms. Regular military forces in most periods have been ill-prepared to cope with the challenges and frustration inseparable from the effort to counter insurgency.

It is a problem for the defence planner that a regular military establishment, somewhat transformed, for example to express the latest version of the preferred American way in high-technology warfare, most likely would fail to satisfy all significant schools of military thought. The forces would be too heavy, and too dependent upon fire support from altitude, to wage war effectively at the human level, up close and personal. The inimitable Ralph Peters states the case with his usual elegant brutality.

> In much of the troubled world, only blood persuades. War and conflict have an enduringly human face. For all of the technological wonders available to Western militaries, we cannot defeat the man with the knife unless we are willing to take a knife – or gun – into our own hands. The basic human dilemmas, of which the

urge to violence is one, still require a human response. That is the lesson of our
Kosovo misadventure, and it is the fundamental principle of warfare that will
endure throughout our lifetimes.[25]

Large regular forces, with their traditional combat vehicles, albeit in
the most modern of guises, would look to be preparing to refight the Gulf
War of 1991, or even the battle of France and Germany, 1944–5. Sad to say,
al Qaeda and its like has shown little inclination to defend some modern
variant of Germany's *Westwall*. It is true that heavy forces, well endowed
with armour and ample additional on-call, if not actually integral, fire
support, proved their worth in Iraq in 2003. But it is ironic that that very
heaviness in armour and weight of firepower has continued to be vitally
necessary, even after the securing of a decisive military victory. With their
much-trumpeted transformation geared to enable them to scale ever greater
heights of military excellence in battle, the US Armed Forces have committed three cardinal sins against the eternal lore of war. First, they have
confused military with strategic success. The former is about defeating the
forces of the foe: the latter is about using that defeat to advance the goals of
policy. Second, the US Armed Forces have confused combat with war.[26]
When the regular style of fighting concludes, the war may, or may not, be
over. Also, there is far more to war than combat. Just how strategically
decisive military success will prove to be will depend on how holistic an
understanding of war has been adopted. Third, as an extension of the
second point, the US Armed Forces are especially prone to neglect the
timeless maxim that war is about peace, not about itself. This, after all, is the
core of Clausewitz's teaching. War is an instrument of policy. It is not a
sporting event to be approached and judged with regard strictly to its own
standards.

Before my American colleagues, fellow defence professionals, take
grave umbrage at the criticisms levelled above, brief justification must be
offered. The US Armed Forces have been singled out for criticism because,
in extraordinary measure, they have demonstrated, and continue to demonstrate, the mistakes identified. This may simply reflect the fact that as an
instrument of the superpower guardian of international order they have

been busier in combat than have other countries' forces. The three sins alleged here are by no means confined to the behaviour of Americans. Nonetheless, American strategic and military culture does have a long-standing tendency to take a narrowly military view of war, which is perhaps understandable for a military culture rigid in its determination to eschew politics, and in practice to discount consideration of, and preparation for, the character of the context of peace that should follow. This is a classic example of an army having the vices of its virtues. The US Armed Forces have a long and praiseworthy tradition of staying out of politics. The military are professionals in 'the management of violence', while policy, the purpose for which violence is managed, is strictly a civilian responsibility.[27] Despite the basic merit in this division of responsibilities, it has the potential for strategic disaster, disappointment at least, if the political and military realms fail to conduct an honest dialogue. That dialogue obviously threatens to draw soldiers into policymaking and civilian policymakers into military planning and strategy. There should be nothing surprising about this condition. After all, Clausewitz argued that:

> Once again: war is an instrument of policy. It must necessarily bear the character of policy and measure by its standards. *The conduct of war, in its great outlines, is therefore policy itself*, which takes up the sword in place of the pen, but does not on that account cease to think according to its own laws.[28]

A little earlier, Clausewitz cautioned that 'a certain grasp of military affairs is vital for those in charge of general policy'.[29] That requirement is far from habitually met, and it points to the need for civilian amateurs to engage with military issues, possibly in opposition to the views of military professionals.

Future warfare must be assumed to encompass both regular and irregular combat. It follows that it is all but trivially easy for critics who focus almost exclusively on one or the other broad mode of conflict, to find fault with defence strategies that appear to lean too far in one direction or the other. Professional soldiers tend to be rightly sceptical of radical visions of new kinds of war in place of old. If, or more likely when, future warfare does not conform to the paradigm proclaimed to be the latest model, soldiers know that they are the ones who will be present at the scene of the proof of error. Planners can return to their sand tables, while armchair strategists can write another book. The historical record does not show it to be a general truth that military establishments prepare for the last war.[30] All too often they forget what their predecessors knew at the close of the last conflict. In addition, soldiers are prone to choose to ignore the lessons of recent warfare, if that experience is rejected because it pertains to a mode of combat that the military organization views with extreme disfavour. This has been the fate of US military expertise in the conduct of irregular warfare in conflict after conflict.[31]

It cannot be denied that military people have a strong preference for weapons and support systems known to work reliably under field conditions and that are under their own control. They are professionally resistant to prophet-salespersons who promise 'victory through ... air power, air mobility and assault, mechanised warfare, decisive manoeuvre, network-centricity', or whatever is the latest gleam in the eye of the fanatical true believer. There has never been a shortage of theorists convinced that they alone had the answer either to the military conundrums of the day or, for those with truly inflated egos, that they had discovered the key to military success in all periods. British theorist Basil Liddell Hart, with his advocacy of an inherently elusive, indeed indefinable, 'indirect approach' to strategy, falls firmly in the latter cluster.[32] Such an approach can have meaning only in contrast to a direct approach. Presumably, the indirect approach is one that the enemy does not expect. Often there will be excellent reasons why the enemy anticipates a direct approach; the indirect may well be geographically impracticable or otherwise fatally flawed. A number of sometime fashionable strategic concepts do not withstand close scrutiny as potential master ideas. The indirect approach, competitive strategy, and, today, asymmetric threats, the OODA loop, network-centric warfare (NCW), Effects Based Operations (EBO), and Fourth Generation Warfare (4GW), all have in common an essential banality overdressed as supposedly brilliant insight. Each of the ideas or approaches just cited is quite a good idea, at least in part. What is more, it always was.

For example, Air Force Colonel John Boyd touted a tactical insight derived from personal experience of aerial combat as a general theory of conflict. His OODA loop, standing for Observation, Orientation, Decision, and Action, is revered by many as summarizing the wisdom of the ages on how to win.[33] The core notion is that success rewards the warrior who can operate within the decision cycle of the enemy. It is a sound idea, but as the philosopher's stone for victory at all levels of warfare it is distinctly sub-Clausewitzian. A major problem with the OODA loop is that its devotees assume that a tactical insight, even principle, will be no less valid at the operational and strategic levels of warfare. It is fairly clear that such is not the case.

The market for panaceas, pretentious expert-sounding jargon, decoration and redecoration of the devastatingly obvious, and rediscovery of ancient wisdom, will never decline.

The dilemma for competent defence planners is that their vision of future warfare cannot be neatly, conveniently, and economically captured by a single paradigm. The United States may have decided that *for the time being*, at least, the defining threat of the new century is international apocalyptic terrorism, a menace that could potentially be enhanced greatly by the acquisition of weapons of mass destruction. In addition it knows that that terrorism has left footprints in the sand leading to such regional powers as Iran and Syria. Also, regardless of the issues associated with terrorism, China as a regional rival in East Asia eventually will need to be contained even more vigorously than was done, and seen to be done, with two carrier battle groups off Taiwan in 1996. Moreover, as the world's sheriff, the principal guardian of the international order of the early twenty-first century, the United States cannot afford to settle upon a preferred mode of combat in the hope and expectation that it will be able to oblige any and all enemies to conform to an American style in warfare.

Distant precision bombardment, with few American boots on the ground, undoubtedly is the preferred new American way in war. It appeared to work well enough in 1999 against a Yugoslavian leadership that was economically on the rocks, and in 2001 against an Afghan theocracy that more or less commanded a military rabble. The new American way of war demonstrated against Iraq in 2003 exercised a variant that employed US manoeuvre forces on the ground – in contrast to the Afghan case – and revealed an impressive competence in combined arms.[34] The military victory was more than a little devalued by the obvious American confusion of combat with the whole of war, as well as by the undeniable fact that the Iraqi foe was extraordinarily incompetent.

The future of regular warfare, that is of warfare between regular troops, should not be predicted too hurriedly on the basis of the wars of the post-Cold War decade, or the US record in Afghanistan and Iraq subsequent to 9/11. Defence professionals know this, which is one reason why they continue to support force structures which allow for sustained heavy ground combat. Also it is why the US Army fought bitterly, if unavailingly, to save its riotously expensive ($11 billion) new self-propelled 155mm howitzer system, *Crusader,* from the transformational axe in Secretary Rumsfeld's budget cuts for Fiscal Year (FY) 2003. Should silver bullets from the sky be slow to arrive, be unexpectedly grounded, or meet unpredicted opposition, there is something uniquely comforting to ground troops about the organic close-support firepower of their own artillery. It is heavy, it is expensive, but it works reliably, always assuming it is not too heavy to be deployable. Jonathan Bailey reports that 'the US Army's *Crusader* (XM2001) was to have been the most advanced SP [self-propelled] piece in the world. The need for field artillery to keep up with the armoured vehicles of manoeuvre arms was revealed during the First Gulf War (1990–91)'.[35] Rumsfeld's transformation zeroed the program in 2002. *Crusader* was judged to be out of step with the path the army was under orders to take. Organic firepower for ground forces would be provided by lighter equipment than the 55 tons, subsequently reduced to 38 (42 with add-on armour), of each of the *Crusader* system's two vehicles. Also, the trend in fire support plainly favours stand-off delivery from altitude. The ill-tempered dispute over *Crusader* was particularly important because it mobilized rival views on the character of, and prospects for, heavy ground warfare in the future.

No other country faces the range and opportunity for military choice of the United States today. Future warfare is a subject of universal concern, but most states and other war-making and violence-organizing institutions (e.g., transnational and subnational bodies, some criminal organizations and some commercial enterprises) are not obliged to guess boldly about the kind of military and para-military perils that they face or wish to pose. After the fashion of Imperial Rome, the United States uniquely, as the global sheriff of the era, must be able to wage and win wars of all kinds.

It is with some reluctance that this text is driven repeatedly to discuss American dilemmas. Such discussion is unavoidable because both technically and politically American arms are at the forefront of our subject. Much of the world will wage future warfare quite contentedly in the same manner that it has waged past warfare, which is to say with AK-47 assault rifles, machetes, cellular phones and drums. The misdeeds of that terrifyingly broad swathe of angry, greedy, status-hungry, fun-seeking, and bored humanity is discussed in the next chapter under the umbrella concept of irregular warfare. It is appropriate however, to close this section with a thumbnail sketch of future regular warfare, American-style.

As recently as the late 1980s the United States and its NATO allies were hunkered down ready to wage all-out conventional warfare, probably to be succeeded promptly by large-scale nuclear and chemical war, in defence of the Rimlands of Eurasia against Soviet assault. Various schemes for grand manoeuvre by sea, land, and air were mooted, but the dread event held every promise of being a decidedly grim exercise in old-fashioned attrition; last army, or country, standing wins. Of course, common sense could have prevailed and hostilities might have been halted after the exchange of token blows. The prospects of that relatively happy outcome were not glittering, however.

How times have changed. The subject of future warfare today embraces a US military establishment transformed in its strategic duties, if not yet in its organization and equipment, a change which takes years, even decades, as, more contentiously, does change in many of its ideas (doctrines) and practices. There can be no doubt as to the sincerity of the Army's commitment to change. In an authoritative document it makes an uncompromising promise. 'The Army will transform its culture, capabilities, and processes as an integral component of Defense Transformation.'[36]

Albeit in microcosm and against a military joke of a regular enemy, in 2001 the American campaign of revenge against the Taleban in Afghanistan and to disrupt the functioning of the al Qaeda terrorist network, did send a clear signal about the state of the art in regular warfare. The RMA discussed in Chapter Three saw action in Afghanistan against pathetic Talebans and the holy warriors of Islam. The foreign fighters were rather less pathetic. This was especially true of those who had graduated from, and been socialized in, al Qaeda's training camps, together with those who had had combat experience in Bosnia, Chechnya and against the Soviets in the 1980s. Judgement on the effectiveness of the American RMA in 2001 must depend upon the standard one applies. What was, or should have been, victory? Was the war conducted in such a way that the subsequent peace enables the creation of a stable political context? The new, at least updated, mix of military elements comprised the synergistic combinations of intelligence for target provision on the ground by special operations forces, and from the air by *Predator* unmanned aerial vehicles (UAVs), which communicated in real time via space systems to the instruments of aerial bombardment. Those instruments included: B-52, B-2, and B-1 erstwhile strategic bombers; tactical strike aircraft from the sovereign decks of aircraft carriers in the Arabian Sea and from local air bases; and cruise missiles launched from submarines and surface ships. The prodigious American firepower, which truly was an exercise in precision, unlike the Gulf War of 1991, was expended initially in aid of local Afghan warlord-allies who were assigned such direct heavy combat duty as might be necessary. Subsequently, when the Afghan allies behaved in traditional Afghan ways, the wonderfully information-led US Armed Forces, the special operations forces and marines in particular, were dependent upon the aerial fireworks to corral the enemy none too effectively in his mountain sanctuaries.

The end result was not overly satisfactory. Culturally alien allies can be fickle and inconveniently unreliable. Moreover, those local players have personal histories, family ties, and traditional habits, that super-soldiers from outside do not immediately understand. American special operations' soldiers did not speak the languages and had not had time to gain the trust of the local warriors. This criticism is less valid with reference to the substantial CIA presence in the theatre of operations. After all, the CIA had conducted history's largest and most successful venture in the covert arming and training of an insurgency, when in the 1980s it sustained the Afghan resistance to Soviet occupation.[37] Ironically, the CIA helped create the battle-hardened warriors who comprise the core of al Qaeda today. The law of unintended consequences strikes again.

In the most vital of respects, the 'Afghan model' of future warfare, to employ a term much favoured by American analysts at the time, was not relevant to the war against Saddam Hussein's Iraq in 2003.[38] Whereas in Afghanistan the United States could leave the lion's share of the ground combat to the warriors of the warlords of the Northern Alliance, in Iraq there was no alternative but to rely primarily upon American troops to secure the military decision. The US plan for the war and the scale and style of military operations reflected a compromise between two schools of thought. On the one hand, the technophiles in senior positions in the Bush administration, much encouraged by their 'Afghan model', believed that Saddam's Iraq could be taken down swiftly by means of a precision high-tech assault on the most vital nodes of the regime, especially the command and control structure, in conjunction with a rapidly moving, relatively small invasion force. The battlespace would be prepared to some useful degree by the extensive employment of special forces, as in Afghanistan, and it was anticipated that much of the country would regard the American and British invaders as liberators. On the other hand, prudent, or conservative, military planners judged unduly risky the Administration's idea of how to bring down Saddam in the shortest time and with the barest minimum of Americans on the ground. In the event, the forces committed to the invasion were a compromise. They were larger than Donald Rumsfeld and other enthusiastic high-technology transformationists believed necessary, but smaller than most safe-siding military professionals judged to be so. In retrospect, there was merit in both points of view. The Iraqis fought harder than American advocates of the new style of war expected, and the local populace did not rise to shower the GIs with flowers and other tokens of gratitude. But the military victory was achieved swiftly, and Baghdad proved not to be Stalingrad on the Tigris.

We are interested in the prospects for future warfare, not in awarding marks for performance in past conflicts. Nonetheless, the Iraq war of 2003 is of particular interest as a partial benchmark, or reality check, on the state of the military art. However, it would be unwise to draw firm conclusions from so one-sided a contest. Above all else, it is abundantly clear that the militarily victorious US troops were hopelessly under-prepared for the long phase of post-war stabilization that succeeded the initial military triumph.

The best of the instant histories of the war, that written by Williamson Murray and Robert H. Scales, Jr, offers a persuasive conclusion that is more than a little reminiscent of some of the military reformist theory from the 1920s and 1930s.[39] Murray and Scales advise that 'the Iraqi campaign re-inforced the lessons of Afghanistan that quality trumps quantity on most modern battlefields'.[40] They contrast the new American way in the conduct of war, a way driven by the personnel limitations of an all-volunteer force as well as by technological opportunity, with the long traditional national style. 'From the Civil War through Vietnam, the American military relied primarily on mass and industrial might to smother its enemies in men and material.' But times have changed. In a panegyric to American military excellence in Iraq, Max Boot provides a convenient summary of the contemporary cutting edge of regular warfare.

> Spurred by dramatic advances in information technology, the US military has adopted a new style of warfare that eschews the bloody slogging matches of old. It seeks a quick victory with minimal casualties on both sides. Its hallmarks are speed, manoeuvre, flexibility, and surprise. It is heavily reliant upon precision firepower, special forces, and psychological operations. And it strives to integrate naval, air and land power into a seamless whole. This approach was put powerfully on display in the recent invasion of Iraq, and its implications for the future of American war fighting are profound.[41]

All of which is true enough, though its omissions are strange, given that Boot is the author of a recent well-regarded work on 'small wars', or wars against irregulars.[42] If war was only about fighting, and if military victory in regular warfare concluded the business at hand, then Boot's up-beat description would be wholly appropriate. But, as he should know, war is about politics.

In less than thirty years the cutting edge of regular warfare has been transformed. From a highly mechanized and imminently nuclear and chemical replay of the Western Front of the Great War, this time close to the then inner-German border, warfare now means a global expeditionary capability to bring precise firepower down on malefactors, preferably strictly from altitude in its American dimension. Whether or not such a practice of regular warfare will be permitted to be the norm, as foes of the American sheriff consider their options (if they have any attractive ones, that is), we shall return to consider critically in later chapters. The fighting is only an instrument of policy, essential but by no means synonymous with war. War is not *about* fighting. The US excellence in fighting demonstrated in Iraq revealed a belief in an unsound equation of military prowess with success in war as a whole. It is prone to privilege firepower over the quality of control that can only flow from physical presence, and as a consequence it can hardly help but regard the enemy as dehumanized targets. For all its technical sophistication, the new American way in regular warfare suffers from two serious weaknesses. It denies Clausewitz and, in practice, equates fighting with war; while in addition it is inclined strongly to reduce combat to the 'servicing' of targets by ever more precise firepower. One need hardly emphasize as a caveat the point that thus far the new American way in information-led war has yet to meet a regular enemy who is competent, cunning, and powerful. The only enemy extant who meets the first two of those criteria, and some would claim the third also, is the distinctly irregular, and network-centric, information-led al Qaeda. Similarly, the Serbs in 1999 were fairly competent and distinctly cunning, but overall lacked the assets to resist in a prolonged struggle.

THE SHAPE OF THINGS TO COME

For all that the future comprises only possibilities, and assuredly will surprise us, it will not happen in a historical vacuum. This concluding section offers a summary of what the author believes to be the major features of the grammar of future regular warfare. Because of their relative novelty, space warfare, cyberwar, and WMD, though covered in what follows here, are analysed in detail in Chapters Seven and Eight.

The first feature we can predict with confidence is that there is going to be a blurring, perhaps we should say a further blurring, of warfare categories. The convenient binary distinction between regular and irregular warfare frequently is going to be much less clear in practice than it is conceptually or in law. The writing of innovative additions to the law of armed conflict continues as a growth industry, but human ingenuity in unpleasantness can make a mockery of the rules. There is an abundance of strategic historical evidence of cases of a fusion of regular and irregular warfare. Regular warfare between states often has included irregular military activity. Sometimes such warfare is waged by regular forces and sometimes by de facto allies who function as associate combatants, or even as all but contract employees. In principle, there is little difficulty distinguishing regular from irregular combat. But in practice, when regular forces adopt an irregular style of war, and when irregular warriors shift back and forth between open and guerrilla warfare, the distinction can disappear. Lest this point seems unduly scholastic, it is of cardinal importance because it bears directly on the vital question of the character of the war at issue. The US Military Advisory Command, Vietnam (USMACV), never did understand the character of war it needed to wage.[43] Failing to recognize the salience of that issue, MACV, under General William C. Westmoreland, waged the aggressive style of large unit war that it preferred. Recall that Clausewitz insists that 'the first, the supreme, the most far-reaching act of judgement that the statesman and commander have to make is to establish by that test [as an instrument of policy] the kind of war on which they are embarking ...'.[44]

It is expedient, generally useful, and legally necessary, to distinguish between regular and irregular warfare. The organization of the analysis here and in the following chapter attests to my belief in the continuing relevance of the distinction. Nonetheless, the identification of categories, even very broad categories of warfare, carries the peril that it may constrict the imagination and impede understanding. Mao Tse-tung's theory and practice of protracted revolutionary warfare posited three stages: the strategic defensive; preparation for the counter-offensive; and the counter-offensive with overwhelming force intended to secure decisive military victory. His stages can be freely translated, successively, as primarily political agitation and terrorism, primarily guerrilla warfare, and primarily regular warfare. Belligerents will shift back and forth in modes of warfare as their circumstances command.

Next, US–Allied experience, first in Afghanistan (2001) and then in Iraq (2003), will remind those who need reminding that there is more to war than combat, just as there is more to combat than firepower. History's lessons have to be learnt over and over again. When war is not simply the sport of kings, but rather engages the passions, if not necessarily the active mass participation, of societies, the verdict of the battlefield may not be accepted by all as the verdict of war. War termination should be much less of a problem for belligerents in regular, as contrasted with irregular, war. The combat in the former generally is conducted with some respect for the law of armed conflict and each side, including the loser, can be presumed to exercise authority over its forces. However, when regular warfare between states is not concluded with a formal armistice or surrender, the victor may discover that the supposedly vanquished foe transitions his activity into an open-ended phase of irregular hostilities. Contrast what has occurred in Iraq with, for some prominent examples, the conclusion of the American Civil War, the First World War and the Second World War. In none of the latter cases did the defeated armies turn to guerrilla warfare and terrorism, once they had been overcome in regular battle. For some time to come those who craft war plans will be unusually alert to the need to make provision for post-battlefield security. More particularly, we can hope that they will remember their Clausewitz and never forget that warfare is a form of political behaviour. If the war planners receive intelligent policy guidance and are themselves strategically educated, they will shape their designs for war with careful regard to the probable impact of their conduct of combat upon the quality of peace that is earned by military victory.

In the regular warfare of the future, as it was in the past, the control of territory with people will be vital. War is about control, as Rear Admiral J. C. Wylie explained with exceptional clarity, and the control that matters most is the control of people. In the Admiral's words: 'the aim of war is some measure of control over the enemy'.[45] Since people can inhabit only one of geography's five dimensions, the sole way to control them is to command the land on which they live. This may seem banal and glaringly obvious, but banal and self-evident or not, it is by no means redundant to insist upon its authority. In future warfare, land power, in key part meaning troops on the ground, will continue to be necessary if anything resembling decisive victory is to be achieved. The high-technology transformation of armed forces, their growing network-centricity, and especially their ability to lay down ordnance precisely from vehicles at altitude or in vehicles navigated precisely to distant targets, are none of them more than enabling features that should contribute to the success of combined arms. War involves death and destruction, possibly inflicted with great precision, just as it can be waged by internetted forces, but that is all instrumental. War is not about the precise infliction of death and destruction, any more than it is about superb communications. Rather, to repeat, war is about the control of people and, of necessity as a consequence, the control of land. The information age will not retire geography as a dimension of war of high significance.

The era of mass armies, armed, equipped, and fed by the mobilized might of the nation, vanished with the demise of total war. 'Demassification' is now the watchword; quality not quantity is the axiom. We have heard this before; indeed we have even seen it before. In modern times, which is to say, somewhat contentiously, from the mid seventeenth century, the era of mass armies, of the nation in arms, can be dated from the French discovery and exploitation of the idea of the nation in 1792–3, until either 1945 or 1989. Historical pedantry aside, there is no argument but that there was a long period when the discovery, or invention, of the nation, married to the industrial and agricultural revolutions, and serviced by radically new means of transportation and communication, resulted in the ever greater massification of major regular warfare. That experience is now definitively over, at least for the more advanced countries. The future of regular warfare will be dominated by combat between professional military champions equipped with weapons that can kill or disable with precision at a distance, including at a very long distance. The demise of mass, sheer quantity, in favour of quality, is today the orthodox understanding of the future of regular warfare in the technically more advanced countries. Armed forces will be smaller and equipped more lightly so as to be more agile in deployment. This agility is to be achieved, *inter alia*: by reorganizing the Army into smaller, more agile, formations for combat (brigades, not divisions), developing lighter classes of armoured fighting vehicles than, say, the extant 70 ton *Abrams* main battle tank; by improving yet further the lethality and timeliness of on-call, as opposed to organic, firepower; and by greatly reducing the weight and amount of the logistic tail. By perfecting true 'jointness', effectively to the point of true interdependence, courtesy of the new network-centricity, diverse forces relatively modest in size can be 'all that they can be'.

The vision, and emerging transformational scheme, is of course pre-eminently American. Also, it is global in the important sense that the Pentagon's drive for military transformation, while admittedly expressing features strong in American strategic and military culture, does conform broadly to the contemporary state of the science of war. That state is transnational. Nonetheless, different cultures will choose to employ technologies in somewhat distinctive ways, and there can be no doubting the relative importance of the ideational over the strictly material. As Paul Hirst has advised: 'War is driven by ideas about how to use weapons and military systems almost as much as it is by technical and organizational change themselves. Ideas are thus crucial....'[46] Just so. A demassification of regular warfare can be presented both as reflecting a global trend in the grammar of warfare, and as expressing an unmistakably American vision of the future. There are some potential, indeed already demonstrated actual, problems with this vision-come-grand design, which we address below. It is necessary to be as clear and specific as possible about the US design for future regular warfare. Since the United States does not, save with minor exceptions, maintain distinctive military establishments for the conduct of regular and irregular warfare, this grand design is the US military story for the future.

Most elements of the 'new American way of war' have been introduced in this text already. Nonetheless, it is useful to corral them together at this juncture, because they do constitute a cohesive whole. Whether or not this American approach will bear the strategic traffic that US foreign policy is sure to send its way is, naturally, another matter entirely. For a final clarification, what follows is the American view of the American conduct of such warfare. By obvious implication, however, Americans assume that enemies will be unable either to deny them the ability to impose their preferred character of combat, or to present a challenge, be it ever so asymmetrical, that newly transformed forces will be unable to meet. So, what are the principal features of interstate, which is to say regular, warfare, in the current dominant American view?

US regular warfare will be largely expeditionary in kind. In sharp contrast to the combat from forward garrison locations that was the pattern of military preparation in the Cold War, it is assumed that US and US–Allied forces generally will need to project power over great distances.[47] This assumption helps explain the enthusiasm for the demassification of forces and their logistics. Future foes may not be as obliging as was Saddam's Iraq in conceding the initiative to the agents of international order. Heavy forces that arrive after the war is over would be less than useful.

The new American way of war embraces the goal of seamless cooperation among forces specialized to excel in each of warfare's five geographical dimensions: land, sea, air, space, and cyberspace. Courtesy of digital communications and sufficient bandwidth, American forces of all kinds should be able to wage war from a script that is truly common in real time. Everyone will know what everyone else knows, including where they are all located. The golden key that enables this transformation from the old days of industrial age combat, with its masses of platforms – tanks, artillery pieces, ships, aircraft, and so forth – is superiority in what has come to be known by the suitably formidable acronym, C^{4}ISTAR, (Command, Control, Communications, Computers, Intelligence, Surveillance, Targeting, and Reconnaissance). Forearmed with that holy grail of war, 'dominant battlespace knowledge', or information superiority, US forces will operate within the decision-cycle time of their enemies. As we noted earlier, Colonel John Boyd, USAF, fighter pilot turned guru, applied his tactical knowledge of air combat to warfare at all levels by means of his simple formula of the 'OODA loop'. Unmatched speed in the sequence of observation, orientation, decision, and action is held to be the key to victory. This insight, banal statement of the obvious, or panacea – take your choice – is probably the most important concept undergirding the current US programme of long-term military transformation. The OODA loop is a formula for decisive success in a manoeuvrist style of warfare. American technology, particularly in the realm of the real-time gathering, processing, and diffusion of information, enables US forces to act effectively with a speed that leaves their enemies gasping in their wake. At least, that is the theory. Also, it is the practice, at least when the enemy elects to stand and fight, as did Taleban Afghanistan and Ba'athist Iraq. We note, however, that when the enemy knows its trade, is technologically sophisticated, and is led by some superior strategic brains, the new American way of war does not perform quite so well. We refer, of course, to the ongoing global campaign against al Qaeda and its franchised associates.

In the preferred American way of future regular warfare, machines will do much of the work and bear most of the risks that used to be the lot of soldiers. There is a clear trend towards the increased use of unmanned aerial vehicles (UAVs), while the next step, the employment of unmanned aerial combat vehicles (UACVs), has already been taken. The latter are flying robots armed with precision-guided weapons. UAVs offer several major advantages over their manned competitors. They can be small, even very small, have long endurance, be procured at a fraction of the cost of manned aircraft, and they do not place American aircrew at risk of death or capture. The much-vexed and amply debated question of an alleged American, indeed general Western, extreme sensitivity to casualties, appears as an analytical conundrum analogous to the dispute over the primacy of the chicken or the egg. The United States has a long history of substituting metal for men in war whenever it could. Indeed, its profligacy in firepower in preference to, as well as in support of, manoeuvre, is legendary. When the battlespace happens to be the territory of an ally, as in South Vietnam, this emphasis on ordnance is a potent and predictable source of political problems.

The new American way of war, actually any American way of war in the future, will depend vitally upon an ever-increasing use of space systems. The C⁴ISTAR referred to already is very much a space story. The history of warfare and the logic of strategy warns unequivocally that the greater the dependence upon the exploitation of space, the greater the need for reliable space control. The strategic significance of space and cyberspace in future warfare is analysed in some detail in Chapter Eight. It is almost a cliché to cite how important is space and cyber prowess to the American way of war. Cliché or not, space and cyberspace now have joined the other three geographical environments as literally essential elements in the architecture of US military power. One should add that that importance, though extreme in the US case, is potentially a global phenomenon.

The United States expects future regular warfare to be conducted more and more by missiles, both ballistic and air-breathing (i.e., cruise). As a necessary consequence of that reasonable assumption, the US defence establishment is committed firmly to the development and deployment of missile defences to partner now traditional air defences. The notice of withdrawal from the ABM Treaty given by the Bush Administration in 2001 was both practicably and symbolically necessary. It was a clear statement that in Washington's view the strategic context had altered radically since the era of strategic arms competition of the Cold War. In those decades, many

Americans of a liberal persuasion were convinced that ballistic missile defence (BMD) would pose a dangerous threat to strategic stability. In principle, such a defence might critically undermine the credibility of the adversary's missile threat, and hence the reliability of its ability to deter. A condition of stable mutual deterrence was believed to rest upon the ability of each superpower to wreak assured destruction upon the other.[48] Appropriately enough, the relevant strategic context was characterized as one of mutual assured destruction, or MAD. The Soviets never subscribed to this theory, but they were delighted to cooperate with Americans who did. If the technologically superior competitor wished to foreclose upon active pursuit of a major sector of strategic arms competition, Moscow was pleased to oblige.[49] In the proverbial nutshell, that is the story of the ABM Treaty of 1972–2002.

Despite the prominence of air power in the American way of war, an effectively strategically insular, albeit continental, United States understands that it must maintain a globally dominant navy. It cannot function as guardian of world order, or even just protect its vital interests, unless it enjoys the ability to assert and defend the sea control it will need in order to secure access to distant landmasses. 'Naval strategy is dead', as Jan Breemer claimed a decade ago, but maritime strategy is very much alive.[50] Regular warfare in the future must require of the US superpower the ability to protect maritime communications, to hover ambiguously in a crisis zone with potent latent force, and to project military power of many kinds from the sea. A cardinal benefit of sea-based power is that its exercise as threat or in action does not depend upon the prior assent of local polities. Naval vessels are sovereign territory. American defence analysts do not anticipate that future warfare will see a return of blue-water combat, with states contesting for control, even command, of the sea. However, they do expect that the US ability to exploit its control of the sea for influence upon the land will be opposed vigorously in some contexts.[51] That plausible expectation has fed a lively debate about the proper character and size of the fleet. Generally it is accepted today that future regular warfare may well see intense combat in the littoral region, as the superpower would strive to enforce strategic access to problem areas ashore, including very deep ashore.

Notwithstanding American appreciation of its dependence upon sea power for force projection of almost any kind, it is no exaggeration to claim that the United States is the world's first air power. In this regard it has been compared by US Air Force historian, Richard P. Hallion, with Rome as a land power and Britain as a sea power.[52] Future regular warfare will be ever more interdependently joint, combined, integrated, and network-centric. But none of that detracts from the American love affair with air power, an enduring condition which is a logical expression of the national faith in technology. There is no doubt that superiority in the air has long been the most distinctive of America's military's strengths. As new technologies have rendered that air power ever more lethal, to strike from the sky has become the preferred American way of war. Over Kosovo, air power seemed to deliver victory by the effect of its own action, unaided by a combined arms story.[53] The reality was rather different, but the belief grew that air power finally had fulfilled its eighty-year promise of winning a war on its own. In Afghanistan, the few American, British, and other special operations forces (SOF) on the ground, functioned principally as target spotters for precision air strikes. Iraq in 2003 was a mixed story. The initial aerial 'shock and awe' bombardment was a military and political failure,[54] but Allied air power achieved disabling attrition against Iraqi forces who otherwise might have been minded, and able, to defend the capital.

Air warfare, certainly warfare from the air, has been and remains very much the leading edge of the American way of war.[55] Obviously, this is more appropriate in regular than irregular warfare.[56] However, states, indeed all belligerents, tend to do that at which they are most proficient, whether or not it is well suited to the case at issue. Anyone planning to challenge the US superpower in regular combat will need to devise tactics and strategy to neutralize, if not actually defeat, the world's most potent air power.

Future warfare of most kinds increasingly will need the services of special operations (SO) units. The US military establishment has a long history of more or less open hostility to the elite irregular regulars of the

SOF.[57] That said, at long last the topmost strata of the American military hierarchy have conceded the desirability, even the necessity, of including the SOF as a vitally important component in the new American way of war. In Afghanistan and Iraq the special warriors performed literally essential duties as enablers for the preferred new national style in demassified, swiftly manoeuvring, and precisely firing forces. So fashionable have the SOF become of late, that, as was to be expected, exaggerated ambitions for their future roles have been mooted. It has even been suggested that the Army should all but transform itself into an SOF establishment on a grand scale. Beyond the absurdities encouraged by undue enthusiasm, there lies, nonetheless, the kernel of a sound idea. It is a fairly safe prediction that future warfare, regular and irregular, will be characterized both by a growing portfolio of vital roles for SOF, and by some noteworthy convergence of skills, style, and training, between regular troops and SOF. Were one of a cynical turn of mind, one might speculate that the US Army harbours a cunning plan to kill off the much detested SOF by means of co-option. If all of the Army supposedly is SO-capable, there are no more *special* warriors. We return to the subject of SOF late in Chapter Six.

The approach to future regular warfare just outlined amounts to a compelling narrative. Moreover it is a story rooted firmly, if not quite unarguably, in the actual historical experience of the past few years. It is not all, or even principally, theory, by any means. Nonetheless, it is necessary to conclude this discussion on a sceptical note. Identification of some caveats makes plain why the future of regular warfare may not conform to the dominant mode of combat anticipated by American theorists and officials. Furthermore, such warfare may not conclude with the decisive victory that seems all but pre-programmed by US military superiority.

Although US transformation of its armed forces is long on the military hitting power effected by precision strike, in its Army variant at least and as should be expected, it does not short-change the importance of the human element. However, little attention seems to have been paid to the critical subjects of the will of the enemy and the determination of friendly forces and the societies they represent. We have argued repeatedly that warfare

ABOVE *Culture can enhance combat performance; ideology matters.*
Recruiting poster for the Waffen-SS in occupied France, 1941. (AKG)

BELOW *Culture can impede performance in war. American culture favours technology and firepower, which can be self-defeating.* An aerial view of bomb damage caused by a US B52 bombing strike north of Dai Tieng, Vietnam, in 1968. (Tim Page/Corbis)

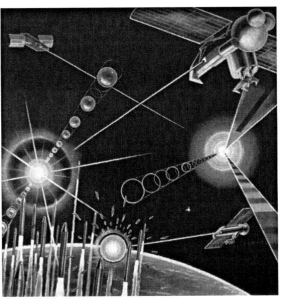

ABOVE *Warfare in geography's third dimension.* Flying Fortresses of the 303rd bomber group dropping a heavy load of bombs on industrial targets in Germany, 19 December 1944. (Bettman/Corbis)

LEFT *Warfare in geography's fourth dimension will be the inexorable consequence of the importance of space systems.* (Science Photo Library)

RIGHT *The effects of climate change may be the dominant stimulus to future warfare.* Sand dunes encroaching on the forest along the Oregon coast, 1986. (Galen Rowell/Corbis)

BELOW *After the First Nuclear Age of the Cold War, we are now in a Second Nuclear Age characterized by the danger of nuclear weapons in the hands of rogue states and terrorists.* Nuclear explosion in the Nevada desert, USA, 15 April 1955. (Corbis)

ABOVE *Holocaust (1): the gold standard; genocide as an industrial process.*
The incinerator block in Crematorium I at Auschwitz destroyed the bodies
of approximately 70,000 concentration camp victims between 1940 and 1943.
(Michael St Maur Shell/Corbis)

BELOW *Holocaust (2): genocide, an ever-popular policy.* A child looks at the human remains
of some 25,000 Tutsis, and some Hutus, who were massacred in and around the
Nyamata Catholic church and in the surrounding Kanzenze community during the
1994 Rwandan massacre, when up to a million Rwandans were killed. (Corbis)

OPPOSITE TOP LEFT *Osama bin Laden: a worthy foe. The brilliant and charismatic leader of a forlorn hope.* A strict Sunni Muslim who became a full-time holy warrior, Osama bin Laden founded Al Qaeda in the late 1980s in order to recruit young Muslim militants for jihad. (Corbis)

OPPOSITE TOP RIGHT *Biological warfare is a terrifying threat, but its strategic effectiveness is highly uncertain.* Workers at Cutters Labs in San Francisco carefully handle a vaccine for the bubonic plague. (Ted Streshinsky/Corbis)

OPPOSITE LEFT *The human face of warfare – past, present, and future.* Battle-weary men of the US 173 Airborne Brigade rest after the battle for Hill 875 at Dak To, South Vietnam in November 1967, some of the bloodiest fighting of the Vietnam War. (Bettmann/Corbis)

ABOVE *The shape of things to come? Warfare as an elite activity conducted by champions.* US Special Forces soldiers jump from a Blackhawk helicopter in the Kuwaiti desert, 35 miles south of the Iraqi border, 19 November 1998. (Reuters/Corbis)

ABOVE *Tomorrow's enemy. The People's Republic of China will challenge US hegemony, initially in East Asia.* A Chinese navy submarine docks at the Ngong Shuen Chau Naval Base in Hong Kong, 30 April 2004. (Kin Cheung/Reuters/Corbis)

RIGHT *The missile age has come to stay. Missile defence is necessary and inevitable.* A Minuteman III intercontinental ballistic missile is launched from a pad on the coast at Vandenburg Air Force Base, California, in the early 1980s. (Corbis)

is about much more than just combat. The US military establishment has yet to demonstrate that it is prepared and able to reform itself to reflect that eternal truth, even though its more thoughtful members recognize the need. Next, it is difficult to ignore the fact that although no country can aspire to construct armed forces that would resemble closely those of the US superpower, an intending enemy of the United States would not need to. After all, war is not a sporting event played according to a common rule book. Regular warfare between a superpower America and a merely regional great power China, for example, would be certain to be characterized by what today is widely known as asymmetrical strategy and tactics. There is a more than marginal possibility that clever and competent defence planners in China's People's Liberation Army (PLA), people who would have been studying the US way of war for many years, might discover ways to offset and diminish nominal US military advantages.

It would be difficult to exaggerate the importance of the reality of the globalization of technological knowledge and artefacts. That globalization guarantees a potentially universal diffusion of the technology, and knowledge of its strategic and tactical value, to anyone for any purpose. It is true that America's military excellence is not merely a matter of the exploitation of technology. As was made abundantly plain in the RMA debate of the 1990s, revolutionary change in military capability requires organization, ideas for doctrine, and training, as well as technology acquired in critical mass. However, most of the technological basis for current and prospectively future US military dominance is readily accessible to a competitor, particularly to one coming up from behind. A rival in pursuit mode has the advantage of being able to pick and choose from among the menu already developed, with variably successful results, by the innovation leader. Also, that competitor should be expected to effect its own 'transformation' in a manner best suited to its unique strategic context and culture, albeit in ways compatible with the general grammar of contemporary warfare.[58]

The preferred US mode of future regular war is designed to yield few American casualties. Unfortunately, this eminently worthy aim will rarely be wholly under American control. A cunning foe, for example, could be one able to disrupt, if perhaps not disable, the functioning of the US Global Positioning System (GPS) of twenty-four satellites in medium-altitude circular orbits at 12,600 miles. Such disruption would cripple US ability to wage a war led by the delivery of extremely precise firepower. Saddam Hussein twice failed to impose a form of warfare upon the United States that would exploit what he believed to be American society's acute aversion to casualties. It would be foolish to assume that all of America's enemies in the future will be similarly incompetent or unlucky.

We have made much of the undoubted global, not only American and European, trend towards military demassification. What we did not point out, though, was that mass, sheer numbers, can be of great importance. A clever foe, China's PLA for an example not selected entirely at random, might be able to blunt America's high-technology military edge through the adroit conduct of asymmetrical 'unrestricted warfare'. In that case, combat could reduce from elegant precise targeting and decisive manoeuvre to an attritional slugging match. As casualties mounted among people and machines, the ancient virtues of mass would become all too clear. This is not a prediction, it is only a caveat.

If air power is to be America's sharpest sword in the future, as indeed it has been for the past sixty years, it is well to bear in mind both the worldview of the airman and the aspirations he encourages on the part of politicians. Notwithstanding its many and varied uses, air power cannot help but view the land and sea below primarily as a source of targets. To air power the terrestrial realm is a dartboard. Moreover, it is a dartboard with a centre which, if struck with devastating force from altitude, should crumble promptly into paralysis, collapse, and defeat. This has come to be called the air centre of gravity, in a dubious application of Clausewitz's potent concept.[59] From early days, air power has carried the promise of a shortcut to victory. Air power's history as an anticipated panacea to the otherwise great messiness and long duration of war, is likely to have an all too healthy future. The tip of the spear of the military transformation that currently is still in its early stages in the United States, is the precise delivery of ordnance from or through the air. Two problems follow. First, a national privileging of air power all but guarantees a distorted understanding of warfare, one that over-emphasizes firepower. Second, excellence in air power, and the placing of undue confidence in its panacea-like qualities, is ever liable to tempt policymakers into imprudent political and strategic adventure.

We choose to defer consideration of the fashionable concept of asymmetrical warfare until the next chapter. It could be discussed under the conceptual umbrellas of either regular or irregular warfare, or both. Since today asymmetrical threats are associated primarily with the approach and deeds of terrorists, for once we bow to popular usage. But, as we shall make abundantly plain, asymmetrical warfare is by no means the exclusive possession of the irregular warrior.

THIS CHAPTER AND the next proclaim boldly that future warfare can be analysed usefully in just two grand categories, regular and irregular. Although these exceedingly broad bands on the conflict spectrum are judged to be the most useful as guides to enquiry, it is necessary to register a host of reservations, complications, and caveats. Above all else, perhaps, in the future, as in the past, there will be a blurring of the line between regular and irregular warfare. The latter sometimes comes to assume distinctly regular forms – recall Mao's third stage of protracted war – while the former may well be prosecuted both by irregular means and by somewhat irregular forces. If future warfare is going to witness an ever-growing role for the super-soldiers of SOF, then irregularity in combat could come to dominate a future era in strategic history. We now move on to discuss this and related possibilities in a detailed exploration of the future of irregular warfare.

Chapter six

Irregular Warfare and Terrorism

AN OLD STORY MEETS POST-MODERNITY

For good reason, definitions and analysis by dissection are the stock in trade of the scholar. The trouble is that a praiseworthy quest for precision can descend into a flattering of tidy minds at the cost of a realistic grasp of the complexity and interconnectedness that is the story of strategic history. Typologies abound of the kinds of warfare explored in this chapter. The concept of low-intensity conflict has long been favoured by the military, while shelves creak under the weight of studies of unconventional warfare, revolutionary war, guerrilla war, terrorism, wars of liberation, insurgency, ethnic war, civil war and many more. Each variant favours a particular method or political character of conflict. Moreover, lest I should appear disdainful of such distinctions, the differences can matter greatly. For example, if al Qaeda is an insurgent *movement* rather than a terrorist organization, which is a plausible, if arguable, proposition, then it poses a strategic challenge of a higher order of magnitude.[1] However, we shall apply Occam's invaluable Razor and insist that the subject here is simply irregular warfare.

Terrorism is appended redundantly within the chapter title for reason of emphasis, not necessity; it is a mode of irregular warfare. Governments must treat terrorists as criminals because the conflict is very much about the respective legitimacy of the two sides in the eyes of society. But just because terrorists have to be countered principally by police forces and intelligence agencies, and are brought to trial for their crimes, we should not be confused about the nature of their activity. Terrorism is warfare and terrorists are soldiers. Needless to say, perhaps, this strategic fact is legally inconvenient. The modern law of armed conflict was not written to define and protect the rights of the irregular, and possibly occasional, warrior. The legal context has been changing in favour of a greater inclusivity, but irregular warfare in all its forms remains a notably under-regulated field of strategic behaviour. Since such warfare is especially prone to register abominable behaviour, the weakness of the relevant law of war is particularly regrettable.[2] However, it is not unduly cynical to say that there are few irregular belligerents who would be likely to take guidance from the precepts of international law. Indeed, they would be foolish if they attempted to do so.

Definitions of terrorism are in plentiful supply, but nearly all are too inclusive. They specify arguable qualities, objectives, or strategic intentions which, though possibly true, still have no place in a definition. For example, in his superior essay on 'Terrorism and Irregular Warfare', James Kiras writes that *'terrorism is defined here as the sustained use, or threat of use of violence by a small group for political purposes such as inspiring fear, drawing widespread attention to a political grievance and/or provoking a draconian or unsustainable response'.*[3] He is persuasive, but he defines too much. I prefer a more austere formula provide by Bruce Hoffman: 'The deliberate creation and exploitation of fear through violence or the threat of violence in the pursuit of political change'.[4] Even Hoffman's definition is flawed, because terrorism can seek to prevent, not advance, political change. Interestingly, Kiras draws a distinction between terrorism and irregular warfare that I recognize, but believe to be more likely to confuse than enlighten. He advises that

> Terrorism is distinguished from irregular warfare by the form that the violence takes. Terrorism seeks to bring awareness to a political grievance but rarely, if ever, results on its own in political change. Irregular warfare by contrast, is an attempt to bring about political change by force of arms.[5]

Kiras is right to point to the limited character of terrorist behaviour and objectives. He explains that 'terrorism does not result in political change on its own, but is undertaken to provoke a response'.[6] Which undoubtedly is correct. However, it is important not to isolate terrorism as a way of war in the manner just quoted, or, to be fair, in the manner plainly implied in the title of this chapter. Terrorism is a mode of irregular warfare. As such it is subject to the same lore of war and strategy as are other forms of warfare, both irregular and regular. Contemporary and presumably future post-modern terrorism is notably different from traditional modern terrorism, but it is still terrorism, which means it is still irregular warfare. Post-modern terrorism is new, at least in recent historical perspective, in its religious motivation, as well as in its extravagant goals, its global domain, and its technical capacity to cause harm.[7] However, it is still terrorism, irregular warfare, and, at root, simply warfare. As a mode of irregular conflict the new terrorism is less novel than was potential nuclear warfare as a new mode of regular combat. Although some theorists disagree, it is plain enough to this author at least that nuclear strategy and nuclear war refer to an identifiable mode of regular warfare. The theory of war and strategy, which is to say the writings of Clausewitz pre-eminently, applies to nuclear, as it does to all other forms of warfare.

Irregular warfare is an exceedingly inclusive concept. The noun matters more than the adjective. The subject of the entirety of this forward-looking analysis is, after all, future warfare. One can lose the plot by becoming over-impressed by the potency or potential of some favoured or antici-pated mode of combat. The quest for panaceas has a long history and undoubtedly will enjoy a healthy future. Defence communities great and small, regular and irregular, are always in the market for some magic device or wonderful new method of warfare that should enable its owner–practitioner to evade the lore of strategy, with all its difficulties.[8] At present, terrorism threatens to occupy the leading edge of strategic potency, much as revolutionary and nuclear warfare appeared to enjoy the blessing of the evil gods of war in the third quarter of the twentieth century.

Readers who suspect that irregular warfare is a convenient catch-all concept are mainly correct. The concept does, however, have a usefully unambiguous core meaning. Irregular warfare is warfare between regulars and irregulars. As a general rule, please note the qualification, such warfare is between a state with its legally constituted official armed forces, and a non-state adversary. We do not have to travel far from the useful core meaning of warfare between regular soldiers and irregular warriors, though, before difficulties appear in ambush. My definition of irregularity rests on the legal status of the rival belligerents, not on the character of the fighting. Successful irregular combatants are likely to become ever less irregular in their style of combat as they acquire the strength to meet the regular forces of the state in open warfare. This is Mao's third stage of protracted war. In irregular warfare, superior official regulars typically are pitted against insurgents whose dominant modes of combat are guerrilla war and terrorism. However, from time to time the irregulars should be able to concentrate superior strength locally in order to secure a politically valuable victory in open conventional combat.

Just as successful irregulars become more and more regular in their mode of combat as they seek decisive victory, so successful regulars become more and more irregular in order to wage the kind of war wherein the irregular enemy can be beaten. Special operations forces (SOF) are the tip of this particular regular spear. Given the contemporary and widely anticipated future dominance of irregular over regular warfare, it is not surprising that SOF around the world appear to be entering a golden era. We discuss this development below.

The guiding light for this chapter must be the prospects for warfare of all kinds other than that between states. It follows that the belligerents will be more or less dissimilar or asymmetrical, in the jargon of today. There will be stark dissimilarities between the relatively small forces of the non-state combatant and the armed forces of the state. Those differences compel the materially disadvantaged party to wage war in a manner that permits the evasion, even paradoxically the exploitation, of its weaknesses, and that turn the nominal strengths of the enemy into handicaps. Such magic is the stuff out of which an irregular style of warfare sometimes is made. Of course, sometimes it is not. The irregular warrior needs to behave covertly with stealth, requires excellent intelligence lest the regular foe is able to concentrate against him, needs to be highly motivated, must have a territorial sanctuary, and cannot persist without the support, active or merely tacit, of at least a healthy fraction of the general public. But descriptions such as that just provided focus on method. Irregular warfare in several forms has attracted a following of what can only be described as admirers and fellow travellers dazzled by what they see as the romance of the enterprise. Anything less romantic than the terms of existence, not to mention the frequently low prospects for victory, of the typical irregular fighter would be hard to imagine. Nonetheless, in the 1960s and 1970s irregular warfare attracted a 'cult of the guerrilla', one greatly propelled by the strange universal appeal of Che Guevara.[9] This new century is already witnessing a 'cult of the terrorist', at least among a segment of Muslim youth otherwise bereft of heroes.

As we have indicated earlier, it is popular to argue that war and warfare is being transformed from the state-centricity of recent times, to a condition where reason of state no longer drives belligerency. The leading prophet for this revelation is Martin van Creveld. With some brilliant, but highly arguable forays of bold theorizing, he has told us that in an ever less state-centric world, the Clausewitzian strategic view of war is now obsolete. Van Creveld informs us, not implausibly, that 'as marriage has not always been concluded for love, so war has not always been waged for "interest".'[10] He claims that 'interest', in the sense of interest, or reason, of state, 'is a sixteenth-century neologism', and he notes that 'the examples provided by the *Oxford English Dictionary* suggest that it was applied first to individuals and only then to states.' His would-be killer assertion is that 'its [interest's] very introduction forms part and parcel of the rise of the modern world view'.[11]

For all his brilliance and historical knowledge, van Creveld is not reliable as a guide to the character of future warfare. There was no distinct Clausewitzian period coterminous with the rise, triumph, and allegedly now the decline of the modern state. Whether or not the states that today still dominate world politics are largely hollow shells, with their one-time monopoly of sovereign power and command of an abundance of loyalty ebbing fast, van Creveld is comprehensively in error when he associates that system with 'the strategic view of war'.[12] For war to be war, and for its conduct to be governed by strategy, there is no reason why the belligerents have to be recognizably modern states. Recall that strategy is about the purposeful matching of forceful means with political ends. Superficially at least, those ends have varied widely over the centuries, but rarely have they been other than 'political', understood in terms appropriate to the time and place. Even when warfare is waged for the glory of God, simply for the joy of slaughter, or for the sake of honour, such potent motivations drive a story with a political dimension. Christ's kingdom is not of this world. The Prophet Mohammed, by contrast, founded both a would-be universal empire by the sword, as well as a religion propelled by his new revelation.

With rather different perspectives, such gifted commentators as van Creveld, noted immediately above, Ralph Peters, and Robert Kaplan, all strive to persuade us that the future of warfare will be largely a tale of irregular combat.[13] These theorists, for all their differences, share a thought-provoking focus upon the human dimension of war, a dimension that the more mainstream strategic literature noticeably short-changes. They see the future as being dominated by intra-state or trans-state conflicts. In a word, future warfare overwhelmingly will be fundamentally irregular in its many manifestations. Peters anticipates a future wherein Western champions of high-technology, civilized warfare are confronted by brutal warriors who neither know nor care about the Geneva Conventions and the Universal Declaration of Human Rights. Kaplan speculates that we are facing a new dark age that will be imposed by 'the coming anarchy'. At least, those who inhabit a large zone of turmoil will be so blighted; a zone wherein chaos rules and Peters' warriors wreak havoc for the hell of it, among a range of non-strategic impulses.

Whether or not the future will be significantly anarchical and its warfare primarily irregular is not the issue at this juncture in our enquiry.

Rather the issue is the alleged novelty of future irregular warfare. The adjective 'new' is greatly favoured by authors, both academics and journalists. We can ignore it, albeit in some irritation, when it seems to be no more than an attention-getter to attract sales. Unfortunately, 'new' is frequently employed by people who believe, largely mistakenly, that transformation of one sort or another is remaking the world. That is an error in need of correction.

The character of warfare is always changing, sometimes quite slowly, as from the mid seventeenth century until the end of the eighteenth, and sometimes rapidly, as in the nineteenth and twentieth centuries. There will be new machines of war and new attitudes towards war and warriors. That is not at issue. What is at issue for the purpose of our mission is whether the future of irregular warfare is likely to warrant description as new, and if so, in what ways. We contend that the new irregular warfare of the future, especially in its terrorist dimension, although different from its recent predecessors, will be only the latest variant in the history of irregular warfare. If that contention is true, it means that there is available a huge reservoir of historical experience relevant to the task of combating irregulars.[14] There is another view of the dominant current trend in irregular warfare well worthy of respect, even though we do not find it sufficiently convincing, for all its seeming plausibility. An exceptionally well-researched study of al Qaeda lays great emphasis upon the novelty of its subject. After all, this is the terrorist organization that is so most post-modern that it all but defines the genre. The author, Rohan Gunaratna, stresses the historical discontinuity between the new post-modern terrorism practised by al Qaeda, and that of nearly all its modern antecedents. The many ways in which al Qaeda is a new enterprise, one that does not have a narrow focus or particular bounded political objectives, places historical experience at a severe discount, or so Gunaratna maintains. We shall let him speak cogently for himself.

> By adapting and seamlessly grafting pre-existing models, Al Qaeda has built an
> Islamist organization full of vitality. Its politically clandestine structure is built on
> the idea of internationalism. Using techniques drawn from Leninism and operating

on the Marxist militant model, it uses *noms de guerre,* adheres strictly to cell structure, follows the idea of a cadre party, maintains tight discipline, promotes self-sacrifice and reverence for the leadership and is guided by a programme of action. Al Qaeda is self-reproducing and therefore hard to defeat.

Because there is no historical precedent for Al Qaeda, the past offers very little guidance.[15]

What Gunaratna says about al Qaeda may well be entirely correct. Where he is less correct is in his claim for the novelty of this post-modern, apocalyptic, catastrophic – select your preference – development in contemporary terrorism. The whole is certainly new, either facilitated or literally enabled by access to the latest communications technology and techniques. But in its many parts, there is nothing about al Qaeda that the world has not seen before. Moreover, even if quantity does change quality, as the rule has it, and the organization truly is historically unprecedented, so what? Gunaratna, for all his profound grasp of the workings of al Qaeda, is guilty of the same error as serried ranks of distinguished predecessors, as well as some contemporaries. He exaggerates the character of the change and inadvertently is misleading on the nature of his subject. Let us repeat our mantra: post-modern terrorism as exemplified by al Qaeda, for all its novelty, real and apparent, is still terrorism, irregular warfare, and warfare.

Time after time new technology, and new – or, more likely, old but adapted – ideas, have been claimed to write a fresh page in the strategic history books. In a technical and tactical sense, there can be literally no exact, or even close, historical precedent for, say, air power, mechanized warfare, nuclear warfare, cyberwar, space warfare, or, in this case, a globally networked, millennial Islamic terrorist organization. That rather obvious truth has, alas, encouraged the fallacious conclusion that our theory of war and strategy must be dumped as obsolete. It takes nothing away from estimates of the apparent potency of al Qaeda for us to insist that it can and will be defeated strategically. Naturally, this malign development on the fringe of Islam needs to be examined on its own terms, but it is far from comprising a strategically unprecedented danger. Al Qaeda is, arguably, one of history's super threats.[16] It is nowhere near as super as the menace of interstate nuclear warfare, but still we should grant that it is an irregular danger quite out of the ordinary. Fortunately, we are well equipped with an empirically based theory of war and strategy that provides most of what is needed for civilization, as this Anglo-American author understands it, to survive yet again. The ever-relevant lore of warfare contains this familiar golden nugget from Sun-tzu, written nearly 2,500 years ago:

> Thus it is said that one who knows the enemy and knows himself will not be endangered in a hundred engagements. One who does not know the enemy but knows himself will sometimes be victorious, sometimes meet with defeat. One who knows neither the enemy nor himself will invariably be defeated in every engagement.[17]

Technology makes a difference, of course; but how much of a difference, and how much does that difference matter? The prospect of WMD in the hands of a globally internetted, cunning irregular enemy is indeed a nightmare without close precedent. Neither WMD in the hands of terrorists, nor the global reach of a loosely interconnected terrorist enterprise, are problems for which there are pre-packaged solutions. But, if interstate warfare is largely yesterday's problem, it is difficult to see how WMD can play much of a role in domestic conflicts. No matter how bitter the contest, if the stakes are control of a particular territory, the use of nuclear, chemical, biological, or radiological, weapons would both compromise the all important legitimacy of the belligerent and damage the prize in the conflict. Unfortunately, however, there is a strand of terrorist activity, epitomized by al Qaeda and its close affiliates, that does see strategic utility in WMD.

There is no question that WMD bring a new scale of danger to irregular warfare in the future. For the moment we will ignore the many severe practical difficulties that must impede the acquisition and effective use of different kinds of WMD by non-state groups. Let us identify bad case and worst case scenarios of peril. Until now, terrorists could kill people by the dozen, or, if they were competent, cunning, and lucky, by the hundred. In a bad case, as with the bombing of Pan Am flight 103 over Lockerbie,

Scotland, in December 1988, (Libyan) state-sponsored terrorists killed 270 people at a single dramatic, attention-getting stroke. That was a bad case, as was the Madrid train bombing in March 2004, which killed 191 people. To date, 9/11 is in a class of its own as a very bad case of terrorist violence. The excellent *9/11 Commission Report* makes the point that 'on September 11, the nation suffered the largest loss of life – 2,973 – on its soil as a result of hostile attack in its history'.[18] The upward trend in the casualty lists from terrorist violence is unmistakable. However, there are severe physical limits to the harm which smaller groups of irregular warriors can cause. Employing either conventional or unconventional, but non-WMD, means (e.g., passenger aircraft as missiles), the terrorist's capacity for mayhem is sharply limited. Unsurprisingly, advances in civil technology as well as in the technology of regular warfare, are certain to provide new tools for the irregular fighter. High explosives in the late nineteenth century (lyddite, 1890; TNT, 1902), plastic explosives after the Second World War, and the abundant availability of personal automatic assault weapons such as the AK-47 and the Uzi, all were adopted gratefully by terrorists.

The possibility or even high probability that in the future terrorists will arm themselves with WMD is far from fanciful. The principal novelty of WMD, of course, lies in the scale of potential damage they could impose. A terrorist organization could acquire the means to kill and injure victims by the hundreds of thousands, perhaps even a million.[19] That, we must emphasize, would be by no means the worst case. If a nuclear device might kill a million people, consider what the consequences could be from the release of a biological weapon. It is not likely that terrorists either would choose, or technically would be able, to cause a global pandemic by the release of biological agents engineered to resist standard antidotes, if indeed effective antidotes exist, which they certainly would not in the poorer parts of the world. It is easy to paint terrifying pictures of a future populated with nuclear and biological catastrophes deliberately manufactured by irregular combatants. Many of those images are technically far-fetched and belong in the historical gallery of popular nightmare. They do, however, feed a burgeoning Homeland Security defence industry. Nonetheless, future irregular warfare has a potential top end that engages the relevance of the old axiom, already cited, that quantity changes quality. Although our culture values each and every human being, a threat to kill people by the tens or hundreds of thousands, if not more, becomes a menace of a qualitatively different character from the terrorism of the past.

The discussion above deliberately highlights significant changes in weapons technology, which make the irregular warrior potentially far more lethal than he has been previously. Were we attempting to present a full, rounded picture at this point, we would have dwelt at length on the utility and easy availability of modern communications of most kinds to our irregular foes. The 'ubiquitous computer' has a lot to answer for.[20] When people contemplate with pride and hope what civil and military technologies are enabling in the field of military transformation, they need to consider also how the unstoppable diffusion of many of the base technologies (e.g., software encryption) can, and will, be employed for nefarious ends.

Despite the material, tactical–doctrinal and organizational (e.g., network-centric), implications of new technologies, important though they are, irregular warfare in its many forms is not at all a new phenomenon. It would be a gross error to discount technologically propelled change in the character of some cases of irregular warfare. But it would be a still greater mistake to exaggerate the importance of the undoubted novelty at the expense of recognizing the extensive continuity in strategic history. Regular and irregular warfare have always coexisted. There has never been a period innocent of irregular combat. It is true that the modern states' system that was considerably formalized at Westphalia in 1648 rests upon the principle that organized political violence is a monopoly of the sovereign power, but in practice warfare has never been confined strictly to the combat of regulars against regulars. To cite just three examples: all but perennial fighting in the Balkans in the eighteenth, nineteenth and twentieth centuries, save only for the forty-five years of the Soviet yoke; murderous partisan warfare against Napoleon's imperium conducted in Iberia, Germany, Austria, and Russia; and a distinctly unofficial war waged by the *franc-tireurs* against the Prussians in 1870–71, following the defeat of France's regular military power. The *franc-tireurs* were army deserters or civilians who acted on their own initiative to harass the invader. The parallel with Iraq today is too obvious to need emphasis. So incensed were the regular-minded Germans at this demonstration of contempt for the proper usages of war that they resorted to exemplary punitive measures in revenge and for deterrence. The most recent study of the Franco-Prussian War, by Geoffrey Wawro, quotes the German soldier, Julius von Hartmann, as stating in 1878 that 'where the people's war breaks out, terrorism becomes a principle of military necessity'.[21] In war after war from 1870 until 1945, German military practice was faithful to von Hartmann's brutal dictum.

It is only fair to observe that irregular warfare almost invariably drives the regular belligerent to behave terroristically towards the civilian populace that provides, or might provide, recruits or support for the guerrillas. The irregular warrior is obliged by his relative weakness to be elusive. That structural reality about irregular warfare tempts the regular combatant – German, French, Russian, British, American, Portuguese, and others – to strike at those it can reach. Those whom the regular can reach are the inhabitants of the civilian sea in which the guerrilla fighter must swim, to employ Mao Tse-tung's famous metaphor. The winning of 'hearts and minds' may be a superior approach to quelling irregulars, but official, or extra-official but officially condoned, military and police terror is swifter and can be effective. The proposition that repression never succeeds is, unfortunately, a myth. Half-hearted repression conducted by self-doubting persons of liberal conscience certainly does not work. That will be as true in the future as it was in the past. Whether or not contemporary and future changes in values in many societies will deny regular belligerents extreme, indeed purposefully disproportionate, terroristic violence as a practical option in the conduct of irregular war, remains to be seen. On the evidence of the on-going Russian brutality in Chechnya, to cite a particularly clear case, it is only prudent to assume that such are the enduring terms of combat in irregular warfare that both sides in desperation are always likely to wage the only war of which they are capable. It is worth noting that the

Russians/Soviets have never shown much respect for a 'hearts and minds' approach to counter-insurgency. Their contemporary counter-terroristic terrorism in Chechnya is as traditional in Russian strategic culture as it is popular with most Russians.

Irregular warfare evolves as technology and culture change, with consequences for the available modes of operation and the dominant beliefs of all parties. However, there is a necessary unity in the essentials of irregular warfare between past and future. That is true whether such warfare is defined politically with reference to the status of the belligerents, or militarily with regard strictly to a mode of operation. The argument that future warfare will be substantially new in character, let alone in nature, is thoroughly unsound. We have debated already the much vexed question of whether or not interstate wars, particularly major interstate wars, are now among the welcome detritus of strategic history. The contention here is that the irregular warfare that many people flag as the wars of the future is new only in that technology will permit the belligerents, regular and irregular, to perform their bloody deeds either in new ways or more efficiently in old. After all, with the exception of WMD, what is or may be significantly innovative about the irregular warfare of the twenty-first century? The nature of such conflict is permanent. In irregular warfare a relatively materially resource-rich regular force is pitted against a resource-challenged foe. Of necessity, the latter must operate by stealth, and has to avoid open combat except under conditions of its own choice. The Romans and their plethora of revolting irregular enemies understood this, as did the colonial powers in modern times, and as should we with respect to the future. Writing a century ago, the British military theorist, Colonel Charles E. Callwell, explained for all time the key problem in the conduct of irregular warfare. It is the difficulty of persuading or coercing an irregular enemy to come out and fight so that he could be duly slaughtered in satisfactorily large numbers. The Colonel advised that:

> Guerrilla warfare is a form of operations above all things to be avoided. The
> whole spirit of the art of conducting small wars [British period term for wars

between regulars and irregulars] is to strive for the attainment of decisive methods, the very essence of partisan warfare from the point of the enemy being to avoid definite engagements.[22]

One of the better reasons for George Armstrong Custer's suicidal impetuosity at the Little Big Horn in 1876 was precisely obedience to the principle enunciated twenty years later by Callwell. Custer had a valid fear, one derived from extensive experience, that unless he pressed the tribes aggressively they would scatter and deny him the opportunity to bring on a decisive battle.[23] In such a case, of course, the relevant principle is, beware of your wishes, they may come true.

Whatever the form of irregular warfare we can anticipate for the future, again with the exception of the WMD dimension and the global character of the major part of the terrorist menace, strategic history has been there already, many times. It may seem to some readers that the two exceptions to historical experience just cited, WMD and effective globality, are matters of the utmost significance. That would seem to be a reasonable point of view, but on balance it is not persuasive. The historically based principles of irregular warfare, its political–military grammar, to borrow and adapt again from Clausewitz, are not negated by technological change, no matter how momentous. The probability that terrorists will make or otherwise acquire a WMD or two, or at least some reasonable facsimile thereof, lends urgency to the duties of counter-terrorists. However, it would not alter the nature of terrorism or the challenge of counter-terrorism. Similarly, the fact that twenty-first century terrorism is a global phenomenon changes neither the nature of the problems it poses, nor the responses that historical experience demonstrates to be superior, if not always wholly successful.

The classics on irregular warfare, in particular the writings of Callwell, Mao Tse-tung, and T. E. Lawrence (of Arabia), will be as valid for the future as they were for the past.[24] That is to say, they will be valid once we make the modest allowances necessary for the changes in political and technological contexts. Terrorism, ethnic intercommunal strife and tribal combat, guerrilla war and insurgency, remain familiar branches on the tree of irregular warfare. Despite the fact that gross errors will be made in the future both by irregulars and by their regular enemies, it is the case that rules for the effective conduct of such warfare by both sides have been all but carved in tablets of stone by past theorist–practitioners.

Terrorism has to comprise the centrepiece of this discussion of irregular warfare. No one writing today about future warfare could reasonably choose otherwise. I must confess, though, to some unease at so 'going with' the crowd' on the hot menace of the moment, or decade, perhaps. An important duty of a book such as this is to extend the horizon of interest beyond the immediate and near term. As they say in journalism, terrorism is a story with legs. It will run and run. But whether it will run as the threat which defines the future of global disorder, I beg leave to doubt. As a precursor to examination of the place and significance of terrorism in future warfare, we need first to locate it in the context of the fashionable concept of the asymmetrical threat.

AN ASYMMETRICAL FUTURE

I explained earlier that the American defence community, with its foreign allies faint but pursuing, is notorious for promoting 'buzzword' concepts that appear profound, but which subsequent close examination reveals as ideas of quite stunning banality. For example, in the 1980s the sensible concept of 'competitive strategies' was touted around the Pentagon as a significant organizing notion for the national defence. After one has reacted to this revelation with a suitable 'Amen', the unavoidable next reaction is to wonder how strategies could be anything other than competitive, at least in the aspiration of their authors. As we all know, war, and therefore strategy, is a duel. For a contemporary example, the US and British armed forces are excited about what they are calling Effects Based Operations (EBO). Once the jargon and acronymic thicket are penetrated, this highly advanced concept amounts to a praiseworthy intention to use military power with a view to its achieving certain specifically desirable effects. No matter how one explains it, the concept, stripped of its protective dazzle, is a statement of the monumentally obvious. How could one conduct operations intelligently in any way other than for the purpose of securing desired effects? If anything, EBO, beyond its unmistakable banality, carries the gem of a dangerous illusion. Specifically, EBO encourages the notably un-Clausewitzian belief that the conduct of war can be precisely orchestrated, with the effects of particular military behaviours reliably predictable. Asymmetry is prominent among the more recent large, even imperial, concepts, beloved by many of those who plan for, and write about, future warfare.

Although asymmetry is strictly a vacuous, literally content-free, concept (for example as in asymmetrical threats and strategy), nonetheless it merits a place in this discussion, and not only because it is fashionable. To deal first with my claim for its vacuity: the dictionary tells us that to be asymmetrical simply means to be different. That is not literally meaningless, but it is certainly naked of particular meaning. Different from what? If I were to assume the august title of Professor of Asymmetrical Strategic Studies, what, exactly, would I profess? Since asymmetry, in common with unorthodox and indirect, can have no fixed abode, it is entirely valueless as an organizing concept. However, banal and circular though it is, it does have some general value worthy of note. Both irregular and asymmetrical warfare usefully contextualize terrorism, if I may be forgiven the ugly adjectival neologism. It is important to recognize that terrorism and counter-terrorism is warfare, albeit warfare of a distinctive kind, irregular and asymmetrical.

Many people decline to think of terrorism as the conduct of war. As a consequence of their confusion they view counter-terrorism as police work, and fail to consider the challenge posed by terrorism in strategic terms. Today, for example, it is commonplace to approach the abominations wrought by the evolving reality of al Qaeda as if they were the work of religious nihilists. We are told that al Qaeda has no genuine political objectives.[25] Allegedly, it commits expressive violence, sanctioned of course by Allah, with death and destruction serving as victory enough in the holy cause. As for suicide, notwithstanding its highly dubious Koranic legitimacy, the martyrs in a Jihad are assured of endless delights in the afterlife.

Undoubtedly many, indeed probably most, of al Qaeda's spear carriers are motivated by anger, a desire for revenge, the sense of empowerment that belonging to a secret elite confers, and other psychological maladies. But the organization as a whole, with its increasingly loose and adaptive framework, does have terrestrial political objectives. Al Qaeda functions strategically, employing exemplary violence instrumentally. Its principal political objectives, of which it makes no secret, are: to expel 'Zionists and Crusaders' (i.e., Jews and Westerners) from Arab lands; to bring down the apostate regimes that currently pollute the Dar ul Islam, the House of Islam; and to restore the united Islamic caliphate as a vast empire of the righteous.[26] In short, we can and should consider ourselves at war with a rational adversary. To be rational is not necessarily to be reasonable. All that one claims with the rationality label is that the enemy purposefully connects its means with its chosen goals. The goals may appear to us unrealistic, not to say appalling, but that is another matter entirely. Also, as in this case, the means may appear wholly inadequate to bear the burden of the goals selected. The purpose of this disquisition is to ensure that the subject of terrorism, even in its post-modern apocalyptic guise, is diagnosed properly for what it is; a mode of warfare that must be analysed and waged strategically.

If terrorism, with several variants, is a mode of irregular warfare, it is also an example of asymmetrical conflict. Indeed, in the current security debate, terrorism, especially when spiced with a WMD dimension, has become the exemplar of the asymmetrical threat. It has become the threat of threats. In the early 1960s, revolutionary 'People's War' or wars of national liberation with the emphasis on the guerrilla mode of combat, was defined officially in the United States as the threat of the era. Naturally, that threat was perceived in the context of the *grande guerre nucléaire* that loomed ever-menacingly over everything. It was precisely the strategic impracticality of nuclear war on the large scale that mandated the prosecution of Cold War hostilities by irregular proxies; at least, so it seemed at the time. Hindsight reveals that although irregular warfare in the Cold War decades frequently was stirred and financed by the superpowers, the motives of the local players typically were both independent and crucial. Although the dominant strategic narrative of the Cold War was the protracted non-event of the great nuclear war-in-waiting, most of those years witnessed the all-too-bloodily real events of the wars of imperial retreat and devolution.[27] The socialist revolution in Portugal in 1974 and its direct consequences for the country's colonial empire, marked the end of the era of the irregular wars of national liberation, always excepting the armed struggles against white Rhodesia and the South Africa of apartheid.

In its very nature irregular warfare is structurally asymmetrical. Two or more very different kinds of belligerents choose to conduct a 'duel on a larger scale' for the purpose of imposing their will on the enemy, as Clausewitz maintains.[28] Irregular warfare is still warfare; it is not some qualitatively different form of behaviour. It is certainly true to claim that there is an important sense in which it is more obviously political than is regular warfare. However, that point must not be allowed to obscure the fact that warfare of all kinds is about politics and should be waged with a view to its political consequences. It was Mao Tse-tung who advised that 'there is in guerrilla warfare no such thing as a decisive battle'.[29] Irregular warfare in its nature is even more obviously a contest of political wills than is regular combat. The principal reason is not hard to unearth, and has been alluded to already. Neither side can win a decisive military victory, because their structural differences, or asymmetries, preclude the conduct of operations that should prove militarily conclusive. Through success on the battlefield one can deny the political will of the adversary free play. If the military victory is sufficiently crushing, he is physically controlled. But in 'the operations of regular armies against irregular, or comparatively speaking irregular, forces', to quote Callwell,[30] the materially weaker belligerent will, certainly should, decline to oblige by placing its limited strength at risk in the open.

There is a great deal less to the concept of asymmetrical warfare than much of the writing on the subject of recent years would have one believe. We discuss it here because, for all the nonsense and exaggeration, it does highlight a most important feature of future warfare. At least for several decades into the twenty-first century, all warfare involving the American superstate cannot be other than highly asymmetrical in character. This less than sparkling insight is simply a translation of the fact that there are, and will be, no belligerents closely resembling the United States. This is not to deny that some aspects of US military prowess will be shared by several, perhaps many, other potential belligerents.

In US perspective, indeed from the point of view of all who will rely upon the United States to perform the sheriff role for global order, it is good news that the ordering power will be militarily superior for many years to come. The less good news, though, is that that superiority in conduct of the latest models of regular warfare, is combat keyed to eviscerate enemies of similar kind. The American sheriff will have systemic difficulty reaching highly asymmetrical enemies. The American military transformation that will be underway for the next twenty or thirty years, with its dependence on excellence in C^{4}ISTAR as the vital enablers, must pose a standing challenge to those who would harass the American-policed world order. The concept of the asymmetrical threat is useful in that, for all its essential vacuity, still it serves admirably to remind people that tomorrow's enemies will be very different from 'us'. In truth, the enemy has always been different, to a degree asymmetrical, but it is remarkable how often policymakers and strategists somehow have neglected that fact. Enemy-independent defence planning is, and long has been, more popular than one might think. Unquestionably, it is convenient to plan campaigns against an enemy who can safely be assumed to behave cooperatively. The greater the military power and reputation of a state, the higher its strategic self-esteem, and the more imposing its recent historical record of victory, the less likely is it to be inclined to approach its enemies adaptively.

Asymmetry is a strategic reality of international life. Every state is distinctive, with unique strengths and weaknesses. In irregular warfare the asymmetries generally are extreme. It is all but certain that the regular forces of most states will be vastly superior by standard military comparison to the forces of irregular, non-state, foes. Terrorism is a mode of warfare at the far extremity of the regular–irregular spectrum. It would be difficult to conceive of two sworn enemies more different in kind than the United

States and al Qaeda. Ironically, they appear to share a commitment to political transformation, albeit of radically different kinds. The American military version of transformation lacks the luxury of being able to focus exclusively upon a single class of enemy, while it is inclined unhelpfully to a somewhat astrategic autism, as noted already.

As with so many of the big ideas that excite the US defence community and even some of its foreign imitator–competitors, the concept of asymmetry expresses nothing more than an eternal truth about warfare. With few exceptions, for example the generality of hoplite warfare between Greek city states, warfare must always be an asymmetrical undertaking.[11] The enemy can never be exactly like us. The question is, just how unlike us is he, and what should that mean for his way of war and, by implication, for ours? History is well populated with cases of belligerents who enjoyed contrasting superiority on land, or at sea, on the plains, or in the forest or mountains, and who, therefore, could not find mutually agreeable terms for conclusive military engagement. The current and future global war on terrorism (or some terrorists), or GWOT in the delightful acronym of the moment, is only an extreme example of the asymmetry that characterizes all warfare.

Asymmetry, as such, cannot be taught or practised. But frequent reminders that current and future warfare is, and will be, asymmetrical, can only have beneficial results. Many defence professionals forget, if they ever knew, that war has a cultural context. An enemy may look militarily familiar in important material ways. But his military culture, with its deep ties to a unique society, is likely to propel his behaviour in directions that are more or less different, which is to say asymmetrical, to ours. Because warfare mercifully is an infrequent occurrence for most societies, the merit or otherwise in a culturally favoured view of particular military innovations can be something of a mystery. As Thomas G. Mahnken claims, 'it is exceedingly difficult to determine the effectiveness of new approaches to warfare in peacetime'.[12] Moreover, even when the actual experience of war does demonstrate the correct, at least better, way to employ new military tools, local culture as well as physical constraints might render slavish adoption of that way impractical. Mahnken compares and contrasts the German, Soviet, British, French, and American approaches to combined arms armoured warfare in the Second World War. He shows conclusively that the achievement of tolerably similar military capabilities across cultures does not necessarily mean the adoption of a single, universally correct model of warfare.

Although the focus in this chapter is on warfare of irregular character, the need to discuss the concept and the practice of asymmetry casts the brightest of lights on the true unity of the awful subject of war. Asymmetry is a feature of all warfare, albeit a more prominent feature in some cases than others. As noted already, terrorism, which pits small numbers of typically fanatical people against the regular might of states, is just the most extreme example of asymmetrical conflict. But regular and irregular warfare frequently are fused. We must beware of the tyranny of categories. It is convenient to analyse regular warfare between states separately from irregular warfare between non-state bodies and states, but it is essential to remember that the distinction may mislead. For a topical example, regular warfare can play a vital role in the defeat, at least attrition, of even the most irregular of enemies. Al Qaeda is not a state that can be taken down definitively, but neither does it exist beyond political and physical geography. The countries that support, or even tolerate, terrorist activity on their terrain, can be coerced by distinctly regular military operations. In principle, at least, this strategic fact explains the fate of Taleban Afghanistan. The asymmetrical dimension to all warfare is about the competitive endeavour to exploit one's strengths and offset one's weaknesses, against enemies whose strengths and weaknesses will be distinctive. Since America's primary strength as hegemon is military, its conduct of asymmetrical warfare is always liable to reduce to the pursuit of political and ideological, or cultural goals by an undue reliance on the use of force. This is not to forget America's other strengths, especially the economic and the cultural.

This discussion of asymmetry will close with another quotation from that gifted military author of imperial Britain, Charles E. Callwell. The Colonel informs us that

> The art of war, as generally understood, must be modified to suit the circum-
> stances of each particular case. The conduct of small wars [regulars versus irreg-
> ulars] is in fact in certain respects an art by itself, diverging widely from what is
> adapted to the conditions of regular warfare, but not so widely that there are
> not in all its branches points which permit comparisons to be established.[13]

In other words, the British Army fought Afghan tribesmen in a
manner radically different from that which eventually was discovered to
be appropriate for meeting the Germans in European continental warfare.
Nonetheless, both were examples of the common phenomenon of war.
Just how uncommon is warfare in terrorist and counter-terrorist mode, is
the topic we move to next.

TERRORISM AS IRREGULAR WARFARE

It is difficult to discount the bias of the immediate. In these earliest years of
the twenty-first century, the threat of the hour, day, year, probably the
decade, and perhaps beyond, is terrorism with a global reach. More specifically, it is primarily the threat posed by religiously motivated, so-called
catastrophic, apocalyptic, or post-modern terrorism, of which the al Qaeda
network is the exemplar.

Al Qaeda ('the base') was not immediately recognized by the US Government and its intelligence agencies as an emerging super threat. The
organization was known, but its scope and operational ambitions were
nowhere near fully appreciated prior to its bombing of the US embassies in
Nairobi and Dar es Salaam on 7 August 1998, even though it had been
founded by Osama bin Laden as early as 1988.[14] In the early to mid 1990s,
Western intelligence agencies believed that al Qaeda was a background
logistical element among radical Islamists, bankrolling warriors and
providing moral support, rather than an enterprise itself committed to
combat. Only recently has it been revealed that that shadowy organization
was responsible for the abortive assault upon New York's 'twin towers' in
1993. Also in that year, al Qaeda coached Somali warriors in how to wage
urban combat against Americans in Mogadishu, with particular reference
to the potential vulnerability of helicopters. Al Qaeda had learnt the hard

way how to deal with helicopters, in the course of the long struggle against the Soviets in Afghanistan. The hard core of 'the base' in the early 1990s and today comprised graduates of the long war in Afghanistan against Soviet occupation. In that war, anti-helicopter tactics and weapons, especially the *Stinger* shoulder-fired ground-to-air missiles provided by the United States, proved critically important for morale and military success, for both sides.

We should take serious note of the operation of the law of unintended consequences, a law whose working can be detected in some of history's ironies. It is ironic that the most potent terrorist menace in world history, that posed by al Qaeda, quite literally was the product of the political and military experience of the anti-Soviet war in Afghanistan which the United States and Britain, among others, supported over-abundantly in the 1980s.[35] Al Qaeda was, perhaps is still, something of a veterans' association for the soldiers of the faith who served the common religious cause in the ultimately victorious struggle against the Soviets. Those veterans were, and are, 'foreign fighters', largely Arab, but also Chechen, Pakistani, Bosnian, and many others. The anti-Soviet insurgency, by another of history's ironies, truly was conducted by an international brigade of Islamic warriors. Except for the contrary outcome, one is reminded of the abortive struggle by the International Brigade of communists and other idealists in Spain in the 1930s in defence of the Spanish Republic.

There is no denying the contemporary significance of al Qaeda. Nor should we forget and neglect the other groups committed to the perpetration of catastrophe terrorism, as well as the terrorists of a more traditional kind (e.g., the Basque separatist ETA, or the perennial soldiers for a united Ireland in the Provisional IRA). But how much attention should a book on future warfare devote to terrorism and its enemies? There is no question but that there is today a global consensus on the proposition that terrorism is the outstanding threat to order, that ever contestable, but essential, value-charged concept and condition. In the 1990s, understandably impressed by the abominations of the Wars of Yugoslavian Succession, by the ethnic genocide in Rwanda, and by a host of inter-communal and separatist conflicts in Africa and Asia (including Chechnya, with its two wars for independence), the threat of the era seemed to many commentators to be 'new wars' of an intra-state, intra-societal, kind. As we noted earlier, for a while in the mid 1990s it was popular to see future international security menaced primarily by a decline in the authority of central government, even merely of governance. A book of the period bore the indicative title, *Managing Global Chaos*.[36] Also, Kaplan's lament upon *The Coming Anarchy* was very much a sign of the times, both as a contributor to, and an expression of, intellectual fashion.[37]

The important issue is not to assess the merit in the period-sited views mentioned immediately above. Rather is it to recognize that there is a recurring tendency among commentators, including those regarded as security experts, to be over-impressed by a contemporary climate of opinion which, invariably, is shaped and driven by reactions to immediate events. The electronic news media has proliferated explosively in its direct access to happenings, in its customer reach, and in the sheer quantity of air time it needs to fill. The result is that the pull of fashion, with its immediacy of focus, has become ever more of a factor in debate. Of necessity, television stations thrive on news, or the facsimile of news. Their need to prevent dead air compels them to employ variably licensed experts, who typically are asked unanswerable questions about the immediate future. This babble of speculation, with opinion often masquerading as expertise, comprises a significant portion of the cutting edge of public debate on security. With its structural bias towards the here and now, or at most the next few days and weeks, the public debate lends itself all too easily to capture by threat projections that lack staying power.

It is appropriate to poke fun at the 'threat of the week' phenomenon, as doomsayers flit from deadly asteroids, to melting icecaps, to global economic chaos and political anarchy, to nuclear- or ecoli-armed terrorists. The problem is not threat invention; the four mega-threats just cited are all potentially real enough. The challenge, rather, is both to assess the severity of the threat at issue and to identify practicable measures for its alleviation, if not outright solution. Also, it is important to contextualize the threat of interest. If, for the sake of argument only, we predict a healthy long-term future for global terrorism of the most unhealthy kind, what else do we believe will be going on in the world at that time? Is an ever more lethally armed terrorism going to be the dominant threat of the twenty-first century? Or will its current prominence at the head of the threat column prove to be only temporary, as other threats, perhaps potentially with more 'mega' horse power, mature? We are in the realm of speculation and guesswork, otherwise dignified as historically educated futurology. Were this study faithful to the main current of opinion today, the exploration of irregular warfare would precede the discussion of regular conflict. The fact that it does not do so reflects the author's inclination to resist fashion. More legitimately, perhaps, the batting order here reveals the conviction that although terrorism assuredly is the leading threat of the 2000s, and probably for sometime beyond, it is not likely to enjoy that star billing for very long into the century. Optimists will say ten years, pessimists thirty-plus. We are in the realm of what is known politely as the educated guess.

I will raise my head above the parapet and offer some points that corral and capture what it is most important to know about terrorism as future irregular warfare. There should be no need for me to apologize for the speculative character of these definite opinions. What follows rests upon my reading of historical experience, upon the logic of strategy, and on my understanding of the probable political and cultural contexts of future warfare. Much of the bold prediction below almost begs to be qualified or otherwise hedged, since none of it can find direct reference support. We shall proceed anyway, accepting the severe limitations on evidence that must reduce the authority of all claims about the future. *Caveat emptor.*

Al Qaeda will be beaten, though not annihilated. The victory will be long in coming and progress will be hard to measure reliably. Furthermore decisive strategic success can be achieved only from efforts deriving from the world of Islam itself. That stands in important contrast to the tactical and operational victories that the non-Islamic world can and must achieve. By its very nature, the threat posed by a terrorist organization is all but impossible to assess with high confidence. Threats of, or in, regular warfare can be calculated by educated guesswork in the strategic art form known as net assessment.[38] Even for a future where quality is nearly guaranteed to beat quantity, and where military inspiration, if not genius, may win the day, the capabilities of a regular enemy will generally be accessible to intelligence probing. Exactly how those capabilities will be used is, of course, always a source of some uncertainty. Terrorist or insurgent organizations provide far less evidence on their capabilities, a systemic fact which encourages both exaggeration and dismissal on the part of the potential victims. Threat assessment is unusually problematic when the terrorist foe comprises a *network* of like-minded organizations that already has demonstrated the ability to adapt and evolve.

There are many apocalyptic-type terrorist groups in the world. For example, the United States is well supplied with extreme fundamentalist Christian groups. Also it is home to many racist, as well as 'patriot' militia, organizations. I must hasten to add that the United States is far from unique in harbouring and nurturing racist groups that are not averse to the use of violence. And we should not forget the disturbed individuals who are willing to exorcise their personal devils by extreme violence. Remember the mentally unhinged Timothy McVeigh, the bomber of the Federal Building in Oklahoma City in 1995. Also recall the lethal venture into chemical warfare by the mystical somewhat Buddhist and somewhat Hindu Japanese sect, Aum Shinrikyo (Aum 'Supreme Truth'), which released Sarin nerve gas on the Tokyo underground in 1995, albeit not to great effect.[39] The reality and probable longevity of the new terrorism is not in question. What is in question is whether it constitutes merely an expensive nuisance or rather a deadly menace to life, political stability, civilized values, and international order. To venture a truly dismissive possibility, does the new terrorism constitute more of a scare-based growth industry than anything of strategic significance?

Everyone knows that al Qaeda is the post-modern terrorist organization from hell. As noted already, it was born out of the prolonged combat experience in Afghanistan and assumed the mantle of an historic victor. Islamic warriors for God had seen off a superpower. This was a heady conviction, one which still plays its role as a potent source of self-confidence and prestige. What was achieved against tough Soviets should be easier against soft Americans. Analysts are in the habit of reciting frightening, if necessarily uncertain, statistics about al Qaeda. Forged by war-hardened veterans of the successful anti-Soviet struggle, al Qaeda processed tens of thousands of young volunteer jihadists through its training camps, principally in Afghanistan, prior to 9/11. This experience was designed as much for socialization and bonding to a new identity as it was for the imparting of technical and combat skills. Al Qaeda employs state of the art communications technology, an asset that enables global networking for security and command and control. At least that used to be the case. 'The base' has learnt that the more sophisticated its communications technology, the easier is it for enemies to monitor. Furthermore, al Qaeda is extremely well funded. Above all else, it is nested in the context of an Islamic world that has been, and continues to be, a material and cultural failure relative to the West in modern times. This thesis has been popularized by the West's leading expert on Islam, Bernard Lewis. His argument has been generally persuasive, though residually controversial.[40] This condition of inferiority stands in sharp contrast to the history of Islam's first millennium. Islam was a great success story from the seventh until at least the seventeenth century.

Al Qaeda has several mutually reinforcing sources of strength. Those strengths include: a unifying and allegedly authoritative religious sanction for the militant variant of jihad; a tradition of victory against a superpower; a hard core of veteran, war-tested warriors; a vast repository of potential new recruits among Islamic youth; inspired, indeed charismatic, leadership that is technically competent and strategically gifted; ample resources to finance operations and service logistical needs; a loose and flexible form of networked organization that is able to adapt to changing conditions; and, last but not least, an enemy from central casting in the form of corrupt and hypocritical, apostate, nominally Islamic Arab regimes. The 'Great Satan' that is the United States is an enemy because it is judged to be the principal external prop for those apostate régimes. Because al Qaeda promotes the *Salafist* Islamic doctrine of a universal kingdom of God, even the version that envisages restoration of the mediaeval caliphate from India in the East to Spain, or France, in the West, its ideological vision is an impossible dream. Such impracticality is useful, because the organization's master goal is not of a kind that lends itself to potential achievement. Hence, al Qaeda effectively is beyond criticism for failing to make measurable progress, at least towards accomplishment of the grandest of its aspirations. What serves as the all-purpose doctrine, however, is the belief that everything that happens reflects the will of Allah and is necessary. This fatalistic doctrine, so alien to Western cultures, excuses and even allows failure, certainly death, to be regarded as victory. Although al Qaeda's millenarian goal is out of reach, we should not forget that its more proximate ambitions may not be. As cited already, it is committed both to expelling Jews and Westerners, especially Americans from the lands of Islam, and to the destruction of apostate regimes.

Belatedly, there are now some useful studies of al Qaeda available; at least we think they are useful.[41] Much about the organization remains unknown and it is far from comprising a static enemy. Representative Adam Schiff, a member of a House of Representative subcommittee on terrorism, stated in April 2004 that 'the Al Qaeda of today is different from the Al Qaeda of 2001'.[42] He went on to note that, 'like a virus, Al Qaeda has evolved and adapted to the US-led war against it. We may have made remarkable inroads in destroying the Al Qaeda of 2001, but are we making progress against the Al Qaeda of 2004?'

In light of the strengths of the enemy outlined above, it may seem as if my claim that al Qaeda will be defeated has to rest more on hope than a realistic assessment of probability. Not only do I claim that al Qaeda will lose in terms meaningful to us, I insist also that we can be confident of that outcome. For all the drama of some of its shocking deeds, it is an organization, perhaps more a cause and doctrine, that is going nowhere and in practice has nowhere to go. Although 'terrorists have learned to think strategically rather than tactically', as longstanding terrorism expert Brian Jenkins of RAND insists, the jihadists of al Qaeda embrace ends that are beyond their means.[43] That would be false only were the rest of the world in effect to surrender comprehensively to its fears. Given that the more extravagant of the religiously sanctioned political goals of al Qaeda are unreachable, it follows that even a Western (and Eastern) determination to appease must fail. Al Qaeda is obeying the will of Allah by fighting the sacred fight. Although that religiously mandated struggle has virtue in and of itself, we must not forget that restoration of the caliphate, at least in some minimal form, may seem to many to be an achievable holy goal. Also, we cannot discount entirely the possibility of an Iran-style Islamic fundamentalist coup in Egypt, Saudi Arabia, or Pakistan.

It is true that al Qaeda has proved itself capable of learning from its mistakes. But it seems as yet unconvinced that the United States and the world order it polices somewhat erratically is a truly robust foe. A standard charge against regular belligerents in irregular wars is that they tend to be abominably culturally ignorant of their enemy, as well as of their local friends and allies. Too little notice is taken of the evidence of the parallel strategic weakness on the part of irregular combatants. For all their intellectual gifts and technical and organizational virtuosity, the leaders of the increasingly loosely connected parts that comprise al Qaeda see the world through the highly distorting prism of fanatical religious conviction. Such a condition is tactically helpful for strength of will, as the German Army in the East, the *Ostheer,* demonstrated in Russia in the Second World War, but it is a severe strategic handicap.[44] Should America's irregular enemies study the superpower's strategic thought and literature with even a fraction of the care currently taken by the Chinese defence community, they might become familiar with an axiom and judgement advanced by Bernard Brodie. He advised that 'good strategy presumes good anthropology and sociology. Some of the greatest military blunders of all time have resulted from juvenile evaluations in this department'.[45] Irregular forces, guerrilla, terrorist, or both, are inclined to make a virtue of the material necessity for their poor person's way of war. That 'way' is obliged to privilege political will and moral qualities as vital offsets for absent legions and missing machines. The trouble is that although it is important to assess the political and moral temper of the foe, a firm conviction of one's own moral advantage is likely to mislead you about the determination of the enemy. Terrorism is a branch of irregular warfare, and its course and conduct is subject to the eternal lore of war and strategy.

It is all but axiomatic to maintain that an irregular belligerent wins by not losing. Somewhat in defiance of that axiom, I will argue that time is not on the side of the catastrophic, post-modern terrorist. The war-hardened multinational cadre of veterans of the Afghan struggle is diminishing rapidly. It has suffered the natural attrition of age and infirmity, as well as the combat attrition inflicted by an aroused bevy of state enemies. Furthermore, although in theory it has a bottomless well of 'useful idiots' from which to recruit, the quality of its army is bound to suffer badly with the loss of well-established training camps and the indoctrination that was effected there. This is not to deny that the arithmetic of the war with al Qaeda will be fairly gruesome for years to come. Between 30,000 and 50,000 would-be jihadists were processed through the organization's boot camps for terror in the 1990s. However, to look on the brighter side, those warriors for Islam cannot be replaced by new cohorts with comparable training and group bonding. Moreover, culture, in the form of religious fanaticism, is not entirely a useful player for al Qaeda. While the divine rewards of jihad comprise a potent incentive to sacrifice, the jihadist can expect to be well rewarded even for strictly temporary, and obviously non-suicidal, service. Many recruits will punch their jihadist ticket and move on to safer activities.

As al Qaeda ages, it is finding at last that the war against 'Zionists and Crusaders' that Osama bin Laden proclaimed in three *fatwas* (decrees) in 1996, 1997, and 1998, has now been joined. Al Qaeda has aroused a formidable array of enemies, within and beyond the Islamic realm. Those enemies now are mobilized for war. Al Qaeda has staged isolated incidents in different countries for little strategic gain. Although bin Laden's religious thugs will continue to promote fear for a long time to come, probably a couple of decades at least, they will be engaged in an ever more punishing rearguard campaign. Not all countries are as soft on terrorists as the United States. For example Turkey and Indonesia are notably unforgiving in their counter-terrorist behaviour. Al Qaeda may suffer no decisive military or political defeat, but it will become increasingly more obvious to the organization's less dedicated members, let alone to potential recruits, or suicide fodder, that the war against Islamic apostasy and the West is an exercise in futility. The attack on the twin towers and the Pentagon was tactically and operationally brilliant. Strategically, however, history will reveal it to have been a Pyrrhic victory. In common with Pearl Harbour, this latest surprise attack on the US homeland could hardly have been better designed were its purpose to arouse the wrath of the American people. Its intention was to demoralize a supposedly cowardly and effete American society. The result, predictable had al Qaeda done its cultural homework, was to commit the United States to a grand strategy to defeat its terroristic foe in open-ended, all-out war. The fury and comprehensiveness of the US response must have come as a sobering shock to those in al Qaeda who believed that as the Soviet Union went down in the 1980s, so the United States will be humbled in the 2000s. A vengeful superpower is a fearsome, and none too discriminating, enemy, as al Qaeda has been learning.

By way of a troubling thought, 9/11 was so spectacular that al Qaeda will appear to be losing its effectiveness if it fails to stage yet greater atrocities in the future. In 2001 it set the bar of demonstrated achievement so high that really only the employment of a nuclear, or at least a 'dirty' radiological, weapon will suffice as the next demonstration of the will of Allah. It is likely that al Qaeda is a victim of its own success. Even the more faithful of its holy warriors will begin to doubt the potency of the organization if its action consists primarily of the delivery of taped messages from undisclosed locations. We can predict with confidence the demise, albeit the slow demise, of al Qaeda, for reasons of natural organizational ageing, the damage wrought by active countermeasures, evolution in the cultural and political contexts of the Islamic world, and its failure to evolve into a full throttle insurgency carried forward by and as a mass movement. Al Qaeda could benefit from studying the writings and practice of Mao Tse-tung. Nonetheless, it is likely that in the course of its protracted decline al Qaeda will join the United States in the very exclusive club of those who have used a nuclear weapon or device in anger. Chemical and biological weapons would be much easier to acquire and employ, but they lack the reliability of effect, both destructive and dramatic, of the nuclear agent. We discuss this danger in some detail in the next chapter.

The roots of post-modern, apocalyptic Islamic terrorism cannot be reached and dug out by Western policy and strategy. As noted already, in the medium to long-term, al Qaeda should fade away through a combination of organizational decay and societal change in the Middle East. Economic modernization leading to political change will alter the social and cultural context sufficiently for al Qaeda and its kind to become irrelevant fringe elements; at least, that is what this author hopes and believes. That happy thought does leave a practical challenge, however: what are the prospects for near-term success for the forces of sanity and order? The rather unsatisfactory answer is that they are mixed. The world's leading economic powers, the G8, let alone the American sheriff and its posse of close allies, lack the ability to remake Islamic states and societies in ways that would deprive al Qaeda of all nourishment. The basic problem is with Islamic societies and their manifest failures to modernize in ways that are competitive in the modern world. By and large, the more determinedly the West seeks to shape the future of the Islamic recruiting grounds for religious extremism, the more counter-productive the activity. Al Qaeda and other Islamic military jihadist enterprises exploit a widespread sense of historical victimization which is at least partially well founded. Somehow, the great empire of Islam fell and was replaced by a century and more of exploitation by 'crusader' polities. And that omits mention of the hated Zionists with their establishment of a new Kingdom of Jerusalem. The fact that Islam's hard times were much accelerated by the corruption of its leaders and the atrophy of its political culture, is not a story that plays too well to audiences eager to blame outsiders for their misfortune. Consistent with taking the precautions necessary for the security of Western societies, the less active we are in attempting to speed reform in the Islamic world, the better. Such reform is the only comprehensively effective answer to al Qaeda, but it cannot be imposed from outside. Evidence of Western effort to accelerate modernization in the Middle East, no matter how well intentioned, as well as obviously self-interested, must delegitimize the local process and slow its pace.

The major problem of Islamic terrorism needs to be alleviated, and can be solved effectively, only by local change in the societal and cultural contexts of the Middle East. Whether or not this will prove possible is very much an open question. In terms of culture, which in this case means largely in terms of attitude to religion, al Qaeda has to be delegitimized theologically. Needless to add, this will be no small undertaking. Where is the Martin Luther for Islam, someone able to sideline Osama bin Laden? Most definitely, however, this does not imply the wisdom of an attitude of quiescence or appeasement on the part of the rest of humanity. The world cannot afford to wait for Islamic civilization to reverse its multi-century decline, reform its religious beliefs and institutions, and join the rat race of profitable economic globalization. Time is on the side of the counter-terrorists, as observed above, but al Qaeda and its murderous martyrs cannot be permitted to fade at a speed set by what may be a glacial pace of societal evolution in the Dar ul Islam.

To understand, even to empathize with, some of the sentiments that lead people on the path of jihad, is not to excuse or tolerate atrocity. Whatever the local Islamic story behind al Qaeda, states have a primary duty to protect their citizens and their citizens' values, including property. It would be well to remember that actual or perceived weakness encourages terrorism. The events of 9/11 were a strategic disaster for al Qaeda because, arrogant in their presumed moral superiority and neglectful or ignorant of Brodie's warning about culture, it was planned to hurt an essentially fictitious American superpower. One is reminded of Adolf Hitler's fatal belief in 1940–41 that his forces only had to kick in the door for the whole rotten structure of the USSR to collapse precipitately. Western scholarship, and much of its liberal-minded journalism, is permeated with attitudes and beliefs that are profoundly inappropriate for the effective future conduct of irregular warfare against the new apocalyptic brand of religious terrorism.

It is fashionable to sympathize with the culture of victimization that is so popular in the Middle East. Someone else has to be responsible for the evil times that have befallen the once great civilization of Islam. Undue sympathy for this self-serving Islamic whinge leads logically to the belief that somehow 'we' are to blame for their troubles, and that 'we' were the true parents of al Qaeda. Vigorous measures of preventive self-defence in counter-terrorism are not encouraged by such an attitude of self-blame. This is another popular Western attitude which, again, is not wholly without merit. It holds that because terrorism is rooted in backward Islamic societies, and is sustained by the systemic unemployment of young people, it can be answered effectively only by change in the local social, economic, and political contexts. This fairly accurate opinion is apt to discourage what are regarded as futile, perhaps even provocative, aggressive measures of irregular warfare. It is true that al Qaeda basically is a problem for the world of Islam. It is true also that Osama bin Laden is more hostile to those he judges to be apostate Muslims than he is to 'Zionists and Crusaders'. But because al Qaeda has chosen to wage war against the West and its interests, it has made itself our problem.

Counter-terrorism against al Qaeda will work if it is approached as a global counter-insurgency. It has to be viewed as a protracted global exercise in irregular warfare, not as a series of isolated, individual raids against leadership targets. Counter-terrorism rarely works conclusively, quickly, or elegantly. But work it does, provided it is conducted on sound principles and with a ruthless determination to persist until a condition of tolerable security is restored. Today it is commonplace to contrast the new post-modern catastrophe terrorism with the traditional terrorism that typically had a specific and limited political agenda for a territorially defined political community. Though largely valid, the contrast can benefit from some modest qualification. Although the new terrorism is characterized by an absence even of theoretically negotiable demands, it is well to appreciate that terrorism not infrequently becomes an end in itself, or degenerates into criminal activities devoid of a political or other higher purpose. The world is well populated with rejectionist groups for most of whose members, or soldiers, the struggle is its own psychological and social reward. When Brian Jenkins writes convincingly of the key importance of the armed struggle to the leaders of al Qaeda, he could be talking about terrorism in either its traditional or its new forms.

> Religious conviction gives them strength, but the armed struggle is what holds them together. Violence is their *raison d'être*. The enterprise of terrorism provides status, power, and psychological satisfaction. It attracts new recruits. It demonstrates their devotion and gives them historical importance. Without terrorism, al Qaeda would collapse into just another exotic sect.[46]

In the ironic words of the title to a recent best-selling book, 'war is a force that gives us meaning'.[47] There is no silver bullet, no single measure or weapon, that can defeat terrorism. Irregular warfare, including terrorism, is a struggle that by its very nature must be conducted on both sides with an attritional strategy. The only exception is the rare case where the regular combatant is able to achieve a definitive victory by means of some political move which thoroughly delegitimizes the terrorist. Since al Qaeda claims its legitimacy from Allah, via the Koran, and has no known political agenda that appears to be even remotely in the negotiable category, a political resolution to this variant of future irregular warfare will not be achieved dramatically by policy design. In order to make political progress towards achieving its grand purpose of restoring the Islamic caliphate, al Qaeda would have to adopt a moderate message calculated to gain widespread support. Only in that way might the organization effect the transition to become a genuine mass insurgency capable of overthrowing regimes it regards as corrupt and apostate.

Al Qaeda is unprecedented in its scale, reach, sophistication, and potency, but so also is its principal non-Islamic adversary, the American superpower. For the reasons cited already, extremist Islamic terrorism cannot be decisively defeated except most probably over the course of several decades as a consequence of organizational decay and regional economic, social, and political change. That granted, it is the duty of states to do what they are able to protect their citizens against mass murder, sacred or other. Fortunately, the counter-terrorist belligerent in future irregular warfare has many powerful tools at its command. Timely intelligence is the core competency required to fight terrorists. Al Qaeda has triggered the creation of a global alliance in opposition. The atrocities of the new terrorism have licensed an inevitable escalation in the boldness and violence in the methods of the counter-terrorist. The United States has declared that those who harbour terrorists will be treated as if they were terrorists themselves. US action to change the regimes in Afghanistan and Iraq, whatever else may be said about it, unquestionably demonstrated a willingness to use extreme force against the political support structure of terrorists. In some ways, the very fragility of the US case against Ba'athist Iraq made the strength of the determination to effect regime change all the more impressive. Sudan, Libya, and even Iran, clearly have read the American counter-terrorist message.

Terrorism cannot usually be defeated decisively, as we have indicated already. But it can be reduced in incidence and severity, driven on to the defensive as it is hounded by aggressive pursuit, and generally set on a curve of historical decline. Islamic extremist terrorism of the apocalyptic kind will not be permitted to succeed in most Islamic countries. The pull of an essentially secular modernity is too great, and the existing political authorities will be compelled to take ruthless countermeasures in self-defence. While such terrorism is unlikely to prosper as a serious political force shaping the history of the Middle East and parts of Southeast Asia (i.e., Indonesia, Malaysia, the Philippines), its strategic prospects there are positively glittering in comparison to its future prospects as a mode of warfare against the non-Islamic world. Apocalyptic terrorism simply cannot succeed, unless, that is, we choose to define success with exceptional liberality. Al Qaeda and its associates will achieve the occasional spectacular event of mass murder. Moreover, one day, perhaps not too far distant, that spectacular event will be notable for the agency of some tool from the basket of WMD. By means of meticulous international police work, occasional preventive military action, punitive discouragement of fellow-travelling state support, and some measures of positive inducement as well as deterrence, the counter-terrorist will defeat most, perhaps nearly all, terrorist spectaculars. However, terrorists cannot reliably be denied access to all lucrative targets. Clausewitz's strictures on the subject of friction and the fog of war apply to irregular warfare, including terrorism and counter-terrorism, as much as they do to regular forms of conflict. Thanks to the diffusion of technology, the unevenness of international development, the imbalance of power between states, and the psychological needs of some people, terrorism will hold a permanent place in future history. The counter-terrorist, though, should be able to render that place more of a nuisance than an apocalyptic menace.

IRREGULAR REGULARS

It is a major contention of this work that warfare is complex, multidimensional and somewhat non-linear. As a consequence, the neat categories produced by defence analysis are apt to be unduly clear cut. Theory is constructed by the making of distinctions. It is an activity at which we theorists are truly expert. Unfortunately, the Cartesian method of analysis, basically to dissect, is always likely to lose the plot, as analysts delve ever more deeply into this or that sharply defined category of military or strategic behaviour. By the ruthless application of Occam's Razor I have reduced future warfare simply to only two clusters of activity, regular and irregular. Now, however, I will show how even this minimalist exercise in organization is by no means wholly satisfactory.

Regular forces, indeed the most elite of highly professional regular forces, special operations forces (SOF), can wage war in an irregular, unconventional way. In fact the history of warfare shows quite clearly that if regulars are to prosper in campaigns against irregulars, they are obliged to adopt at least some of the characteristics, including the modus operandi, of the irregular enemy. Regular forces generally are trained, equipped, and organized to fight other regular forces in recognizably symmetrical modes of combat. SOF, in contrast, are trained, equipped and doctrinally prepared both to conduct unconventional, irregular warfare against a regular enemy, and to fight irregular foes irregularly. SOF can be described as our guerrillas in uniform, or, in a more pejorative vein, as our terrorists in uniform. It is essential to think operationally as well as tactically. While SOF need to function in irregular modes, it is even more important that they function as a countervailing network. The relevant rule is that it takes a network to defeat a network. Many people believe that SOF need to operate in uniform so as to comply with the laws of war and, most importantly, be able to claim legitimate combatant status should they be captured. The elite warriors of the SOF tend to be handled roughly when they fall into hostile hands, but at least they can claim notional legality under the Geneva Conventions. However, Geneva sometimes is not as important as access and stealth, tactical matters with life or death consequences which cannot be conducted in uniform.

Although special operations have a history traceable to the Old Testament, the organization of dedicated SOF was an innovation of the Second World War.[48] Britain provided an especially encouraging context for the raising of SOF. Its regular army was condemned by events, geostrategy, and its own deficiencies, to wage war only on the margins of the Axis empire from 1940 until June 1944. The fact that the Prime Minister was romantically attracted to adventurous, unconventional ways of war, did not hurt either. Other countries followed suit with SOF, some more successfully than others. Naturally enough, those others went down the SOF path in ways that reflected their political and strategic contexts and, perhaps above all else, their particular strategic and military cultures. SOF always need powerful political sponsorship, because they are typically more or less anathema to regular-minded regulars. The international SOF story is well known and is relevant here only as useful background for consideration of its significance for future warfare. Suffice it to say that the institutionalization of SOF in many countries was an important military innovation of the 1940s which, not without many difficulties, survived into the post-Cold War years.

SOF have been treated differently in different countries.[49] Some armies are not enthusiastic about elite, let alone super-elite, 'special' troops, because their very designation as such tells the rest of the forces that they are not so elite or special. The United States military proved to be especially stony ground for growing cadres of special warriors. SOF were briefly fashionable in the early 1960s, when the 'Green Berets', the Army's SF, were all but adopted by the Kennedy Administration as the military epitome of the bold and youthful spirit of the 'New Frontier'.[50] Their extensive employment in Vietnam, including much faulty employment and association with the CIA, provoked hostility from more regular soldiers. Moreover, the SOF suffered from guilt by close identification with a mission that the Army, and the country as a whole, was eager to forget. Courtesy of Congressional backing, however, American SOF limped on to the end of the century. But times have changed, and changed rapidly.

Quite suddenly the SOF have become popular, though still, one suspects, not among the regular rank and file who must perform the military heavy lifting. After the swift Afghan campaign of 2001, SOF were identified as key to a new American way of war, or 'way of battle', as Lieutenant Colonel Antulio J. Echevarria insists.[51] The US Army could conclude its campaign against the Apache irregulars in the American South-West only by employing Apaches. That most experienced of Indian fighters, Brigadier General George Crook, declaimed firmly that

> To operate against the Apache we must use Apache methods and Apache soldiers – under, of course, the leadership of the white soldier. The first great difficulty is to discover the whereabouts of the hostiles, and this can be done well only by Apache scouts.[52]

The general explained to the journalist Charles R. Lummis his approach in terms that have resonance and relevance to the future irregular warfare of the twenty-first century.

> In warfare with the Indians it has been Crook's policy – and the only effective one – to use them against each other. 'To polish a diamond there is nothing like its own dust,' he told me. 'It is the same with these fellows. Nothing breaks them up like turning their own people against them. They don't fear the white soldiers, whom they easily surpass in the peculiar style of warfare which they force upon us, but put upon their trail an enemy of their own blood, an enemy as tireless, as

foxy, and as stealthy and familiar with the country as they themselves, and it breaks them all up. It is not merely a question of catching them better with Indians, but of a broader and more enduring aim – their disintegration.' [53]

America's irregular enemies in the twenty-first century will be taught the error of their ways by handfuls of professional elite, regular warriors, who behave as unconventionally as circumstances require, the terms of engagement permit, and the laws of war, probably somewhat stretched, will tolerate. SOF, being small in number, are wholly unsuited for sustained regular or irregular heavy combat.

The US defence community is persuaded that in future warfare against regular and irregular enemies, SOF will provide the vital link with local allies, who must do most of the fighting on the ground for themselves. The SOF will connect the needs of the local battlespace with the on-call precision firepower that the ongoing US military transformation will provide. If the Afghan model is valid, SOF mean relatively few American boots on the ground, and therefore low American casualties. Also, with their real-time knowledge of combat conditions, they can ensure that maximum leverage is secured from stand-off precision firepower. In short, thanks to the wonders of C⁴ISTAR, to which the SOF should make a major contribution, the special warriors can function as a force multiplier for friendly regular troops. At least, this is the theory. Iraq 2003, and subsequently, has not entirely demolished that vision of the new American way of war, but it has revealed to those who saw SOF as a silver bullet, a panacea even, that there is more to war than battle.

Earlier in this text we expressed considerable scepticism about strategic, or any other kind of, futurology. However, we do predict that SOF will enjoy a golden era in many countries in this new century. They are regular troops, rigorously selected – the meaning of elite – and trained to effect tasks that fall outside the normal run of duties in war. Thus far, the water here has not been muddied with a definition of SOF or SO. As with terrorism, a fully satisfactory definition remains elusive. The best available is a rather elaborate formula devised twenty years ago by Maurice Tugwell and David Charters. By the terms of their definition, special operations are 'small-scale, clandestine, covert or overt operations of an unorthodox and frequently high risk nature, undertaken to achieve significant political or military objectives in support of foreign policy'.[54]

Special operations can be executed both to 'kick in the door' for the follow-on regular forces to whom they are adjunct enablers, or they can be independent, stand-alone missions intended to have effect at the operational or even strategic levels of war. Whether SOF and special operations should be regarded as integral to the future of regular or irregular warfare is a question that would interest only a pedant. SOF, as more or less 'super-soldiers', are vulnerable to misuse by military superiors and political sponsors who fail to recognize their limitations. They may be assigned impossible missions, or they may be used, briefly, as shock troops. Alternatively, they may be trained and ready, but have nowhere to go, because the regular minds of higher military command has no real comprehension of how SOF should be employed. Readers may have noticed that although there is an abundance of literature on the unconventional tactical derring-do of SOF, discussion of their strategic value is all but non-existent.[55] That is a story much in need of telling, particularly since SOF assuredly will figure with increasing prominence in the strategic history of future warfare.

Notwithstanding the many kind words offered in the paragraphs immediately above, three questions in particular need answering about the role of SOF in future warfare. First, will SOF be permitted to operate globally with sufficient independence as well as in sufficient strength, so that they can exploit their inherent strengths? There are two principal hindrances to such exploitation. On the one hand, there are the fears of higher command that SOF units may go 'off the reservation' and operate as they themselves prefer, rather than as they are tasked. In short, SOF will not always be trusted with independent missions. On the other hand, as the popularity of SOF leads to an expansion in their numbers, it is probable that they will suffer both some dilution in quality and will be misused in a shock-troop, fire-brigade role.

Second, if SOF are to provide the main military contact with alien societies, both those that are generally friendly and others that are less so, how do they gain access to all but impenetrable cultures? In many cases it will not suffice to grow a beard, wear tribal clothes, and speak a few words of a local dialect. As SOF numbers expand, this problem must assume ever greater importance. In the past, SOF typically have been manned by long-serving, mature and experienced soldiers. As SOF numbers rise rapidly to meet the needs both of fashion and of new or expanded duties, they will recruit much younger soldiers who lack the maturity and experience to function discreetly in the quasi-diplomatic role that is assigned them towards allies with unfamiliar cultures.

Third, is it likely that SOF will become so fashionable and, in principle, so useful, that like the Mongols in Imperial China they will be changed critically by the consequences of their success? If the US Army transforms itself to be much more SOF-like, a popular view today, what will distinguish SOF from the more regular of regular forces? Today it is commonplace to claim that the future of warfare will not so much belong to SOF, but rather to regular forces that have stolen SOF's clothes. Unsurprisingly, this possibility is especially relevant to debate over the future character of the US Army. Inevitably, US defence policy invests heavily in the preferred capabilities of the era. By and large this is sensible and is effective in providing the support needed for the foreign policy of a very great power. However, there are some military, and strategic, missions that need to be addressed under the guidance of the maxim that 'more is less'. There is a non-trivial danger that the US military establishment might abolish much of its true SOF capability as a consequence of attempting to transform too large a fraction of its forces into SOF-like units. If most, even just many, soldiers and marines are SO-capable, what need is there for dedicated SOF? One need hardly stress the point that the motives of many soldiers with non-SOF careers may not be entirely professional and beyond reproach. If SOF cannot be killed bureaucratically by direct opposition, a more effective alternative may lie with friendly emulation, co-option, and absorption.

THIS ANALYSIS OF THE future of irregular warfare in general, and terrorism in particular, has been deliberately light in its treatment of WMD, and in the weapons of mass disruption that lurk so obviously in the internetted computer. It is to this dimension of future warfare that we turn next. The exploration in Chapter Seven flows naturally from the discussion just concluded, both conceptually and practically. With regard to the latter, WMD, unfortunately, will play vitally important roles in future warfare, regular and irregular. As to the former, WMD as a relatively novel dimension of warfare will be shown to be governed as much by the general lore of war and strategy as are the familiar operations of land power, sea power, and air power. In this chapter we have argued that terrorism is warfare, albeit in irregular mode, and that it too functions strategically and in terms thoroughly comprehensible via the classical theories of war and strategy.

Chapter seven

Old Rules for New Challenges I: Weapons of Mass Destruction

SILVER BULLETS AND COMBINED ARMS

Thus far we have tried to approach future warfare holistically. The choice of such grand aggregations as regular and irregular warfare reflects an effort not to be sidetracked down secondary pathways of military particulars. Throughout, we have been at some pains to insist that belligerents wage war, they do not wage land, sea, air, or space war, though they do wage war on land, at sea, and in the air and in space. The difference is vital. The menace from different kinds of threat and the promise in distinctive forms of military power, all have their closely attentive publics and lobbyists. As a consequence, future-oriented discussion is ever liable to capture by one or more extravagant story. When a favoured way of war, or weapon, is presented as the key to future military, even strategic, success, appreciation of the importance of context is an early victim of neglect. When one is selling a 'silver bullet', all the other elements that contribute to military and strategic effectiveness, the several contexts discussed earlier, tend to fade into the background. The political and strategic contexts are of war or the threat of war, considered as a whole. No matter the quality of silver in the bullet, it must not be analysed outside the context of war, including the prospects for deterrence.

The discussion in this chapter and the next is only an apparent deviation from the commitment to holism. The mission in these chapters is to examine three kinds of military power, each of which attracts stand-alone theories of war and strategies. In short, each has silver bullet qualities, at least in the minds of some of its less critical adherents and opponents. The three topics to be considered are WMD, space power, and cyber power.

While WMD have a long history, space power and cyber power are both relative newcomers to the feast of war. Moreover, WMD is a potentially misleading acronymic aggregation of a hugely diverse reality. We must make it crystal clear that our subject is not nuclear, biological, chemical, and radiological war, space war, or cyberwar. Rather is the focus on WMD, space power, and cyber power, in future warfare. There is an obvious sense in which the analysis in these chapters treats three hugely different challenges. For all their interdependencies, WMD, space systems, and computers, nonetheless must each be treated on its own terms. Each has distinctive military and strategic meaning. However, the three have in common subjection to the enduring nature of war and strategy. Even if one or the other of them should have such extraordinary potency as occasionally to merit the silver bullet label, still it cannot function beyond the constraints in the contexts of war and strategy.

If some readers are beginning to feel that I am belabouring the obvious, they should be reassured to learn that it is not so, appearances to the contrary notwithstanding. Classical strategic thought, with its foundations dug from historical experience, is a living tradition, at least to those who allow it to be so. As a consequence it has much to tell us about the high-technology subjects of these two chapters. WMD, space power, and cyber power, are all novel, or comparatively novel, departures within the grand narrative of strategic history. But we know a great deal about each because we are well educated as to the nature of war and strategy. Each of these topics has seduced some commentators into analyses which effectively assert that their subject transcends, or soon will transcend, war and strategy as they have been known to date. We argue that that is not, and cannot, be so.

WEAPONS OF MASS DESTRUCTION (WMD)

WMD is shorthand twice over for a complex reality. The acronym suggests, indeed asserts, a unity that does not exist. Moreover, the very ease of familiarity with which the acronym trips off the tongue or the keyboard obscures the fact that a host of important political, strategic, and moral issues remain ill understood. Rarely is it more true to claim that one size does not fit all with ideas for the meaning of what is supposedly a whole category of weapons, than with respect to WMD. As well as being an obvious convenience, the term probably hinders consideration of their possible roles in future warfare more than it assists. However, it is a favoured acronym of our era and as such is unavoidable; hence, the reluctant surrender here.

What are we discussing? What are these so-called WMD? In summary terms, they comprise nuclear, biological, chemical, and radiological weapons.[1] Strictly speaking, radiological weapons are not WMD at all. They are weapons designed to have conventional explosives (e.g., semtex or TNT) scatter radioactive material. There would be no nuclear explosion and no mass destruction. Even weapons that fall incontestably within the nuclear category can be hugely dissimilar. For example, a primitive atomic device home-assembled by ambitious DIY terrorists might achieve an energy yield the equivalent to 100 tons of TNT. Such a device undoubtedly would be a nuclear weapon, and that status would cause its employment to trigger political, strategic, and moral shock waves. A taboo, a supposed taboo we should add, would have been flouted, and its possible meaning as a precedent would be deeply worrying. However, the crude device in question would be unlikely to kill more than a few thousand people, though it would cause immediate and long-term injury to many more. Moreover, its effects, including the radioactive contamination it must cause, would be geographically highly restricted. At the other end of the scale from the terrorist's efforts with home assembly are the 5-megaton warheads which are believed to occupy the business end of Chinese ICBMs (intercontinental ballistic missiles). The other states that have long-range ballistic missile holdings, including SLBMs (submarine-launched ballistic missile), which is to say the United States, Russia, France, and

Britain, have all achieved accuracies which permit warhead yields of no greater than 750 kilotons. Between the terrorist's 100-ton device, and the Chinese 5 megatons, there is a monumental practical difference. The former, even though it would achieve ten times the energy yield of the largest conventional weapon on record (10 tons), would damage a neighbourhood. The latter would destroy a major city and almost certainly cause fatalities on the order of 5–10 million, depending on the target. This assumes that the target in both instances would be an urban area. This is a reasonable assumption, given that both the terrorist and the Chinese would have nuclear arsenals on the sparse side; probably only one weapon in the terrorist case. China's strategic arsenal currently comprises only approximately 252 warheads, a number which stands in sharp contrast with the US total of 5,968, and the Russian of 4,978. Table 7.1 summarizes what is known or estimated to be the state of the world's operational nuclear arsenals as of late 2004.[2] In the American and Russian cases, the numbers could easily be doubled, and more, were we to account also for weapons that are not currently operational.

TABLE 7.1 *Operational Nuclear Warheads, 2004*

	Strategic	Sub-Strategic	Total
USA	5,968	1,120	7,088
Russia	4,978	2,980	7,958
France	338	10	348
China	252	150	402
UK	185		185
Israel		200	200
India		40+	40+
Pakistan		40+	40+
N. Korea		±2	±2

Source: International Institute for Strategic Studies, 2004

For good or ill, though probably on balance mainly for the former, nuclear WMD have been singularized and stigmatized. No matter whether the weapon is thermonuclear in the megaton range, or whether it would struggle to achieve 100 tons, it is held to be different, unconventional, and in the opinion of many people beyond the pale of civilized warfare. Indeed, nuclear weapons, generically, are held widely to have changed the nature of war, since, allegedly, they fracture the Clausewitzian connection between the military grammar and the policy logic of it all.[3] War with nuclear weapons would not be war, and strategy for the employment of such would not be strategy, so the argument insists. We shall deal later directly with this plausible fallacy.

Biological and chemical weapons present vastly more complex pictures than do their nuclear WMD stablemates. Both are illegal. The Nuclear Non-Proliferation Treaty (NPT) of 1970 recognizes and contingently condones the nuclear weapon states extant when it was opened for signature, non-coincidentally the five Permanent Members of the UN Security Council. By contrast, the treaties governing biological and chemical weapons make no allowance for any privileged status. The Biological and Toxin Weapons Convention (BWC) of 1975 bans the development, production, and stockpiling of biological and toxin weapons. In addition, it requires the 'destruction of the agents, toxins, weapons, equipment and means of delivery in the possession of the parties'. As of 2002, 145 countries had ratified the Convention, while another eighteen had signed it. The radical scope of the BWC is a little less impressive than its wording suggests, since it makes no provision for the verification of compliance. As Frank Barnaby notes, 'a significant number – probably about eight – of the parties are suspected of developing biological weapons'.[4]

The Chemical Weapons Convention (CWC) of 1993 had antecedents in the Hague Conventions of 1899 and 1907, and the Geneva Protocol of 1925.[5] The Protocol prohibited 'the use in war of asphyxiating, poisonous or other gases, and of bacteriological methods of warfare'. Actually, the Protocol only bans the first use of such weapons. The CWC bans any use of chemical weapons as well as their development, production, acquisition, transfer, and stockpiling. Also, stocks and production facilities are to be destroyed. However, the treaty does permit research 'directly related to protection against toxic chemicals and to protection against chemical weapons'. In stark contrast with the BWC, the CWC does make some provision for verification. An Organization for the Prohibition of Chemical Weapons (OPCW) was established in the Hague. It dispatches inspectors to monitor compliance. Again, as of 2002, 145 countries had ratified the treaty.

Before we delve briefly into the noxious character of these weapons, it is worth mentioning that many studies of arms control regimes blur the vital difference between treaty monitoring and treaty verification. Thus far we have referred to verification, choosing ease of communication over strict accuracy. The distinction is not a trivial one. To monitor treaty compliance means simply to gather intelligence on what is, is not, or may be, underway that might be of a prohibited nature. In contrast, verification of treaty compliance or non-compliance is a political, not a technical, judgement. Intelligence agencies cannot verify compliance; only governments or other authoritative agencies can do that. However, it is prudent to be alert to the hardy perennial dilemma of negotiated arms control, 'after detection – what?' as Fred Charles Iklé expressed it pungently way back in 1961.[6]

It is no easy matter to make sense of the possible roles of biological and chemical weapons in future warfare, and to speculate on what the consequences might be. Unfortunately, the technical dimension of this subject is as clear as the political and strategic are opaque. There is near universal condemnation of biological and chemical weapons.[7] They are widely regarded with a particular horror, and both treaty and customary international law prohibit them. Nonetheless, it is little short of amazing to discover just how much information about them, and about their nuclear cousins also, is readily available. Moreover, as often as not that helpful information is provided from such authoritative sources as the US Government and distinguished scientists associated with peace research institutes. While there is much to be said in praise of a technically educated citizenry, what is easily publicly available today amounts to manuals and guides that could serve as the intending proliferator's friend. Between websites and more traditional sources, determined WMD proliferators in search of practical advice inhabit a world of plenty. Such people would find exceptional value in a 1993 study by the Office of Technology Assessment (OTA) of the US Congress, entitled *Technologies Underlying Weapons of Mass Destruction.*[8] Or, for a more modest guide, there is physicist and peace researcher Frank Barnaby's small book on *How to Build a Nuclear Bomb and other weapons of mass destruction.*[9] Fortunately Barnaby's short treatise does not sustain the promise in its exciting title, but still it does offer information useful to the enemies of civilization as we know it.

Since the essential technical details about WMD are so freely and authoritatively available, and because they are not controversial, we shall deal with them here only in summary ways. It is their implications for the future of warfare that concern us, not their scientific or technological feasibility. The latter, to repeat, unfortunately is not in dispute.

NUCLEAR WEAPONS

Rather than reinvent the wheel, we reproduce here the excellent table from the OTA study cited above which summarizes the technical hurdles to be overcome on the road to nuclear, biological, and chemical weapons capabilities.

Nuclear weapons come in three varieties: fission, boosted-fission, and fusion. There is no theoretical limit to the energy yield of fusion weapons. As missile accuracy improved from a mile or more over intercontinental distances in the early 1960s, to perhaps a hundred yards in the 1980s, it was only sensible to reduce weapon yields from the megaton to the kiloton range.[10] Newly nuclear proliferant states, if they are accuracy challenged and short of nuclear ammunition, may not care very much about navigational precision or collateral damage. Their small nuclear arsenals will serve political and strategic, not military, purposes. Atomic fission weapons do have a practical upper yield limit of approximately 50kt. To obtain an explosion of much greater magnitude the fission weapon needs to be boosted with the insertion of fusion material, a step that allows a tenfold increase in yield. While it is difficult to acquire a sufficient mass of the enriched uranium or the plutonium – the alternative nuclear materials necessary for bomb production – there are not really any significant nuclear secrets remaining.

TABLE 7.2 *Technical Hurdles for Nuclear, Biological, and Chemical Weapon Programs*

	Nuclear	Biological	Chemical
NUCLEAR MATERIALS OR LETHAL AGENTS PRODUCTION			
Feed materials	Uranium, ore, oxide widely available; plutonium and partly enriched uranium dispersed through nuclear power programs, mostly under international safeguards.	Potential biological warfare agents are readily available locally or internationally from natural sources or commercial suppliers.	Many basic chemicals available for commercial purposes; only some nerve gas precursors available for purchase, but ability to manufacture them is spreading.
Scientific and technical personnel	Requires wide variety of expertise and skilful systems integration.	Sophisticated research and development unnecessary to produce commonly known agents. Industrial microbiological personnel widely available.	Organic chemists and chemical engineers widely available.
Design and engineering knowledge	Varies with process, but specific designs for producing either of the two bomb-grade nuclear materials can be difficult to develop: ★ Separation of uranium isotopes to produce highly enriched uranium; ★ Reactor production and chemical processing to produce plutonium.	Widely published; basic techniques to produce known agents not difficult.	Widely published. Some processes tricky (Iraq had difficulty with tabun cyanation, succeeded at sarin alkylation;however, sarin quality was poor).
Equipment	Varies with different processes, but difficulties can include fabrication, power consumption, large size, and operational complexity: ★ Electromagnetic separation equipment can be constructed from available, multiple-use parts; ★ Equipment for other processes is more specialized and difficult to buy or build.	Widely available for commercial uses. Special containment and waste-treatment equipment may be more difficult to assemble, but are not essential to production.	Most has legitimate industrial applications. Alkylation process is somewhat difficult and is unusual in civilian applications. Special containment and waste treatment equipment may be more difficult to assemble, but are not essential to production.

TABLE 7.2 *Contd.*

	Nuclear	*Biological*	*Chemical*
Plant construction and operation	Costly and challenging. Research reactors or electric power reactors might be converted to plutonium production.	With advent of biotechnology, small-scale facilities now capable of large-scale production.	Dedicated plant not difficult. Conversion of existing commercial chemical plants feasible but not trivial.
Overall cost	Cheapest overt production route for one bomb per year, with no international controls, is about $200 million; larger scale clandestine program could cost 10 to 50 times more, and even then not be assured of success or of remaining hidden. Black-market purchase of ready-to-use fissile materials or of complete weapons could be many times cheaper.	Enough for large arsenal may cost less than $10 million.	Arsenal for substantial military capability (hundreds of tons of agent) likely to cost tens of millions of dollars.

WEAPONIZATION

	Nuclear	*Biological*	*Chemical*
Design and engineering	Heavier, less efficient, lower yield designs easier, but all pose significant technical challenges.	Principal challenge is maintaining the agent's potency through weapon storage, delivery, and dissemination. Broad-area dissemination not difficult; design of weapons that effectively aerosolise agents for precision delivery challenging (but developed by US by 1960s).	Advanced weapons somewhat difficult, but workable munition designs (e.g., bursting smoke device) widely published.
Production equipment	Much (e.g., machine tools) dual-use and widely available. Some overlap with conventional munitions production equipment.	Must be tightly contained to prevent spread of infection, but the necessary equipment is not hard to build.	Relatively simple, closely related to standard munitions production equipment.

Source: US Congress, Office of Technology Assessment, 1993.

FIGURE 7.1 *Technical Routes to a Nuclear Weapon Capability*

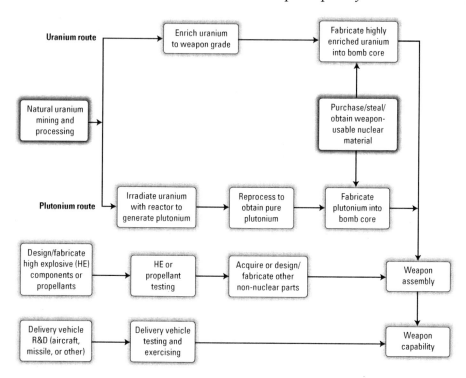

Source: US Congress, Office of Technology Assessment, 1993.

For a state or a terrorist organization to become a nuclear power is expensive and difficult, but there are no insuperable technical barriers once an adequate supply of uranium-235 or plutonium-239 has been secured. Scientists warn us unequivocally that the days of nuclear mystery are long gone. Barnaby, for example, emphasizes the ease with which a terrorist group could acquire weapon-grade plutonium from civil mixed-oxide (MOX) nuclear fuel.

> None of the concepts involved in understanding how to separate the plutonium are difficult; a second-year undergraduate might be able to devise a suitable procedure by reading standard reference works, consulting the open literature in scientific journals and by searching the World Wide Web. The progress of

the separation can be estimated easily at different stages by measuring the concentrations of uranium and plutonium, by, for example, ultraviolet spectrophotometry, using cheap and readily available equipment.[11]

Earlier, Barnaby warns that

A group of two or three people with appropriate skills could design and fabricate a crude nuclear explosive. It is a sobering fact that the fabrication of a primitive nuclear explosive using plutonium or suitable uranium would require no greater skill than that required for the production and use of the nerve agent [sarin] produced by the AUM group and released in the Tokyo underground.[12]

The key challenge to the would-be nuclear proliferator is acquisition of the nuclear material, enriched uranium or plutonium. That is the *sine qua non*. There is a wide range of possible means of delivery. Ballistic missiles have great advantages of availability – thirty-six countries produce them, at present – speed and relative reliability. But nuclear delivery could be achieved by ship, aircraft, cruise missile, car, backpack, donkey cart or almost anything available. Naturally, the technical characteristics of the weapons and their means of delivery must have implications for the suitability of this option for particular missions. Even this terse discussion indicates plainly that nuclear proliferation is far from comprising an insuperable challenge to those who are: well funded; sufficiently determined; cunning in using the global black market in nuclear material, equipment and expertise; and not overly concerned about the technical excellence, or otherwise, of the end product. This discussion ignores, of course, the possibility that nuclear weapons may be stolen, bought, or acquired by gift.

BIOLOGICAL WEAPONS

The nuclear story is strewn with significant barriers to acquisition when it is compared with the technical dimension to biological and chemical weapons. What is a biological weapon? The OTA study referred to already notes that 'biological and toxin warfare has been termed "public health in reverse" because it involves the deliberate use of disease and natural poisons to incapacitate people'.[13] It employs pathogens as weapons.[14] Pathogens are the micro-organisms – whether bacterial, viral, or protozoic – that cause disease. Biological weapons are distinguished by being living organisms that reproduce within their host-victims, who then become contagious with a deadly, if weakening, multiplier effect. Toxins, in contrast, do not reproduce in the victim and need only the briefest of incubation periods; they kill within a few hours. The living biological agents of interest to this enquiry have incubation periods ranging from twenty-four hours to six weeks. Toxins are poisonous chemicals produced by living organisms. Their scientific character is a combination of both chemical and biological agents.

There are four kinds of biological warfare agents: bacteria, viruses, rickettsiae, and fungi.[15] Bacteria, simple-cell micro-organisms, cause anthrax, cholera, pneumonic plague, and typhoid, for leading examples. Viruses, the simplest of organisms, cause such diseases as ebola, aids, flu, polio, and smallpox. Rickettsiae are micro-organisms, biologically intermediate between bacteria and viruses, and can spread typhus, Q-fever, and Rocky Mountain spotted fever. These potentially lethal micro-organisms are carried by lice, ticks, and fleas. Fungi are more complex organisms and reproduce by forming spores. They cause diseases like coccidiomycosis. In contrast to the biological agents just cited, all of which spread disease by human contact, toxins do not have the quality of contagion. The micro-organisms that produce toxins can cause botulism, for a single example. The technical details vary from agent to agent, while the prospective casualty count will depend not only on the virulence of the biology, but also on the efficiency of the means of delivery as well as on vital environmental factors. Biological warfare agents can be delivered by a distressingly wide variety of means. Effective delivery naturally would be subject to the technical requirement for biological survival, a standard which in many cases would be very strict; after all, the agents in question are living organisms. Ballistic and cruise missiles, artillery shells, spray tanks on aircraft, and human delivery, are just some of the possibilities.[16] The more highly favoured agents include inhalation anthrax, which has advantages offering 95 per cent lethality but no contagion from the victim to others; smallpox, which is, of course, extremely contagious; and ricin, a toxin produced from castor beans.

FIGURE 7.2 *Biological Weapon Acquisition*

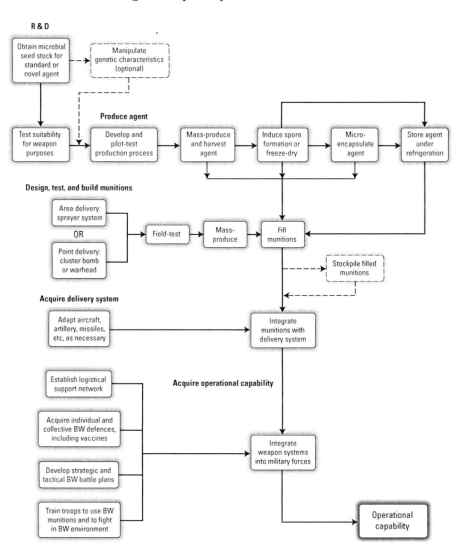

Source: US Congress, Office of Technology Assessment, 1993.

TABLE 7.3 *Effects of Chemical and Biological Weapons*

Chemical

Nerve agents (persistent): Convulsions, cessation of breathing, vomiting, paralysis, death within minutes if not treated. A minute amount is lethal.
- ★ Novichok (Russian agent recently developed)
- ★ VX
- ★ Tabun (GA)
- ★ Sarin (GB)
- ★ Soman (GD)

Biological (non-engineered)

Bacterial – Usually in the form of dry powder or spores. Far more lethal per pound per per agent than CW due to smaller lethal doses, infectivity, and epidemicity.
- ★ Anthrax: Cutaneous or inhalational, incubation period 1–7 days, death from inhalational form within 24 hours, fatality rate 90 per cent if untreated, low epidemicity. Symptoms. include fever, shock, and formation of malignant pustules on skin, difficulty in breathing, tachycardia, cyanosis and death.
- ★ Plague: (Bubonic or Pneumonic Plague/'The Black Death') Incubation period is 1–6 days, death within 1–2 days, fatality rate is 70 per cent for pneumonic plague and 40 per cent for bubonic plague. Symptoms include high fever, headache, glandular swelling, haemorrhages in skin and mucous membranes, extreme lymph node pain, haemorrhagic pneumonia.
- ★ Tularaemia: Incubation period is 2–10 days, highly infectious. Lethality rate varies according to particular strain. Symptoms include sudden onset of chills, fever, headache, muscle aches, fatigue, loss of body fluids. Skin infections characterized by deep ulcers on skin.

Blister agents (semi-persistent): Hours after exposure symptoms include eye irritation, burning of the skin, difficulty in breathing. Lewisite and CX produce severe pain, which does not decrease but increases. Skin damage leading to large blisters, damage to eyes, airways, and internal organs.
- ★ Distilled Mustard (HD)
- ★ Nitrogen Mustard (HN)
- ★ Sulfur Mustard (H)
- ★ Phosgene Oxime (CX)
- ★ Lewisite (L)

Viral – Usually powder or liquid – ideal for genetic engineering.
- ★ Ebola: Virus transmissible by touch or possibly inhalational. Incubation period of 2–21 days. Fatality rate of 90 per cent. No cure or vaccine. Sudden onset of fever, weakness, muscle pain, followed by vomiting, diarrhoea, rash, limited kidney and liver functions, both internal and external bleeding five days after symptoms begin. Finally convulsions and 'bleed out' through spontaneous tears in the skin, spreading infected blood throughout the immediate area. The body liquefies, sloughing off the skin, the brain divides as the virus consumes the body.
- ★ Smallpox: High infectivity and epidemicity as well as suitability for 'chimera virus' engineering (i.e., smallpox-Ebola chimera). Incubation period averages 12 days. Lethality averages 30 per cent. Symptoms include high fever, malaise, rigors, vomiting, aches, and delirium. Skin rash covers the body, which becomes pustules.

Choking agents (semi-persistent): Shortness of breath growing worse, coughing becoming severe hacking cough with large amounts of clear frothy sputum. Rapid fluid loss.
- ★ Diphosgene (DP)
- ★ Phosgene (CG)
- ★ Chlorine (CL)
- ★ Chloropicrin (PS)

Rickettsiae – Mainly incapacitating agents, usually not lethal.
- ★ Rickettsia Prowsecki–Endemic Typhus: incubation period of 6–14 days. Symptoms include headache, high fever, general aches and pains, chills and rash.
- ★ Coxiella Burnetti (Q Fever): 2–3 week incubation period. Sudden onset of fever, headache, chills, weakness, perspiration, upper respiratory problems, coughing.

Blood agents (semi-persistent): Dizziness, weakness, anxiety, loss of consciousness, convulsions, cessation of breathing, paralysis, and death within minutes of a large dose.
- ★ Hydrogen Cyanide (AC)
- ★ Cyanogen Chloride (CK)

Toxins – Usually liquid, mainly lethal.
- ★ Botulism: Incubation period is 1–12 hours, lethality is 60 per cent if untreated. Death from muscle paralysis and asphyxia.
- ★ Ricin: Incubation is 1–12 hours, death within 36–48 hours from failure of respiratory and circulatory system.

Source: Davis and Gray, 2002.

As noted already, those wishing for further detail will find their mission almost childishly easy to complete. Information is abundant. An important feature of a biological warfare arsenal is the fact that it is effectively undetectable with certainty ahead of its employment, and perhaps not even then with respect to its parenthood. A military programme designed to develop and stockpile biological agents for offensive use can be hidden near perfectly within legitimate, or legitimate seeming, medical research facilities, as well as in the laboratories of a pharmaceutical industry. In addition, for the frustration of arms controllers, there is no real technical difference between a programme of scientific research on biological weapons for offensive ends, and one motivated strictly by the needs of defence. As if those details are not sufficiently discouraging, it is a regrettable fact that biological weapons, being self-reproducing in the right conditions, do not have to be stockpiled in large quantities. Unlike a nuclear or chemical weapons programme, distinctive physical evidence of preparation for the conduct of offensive biological warfare is all but completely absent.

CHEMICAL WEAPONS

Chemical weapons are inert agents that come in four categories of horror: choking, blister, blood, and nerve.[17]

The first modern employment of a choking weapon was the German introduction of chlorine gas in the Second Battle of Ypres on 22 April 1915. The Germans also led the way when they used phosgene and then mustard gas on 17 July 1917, again at Ypres.[18] Since Germany was the world's scientific and industrial leader in developing and manufacturing chemical agents to meet commercial demands, it is not surprising that they should have led the way in gas warfare. The continuing popularity of the German innovation of 1917 was attested by Iraq, and then Iran, when both resorted to mustard gas in their attritional war of 1980–88. Never one to be backward in dispensing death, Saddam Hussein's Iraq also used tabun nerve gas. It may be needless to add for the cynics amongst us that both countries were signatories to the 1925 Geneva Protocol which forbids their (first) use.

For prompt lethality, a quality of particular military, if not necessarily

FIGURE 7.3 *Chemical Weapon Acquisition*

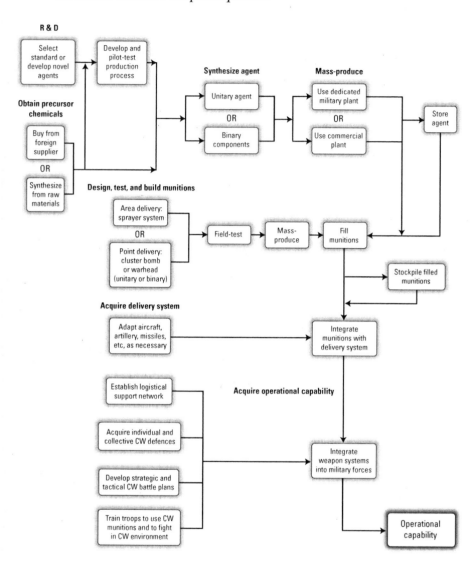

Source: US Congress, Office of Technology Assessment, 1993.

strategic or political, value, the chemical agent of choice in future warfare is most likely to be one or more of the nerve agents. To date, and we need to remember that biology and chemistry are highly dynamic disciplines, the principal nerve agents of note are VX, tabun, sarin, and soman (see table 7.3, p. 267). Biological warfare has no recent history, notwithstanding the fact that during the Cold War both superpowers developed and deployed offensive biological weapons for delivery by ballistic missile. The same cannot be said of chemical warfare, however. Chemical weapons were used by the Italians in Ethiopia, 1935–6; occasionally by the Japanese in their long war with China, 1937–45; by the Egyptians in Yemen, 1963–8; by the United States in Vietnam and Laos, 1965–73 (the defoliant, Agent Orange); and on a massive scale by the Iraqis as a desperation measure to offset Iranian successes on the ground in their bloody war in the 1980s. In a notorious but sadly strategically rational act of bestiality, the Iraqi Air Force launched a chemical assault upon their own town of Halabja, in Kurdistan, on 16 March 1988, employing mustard gas, nerve gas, and cyanide. Four thousand people died in Halabja, most of them civilians. Situated some 15 miles inside Iraq, the town was populated by Kurds hostile to Baghdad; it had been captured by the Iranians on the previous day. Naturally, Teheran made propaganda capital out of the Iraqi atrocity, but in so doing they served Saddam Hussein's strategic purposes. The Iranian propaganda frightened its own city dwellers and offered yet more encouragement to the international community to put pressure on Ayatollah Khomeini to consent to a cessation of hostilities.[19] Tactically, if only arguably strategically, chemical weapons proved highly effective in blunting Iranian ground offensives. Both the reality and the fear of poison gas proved crucial in defeating offensive after offensive launched by Iran. Similarly, the fear of poison gas contributed significantly to war weariness on the part of Iran's poorer city dwellers, the very people who provided the core of support for the new revolutionary regime. Recall that this was a contest wherein the Iraqi enemy already had attacked Iranian cities with conventionally armed ballistic missiles.[20]

Expert technical commentaries agree that 'of the three types of weapons of mass destruction – chemical, biological or nuclear – chemical ones are the most accessible to terrorists'.[21] Scientist Frank Barnaby conveys the ill tidings that 'the chemicals required to manufacture nerve agents are readily available and no specialized chemical equipment is needed for the preparation; a competent chemist would have no difficulty in making tabun, sarin, or soman, all with ingredients legally obtainable'.[22] If it would fall short of a heroic technological achievement for terrorists to make chemical weapons, consider the ease with which states could acquire them. With respect to chemical weapons, any country with a chemical industry, especially one that manufactures fertilizers, would have no difficulty producing a chemical arsenal. Not many states would fail the test of minimal but adequate industrial competence.

If we assume that the acquisition of WMD by states generally will be a clandestine activity, we must assume also that, by and large, they will succeed in evading detection. Of course, such secrecy would be counter-productive if the main purpose behind the acquisition was deterrence. However, even if deterrence was the dominant motive, say of American intervention in a regional quarrel, the need for secrecy would still be paramount in this era of proactive counter-proliferation strategies. We discuss the political and strategic dimensions to WMD immediately below. The issue to clarify here is the technical one of the relative simplicity of covert WMD development.

The central problem for the determined counter-proliferator is the unalterable technological fact of dual use. All three categories of WMD can be produced on the backs of legitimate scientific and commercial industrial activity. Moreover, with regard to biological and chemical weapons, at least, it is improbable that any regime of international inspection for treaty compliance could provide assurance of an absence of weapons. An intending proliferator would not need actually to produce WMD; it may well suffice for WMD options just to be within easy reach. Countries with a civil nuclear power industry, and currently there are thirty of them with no fewer than 438 reactors for the generation of electricity and for research, already have most of the physical and human infrastructure necessary for a swift move into nuclear weapon production. Iraq, Iran, and North Korea, have demonstrated how simple a matter it is to hide a weapons programme under the cover of a legitimate, *and internationally inspected*, civil programme. For the production of chemical weapons, so mundane are the general run of necessary ingredients, though perhaps not in the quantities required for weapons, that industrial conversion from civil to military use could be accomplished in only days or weeks.

By way of a summary of the discussion so far, and as a bridge to the strategic analysis that follows, we maintain that nuclear weapons are the most rewarding of WMD to develop or otherwise acquire, for reasons highlighted below, but they are also by far the most expensive and most difficult. Chemical weapons are by far the easiest to acquire, but they lack the political cachet of their nuclear cousins. Also the effects of these weapons are apt to be strictly limited, which could be a benefit, of course. Biological weapons are the easiest to prepare in secret, though they are not the easiest to develop, handle, and deploy. They share with nuclear weapons a high score on the fear scale. Because, except for toxins, they are living organisms, biological agents of warfare are extraordinarily sensitive to environmental conditions. It is one thing to develop a monstrous biological masterpiece in the laboratory, and then to store it most carefully until needed for reproduction as a weapon. It could be quite another to be able to disseminate the military pathogens in such a way, by aerosol or explosive, say, that they neither died *en route* to their targets, nor suffered a catastrophic loss of potency. I am pleased to report that the way of the biological warrior is certain to be fraught with deep, and one hopes, deterring uncertainties.

A STRATEGIC PERSPECTIVE

Now we must turn from the technical essentials of WMD to judgements about the political and strategic meaning of it all. What can be said about WMD and future warfare?

It might be thought that we are already well blessed, or cursed, with a mature body of strategic lore on nuclear matters. After all, modern strategic studies was born in the 1950s in order to answer the challenge of the terrifying new weapon.[23] Today, sixty years on from Hiroshima and Nagasaki, and certainly fifty years on from the first elaborations of deterrence theory, surely there cannot be much about the strategic meaning of nuclear WMD that remains unknown? Unfortunately, perhaps, the beliefs and practices that obviously served well enough during the Cold War, which we should think of as the First Nuclear Age, are not obviously comprehensively relevant today or for the future. That judgement refers only to the radical shift in the context of threat; it ignores the grounds for doubt about the wisdom of the ideas, policies, and programmes for nuclear arms and arms control with which the Cold War was waged in the First Nuclear Age. As I have attempted to explain in a book assertively titled, *The Second Nuclear Age,* the near-term, and just possibly medium-term, strategic future will bear little resemblance to the context of the great Soviet–American struggle.[24] I admit freely, if with some slight embarrassment, that by conceiving of two distinct 'nuclear ages', I am guilty of that resort to a simple grand narrative that I condemned in Chapter Four.

Today, there is no central strategic balance, despite the apparent evidence to the contrary provided by the Russo-US treaties that schedule sharp reductions in strategic nuclear arms. It is highly likely that over the next decade, as prescribed by the 'Strategic Offensive Reductions Treaty' of 24 May 2002, both countries will reduce their operational long-range arsenals to a level close to 2,000 warheads, though many more will be held in storage as insurance against the unexpected. Since there is now no acute political antagonism between Moscow and Washington, there is no strategic arms competition between them. That is almost true as stated. In practice, the current superpower and its lapsed, politically defeated, ex-superpower enemy, naturally are attentive to each other's military prowess. The Russian Federation is particularly sensitive about its reputation for nuclear excellence, because of the poor condition of its conventional forces, and the precipitate weakening of its geopolitical position and consequently of its resources base. The United States is so strong today in its conventional military power that it seems to many people that it has scant need of nuclear weapons beyond their role in the deterrence of others, if indeed the others of future concern should prove deterrable. Not so the Russian Federation. It is worth noticing that the most recent US Nuclear Posture Review, announced as policy and strategy in 2002, found nuclear weapons to have important war-fighting, as well as deterrent, tasks in the future.[25]

In this Second Nuclear Age the security problems posed by nuclear WMD are quite novel. The new difficulties are additional to whatever trouble may lurk with the nuclear powers of the First Age. None of those states with arsenals or policies of note have disinvested themselves of their nuclear WMD, it must be emphasized. The Soviet–American contest was between superstates with roughly balancing asymmetries. The US lead in high technology, particularly as it related to the ability to strike the Soviet Union over an intercontinental distance, was offset for most of the period by the fairly credible Soviet threat to overrun peninsular Europe. Furthermore, the superpowers were risk-averse. That was both because of their fear of being anything else, and because neither held an ideology which commanded aggressive near-term action. Despite decades of close study, neither side understood the other particularly well, a fact that many Americans arrogantly resisted believing. Not unreasonably, but still incorrectly, it was believed that nuclear weapons cancelled the effect of local political and strategic cultures. American culture as it bore on nuclear matters was confused with a universal strategic enlightenment. Be that as it may, the fortunate central strategic reality of the First Nuclear Age of the Cold War was that neither side, including their nuclear armed allies, wanted to use nuclear weapons. Moreover, everyone with a finger on the nuclear trigger went to great lengths to ensure that while on the one hand, the nuclear forces should be ready to launch when so ordered, on the other hand they must be so well fitted with brakes that they would never launch without orders from the highest political authority or its designated successors. This is not to claim that command and control was error-free, let alone error-proof.[26]

Contrast that situation with the historical context of this Second Nuclear Age. In its terrorist dimension, there may, eventually are well nigh certain to be, organizations that actually want to use nuclear weapons.[27] Al Qaeda and others of an apocalyptic kind, especially when liberated and encouraged to commit mass murder by religious sanction, cannot be deterred. This is not to say that deterrence is irrelevant. Terrorists must have the support or acquiescence of states. There will be friends of catastrophic terror who should prove eminently persuadable as to the wisdom of distancing themselves from the use of nuclear, and other, WMD. But the terrorists who will positively yearn to make their mark with a nuclear device by no means comprise the whole of the problem. Also, there will be states, so-called rogue as well as others of more sober character, who will have relatively few nuclear weapons, will lack many, if not all, of the safety technologies and procedures pioneered during the Cold War, and who will almost certainly exist in an international political context of acute hostility. If the last point is not so, why would they expend the treasure and take the risks necessary to acquire nuclear weapons? A fairly benign answer would be to the effect that nuclear status confers general benefits. But it is prudent to assume that states, and non-state groups, will 'go nuclear' only for serious and pressing reasons of perceived necessity. Finally, in this Second and very different Nuclear Age, understanding of the pertinent culture of the new proliferants is near certain to be perilously fragile. When we consider the poor quality of Western intelligence on Saddam Hussein's Iraq in 2002–2003, especially in connection with its WMD programme, it is troubling to speculate on what might have occurred had Saddam been nuclear armed. The long-standing US record of weakness in achieving cultural understanding of its enemies does not bode well for the future of nuclear deterrence, even in those circumstances when deterrence may be feasible.[28]

Future warfare will see the use of WMD, including those of a nuclear variety. There are two main reasons why we can assert this unwelcome conviction with such high confidence. First, today and in the future WMD are the weapons of the relatively weak. Relative to the military power of the American sheriff, everyone, greater polities, lesser polities, and transnational anti-polities, is more or less weak. It has to follow that anyone who intends mischief in his neighbourhood must take steps to neutralize US influence for order and discourage its intervention. The quintessential tool of the strategically disadvantaged who desperately requires an asymmetrical edge, lies in the basket of WMD options. We have to take seriously the probability that just because WMD are culturally anathema and are widely believed to be militarily marginal, save for deterrence, in the West, it does not follow that the alleged nuclear, biological, and chemical taboos carry much traffic elsewhere. Signatures on the appropriate conventions would count for little or nothing. As German Chancellor, Theobald von Bethmann Hollweg, said on 4 August 1914, with reference to his country's violation of Belgian neutrality, 'necessity knows no law'.[29] Particularly is this so when the law in question does not express a deeply treasured belief. The rights of small countries did not rank high in the official German creed (or the British, one might add).

Second, this author is impressed by the suggestive strength of statistical probability. We should pass over the prospects for the use of chemical weapons in future warfare, if only for the excellent reason that the world's leading militaries are all convinced that such horrors will be unleashed again. The question devolves, rather, upon nuclear and biological possibilities. As a scholar I am not completely comfortable with an argument which amounts to a claim for what 'stands to reason', given the cultural bias in the reason and the certainty that future history will lay on some noteworthy strategic surprises. Nonetheless, it is only prudent, as well as reasonable, to assume that nuclear and biological weapons will be used in future warfare. There will be too many conflicts of all kinds, and nuclear weapons or devices will be too accessible, for motive and WMD means not to achieve some marriages of malign strategic convenience. No comfort should be taken from the facts that neither nuclear nor biological weapons have been used for more than half a century. The force of a would-be universal taboo against these weapons, one supported and strengthened by treaty and customary international law, not that nuclear use is illegal, we must add, will prove robust only when it is not severely tested. For catastrophe terrorists the power of culture ensures disdain for any taboo on WMD employment.

For the practical reasons of relative ease of access, terrorists and regional rogue states are likely to find their choice among WMD seriously constrained. Both kinds of troublemaker will be able to acquire chemical, biological, and radiological weapons long before nuclear explosives are available to them. However, there is no doubt that the gold standard among WMD is the nuclear weapon, even if only a crude device, machined and assembled in a basement, and likely to produce an energy yield equivalent only to 100 tons of TNT, or less. Nuclear weapons are perceived to be different from all others. At least that is probably still true, even though the often rather thoughtless aggregation now known by the shorthand acronym, WMD, poses a challenge to the singularization of the nuclear category. We discuss below whether or not all kinds of WMD are created, and should be regarded as, equal.

Nuclear weapons enjoy a reputation for being the ultimate horror, which they may not deserve when they are compared with some of the more lethal and contagious of biological warfare possibilities. There are several major advantages to the nuclear option, and these will continue to be attractive. In addition to the unique status they enjoy, and hence the reputation for high achievement they confer on their owners, nuclear weapons promise a certainty, a reliability, of immediate performance. The delayed damage from radiation effects can be viewed either as a bonus, or as regrettable, but alas unavoidable. Biological weapons are relatively, even hugely, uncertain in their effects. Leaving aside the theoretical, but improbable, possibility that the target population might be vaccinated against the particular pathogens in question, the performance of biological weapons must be highly dependent upon environmental and human factors. The extreme care with which the living cultures need to be grown, stored and delivered, virtually ensures a field day for everything that Clausewitz included in his compound concept of friction. There will be an awful lot that could go wrong. In addition, whereas nuclear weapons do their worst instantly, or fizzle instantly if the DIY assembly was less than competent, all biological weapons work only after an incubation period within their human victims. For some purposes that may not matter. One might argue that there is a horrific quality to the deliberate spread of disease as a weapon of war, which even nuclear weapons cannot match. Nonetheless, no state or group striving to add WMD to its arsenal will decline the nuclear option if it is believed to be achievable and affordable.

The motives for WMD acquisition will not always, perhaps not even frequently, reduce to a determination to secure an asymmetrical offset to the all too usable conventional power of the United States. States and groups will have political and strategic needs that are domestic, local, and regional.[30] The strategic utility of WMD to help deter intervention by a superpower, or anyone else from a distance, would be a bonus, but not the prime stimulus to proliferate. WMD proliferation invariably has mixed, and generally many, motives. We need to beware of falling into the trap of interpreting such proliferation through the unreliable lens of rational strategic choice. The Soviet space programme had major and direct military applications. It was also intended as a ringing affirmation of the superiority of the socialist system in the high prestige realm of science and technology. Similarly, the Soviet build-up of their strategic missile arsenal in the 1970s, which so worried Western governments, had obvious military applications. But we know now that Soviet domestic politics played at least as large a role as did strategy. The Soviet strategic missile force was shaped not so much by the military requirements of the war plans of the General Staff, as by the interests of the party–industrial complex that churned out missiles.[31]

Despite the highly arguable cultural claim of there being a near universal taboo against nuclear weapons, a development since the initiation of the NPT regime in 1970, these weapons have not lost much of their glitter. In comparison, chemical and biological weapons are regarded widely, if not necessarily universally, with great revulsion. Whereas a state or group would anticipate some gain in respect for acquiring nuclear weapons, or at least a near nuclear option, no prestige attaches to the other kinds of WMD. It is not just that biological, and especially chemical, weapons are considerably easier to acquire than are nuclear. Chemical weapons, 'poison gas', has never regained the respectability that it earned in the First World

War. By 1917–18, the massive use of gas shells by both sides was entirely routine as a regular component of artillery fire plans. Poison gas became an integral part in the new style of combined arms warfare. The British always lagged behind German chemical prowess. For example, the British Expeditionary Force (BEF) was unable to follow the Germans with their 1917 use of mustard gas shells until September 1918.

The story of poison gas in modern war is particularly instructive in two respects that have implications for future warfare. First, some of its advocates hoped that gas would prove to be the key that unlocked the Western Front. It was viewed as a potential War Winning Wonder Weapon. This hope-come-belief figures so frequently in the history of warfare that it might be worthy of joining the legion of acronyms as the cropped and economical W^4. The reality of the impact of gas on ground combat in the First World War was that it was useful as part of the combined arms team. Historian Gary Sheffield has this to say in a well-regarded study of the BEF's performance:

> Rather than underlining the reactionary conservatism of the British high command, the story of gas at Loos [1915, first substantial British offensive on the Western Front] shows that too much faith was placed in a single unreliable and untried weapon. Subsequent years were to demonstrate that chemical warfare had its place on the battlefield, but as an auxiliary to artillery and infantry, not as a primary weapon.[32]

Both sides discovered that gas delivered from cylinders in the front lines would only arrive in the intended target area if the wind obliged. If the wind did not oblige, the release of gas meant that friendly assault troops would be choking in their own trenches. The only way to defeat the most harmful vagaries of wind direction and velocity was to deliver the gas by shell fire.

The second point worthy of particular note about the experience with gas in 1915–18, is that the cultural, perhaps ethical, response to its employment was out of all proportion to its military or strategic significance. In his careful study of the Hundred Days campaign of August–November 1918, J. P. Harris concludes thus: 'In the final analysis, while gas added another dimension of fear and unpleasantness to warfare, its casualty-producing power has been much exaggerated and its influence on the course of operations during the Hundred Days was generally small.'[33] Despite the modest military significance of the choking and blistering effects of the chlorine, phosgene, and mustard gases, chemical (and biological) warfare was singled out for prohibition and, in consequence, opprobrium, in the 1925 Geneva Protocol for the Prohibition of the Use in War of Asphyxiating, Poisonous or other Gases, and of Bacterial Methods of Warfare.[34] The Protocol did not specify an absolute prohibition. The signatory states agreed to its provisions subject to the vital reservation that their compliance was conditional upon their not being the victims of attack by the weapon in question. Despite the existence of the Protocol, it was assumed by all of the great powers that in a future major war among themselves gas either would be used, or at least well might be. Recall that throughout the Second World War all British subjects were required to carry gas masks. It was anticipated that bomber fleets would drop gas-filled bombs on to panic-stricken civilian population centres. Armed with gas, fire, and explosives, air power would overfly, and thus evade, the problem of deadlock on the ground à la 1914–18. Here was a W^4, a war winning wonder weapon, or so its advocates believed and even its sceptics feared. Of course, air power was to achieve wonder weapon status, but only when it was married to weaponized nuclear science. Paradoxically, nuclear-armed air power was to prove so wonderfully potent as to be all but unusable save in purposeful non-use, as Bernard Brodie expressed the matter time and again. As early as 1946, he declared that 'thus far the chief purpose of our military establishment has been to win wars. From now on its chief purpose must be to avert them. It can have almost no other useful purpose'.[35]

It can scarcely be doubted that a taboo, a social or cultural prohibition, has attached to chemical warfare.[36] In the Great War, injuries from poison gas generally were less lethal than were those from conventional artillery shells, the leading killing agent in the war. However, the nature of gas injuries was so gruesome, or was perceived to be such, even if short-term survival rates compared favourably with other varieties of wounds, that poison gas was ring-fenced as incompatible with civilized ways in warfare. Today, eighty years on from the Geneva Protocol, we need to know what to make of the legal and cultural constraints on WMD. I have limited this discussion thus far to the chemical taboo, but the popularity of the thesis that there is a nuclear taboo also, is a claim of even greater interest for our study. The combination of longevity, 1925 to the present for chemical and biological weapons, and with the NPT from 1970 to the present for nuclear, certainly places barriers of treaty and customary international law in the way of the would-be WMD wrongdoer. In addition to the force of law, the fact that nuclear weapons have not been employed in anger since 1945 leads many people to believe that a potent tradition of non-use is now extant. A similar tradition pertains to biological weapons also. But, as strategists are obliged to ask, so what?

Terrorists, who stand outside the law of nations and reject the values that help provide some cultural rules for the governance of warfare, generally are unmoved by the sentimental and prudential taboos of ordinary mortals. An important exception to that fact would be if a terrorist organization believed that the use of WMD of some variety would constitute an own goal, losing it support and legitimacy. Of course, post-modern terrorists might not care about pubic opinion. They may believe that they will gain political strength from the awe in which their breaking of a taboo is regarded. In that case, the hope that essentially ethical, cultural norms will restrict violence, must prove forlorn.

The idea behind the WMD designator itself poses an increasingly serious problem for the deterrence and conduct of future warfare. This highly aggregating, inclusive acronym implies strongly that all WMD are equally vile and, presumably, all are equal in the eyes of Strategic Persons. Politically it may be sensible to assert a common villainy to all kinds of WMD, but it is a strategic absurdity. Bear in mind that the Western powers at least have no offensive capability to wage chemical or biological warfare, not even the ability to respond in kind. The Russian Federation ought to be similarly bereft, but we cannot be certain that that is so. The United States and its allies cannot deter, or promptly wage, chemical or biological warfare, by means of threats or retaliatory action in kind. As a consequence, in declaratory policy at least, they have elected to emphasize the unity of all WMD. For a well-known example, prior to the Gulf War of 1991 Iraq was warned that any use of its chemical arsenal against Coalition forces would, or most probably would, result in a nuclear response. In a rather softer vein, American and British spokesmen let it be known that any use of WMD on the Iraqi part would licence a WMD reply, which could only have a nuclear character. This was a bluff, but Saddam Hussein's restricted understanding of the outside world, buttressed by the tame, submissive intelligence agencies that served him, inclined him to the conviction that the Western threat was real.

There is obvious deterrent merit in asserting the political, strategic and ethical, equivalence of all WMD. The US Government has declared that any use by terrorists and their state supporters of WMD of any character against American interests, forces, or allies would call forth an 'extraordinary response'. It is expedient for the United States to encourage the world to believe that that opaque verbal formula is a lightly coded reference to nuclear weapons. In prospective reality, however, the opacity of the concept of an extraordinary response should be taken at face value. No country wants to box itself into a position where it is publicly committed to nuclear action, especially when such behaviour would make no strategic, and even less political, sense. Plainly, a conundrum has arisen. What should be done to deter, or respond to, the use of biological or chemical weapons, when the most effective reply would certainly take the form of conventional military action? The US Government does not want to say, 'wage biological, chemical, or even nuclear, war against us, and in reply we will defeat you with conventional means'!

The question of how best to deter and, if need be, respond to WMD attack is a central problem of future warfare. Given the measure of US conventional military superiority, and the robustness of the societal infrastructure on which it is founded, America's foes will need to devise strategies that bid for leverage in asymmetric ways. The most obvious among the possibilities is to threaten, or employ, WMD against the superpower.

WMD will be the weapons of the materially weaker side in future warfare; of that we can be certain. Those weapons are taken seriously today. Witness the enervating special protective clothing worn by allied forces in Iraq, and the slightly perilous vaccinations mandated for the troops. Future warfare, however, will not be conducted solely against decaying regimes led by strategic incompetents. And we should not forget that, for all its errors, Ba'athist Iraq did succeed in using chemical weapons effectively as a vital combined arms player in their Western Front-style frontier defence against Iran in the 1980s.

WMD are useful. That utility can be political, strategic, operational, and tactical. Politically and strategically, the certainty of further WMD proliferation means an elevation in the stakes of the conflicts at issue. In wars between regional rivals, WMD use of any kind will likely mean a longer casualty list and, possibly, but only possibly, much greater and persisting environmental damage. This is not to forget that chemical and biological agents, in common with the effects of neutron bombardment from a so-called neutron bomb, would harm people but not property. With respect to actual or potential warfare between the superpower and a regional state, say Iran or North Korea, knowledge or strong suspicion that the regional foe had operational WMD capabilities must encourage some policy pause. The United States, or indeed any great power or coalition considering intervention to impose discipline, and restore order in a region, would demand of its military an iron-clad assurance that any WMD menace would be neutralized before it could be employed. Given the inherent uncertainties of intelligence, and the ever-lurking threat of friction, no responsible military organization would be likely to give such an assurance. What if it proved ill founded? Heads would roll. A strategy of preventive, or at worst, pre-emptive anti-proliferation, would be essential, if the diffusion of WMD were not to be allowed to paralyse the forces of international order. That judgement, offered without apology, is of course politically and culturally biased.

Even if in principle there exist effective military answers to regional WMD dangers, the practical difficulties and risks that must attend an effort at forcible disarmament mean that the regional proliferant will have raised the stakes of conflict hugely. Pending the return of balance of power struggles among great powers, when history's cycle turns yet again, the superpower sheriff of world order generally will be confronted with possible wars of discretion rather than strict necessity. Obviously, the struggle against al Qaeda and other murderous entities of similar ideological persuasion comes under the aegis of necessity. Al Qaeda has to be destroyed as a global network capable of mounting operations. In the medium and long run that destruction can be achieved only from within the Islamic world. In the nearer term, however, an al Qaeda with access to WMD must be prevented from using them. Whereas regional states with WMD, especially of a nuclear kind, could threaten the basis of the superpower's, or even the somewhat mythical international community's, policy and strategy for enforcing order, apocalyptic terrorists with WMD give the agents of order no choice. When a regional power such as Iran acquires nuclear weapons it threatens US strategy. That case of proliferation would have the effect of disconnecting America's, or anyone else's except for Israel's, strategic means and ends. Since Iran must care more deeply about the interests at stake in the Gulf region than does the United States, oil and the global economy notwithstanding, a nuclear option for Teheran would menace the integrity of US strategy. While the prospective benefits of taking military action against Iran would be unchanged, the risks would be raised astronomically. Sea-based theatre missile defence should neutralize an Iranian nuclear-armed missile threat, but there are many ways to deliver nuclear weapons. The Islamic Republic of Iran has a history of tactical flexibility and a willingness to chance its arm militarily in unconventional ways. The United States discovered this dimension to Iranian strategic culture during the 'tanker war' in 1987–8.[17] Members of the Revolutionary Guards Corps manned a fleet of small armed assault craft, a fleet that included inflatables which yielded a low or zero radar cross-section.

This is not quite to predict that a nuclear-armed Iran would be safe from violent expression of American, let alone Israeli, wrath. However, it is to state that anyone contemplating war with such an Iran would be obliged to hesitate long and hard given what the consequences could be if its initial military action was conducted less than immaculately. Experience, the theory of war, and our old ally, common sense, all advise that Murphy works particularly hard in wartime. Clausewitz tells us that the climate of war comprises 'danger, exertion, uncertainty, and chance'.[38] It is one thing to accept uncertainty in a strictly conventional conflict, it would be quite another were risks of a nuclear kind. Not only is this self-evidently true; we learnt to respect nuclear peril through forty-plus years of the Cold War. Anyone who believes that the solution for international order lies with a new (American) way of war, one that privileges and exploits true excellence in C4ISTAR, precision firepower, and agile elite light ground forces, needs to be reminded of an ancient truth. In the sage words of Rear Admiral J. C. Wylie, USN: 'planning for certitude is the greatest of all military mistakes, as military history demonstrates all too vividly'.[39] When politicians interrogate their military advisers about the prospects for victory in planned operations, we can assume that they will demand an unrealistic certainty of swift decisive success when the enemy is armed with nuclear weapons. It may be worth recalling President Kennedy's unhappiness with the honest, hedged answers he received from his advisers during the Cuban Missile Crisis. Despite the apparent fact that the Soviet medium and intermediate-range missiles were far from elusive, their mobility being more notional than real, the President remained less than completely reassured. Lawrence Freedman records that 'Kennedy kept coming back to the likelihood of some missiles firing during the course of an American attack of any sort. Nor would he have been encouraged by McCone's [John A. McCone, Director of the CIA] own sober warning about the hazards of land invasion, even with command of the air'.[40] The presence, even just the suspected presence, of WMD, nuclear especially, tends to make super cautious, if not downright cowardly, policymakers of us all. It is not difficult to see why the anti-proliferation strategy of a state that bears the heaviest load for international order is likely to include the option of preventive military action. If nuclear-armed rogues are unacceptable, and if pre-emption is far too risky, preventive invasive surgery is the obvious, indeed the only, answer remaining.

Biological weapons could in theory wreak more havoc than the nuclear arsenal of any regional power, let alone any nuclear capability likely to be cobbled together by terrorists. However, the biological threat loses much of its strategic potency because of the extreme uncertainty over both its success in delivery and its consequences. Notwithstanding the night and day difference between a 5-megaton ICBM warhead and a 100-ton device, nuclear weapons carry a generic stamp of quality assurance as the 'Class A' menace. They are prompt in most of their effects; they are technically reliable, which may not necessarily be a sound assumption; and they are universally understood, feared, and respected.

What distinguishes al Qaeda and similarly motivated terrorist organizations with regard to WMD is that they actually want to use them. That is why normal risk-benefit analyses cannot apply either to them or to their enemies. To disarm an apocalyptic terrorist group of a nuclear or biological capability would be an overriding policy priority. Whereas states that acquire nuclear WMD are likely to find the outside world seeking ways to adjust to the new unwelcome reality, except in the case of Israel vis-à-vis an Iranian 'bomb', apocalyptic terrorists so armed would have to be destroyed.

WMD of all kinds will continue to proliferate because they are useful. It is worthwhile to harass, slow, and occasionally reverse the pace of proliferation, but fundamentally the task is mission impossible. Such meritorious, if somewhat self-serving, Western endeavour is akin to the determination to keep outer space supposedly pristine and free from weaponization. We pursue that contentious matter in the next chapter. It does not require extensive expertise in strategic history to appreciate that states sign on for arms control regimes that serve their interests. Sometimes they even sign for the purpose of acquiring useful cover for evasion. Such was our experience with Iraq, North Korea, and the eighteen years of lies with which Iran outwitted the inspectors of the International Atomic Energy Authority.[41] We can be certain that WMD have a prosperous future as a dimension to future warfare, because for many belligerents, or states and groups contemplating belligerency, there are no superior alternatives available to them.

It is difficult to conduct realistic debate about the political, strategic, and military utility of WMD in Western security circles. We are so fixated on our commitment to arrest or reverse the pace of proliferation, that our focus overwhelmingly is on the great and complex challenge of arms control and disarmament.[42] Without disagreeing with the determination to minimize WMD proliferation, certainly to retard it where we are able, it is the view in this text that more attention needs to be paid to the prospective utility of these weapons to possible proliferants. Audiences of decent, right thinking folk, including some defence professionals, are easily shocked by the argument that nuclear weapons are useful. If they are not useful, why do the declared nuclear weapon states continue to hold them and why do others aspire to join their ranks? It so happens that biological, chemical, and radiological weapons also can be useful. The phenomenon that impedes comprehension and strategic empathy amounts to nothing less than demonization. By analogy, those who would explain Nazi Germany overwhelmingly in terms of its obedience to a Fuehrer who was allegedly a madman, or simply an evil monster, rarely feel obliged to probe any further. The demonization of Adolf Hitler provides a convenient catch-all explanation for events. The fact that it is a grossly flawed and inadequate thesis has difficulty penetrating the protective wall provided by vilification. So it is with WMD also.

At every level of analysis – political, strategic, military, operational, and tactical – each of the nightmare brands of WMD discussed in this chapter will have greater or lesser utility for some belligerents in future warfare. As the commonplace axiom insists, accurately for once, in common with terrorism WMD are the weapons of the relatively weak. Naturally, the specific technical details of weapon effects, as well as ease of acquisition, secure storage, and delivery, matter enormously for judgements on utility.

Politically, only nuclear WMD carry the cachet of legitimate major accomplishment. Readers are advised to dismiss as a plausible Western fallacy the attractive thesis that there is a global nuclear taboo.[41] Strategically, nuclear WMD, and just possibly some biological, carry the promise of restructuring the terms of a conflict. They alter cost-benefit calculations markedly. For states desperate to discourage intervention in their locality by an interfering sheriff protecting Western notions of international order, nuclear status is the best-looking answer to the local strategist's prayer. At the operational level of war, both nuclear and biological weapons have important, possibly decisive, roles to play. The logistic infrastructure of a militarily superior enemy is the target set from central casting for the nuclear and biological proliferator. Ports of regional entry and other communication nodes, bases, and large assemblies of troops and those that must support them, would all be at risk to WMD attack. If a war is a protracted one by contemporary standards, then the incubation periods of biological agents would scarcely matter. Moreover, it is well worth noting that the fear of biological assault, an understandable dread of unknown horrific infection, would be likely to have a seriously adverse effect on morale. And that is an understatement. Obviously, both nuclear and chemical weapons could inflict immediate harm on a scale that a conventionally weak combatant would be unable to accomplish by any other means. Finally, at the tactical level of war, chemical agents come into their own. Whether or not they are highly lethal, as is the case with a nerve agent such as VX, their presence in the arsenal obliges a prudent enemy to take enervating precautions by way of wearing protective clothing which inhibits military performance. For example, in the gigantic battles of 1918, relatively primitive chemical choking agents were extremely useful to both sides in the artillery counter-battery role. Their mission was not to kill enemy soldiers, but rather to drive them away from the guns that they should be serving and, if they stood to their posts, to slow the pace of their firing. Biological agents have no obvious tactical role, since the military need is for immediate results to affect the course of battle.

The abominable agents of destruction discussed above have to be regarded in strategic perspective. Once one has expressed distaste, or more, for the agents at issue, one has to move on to the practical task of thinking about them strategically. WMD may be approached in several ways, and this book has no quarrel with those who devote their attention to pertinent ethical, political, or environmental topics. All that we insist upon here is that the strategic perspective must be accorded its due. And in practice that particular due is always likely to be the dominant consideration. As threat for deterrence or coercion, or as military instrument for actual use, all WMD fit into the means–ends framework that characterizes strategy. Strategy is about the purposeful threat or use of force to achieve desired goals. There is some merit in the argument that the 'M' in WMD destroys the very basis of the Clausewitzian theory of war. War, allegedly, can hardly be an instrument of policy if it would entail mass slaughter, especially reciprocal mass slaughter. Alas, that all too reasonable point of view is not correct. Nuclear strategy is not an oxymoron, and nor is the idea of strategy for highly contagious biological agents. The strategy may be poor, not to mention morally and legally indefensible, and it may not work well, but strategy there will be. In this book we refer to the eternal and universal lore of war, the features of belligerency that are unchanging because they stem from war's very nature, its 'objective nature' in the Clausewitzian term. That persisting lore of war applies no less to WMD than to all other kinds of weapons.

HERE ENDETH PART ONE of the lesson on the relevance of strategic ideas and analysis to new varieties of warfare, or to new forms of old varieties. Part two of this story, in the next chapter, ventures into realms radically different from those probed above. However, the essential argument is the same, as is the most prevalent pitfall for the unwary. Space power and cyber power, as with WMD, both suffer in understanding from a continuing reluctance on the part of analysts to approach them strategically. They are all so different, so distinctive, from the common run of warfare with which we are all too familiar. In the minds of many, WMD, space power and cyber power bear such high promise of delivering extraordinary consequences from use that they are treated as if they transcend discipline by the lore of war. Now we move onward and upward to extend the argument for the relevance of the historically based theory of war and strategy into outer space and cyberspace.

Chapter eight

Old Rules for New Challenges II: Warfare in Space and Cyberspace

THEORY FOR NEW GEOGRAPHY

Future warfare will include war in space and cyberspace. That is a claim one can make with complete confidence. To date, both outer space and cyberspace have been extensively militarized, but neither geography has seen combat; they have not been used in more than marginal ways for offensive strategic purposes. That is certain to change. Indeed, it is changing already since low-level cyber-terrorism and efforts at information warfare now occur on a daily basis. The discussion here shares with the examination of WMD the task of explaining how even distinctly non-traditional kinds of military power must function according to the general lore of war. That is to say, the 'objective nature' of war described by Clausewitz is enduring and universal regardless of the geography of combat.[1] It is useful to remember that for some decades into the twentieth century the use of aircraft in war was emphatically non-traditional. It is ironic that although the development of air power was vastly accelerated from what we might term a normal pace of evolution by its military co-option in the First World War, even now, a century on from the first flight at Kitty Hawk on 17 December 1903, its role in war remains controversial. Outer space and cyberspace are simply the latest geographies to be exploited for military purposes.

WMD, spacecraft, and interconnected computers or cyber power, all share the significant characteristic of being radically different from the military systems that preceded them, and to some degree which continue to operate in parallel. In the 1940s and early 1950s, future warfare, except of a colonial kind, was expected by both East and West to be nuclear. The Eisenhower administration made it clear that it regarded nuclear weapons as just the latest of military developments; it expected to use them in wars of all kinds, save for the smallest, as a matter of routine. That attitude did not long survive the arrival of fusion weapons in the megaton range and the explosive expansion of the scale of the nuclear arsenal. Above all else, the reality of a principal enemy who was similarly arming promoted sober second thoughts, even though that enemy lagged seriously in the nuclear competition until the late 1960s. By the end of the 1950s at the very latest, everyone agreed that nuclear WMD were so different as to be unique. Indeed, it was not entirely self-evident that they should be treated as weapons as traditionally understood at all. They appeared to effect a gigantic non-linearity in strategic history. If these were weapons that had utility only in non-use, and if the overriding mission of nuclear-armed forces was to prevent war, rather than to wage it, was not this so stark a historical change as to be a revolution in the nature, and not merely the character, of war?

All too obviously, nuclear WMD have not abolished warfare, though they did contribute to an unusual caution during the First Nuclear Age of the Cold War. Their unique features were slowly appreciated and exploited, and they were accommodated in their turn in modern strategy and prospectively in modern warfare. Neither biological nor chemical WMD have triggered much of a strategic literature, which is scarcely surprising given the fact that the former has no modern history. The latter, following its extensive outing from 1915–18, was singularized in international law – along with biological agents – as a class of weapon beyond the pale of tolerable awfulness. Had biological and chemical weapons played an important role in the strategic history of the twentieth century, we can be certain that their political owners and military users would have been obliged to devise a theory to explain their utility and doctrine to guide their employment in combat.

Space and cyberspace share with WMD the feature of military, and arguably strategic, historical non-linearity. In common with air power, space power and cyber power refer to the military exploitation of a new geographical environment, if one may be permitted so to identity the electromagnetic spectrum. Space power is an obvious historical departure. Prior to the achievement of Earth orbit by Sputnik in 1957, outer space could be used, somewhat unreliably, militarily only as a medium for the rapid transit of ballistic missiles.[2] Space systems involve vehicles, satellites, that can achieve orbital velocity (17,500 mph). Cyber power, a potent if somewhat mysterious neologism if ever there was one, refers to human military exploitation of a new geography, albeit one that has been used for a hundred years, thinking of radio. However, the computer, specifically the internetted computer, and even more specifically the internetted computer that has orbiting spacecraft as servants, amounts to a radical change in technological context. Moreover, if there are grounds for questioning the weapon character of nuclear WMD, because of their alleged destruction of the Clausewitzian connection between power and policy, what are we to make of cyber power as a weapon of mass disruption that cannot itself actually spill blood. This is not to deny that cyberwarfare might cause planes to crash, trains to derail, and other disasters.

Since Clausewitz tells us that *'war is thus an act of force to compel our enemy to do our will',*[3] how can cyberwar qualify? The answer is twofold. First, war is conducted to serve policy and a political vision that inspires policy, and policy has many instruments with which 'to impose our will on the enemy'. Cyberwar, in the particular sense of strategic, stand-alone, information warfare operations, can be seen as a reasonably distinct tool of grand strategy. A country may wage economic warfare also without using force. Coercion can take many forms. Second, cyberwar generally will be a team player to provide more or less direct support for the sharp end of the spear. Even if cyber combat has some stand-alone qualities, still it must occur in the political and strategic context of warfare. In other words, provided we are intelligent in thinking about new military instruments according to their unique natures, a traditional definition of war will not trouble us. Cyber power, and indeed space power in its current, though not future, form, cannot itself apply organized violence, or force. But so what?

In this chapter we explore the roles and significance of space power and cyber power in future warfare. The sharpness of their strategic novelty inevitably has fuelled speculation that each might offer the golden key to military success and political hegemony. The market for grand, if simple, solutions, for panaceas, is always open. Space power and cyber power provide near perfect material to test the leading arguments of this book concerning the essential historical continuity and holistic nature of warfare.

CLAUSEWITZ IN ORBIT

If we discount the shocking strategic surprise of Hitler's V-2 rockets, first test-fired in 1942, and then launched against England in 1944–5, the space age began in the mid 1950s.[4] The Sputnik satellite in 1957 was a political stunt, but it had profound military implications in that the ability to achieve orbital velocity had to mean that the Soviet Union had rockets powerful enough to function as ICBMs. Since the late 1950s, with the United States typically in the lead, despite the embarrassment created by Sputnik, both superpowers exploited Earth orbit for an expanding set of vital functions.

The United States and the Soviet Union / Russia have been followed distantly by other states in the acquisition of space systems both for reasons of national security, as well as by commercial and scientific operations. Bearing in mind what we said in Chapter Seven about the problem of dual-use with respect to materials and facilities that can serve both innocent civilian, and deadly military, purposes, the same phenomenon applies to space systems also. States invest in dedicated military satellites. These are vehicles increasingly built to meet military specifications to resist electronic attack, directed energy weapons, electromagnetic pulse (from nuclear or carefully tailored conventional anti-satellite weapons), or physical

FIGURE 8.1

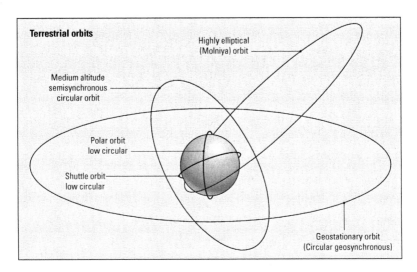

Source: Everett C. Dolman

interception. However, military space power is heavily dependent upon the commercial space industry. The United States, for example, rents access to terminals on commercial communications satellites to augment, and as back-up to, its dedicated military systems.

FIGURE 8.1 SHOWS the most basic geometry of the options among possible Earth orbits. The choice of orbit is driven by the mission of the space system. That choice is driven also for would-be space ventures by the high cost of reaching some Medium Earth Orbits (MEO, 300 to near 22,300 miles) with worthwhile payloads. Low Earth Orbit (LEO, 60 to near 300 miles: the forbidding Van Allen radiation belts lie close above the upper limit of this range) has obvious advantages for reconnaissance and surveillance missions, particularly of the photographic kind. However, spacecraft in LEO pay for the excellence of the resolution of the imagery they provide by requiring frequent engine firings in order to keep station and combat re-entry. Satellites occupying orbits in the very low range of 60 to 100 miles need repeated engine activation to fight the effects of atmospheric drag. If they cannot manoeuvre for station-keeping they will re-enter the Earth's atmosphere within twenty-four hours. Only at orbits higher than 1,200 miles, in the hard vacuum of space, can space vehicles remain in their intended orbits indefinitely without the need to fire engines to sustain altitude. In addition to the difficulty of maintaining station against the force of atmospheric drag and the pull of Earth's gravity well, satellites in LEO obviously can offer only a very restricted line of sight coverage of terrain of interest. As one space expert explains, 'during a typical orbit by a satellite at LEO altitude, its field of view is a narrow ribbon of the Earth's

FIGURE 8.2

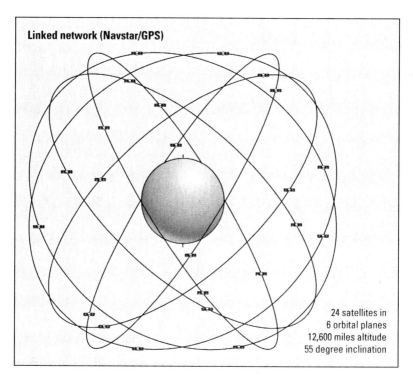

Linked network (Navstar/GPS)

24 satellites in
6 orbital planes
12,600 miles altitude
55 degree inclination

Source: Everett C. Dolman

FIGURE 8.3

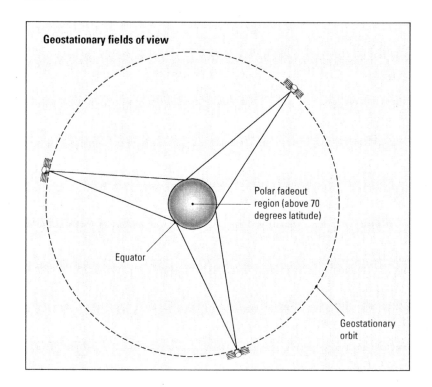

Source: Everett C. Dolman

surface about as wide as a large metropolitan city, and equal in area to less than one per cent of the Earth's surface'.[5] A satellite in LEO takes between an hour and a half and two hours to complete an orbit. The lower the orbit, the greater the number of satellites required to provide extensive terrestrial coverage. Also, spacecraft that are, say, 250 miles high, are a great deal easier for an enemy to reach than are those in MEO at, say, 12,600 miles, like the vehicles of the crucial Global Positioning System (GPS) constellation (see Figure 8.2) let alone the communications and missile early warning satellites in GEO at 22,300 miles (see Figure 8.3).

Satellites at any altitude can manoeuvre on command, provided they have sufficient fuel in their small thrusters' engines. But in order to change orbit spacecraft must effect a delta-v (Δv), or change (actually two changes)

FIGURE 8.4

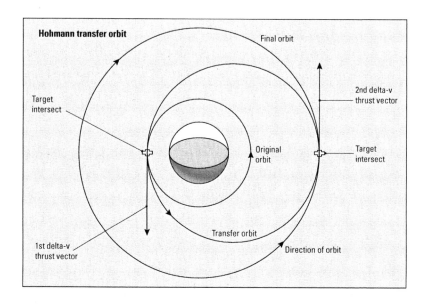

Source: Everett C. Dolman

in velocity. To shift to a much higher orbit, a satellite first must accelerate so as to thrust itself out of its existing orbit with a Δv into an elliptical orbit known as a Hohmann transfer orbit. When the transfer orbit intersects the desired orbit the satellite effects another Δv, this time to decelerate, in order to lock itself on to the new path (see Figure 8.4).

Space theorist Everett C. Dolman predicts that *'the future lanes of commerce and military lines of communications in space will be the Hohmann transfer orbits between stable spaceports'.*[6] Dolman is one of the few analysts who have attempted seriously to accomplish a Hohmann transfer of their own. He has advanced from the uncontentious astrophysics of orbitology to the controversial question of the strategic meaning of the technical story.

Readers may be wondering why I have delayed the strategic consideration of space power in future warfare even with the barest of bare technical
essentials just presented. The answer is that each geographical environment imposes distinctive constraints, just as it offers unique advantages.
To assess the importance of outer space in future warfare, it is necessary
first to grasp the more important influences on military behaviour that
derive from physical realities. That story changes with technology, but
geography always matters. Ideas about joint and integrated warfare are
popular, while the thesis that there is a need for warfare to be approached
as a whole meets with general approval, though not widespread understanding. It is simply a physical fact that the land, sea, air, space, and cyberspace comprise five unique dimensions, whose distinctive geographies
dictate: how humans can behave in, on, or through them; the range of
feasible technical choices; and the scope for tactical behaviour. This is not
technical determinism. Rather is it to recognize the fact that warfare on
land, at sea, in the air, in space, and in cyberspace cannot be other than
dominated technically and tactically by the constraints of each distinctive
geography. This old, old story has applied to the coming of air power, while
now and in the future it must dominate the evolution of space warfare and
cyberwarfare.

Space power in history is a dynamic tale, but so is the record of land
power, sea power, and air power. Our argument is to the effect that, on the
one hand, we understand the nature of war and strategy, courtesy of the
insights bequeathed to us by the classical theorists. On the other hand, we
grasp the physical possibilities and constraints that apply to shape behaviour
in each geographical environment. Between them, an understanding of
the general theory of war, and a mastery of the geographical dimension
to the technical–tactical grammar of warfare, should equip us well enough
to venture into the *terra incognita* of future warfare. In this case with specific
regard to the use of space and cyberspace.

Geographically speaking, space warfare, indeed the use of orbital space
for any purpose whatsoever, is dominated by the need to overcome the
pull of gravity (see Figure 8.5). Whereas an aircraft can move at will in any

direction, the movement of a spacecraft is governed rigidly by astro-dynamics, by the effects of gravity as expressed formally in Johannes Kepler's three laws of planetary motion. These laws govern orbital characteristics. I will adapt the wording for greater ease of understanding by those among us who are not physicists. The First Law of motion states that the orbit of a satellite forms an ellipse with the centre of the Earth at one focus. The Second Law holds that as a satellite moves around its orbit, an imaginary line (radius) joining it to the centre of the Earth sweeps out equal areas in equal amounts of time. Translated further, the First Law gives the shape and inclination (relative to the plane of the equator) of an orbit, while the Second Law describes the speed of a satellite relative to its orbital position at any point in time. The Third Law, in plain English, maintains that the period, which is to say the length of time, a satellite takes to complete one revolution of the Earth is dictated by the size, not the shape, of its orbit. The US Air Force (USAF) has always favoured the neologism of aerospace, as if the air and space environments essentially were one. In fact what they have in common amounts to little more than: a common status as the lesser and greater overhead flanks of terrestrial action; a form of high, and yet higher, ground; a global ubiquity; and adjacency. For many years, the USAF regarded the subject of doctrine for space operations as being totally sub-ordinate to air power doctrine.[7] Times have changed and space forces in the future will be directed according to a grasp of what astrodynamics mean for the grammar of war to, in, and from outer space.

Satellites must move in ways mandated by Keplerian law. They have to orbit, since gravity rules in the space of interest to us. This inflexibility, and predictability, is as different from the freedom of movement of aircraft as one could imagine. It is true that spacecraft can manoeuvre, but to do so frequently costs fuel, the weight of which detracts from the payload the vehicle otherwise could carry in order to perform its intended functions. Predictability in orbit is useful, actually vital, in that in principle a country can plan, precisely, exactly which military capabilities it will have at which point over the Earth at which times. The downside of the upside, naturally, is that the laws of planetary motion are not a state secret. Enemies will

FIGURE 8.5

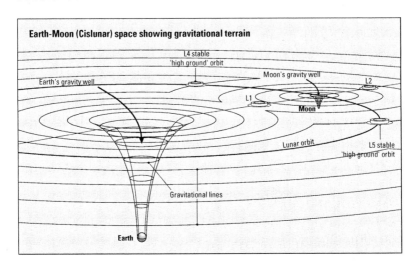

Source: Everett C. Dolman

know exactly where your spacecraft will be at any point in time, because their orbital paths will be precisely predictable, notwithstanding the possibility of some limited tactical manoeuvre.

A number of theorists, particularly those with some maritime affiliation, assert that 'space is an ocean' and oceans are where navies go.[8] It is not surprising that the heaviest user of space systems among the American armed services is the Navy (USN).[9] The all-but-global geography of naval deployments, the nature of the sea environment, and the relatively isolated status of warships often far from home ports, all drive the USN to depend more and more on information flows over the horizon via space systems. Theorists have noticed that the territorial ocean and the space ocean share the militarily key phenomenon of the chokepoint. It is argued, with some plausibility, that orbital space offers the equivalent of maritime chokepoints. In 1904, Britain's pugnacious First Sea Lord, Admiral Sir John Fisher, claimed that 'five strategic keys lock up the world!'[10] Those keys comprised

Singapore, the Cape of Good Hope, Alexandria, Gibraltar, and Dover. And Britain owned, or at least held, them all and guarded them all with its naval power. Because 'all the seas of the world are one', as J. H. Parry tellingly notes, it is possible for a great naval power at least to approach the achievement of global maritime control.[11] Fisher exaggerated, as was his habit, but his geostrategic logic was sound enough, as German naval theorists were obliged to concede in the inter-war years, when they reflected on the reasons for the impotence of their country's High Seas fleet in the Great War.[12]

If 'all the seas of the world are one', how much more unified is the all-enveloping vacuum of outer space. And are there chokepoints for space blockade, control of which would grant control of the whole space environment? The answer is yes, there are such chokepoints. Vast, indeed theoretically infinite, though the space environment may seem to be, in practice there are only a few orbits that attract heavy traffic. Specifically: LEO from approximately 150 to 300 miles altitude is heavily used for reconnaissance that needs imagery with high resolution; semi-sun synchronous twelve-hour orbits in MEO are ideal for the deployment of satellite constellations devoted to navigation (e.g., GPS); while the highly prized, limited number of orbital slots in GEO are perfect for communications and early warning of missile firings, *inter alia*. Furthermore, the physics of it all mandate the so-called antipodal rule. The rule specifies that any spacecraft must pass over the precise spot on Earth antipodal to its launch point before it completes its first orbit. Since spacecraft tend to be launched only from well-established spaceports that can provide the elaborate logistical support that they require, it does not take military genius to discern the possibility of enforcing a blockade of access into orbit. It is necessary to point out, however, that 'Jackie' Fisher's Britain had five fleets to hold his five strategic keys. A strategy of space blockade similarly would require the deployment of weapons, probably including some in space. As we explain below, space weapons remain controversial, albeit legal (provided the weapons are not WMD).

But what are space systems? Of what do they consist? Since our topic is space warfare, must this mean, strictly, warfare *in* space? It could, but it need not. A space system has three segments, each of which, in principle, offers opportunities for attack to an enemy. The system comprises: the satellite, perhaps the constellation of satellites, in orbit; the up and down links to and from the orbiting vehicle, commands from the ground stations and information flows from the satellite; and the ground station that controls the behaviour of the satellite and distributes its information to the users. In addition, though this probably would not be dedicated to a particular space system, a space force must have sophisticated launch facilities with all the logistic back-up necessary. In the jargon of today and to resort to a concept already introduced in this enquiry, Effects Based Operations (EBO) are focused on consequences, not upon particular means. While space warfare may well include some shoot-outs in orbit, it is more likely to be characterized by electronic assault upon the signal flows between orbit and ground. It should go without saying that the more direct is the access to data from orbit enjoyed by the ultimate military user, the less vulnerable is the system to a devastating, even paralysing, blow. If all satellite information must be distributed from only a handful, or fewer, of ground control stations, those facilities must be the targets of choice to the enemy. They may be protected politically to some degree because of their usual location on sovereign territory, at least if the combatants are striving to control escalation, but the pay-off from such an attack could be so large as to be a temptation that defies refusal.

As to the uses of space systems in future warfare, there is no single answer that will cover all cases. The most appropriate analogy, albeit necessarily inexact, is with the growth of dependency upon air power over the past century. From the humblest of military duties, providing reconnaissance as an alternative to the cavalry, and reporting the fall of shot for the artillery, air power has evolved into what some regard as the leading edge in war. Even those who are sceptical of air power's potency, especially as an independent war winner, acknowledge that in regular warfare a friendly air environment is literally essential. Today and in the future, it is all but inconceivable that regular warfare could be waged successfully in a context where the enemy ruled the skies. In the 1920s, say, the future of air power was deeply uncertain in detail, but one could predict with total confidence that that future must witness ever more diverse and heavier use, leading both to new dependencies and new forms of warfare. Much the same can be said today about space power.

The uses of space power to date include: reconnaissance and surveillance of many kinds (optical, infra-red, radar pre-eminently); electronic intelligence gathering; communications; navigation; meteorology and environmental monitoring; missile early warning and nuclear burst detection; and cartography and geodesy. Space has been militarized since the United States successfully deployed its first photo reconnaissance satellite, SAMOS 2, in 1961, and its first satellite constellation for navigation, to support the new Polaris SLBM force, in 1963. But, to date, weapons have not been deployed in space. There are several reasons why that is so. Primarily, thus far, because there has been no pressing need for such a development. We must note, though, that the long march to acquire ballistic missile defence (BMD) capabilities that should work effectively, from time to time has seen active consideration of weapons, as well as detectors, in orbit. Almost as important as the absence of a convincing military case for space weapons has been, and remains, the political, ethical, perhaps cultural, objection to the putative pollution of this pristine environment. Outer space, in common with Antarctica, has attracted the attitude that favours it being treated as a sanctuary from the standard run of human beastliness. Antarctica has a much greater chance of retaining its pristine character than has orbital space. In the latter case, the lady's virtue is already deeply compromised by the deployment of military space systems. All that are lacking today are weapons in orbit.

There is an enormous library of studies about outer space, spacecraft design and operation, astrophysics, and space arms control. What is missing, however, are first-class theories of space power. This is the same deficiency we noted in Chapter Six with respect to special operations. The shelves groan with exciting tactical tales of brave men and daring deeds, but one searches in vain for anything worth reading on the strategic meaning and value of all that heroism and tactical excellence. So it is for space power also. In an essay published in 1996, this author posed two challenging questions that were not solely rhetorical: 'Where is the theory of space power? Where is the Mahan for the final frontier?'[13] The answer is still, 'nowhere in sight', at least not yet. That condition of strategic conceptual neglect certainly will alter. Strategic ideas are forged, or disinterred and dusted off, in response to the needs of the period. Strategy and strategic studies is a practical enterprise, and few dimensions of future warfare will be in more urgent need of practical strategic guidance than will space warfare. The eminent American defence analyst and strategic theorist, Eliot Cohen, offers the following far-reaching, if contingent, judgement:

> The opening of space to full-fledged warfare would be as large a change as the opening of the air was during the First World War. New organizations, new operational conditions, new incentives to strike first, new ways of war, will blossom overnight.[14]

Cohen is almost certainly correct. But note the contingency in his claim. He predicts for a context wherein space is open to 'full-fledged warfare'. In other words, belligerents would treat the space environment in no way differently from their approach to the land, sea, air, and cyberspace (see below). Space would be an environment for war, as are the other geographies. If and when it was expedient to do so, weapons would be deployed in orbit. Those weapons could be directed against other spacecraft, against ballistic missiles, or for the purpose of terrestrial bombardment.[15] They might be nuclear WMD, which would be illegal under the terms of the Outer Space Treaty of 1967. They might be directed energy weapons, lasers in particular, since laser beams do not suffer attenuation in the vacuum of outer space. Or, they might be conventional explosives designed to propel lethal shot at, or in the predictable path of, an enemy's spacecraft. Perhaps as likely as the above would be the deployment of killer satellites whose weapon would be itself. Satellites are delicate vehicles, though they can be armoured and otherwise protected, albeit at a heavy cost in weight, and would not fare well in a contrived collision with a suicidal killer satellite. For terrestrial bombardment, the weapon could comprise metal rods shaped to survive re-entry into the atmosphere and calculated to impact with precision at a hypervelocity imparted by friendly gravity. These solid rods, deployed on arsenal platforms in orbit, would strike with a devastating kinetic energy.

In broad terms, the importance of space for future warfare is as easy to predict as the details are murky at best. We can be certain that future warfare will include warfare in space, at least warfare to contest the control of space. The reason is that space systems already have become vitally important to the military performance of the greater powers, and to the US superpower most especially. Belligerents will be unable to afford the luxury of according Earth orbit a geographically unique sanctuary status, because space is already extensively militarized. Were it, in common with Antarctica, to have little if any known value as an environment for military exploitation, then, indeed, space warfare might be postponed indefinitely. However, most emphatically such is not the case. Space systems have become not simply useful tools to enhance American, *inter alia*, military performance. Instead, some of those systems are literally essential if the US Armed Forces are to function at all. The information dominance that in aspiration is at the core of the US approach to future warfare, and the capability for distant precision strike, are feasible, even in theory, only because of the C^{4}ISTAR benefits conferred by imaging, communications, and navigation satellites. It should be needless to add that this now mature state of US space dependency is common knowledge on the planning staffs and in the military colleges of America's potential enemies. It is true that space dependency is not solely an American condition. But it is the case that America's geopolitical situation, its global security duties, and its leadership in the higher technology of both commerce and war, all combine to ensure that its space dependency will long outstrip that of regular rivals.[16] In future warfare, regular and irregular, the United States and its allies will be fighting, or violently peace-enforcing, very far from home. Enemies are near certain to be operating either at home or at least in close proximity thereto. It follows that the extensive use of space must confer unequal advantages in favour of the United States. This structural inequality is one enormous reason why America's foes will have every incentive to seek to distress their superpower enemy's space systems.

It is a rule in strategy, one derived empirically from the evidence of two and a half millennia, that anything of great strategic importance to one belligerent, for that reason has to be worth attacking by others. And the greater that importance, the greater has to be the incentive to damage, disable, capture, or destroy it. In the bluntest of statements: space warfare is a certainty in the future because the use of space in war has become vital. Warfare on the high seas developed in the late sixteenth and seventeenth centuries, waged by dedicated warships and newly naval professional sailors, precisely because control of the sea lines of communication had become crucial to the wealth, and hence the strategic staying power, of states. This is one subject on which there can be no argument. Regardless of public sentimental or environmentally shaped attitudes towards space as the pristine final frontier, space warfare is coming. In theory, the only way to falsify that resolute claim would be for the technically more advanced nations all to cease to employ Earth orbit for military purposes. In practice, though, even such improbable self-abnegation would not work. The dual-use problem to which we alluded in the previous chapter applies with even greater force to space than it does to biological and chemical facilities. There is really little difference between commercial, scientific, and military space systems. This is true despite the survivability features of dedicated military space vehicles, while some of the military uses made of non-dedicated satellites entail special measures for security. For the first of two historical analogies, modern warfare was enabled by the building of railways.[17] In most countries railway construction was driven far more by commercial than by official strategic considerations. Moving on to the second analogy, in the inter-war decades worthy efforts to ban aerial bombardment ultimately were frustrated by the inconvenient fact that a modern bomber or troop carrier of, say, 1930 vintage, was essentially identical to a modern civil airliner modified with a bomb bay and a strengthened floor. To ban the bomber, one would have to ban civil passenger aviation.[18] The latter could be readily militarized, even 'weaponized'.

Perhaps the simplest yet most dramatic way to illustrate the technical unity of the civil and the military in space, is with reference to anti-satellite weapons. The same geography and physics of orbital space govern the design and operation of all space systems, military or civilian. Literally any vehicle can function as an anti-satellite weapon if it can approach sufficiently close to its intended victim. The anti-satellite weapon might be a missile ascending directly from Earth, a missile launched from a high-flying aircraft or drone, or it might be an innocent-seeming satellite that manoeuvres either modestly or grandly via a Hohmann transfer orbit, as described earlier, on to a collision course.

Five points serve to summarize the significance and role of space power in future warfare. First, because space forces have become literally essential, even key, to effective performance in the conduct of post-modern war, there will be a paramount need to gain and keep space control. The military transformation underway in the United States, depending on excellence in C^{4}ISTAR, and which is being emulated in cheaper modes by others around the world, would be impossible without support from orbit. The potential vulnerability of US military power to attacks on its essential space systems is well recognized. 'Enhancing Space Capabilities' is one of the Pentagon's six official transformation goals.[19] Secretary of Defence Donald Rumsfeld has written that 'in addition to exploiting space for their own purposes, future adversaries will likely also seek to deny US forces unimpeded access to and the ability to operate through and from space'.[20] He proceeds to insist that 'U.S. forces must ensure space control and thereby guarantee U.S. freedom of action in space in time of conflict'. Adversaries of the United States who aspire to mount a truly serious military challenge will have no practical choice other than to attempt to harass and damage the US ability to use space at will. This is a familiar story with direct parallels in the history of sea power and air power.

The strategic issue will be space control. To have it means that a belligerent force is able to use Earth orbit as it wishes, reliably, while its enemy is denied such freedom of reliable action. Conceptually, and in its operational implications, space control is identical to sea control and air control.

In those earlier, but still relevant, cases it does not mean that the enemy cannot sail or fly at all; the concept does not imply a totally preclusive command. But it does mean that the foe should be unable to plan or conduct military operations that would require reliable assistance from orbit. That assistance may, or more likely, may not, be available. That is what is meant by space control. It is important to note that space control, in common with sea and air control, has both positive and negative aims. Enemies of the United States in future warfare may well be far more interested in space denial than in space control. They will want to deny the superpower reliable use of the most vital of its space systems, NAVSTAR GPS, for example, the dedicated defence communications satellites, and the early warning vehicles, notwithstanding the high altitudes of their orbits (in MEO and GEO).

Second, by extension from the first point, the increasingly heavy use of, and growing irreversible dependence upon, space systems, must lead inexorably to space becoming yet another environment for warfare. To date, outer space has functioned as a global sanctuary for the conduct of militarily useful, even essential, tasks, but it has not itself contributed to the total contested battlespace of modern war. The Gulf War of 1991 was described as the first space war, because it was the first conflict wherein systematic use was made of space systems for such vital tasks as reconnaissance and surveillance, navigation, communications, missile early warning, meteorology, and environmental monitoring.[21] Since 1991 the space contribution to the American way of war has continued to grow and become routine. Space has become a team player in the planning for, and conduct of, joint warfare. Even for the task of pilot search and rescue, satellites provide the vital link between the distressed, downed airman who is seeking to escape and evade, and the special forces rescue team. For our purposes the details matter less than the trend. Heavy and growing military dependence on space is here to stay and is a trend that cannot be reversed. Early critics of the use of railways for military purposes feared that the lines would be vulnerable and, even more, that they would inhibit operational flexibility by channelling operations to suit the geometry of the rail system. They were voices crying in the wilderness. Because space is here to stay as a permanent dimension of warfare, its use will be contested according to the strategic interests and military capabilities of belligerents. Thus far, although space systems featured both in the Cold War and in every conflict that has involved the United States (and a few others), since then, no one has challenged forcibly the use of Earth orbit. That de facto sanctuary condition cannot possibly endure.

Third, it follows from the analysis above that arguments pro and contra space weaponization are simply irrelevant. There will be ample scope for argument over whether particular weapons should be deployed in, or should be rapidly deployable to, orbit. But there can be no intelligent debate over the desirability of placing weapons in space. Space weaponization is not at all analogous to poison gas and lethal pathogens, as categories of nastiness that nearly all countries can agree to prohibit. The history of arms control reveals the relative ease with which states are able to agree not to do that which they have no wish to do. Unlike chemical and biological weapons which must target people, weapons in space most probably would be directed primarily against other space vehicles, either satellites or ballistic missiles in transit. Many people believe that the now longstanding absence of weapon deployment in space can be made permanent, both by treaty and culturally by taboo. This is a nonsense. It is foolish on two lethal counts. First, it disregards the strength of the strategic incentive to contest space control, at least in pursuit of some prowess in space denial. While second, it is technically absurd because space weaponization is an unduly general conflation of all sorts of means of waging space warfare. As we noted earlier, space systems have three segments: spacecraft; communication links; and ground control stations. Space weaponry is impossible to define tightly. This author happens to know this because he attempted, and failed, to craft such a definition for the US Government in the early 1980s, in preparation for possible superpower negotiations on anti-satellite weapons. One discovers rapidly that an anti-satellite weapon can be anything, yes anything, that inhibits the performance of a satellite. That 'anything' includes vehicles in orbit that can manoeuvre for a fatal collision, signal jamming transmitters on the ground, direct ascent rockets, again deployed on the ground, and many more. So what is a space weapon, or even a weapon in space? Plainly, this is not a productive field for arms control endeavour. The familiar problem of dual-use intrudes also. Ballistic missile defence (BMD), save of the most modest kind, can hardly avoid providing anti-satellite capability against spacecraft in LEO. Satellites are far more fragile than are re-entry vehicles with warheads.

Fourth, although arguments about space weaponization eventually will prove irrelevant, despite their high political profile today, debate over the degree to which dependency on space systems should be tolerated certainly will not. This discussion inadvertently may have given the false impression that in future warfare there will be no alternatives to the use of space systems. The truth is that for certain functions, very long distance communications, navigation, wide-area surveillance, and missile early warning, for some examples, there is, and will be, a lack of good alternatives. Governments in the future will need to consider far more seriously than they have to date where the balance among risk, benefit, and cost lies in their use of orbital vehicles. Only comparatively recently has the question of space system survivability been addressed rigorously. The advantages and disadvantages of a growing space dependency look very different if, on the one hand, outer space is assumed to be a sanctuary from hostile military action, or, on the other hand, if it is assumed to be an integral part of the general battlespace. Moreover, the vulnerability of space power to enemy action is not only a matter of hostile behaviour towards vehicles en route to, or in, orbit. A space system can be neutralized just as effectively by an electronic 'soft kill', by the jamming of its transmissions, or by the disabling or destruction of its control and data distribution stations on the ground. None of these menaces, among others, are showstoppers for space systems, but they do mean that states will have to approach space as they do the other geographies of war. As we keep insisting, war is a duel with an intelligent and highly motivated enemy, even if frequently one asymmetrically materially inferior. Security in orbit cannot be assumed to be a gift of some global cultural taboo or the like. It must be assumed that

deployed space forces will take losses and therefore be in need of replacement, at least if spare satellites are not already in orbit waiting to be
activated. It is going to be increasingly difficult for Americans, in particular,
to remember what war was like before the space age. They may benefit
from a reminder that between 1941 and 1945 their country waged what
amounted to two strategically distinct wars half a world apart, without
the aid of space power. More attention will need to be given by all space-
faring potential belligerents than is evident at present to finding good
enough, albeit much inferior, alternatives to space systems. It is entirely
predictable that in wartime those systems will suffer degradation because
of their status as prime targets.

Fifth and finally, attempts to understand future warfare must treat war
to, in, and from space in the context of war as a whole. Just because space
warfare is a novel idea and, as yet, naked of empirical evidence, it does not
follow that it can be appreciated in isolation. No one is going to fight a
space war or, anticipating the next section, a cyberwar. Space warfare will
have a political and strategic context. To claim otherwise would be identical
to an argument for sea war or air war. Single-environment views, theories,
and doctrines, continue to harass sound strategic debate. Warfare inherently is a joint undertaking, requiring the efforts of all kinds of military
power, though one or another military varietal probably will play the
leading role, according to the character of the conflict. These comments
are written in the light cast by the eternal strategic fact that military victory
ultimately can only be secured by control of the enemy's territory and
people.[22] Only land power can be decisive, notwithstanding the enabling
assistance it is given by sea, air, space, and now cyber, power. As space
warfare is an integral dimension to warfare as a whole, so it is governed
by the general theory of war as developed in the classics, Clausewitz's *On
War* and Sun-tzu's *Art of War* most especially. No matter how unfamiliar
the military technologies, or strange the geography, warfare is still warfare.
Some people believe that because Clausewitz was a continentally minded
Prussian, who made no effort to accommodate a maritime dimension in
his grand theory, he wrote only for land power. That view is incorrect. It

is true that the one hundred and thirty battles that constituted his empirical base were all continental,[23] but the absence of naval, air, space, or cyberspace dimensions, though noticeable, does not really matter. Clausewitz recognized a duality about war. He agreed that it had both an eternal and universal 'objective', and an ever-changing 'subjective', nature. The grammar of war is always evolving, albeit at a rate that varies over time and among polities and other belligerents. Our argument is that the novel evolving grammar of space warfare will be subordinate to political purpose, and also to the features that comprise war's objective nature.

Strategic thinking about space is rare. The evidence available is all about the technologies, their utility in war when uncontested, and their high value in peacetime. For all its deficiencies, understanding of the roles and significance of space power is mature in comparison with the state of comprehension of the meaning of cyber power for future warfare.

CYBERWARFARE IS *STILL* WARFARE

The newest, at least the newest sounding, mode of warfare is cyberwar, sometimes known as information warfare. As a concept in the public market place of strategic ideas, information warfare was invented and explained by Boeing scientist Thomas P. Rona in a study in 1976: *Weapons Systems and Information Warfare.*[24] The provenance of cyberspace owes much to science fiction, but the term cyberwar was first advanced in an influential essay by John Arquilla and David Ronfeldt published in 1993. They startled the unwary with an uncompromising prediction as their title: 'Cyberwar is Coming!' More than ten years on from the appearance of that thesis, and thirty from Rona's innovative study, no one would deny that those theorists were correct. However, as usual the really important question is 'so what?' Whenever a new mode of warfare is on the horizon, or in its earliest manifestations, it is standard form for the prophet–advocates, as well as many usually sober thinkers, to proclaim that everything about war will change. The new mode of warfare usually is enabled by a dramatic new technology. At the end of the nineteenth century a revolution in land warfare was predicted to follow from the combined effects of high explosives, magazine-fed rifles, machine guns, smokeless powder, and recoilless quick-firing field artillery. A little later some believed that the apparent perfection of the torpedo, when used to arm dedicated torpedo boats and, one day, who knows, perhaps a swarm of submarines that worked reliably, would utterly revolutionize war at sea. Twenty years on, the prophets of air power proclaimed the obsolescence of land and sea forces. A quarter century later, it seemed to the most prescient of America's strategic thinkers that the appalling, sudden, appearance of atomic weapons had not merely revolutionized warfare, but rather had rendered war intolerable. Space power in its turn has not lacked for promoters. In the 1950s and 1960s, reflecting the excitement of novelty, the view that victory in space meant victory on earth gained some adherents. And now history is in the process of repeating itself over cyberspace. *Plus ça change!*

Lest we be misunderstood: each of the succession of great claims just cited was correct, *up to a point*. That is the trouble. History, certainly strategic history, is irregularly cyclical. We should not be surprised that the novelty of cyberwar is attracting the traditional bevy of over-excited theorists. Unknowingly following their strategic antecedents, these theorists claim either that the sky is falling or that the magical new capability is the key to certain victory. We have seen it all before. Readers might care to recall that a central argument, really a central premise, of this book is the insistence that the past offers by far the best, in fact the only, guide to the future. And yet again the prophet–advocates are substantially correct. Cyberwar certainly is coming. But we are not in advocacy mode here, nor primarily in descriptive either. Rather must we tackle that nagging strategist's question, 'so what?'

The first observation that needs to be registered about cyberwar, war in the fifth dimension of the 'infosphere' as David Lonsdale has called it in an outstanding study, is that under close examination its novelty begins to fade a little.[25] It is somewhat to their credit that Arquilla and Ronfeldt recognized historical antecedents to the information revolution about which they theorized. They advised that 'cyberwar refers to conducting, and preparing to conduct, military operations according to information-related principles'.[26] They discuss 'an early example of cyberwar: the Mongols' and consider 'German *blitzkrieg* doctrine' to have been 'in some ways a forerunner of cyberwar ...'.[27] It is less to their credit that, notwithstanding their appreciation of some historical continuities, they almost certainly exaggerate the potency of their invention. But such is the character of prophecy, strategic and other.

A serious difficulty with cyberwar is the rather mundane matter of uncertainty over the identity of the subject. Cyberwar obviously refers to warfare in cyberspace; bloodless electronic warfare in the struggle to deny or gain information. Plainly, cyberwarfare is all about information. Such is made clear in its alternate title, information warfare, though that clarity is something of a mask for much imprecision. The Pentagon's Office of Force Transformation, which during its brief existence was the sharpest part of the cutting edge of US official thought on future warfare, issued what amounted to a manifesto. In *Military Transformation: A Strategic Approach*, it explained what it calls the 'governing principles of a network-centric force'.[28] Network-centricity is the reigning jargon for an organization, military or civilian, that thanks to the computer is tied all together digitally with common access to information in real time. The vision of future network-centric warfare (NCW), while reasonably plausible technologically, nonetheless is disturbing in its strategic naivety. *Transformation* tells us that

> NCW is not just dependent on technology per se; it is also a function of behavior. Fundamentally it is about how wars are fought and how warfighting power is developed. During the industrial age, power came from mass. Increasingly, power tends to come from information, access, and speed. NCW will capitalize on capabilities for greater collaboration and coordination in real time, the results of which are greater speed of command, greater self-synchronization, and greater precision of desired effects. It will enable the merging of our current warfighting capabilities into a seamless, joint force that is highly agile and capable of locking-out its opponent's ability to respond to high rates of change.[29]

The leading item in what are identified as the 'new rules of information age warfare', is necessarily, the command to 'fight first for *information*

superiority.[30] NCW, enabled by an information dominance thoroughly
dependent on the proliferation of computer terminals, is open to a number
of technical caveats, if not objections. However, the technical issues are
less significant than the strategic difficulties. Not to mince words, the
current official American vision of NCW is an example of a technophilia
undisciplined by recognition of the enduring nature of war. Lieutenant
Colonel Antulio Echevarria hits the mark unerringly and mercilessly in a
brutal critique of the current official US approach to computer-dependent
warfare. He is worth quoting at some length.

> Much like its predecessor, the current American way of war focuses principally on
> defeating the enemy in battle. Its underlying concepts – a polyglot of information-
> centric theories such as network-centric warfare, rapid decisive operations, and
> shock and awe – center on 'taking down' an opponent quickly, rather than
> finding ways to apply military force in the pursuit of broader political aims.
> Moreover, the characteristics of the U.S. style of warfare, speed, jointness,
> knowledge, and precision – are better suited for strike operations than for trans-
> lating such operations into strategic successes. Defense Transformation
> concentrates primarily on developing concepts and capabilities for getting
> to the fight and for conducting combat operations once there. Similarly, the
> capabilities-based [instead of the threat-based] approach to defense planning,
> which underpins Defense Transformation, focuses chiefly on the hardware
> needed to move, shoot, and communicate across a global battlefield; in other
> words, capabilities-based planning is about winning battles – not wars – in the
> information age.[31]

The conclusion is irresistible, and scarcely surprising, that the computer,
cyber power generically, enables old strategic sins to be committed with
new machines. The result, however, is the same. We must conclude that
some of the cyber prophets are guilty of repeating an ancient sin against
all strategic experience as well as simple logic. New tools and methods of
war are confused with a fundamental change in war itself. Arquilla and
Ronfeldt have provided a perfect illustration of this error.

> Our contention is that netwar and cyberwar represent new (and related) modes
> of conflict that will be increasingly important in the future. The information

revolution implies – indeed, it assures – that a sea change is occurring in the nature of conflict and warfare.[32]

The first sentence quoted is relatively uncontentious, though it does risk exaggerating the novelty of the focus on information. The second is a complete non sequitur. The error is highlighted usefully if we substitute airwar for netwar and cyberwar. For all its novelty and great importance, over the course of a century air power has not wrought a change in the nature of conflict and warfare. The tools and agents change, along with the many contexts, but war and strategy do not change their nature. Why would cyberwar change war's nature, if air power, and even nuclear weapons, have not? For further illustration of the mistake in confusing the changing character of war with a change in its nature, which would have to mean that war becomes something else, Bruce Berkowitz begins his excellent study of *The New Face of War* with two bold, but alas erroneous, claims. 'The main message is this: the Information Revolution has fundamentally changed the nature of combat. To win wars today, you must first win the information war.'[33] It is a challenge to decide which of the two claims is the more serious fallacy. The nature of combat is, and will remain, the same in the information age as it has been in all past ages. But as Jeremy Black reminds us, 'the sameness of battle', involving 'men being willing to undergo the trial of combat', can conceal important differences.

> In practice, the understanding of loss and suffering, at both the level of ordinary soldiers and that of societies as a whole, is far more culturally conditioned than any emphasis on the sameness of battle might suggest. At its bluntest, the willingness to suffer losses varies greatly.[34]

Black omits to note that the willingness to suffer losses is always closely related to a society's perception of the importance of the stake that it has in a conflict.

In the words of the Prussian master, which we have need of repeating, 'four elements make up the climate of war: danger, exertion, uncertainty, and chance'. Information superiority should lessen the salience and effects of those elements, but it cannot eliminate them. Such superiority, when attainable, will not be a panacea, a philosopher's stone for the otherwise bewildered warrior.

Berkowitz's second claim, 'to win wars today you must first win the information war', is at the very least seriously misleading. It implies that victory in the information war should lead to victory in the war as a whole. More directly, though, it claims unambiguously that wars today cannot be won unless the war for information is won first. These are not unreasonable arguments, but they happen to be untrue. Information superiority is no guarantee of a superiority, even adequacy, of understanding of the meaning of that information, while, to adapt an old maxim, 'information sinks no ships'. Someone actually has to do it, tactically. It is one thing to have access to a relative superiority of information; it can be quite another to be able to do anything decisively effective with that data. As for Berkowitz's claim that 'wars today cannot be won unless the war for information is won first', the appropriate response is to emphasize the reminder that war and strategy have many dimensions, of which intelligence, or information, is only one.[35] Nothing in strategic history, past or present, suggests persuasively that a clear superiority of information is a prerequisite for victory. One might try to argue that the quality of information superiority enabled by the C⁴ISTAR of today and tomorrow, amounting to information dominance, has altered radically as compared with times past. There are ample grounds for scepticism, though. No measure of information dominance will compensate for low morale, poor discipline, or inappropriate or otherwise inadequate training on the part of the troops at the sharp end of war. Similarly, information dominance will not rescue a military venture that is poorly conceived strategically or incompetently commanded. Warfare is just too richly textured, too multidimensional, to be reduced to decisive resolution by information superiority.[36] Moreover, with Iraq in mind as a reminder of several important caveats, it is obvious that the very notion of information dominance, a concept iconic to many of America's more starry-eyed technophilic military transformers, is hopelessly misleading. America's military–technical transformation thus far has been keyed to an unduly technical and narrowly military understanding of the information necessary as the great enabler of victory. Events in Iraq have illustrated the relevance of the enduring truths that information, knowledge, and understanding are different. Furthermore, much of what one most needs to know about the enemy cannot be collected by technical means. For example, will he stand and fight? And, how skilful are his commanders? Information superiority, while always desirable, will not eliminate the crucial importance of factors that cannot be imaged, counted, or tracked.

For convenience and to abide by common usage, we have referred to cyberwar and cyberwarfare as if they were synonymous. In fact there is a distinction between the two that is of the utmost importance to our analysis. As war refers to a relationship or to the whole of a conflict, so warfare is the generic activity that occurs in war. Whereas cyberwarfare, together with land, sea, air, and space warfare, identifies a distinguishable dimension of the whole conflict, reference to cyberwar means, or implies, a war confined to cyberspace. Such a war is extremely unlikely, as would be a space war, a sea war, or an air war. But the novelty of cyber power has attracted speculation that whole wars might be waged in cyberspace, and won or lost in that fifth anti-geographical dimension. There is an understandable excitement and enthusiasm over exploiting cyberspace for offensive and defensive purposes. After all, one is considering nothing less than the force multiplying, properly networked, nervous system of an information-led way of war. But that technical and military enthusiasm, whether for cyberwarfare as an element in the joint forces team, or as an independent agent, has yet to spur much that is recognizable as strategic thought.

We commented earlier that a strategic theory of space power was noticeable by its absence. That observation applies no less pointedly to cyber power. To be fair, we still do not have a satisfactory theory of air power. Twenty years ago David MacIsaac wrote as follows:

> Air power, the generic term widely adapted to identify this phenomenon [the use of aircraft in war], has nonetheless yet to find a clearly defined or unchallenged place in the history of military or strategic theory. There has been no lack

of theorists, but they have had only limited influence in a field where the effects of technology and the deeds of practitioners have from the beginning played greater roles than have ideas.[37]

MacIsaac goes on to lament that, 'despite the efforts of Douhet and Mitchell [the two principal air power theorists, respectively Italian and American], neither proved to be a Mahan or a Jomini from whom the air power enthusiasts could draw the secrets of the third dimension in warfare'.[38] Since a century of experience with air power still finds this form of military power to be very much a contested realm, we should perhaps not be surprised by the strategic vacuum that matches the vacuum in which spacecraft ply their business. True to the precedents set by air and space power, the potential of the internetted computer, cyber power, currently is untroubled by serious strategic thought.

It is not unusual for military capability to precede strategic thought. That thought usually, though not invariably, catches up before long. For example, the atomic, then nuclear, revolution was at least a decade old before strategic concepts and official policy and strategy had come to terms with the new, and still rapidly evolving, technological context. In the United States, information operations, or cyberwar, today are part of the impressive empire owned by Strategic Command. Such operations, together with strategic nuclear and conventional strike options, as well as space warfare and BMD comprise a daunting menu of offensive and defensive possibilities. To date, though, officials admit freely that technology has run ahead of policy and strategy. The United States is technically capable of waging cyberwarfare, but its cyber warriors lack doctrine and strategic and policy guidance. United States Strategic Command believes in the future of information operations, but it is deeply uncertain about their effectiveness, or indeed about how that effectiveness can usefully be assessed.[39] For some years to come cyberwar will be a weapon not at all well understood by its practitioners. Of course, this should not be true of some specific cyber missions. At present, however, it is no exaggeration to say that cyberwar is a weapon that its warriors: do not fully understand; do not know how to use effectively, which is to say strategically; do not know what they will be allowed by policy to attempt; and do not know how to measure the damage they might achieve. This paragraph is not intended to read as blistering criticism. What we report here is simply the state of play in the early stages of a new form of warfare.

While it is understandable that consideration of cyber power in future warfare appears suffused by a seemingly irreducible ignorance, in point of fact we know a great deal about this fifth dimension of warfare. Of course, cyber warfare must obey its own technical grammar. In common with land, sea, air, and space power, cyber power has distinctive attributes and capabilities, strengths and vulnerabilities. Exactly what those are, or will transpire to be, only experience in future warfare can reveal. The grammar, or technical–tactical characteristics, of cyber power is unique. It is, however, scarcely more startlingly distinctive than the grammar of air power and space power. To a military profession for whom warfare was, and had always been, a two-dimensional affair, the idea of flying machines with serious military value was an all but unthinkable prospect. Half a century on, the anticipation of spacecraft in orbit, as opposed merely to passing through en route to deliver a deadly warhead, heralded a new military context with unknown features. It is useful to think of the grammar of the computer-driven fifth dimension of warfare as being entirely comparable, generically, to the unique grammar of warfare in the air, in space, and indeed on land and at sea also.

What do we know about cyberwarfare? The technical story that under-girds it is evolving more rapidly than is the ability of military organizations to procure, and learn to use profitably, the latest products of the innova-tors. Cyber power is one of those areas where technological advance is pulled forward more by what the technologists find they can do than by genuine need. That need would be a push from customers, including the military, who have jobs for new capabilities. For the purposes of this enquiry the technical details of cyber power in the future really do not much matter. It is probable, actually inevitable, that the technical basis for the information revolution will slow down. There will be limits to the rate of increase in the number of transistors that a manufacturer of microprocessors can fit on to a microchip. All technological developments, bar none, are subject to the workings of the law of diminishing returns to effort. The fact that the curve of additional performance – of computing power to size, weight, and price – is still ascending, means nothing. The computer age is still young.

To return to the important question, what do we know about cyber warfare that we can be confident will be robust in the face of relevant technical innovation of any pace? It is necessary to specify the main characteristics of cyber power. If a strategic theory for cyber power is to emerge, it will have to be constructed from appreciation of these features.

1. *Commerce rules!* The information age is led technologically by a literally global industrial pull. The cutting edge of cyber power is developed for commercial motives, as well as simply because it can be done. The technology, the hardware and most of the software, is effectively in the public commercial domain. Today, cyberwarfare probably describes the cut-throat commercial rivalries between the industrial empires of the information age, rather more than it does the use of computers for the performance of other than mundane military tasks.

2. *Bloodless warfare.* Cyberwarfare appeals to some people because, uniquely among the current five dimensions of combat, it is itself non-lethal. Now what it enables other, lethal forces to do is, naturally, another matter. So different is a non-lethal dimension of warfare that some theorists are seduced into believing the fallacy that the computer is changing the nature of warfare. It is a plausible fallacy, one must concede. Electronic warfare, my electrons against yours, producing no direct human casualties, is indeed a radical standout from what traditionally we understand by warfare. Those tempted by the heresy that the emergence of cyber power is changing war's very nature should appreciate their error when they reread, or just read, the first page of Clausewitz's masterwork. To repeat the formula yet again, he tells us that *'war is thus an act of force to compel our*

enemy to do our will'. He proceeds in a manner most apposite for this discussion, by noting that 'force to counter opposing force, equips itself with the inventions of art and science'.[40] Of course, Clausewitz had physical force in mind. However, to regard cyber power as an agent of coercion is entirely consistent with the logic of his definition. While being faithful to the theorist's meaning, it is only sensible to interpret his argument in a way that is consistent with changed material circumstances.

3. *Cyberwarfare is instant warfare.* Cyber power is exercised at the speed of light. Cyberwarfare is instant combat. Whatever the strategic purpose to which the computer is committed, the execution is immediate, always assuming that it functions as it should. The caveat is not merely decorative. Friction is ubiquitous in warfare of all kinds, certainly not to the exclusion of the high-tech wonders of cyber combat. A downside of the upside of the bloodless soft-kill effect of cyber power, is an inevitably uncertainty as to whether or not the cyber action has worked as intended. Old fashioned 'hard kills', provided they can be monitored, do not have this difficulty. Damage prediction and assessment is extremely important. Cyberwarfare poses a large problem in that respect. It is not unique, however. Biological attack also is subject to considerable difficulty of prediction and assessment. If we include political warfare within the scope of information warfare, as we should, the uncertainty of consequences can be so severe as to be a candidate showstopper. Military planners and their political masters tend to favour reliable agents of coercion and persuasion, perhaps one should say coercive persuasion. That is the reason why the nuclear option among WMD is so highly valued.

4. *Cyberwarfare is global.* At least it should be global if the computers are connected by reliable communications. We must hasten to admit that there is nothing new about global electronic communications. With the electric telegraph Britain wired the world that mattered most to it in the nineteenth century. And with the Royal Navy supreme in blue water, Britain guaranteed that it alone controlled access to the world via the submarine cables of the

telegraph. This strategic fact drove Imperial Germany to take the lead in long-distance radio technology. Notwithstanding the partial precedents of history, cyber power has a quality of globality, and instant globality at that, which is unique, characteristic, and defining. Inevitably, even unfortunately, need one add, this globality is not a gift of some quality immanent in information technology. Cyber power is global only because computer terminals are able to transmit and receive signals around the curvature of the Earth. To defeat global geography the cyber warrior requires the reliable services of terminals on vehicles in orbit. There are other ways of sending radio messages, but spacecraft have become by far the most convenient and reliable – reliable, that is, in time of peace.

5. *Cyber power is accessible to all.* Significant land power, sea power, air power, and space power all carry price tags, among other difficulties, which impose serious, not to say prohibitive, constraints on the ambitious. Cyber power appears uniquely to fracture the nexus that usually binds strategic strength to wealth of material and human assets. We must qualify this vital point, because it is not by any means as valid as it can be made to seem. What is certainly true, as well as unique about this fifth dimension of warfare, is that it is possible to enter the lists of combat and cause noteworthy harm on the basis of only a modest investment. The technologies of cyberwarfare, including many of those for cyber security, are accessible, economically, to all. The computer industry in all its facets is truly global and, to repeat, is led technologically by commercial enterprise for financial motives. This means that a state, or even a group, can equip itself at affordable cost with the technical means, and the human skills, to hurt the mighty. Nonetheless, though affordable compared with armies, navies, and air forces, substantial resources would be required for a sustained cyber assault, and the attack may fail to inflict critical damage. Even if the enemy is disrupted by cyber attack, what happens next? Cyber power is unlikely to be a reliable panacea that miraculously enables the weak to operate as giant killers. Although there are historical precedents, including some contemporary ones, for weak belligerents over-performing against great

powers, nothing quite like cyber threats has been seen before.[41] Organized and directed with the aid of state of the art information technology, 9/11 was a monstrous act of strategic genius that employed emphatically non-futuristic means. Box-cutters and passenger aircraft are not exactly frontier weapons, save in their all-important unconventionality. As always, the brain, the idea, is more important than the machine. The neglected factor of strategy is the reason for caution in assessing the implications of the global accessibility of information technology.[42] A materially hugely challenged enemy of the United States might well succeed in hacking its way into the programmes that control some element of the Critical National Infra-structure (CNI). The CNI generally is understood to comprise twelve processes.[43]

- Telecommunications
- Electricity
- Fuel supplies for transport
- Road infrastructure
- Clean water
- Fund transfers
- Postal Service
- Gas supplies
- Sanitation and waste disposal
- Fire and rescue service
- Weather information
- Rail transport

Among other possibilities, one may choose to add air and sea transport to the shortlist. The strategic question will not depart, however. So cyber attack does damage, even serious damage, to some critical pillar of modern society. So what? Strategically speaking, what goal is advanced thereby?

6. *Cyberwarfare is a joint team player or it is inconclusive.* In an effort to focus on the essentials, I have deliberately obscured some important dis-tinctions. The concept and reality of cyberwarfare covers a wide range of strategic behaviour. We know for certain, for the most mundane of sig-nificant claims, that cyber power, the use of networked computers, will be all but ubiquitous in future warfare between belligerents of all kinds, states and others. Like the aeroplane and the satellite, the computer and its host of issues is here to stay. Cyber power, its strengths and weaknesses, has joined the arsenal of war on a permanent basis. Computers, and hence

cyber power, will feature directly or indirectly in warfare at every level and of every variety. Given the most notable feature of cyberspace, its immateriality, it is highly improbable that any security community will proudly advertise itself as a Cyber Power, after the precedent of Britain's pride as a Sea Power, and – today – the United States as an, perhaps the, Air Power. There is too little that can be done with cyber power to attract its identification as being strategically defining. Cyberwarfare, certainly the use of networked computers, will figure in all aspects of belligerency. Tactical, operational, strategic, and political operations will all be assisted by cyber power, or, in the strategic and political cases, will be conducted by information technology alone. To repeat, the computer and its myriad, though severely limited, uses will be ubiquitous as a feature in warfare. That ubiquity will mirror its presence in the life of societies globally. This is not to ignore the sharp differences among societies in their degrees of computer dependency. The point is that the trend is set and, in this case at least, is unalterable.

The title to this sixth point differentiates between cyber power on the one hand as a team player in joint warfare, and the other as an independent strategic agent. Despite the catastrophe scenarios that can be written easily enough about the allegedly lethal consequences of strategic information warfare (SIW), those fictions tend to be fatally weak in at least two key respects. They assume a vulnerability of the CNI which is probably exaggerated, and they lack a convincing strategic rationale.[44] There is no doubt that much mayhem could be caused by SIW, but we must insist that the strategic question not be evaded, so what? Damage from cyber assault would be repaired, hopefully with lessons learnt. What would the cyber attacker have gained? There are no grounds for complacency, however. Some malevolent rogues in the future may be moved by locally convincing answers to the central strategic question that I keep repeating. Also we should not forget the power of the ingenious private and amateur hacker to make mischief. Hacker groups, who would not qualify as security communities, have the potential to create temporary chaos or to achieve stealthy access for fun and profit.

7. *Cyberspace and cyber power are lawless.* Currently there are no laws, rules, or norms providing governance for cyberspace. There are suggestions that with cyber power now integral to the military plans of just about every potential belligerent on Earth, it is time for cyberwarfare to figure in the laws of wars.[45] It has been suggested that measures of operational arms control might be negotiated, in order to limit the collateral damage that cyber attack all too easily could wreak. For all its apparent precision and benign non-lethality, cyber power is apt to be as blunt a strategic instrument as is economic blockade or area bombardment from altitude. Strategic Information Warfare (SIW) successfully targeted upon some elements of a country's Critical National Infrastructure (CNI) inevitably must hurt innocent and guilty alike. Because of its impact upon the general public, some true optimists suggest that SIW might be prohibited altogether. It is hoped that whether or not such a ban would prove negotiable, a global norm should be promoted, vilifying SIW as unacceptable.

In the opinion of this author, cyberspace is doomed to remain beyond the dubious benefit of regulation by international law. In addition, the prospects for creation of a cultural barrier to strategic cyberwarfare, a global taboo, are as close to zero as makes no difference. Computers are too useful, and therefore too attractive as targets, for law or custom to stand a chance of erecting constraints on their use in war. Moreover, compliance with any agreement that should prove negotiable would be utterly beyond any practical system of monitoring and verification.

8. *Cyberwarfare is warfare: Clausewitz rules!* We know that future warfare will be waged in cyberspace as well as in at least one of the other environments for war. Future warfare must be waged on land, generally for territorial goals. All warfare ultimately has to be about shaping, or physically overcoming, the will of an enemy. As often as not, that requires the presence of *'the man on the scene with the gun'*.[46] Despite its undoubted strangeness, cyberwarfare cannot alter the nature of war. The theory of war developed by Sun-tzu and Clausewitz in particular, holds for cyber power as it does for every other mode of combat. This is fortunate, because were it not so

we would need to delve into military–technical detail in the attempt to understand cyberwarfare. As it is, nearly all of the Prussian's more potent ideas, some of which admittedly he left underdeveloped, help us understand cyberwarfare as warfare.

Cyberwarfare is not a new stage in warfare, one to which Clausewitz and the classical theory of war and strategy does not apply. Its elements of novelty, as noted above, are no more challenging, possibly less, than were the new features brought to warfare by air and space power. A strong, though not uncritical advocate of cyber power as 'the new face of war', such as Bruce Berkowitz, insists that 'security in the information age depends heavily on who has "command of the nets" – that is, who has greater control over the design, manufacture, and operation of information technology'.[47] Analogies from other environments need to be employed carefully and accurately. David J. Lonsdale reminds us that 'in line with Sir Julian Corbett's theory of sea power, at the global level the infosphere will commonly remain in an uncommanded state'.[48] Later on he coins the worrying maxim that *a little information power goes a long way*'.[49] In other words, in an infosphere, or cyberspace that typically cannot be commanded reliably, enemy cyber warriors at any level of conflict might well get lucky. Recall that Clausewitz warns us that war is the realm of chance, risk, and uncertainty.

Cyber warfare is not going to deliver defeat or victory. But it is going to play an increasingly important, even literally vital, role as an enabler and force multiplier for the modes of warfare that do draw blood and break things. There will be cyber combat, with wins and losses on both sides. While it is true that acquisition of some cyber strength will empower the weak to reach out, even globally, to harass and damage the strong, that fact is not going to change the course of history.

BOTH OF THE SUBJECTS of this chapter are already integrated into military plans, indeed they have become vital enablers for those plans, although their relative immaturity leaves open many questions about the future. Is space power the key to strategic success in the future? Is cyber power? Does either have an all but magic ingredient that renders it a potential stand-alone war winner? Does cyberwarfare, with its physical restriction to electronic force only, change the very nature of war as we have always known it? There is room for argument on these matters, but we are confident in the resilience of the argument that has run through this chapter, and indeed through the book as a whole.

The emergence of space power and cyber power has to be approached as was, or should have been, the arrival of air power. None of the three transformed warfare; they added to its complexity. There are two obvious reasons why the impressive exploitation of a new geographical dimension of war repeatedly fails to be transformative. First, there is no final move in the flow of new tools of warfare. Beginning with the industrial revolution, innovation has been routinized. The greater powers support large official and commercial establishments that live by their wits, and on patronage, in producing new engines of destruction or, more accurately these days, new systems of C⁴ISTAR to enable precise destruction and decisive manoeuvre. Second, as we keep repeating, following Clausewitz, war is a duel. An American colonel has reminded us of the highly probable truth that 'our advantages in information technology are ephemeral given the cycle of advancements in that field'.[50] Amen, is our response to that warning.

There is no doubt that space power and cyber power are radically different from other forms of military power. However, they fit comfortably enough into the increasingly joint trend in warfare characteristic of recent strategic history. Space power is unique in that it continues not to be expressed in weaponry, despite its high measure of militarization. To date, there has been no pressing need to deploy weapons in orbit. Because of the great expense of lifting weight up the gravity well, and servicing and replacing assets there, it is a general rule that one only employs space power for vital duties that cannot be performed in other, more convenient and cheaper, ways. A further explanation for the absence of space weapons is normative. There is considerable political opposition to proposals to place weapons in orbit. With the exception of WMD, this is not a matter of law, but of culture. Whether or not it warrants labelling as a taboo is a matter for choice. Cyber power is distinctive, of course, in the fact of its direct, though not indirect, non-lethality. Unlike space power, however, no notable inhibitions are emerging which restrain the use of cyber power from use for offensive purposes.

After the lengthy discussions here and in the preceding chapters on the future of warfare in its several modes, it is necessary to consider the state of our armoury for the control of organized violence for political ends. What will, or might, serve to control future warfare? And how successful should we expect the forces of control to be? These are the questions to which we now turn.

PART THREE

Taming the Beast

Chapter nine

The Control of Wars

IS WAR USEFUL?

In the Introduction we stated without qualification that war and warfare will always be with us: war is a permanent feature of the human condition. That assumption and prediction is a deliberate overstatement. The occurrence of war is not akin to the law of gravity or the laws of planetary motion. Humans have choices; they have to choose to wage war. They could, and frequently do, choose otherwise. It is not sufficient to argue that war must persist for so long as security communities have interests they deem worth fighting about. That circular logic evades the crucial question, why threaten or use force? Conflict may be endemic to man's social estate, but does it need to be violent conflict? Must war persist?

This chapter brings both bad news and good news, if I may be permitted the cliché. The bad news is that there is war in our future, as there was in our past and is in our present. The good news is that both the incidence of war and the conduct of warfare can be controlled. There are those who believe that commitment to the control of war is fundamentally misguided. The problem, so it can be said, is war itself, not the manner of its conduct. It would follow that the real challenge is to prevent war, not to look for ways to civilize it. I find little merit in such an attitude. The approach favoured here is that war should be prevented when that is feasible and desirable, while it should be as controlled as, again, proves possible and desirable. I am nailing my colours to the mast with those formulas. They mean that in the author's opinion there are wars that should be waged. Furthermore, the degree of control that is sought and accepted should not be so restrictive that the political purposes of the war in question cannot be achieved. In practice, there is, at least there should be, a constant dialogue between military effort and political goals. If one accepts war as a legitimate, albeit regrettable, occasional necessity, the overriding purpose of policy cannot be to wage it in as modest a fashion as the enemy permits. If the occurrence or control of war is the centrepiece of one's policy, not only is such a policy both apolitical and astrategic, more seriously it is liable to be fatal for the national security. When rivals are nuclear armed it is entirely understandable that war prevention and, possibly, war control, should be accorded very high priority. However, even nuclear weapons serve political and strategic purposes. That is a controversial claim in some quarters, but it is stated here without apology or qualification.[1]

The assumption that the future will hold an ample measure of warfare has been one of the foundations of this text. Also, thus far, no explicit analysis has been offered on the subject of the control of war. Although we addressed the nature of war and staked out a clear position in Chapter One, at that early juncture we did not trouble the reader with a detailed consideration of war's future as a social institution. The reason was not indifference. Rather was it the reasoned conviction that the question, and hence all possible answers, is futile. Strategy is a practical endeavour, and this author is an academic strategist who sometimes works for the government. Also, this book is an exercise in policy science, which means that it seeks to explore and explain the structure of an issue; hence the attention paid in Chapter Two and here to war's contexts and complementary historical narratives. Nonetheless, it is important not to dismiss peremptorily, or even to appear so to dismiss, attitudes and theories that are not favoured here. Given the importance of the subject of future warfare, the fact that the future is certain to contain many surprises, and the author's recognition of the possibility of his being in error, some contrary views will be discussed. However, no effort will be expended in an attempt to be even-handed between what is judged to be true and what is judged to be false.

On balance, this chapter carries a positive message. It is organized so as to demonstrate how truly high ambition for the abolition or rigorously severe control of war, must prove self-defeating. Succeeding sections contrast 'grand solutions' to what some misguided, if well-intentioned, people regard as the problem of war, with approaches and measures that actually work. They will not always work, but did not Clausewitz advise that war is the realm of chance and uncertainty? We can safely extend that judgement to include pre-war periods. In the discussion of approaches to the control of war that stand a reasonable prospect of working, we will not neglect the broad church known as 'peacekeeping'. Peacekeeping can fuse with peace enforcement and, controversially perhaps, certainly paradoxically, it is plausible to regard it as a mode of warfare. After all, it does entail posing the threat and occasionally ordering the use of force for political purposes. If it is most relevant to situations that are not quite of war, but certainly are warlike, it is hardly necessary when peace reigns.

It is standard, even just common sense, while assuredly it is politically correct, to assume that the control of war is desirable. As a general rule such control can hardly be other than welcome. However, as noted already, there are occasions when peace is not desirable. Many aggressors offer an immediate cessation of hostilities, even the prospect of a far-reaching treaty of peace, once they have secured their immediate objectives. For a classic example, Britain could have had 'peace' with Nazi Germany in the summer of 1940. In fact, Hitler waited quite a while for his offer of peace and friendship to be accepted, before he was compelled to recognize that no British government headed by Winston Churchill would come to terms of any kind with his regime. A government led by Lord Halifax or Lloyd George would have been another matter altogether. War termination by agreement can be hugely challenging to effect.

In addition to the problems of ideological rancour, sacrifices already made, and a public that has been fed promises of inevitable victory, it can be all but impossible for both, or all, belligerents to want peace simultaneously and to roughly and negotiably the same degree. By and large one belliger-ent is too strong, or too weak, to favour a negotiated peace. Even when contemporary military and strategic stalemate is undeniable, one or both sides will be likely to expect to do much better in the next campaign. For example, one might be tempted to regard the many peace overtures, usually only semi-official at most, of 1914–18, as a series of lost opportunities. That reasonable thought would not be well founded. Neither side ever was able to assemble a peace offer that the other was at all likely to deem accept-able.[2] Moreover, a coalition war, as was 1914–18 on both sides, is especially difficult to conclude by agreement. There are too many diverse interests at stake, and the pressures for peace will be different from ally to ally. Needless to say, perhaps, the threat to make a separate peace, or just the ally's understandable fear that that might happen, a fear that can be fed deliberately, is integral to the political context of war. In 1914–18, France played the 'failing ally' card repeatedly and to good effect in its impact on British war-making.[3] In 1941–4, Soviet Russia proved adept at stirring deep Anglo-American anxieties by threatening to sign a separate peace. In the autumn of 1941 Stalin probably was not bluffing. However, as Simon Montefiore comments: 'Stalin was probing German resolve [7 October 1941] but there was no moment when Hitler was less likely to make peace than when Moscow appeared to be falling'.[4]

Primarily because of war's horrors, actual or by escalation more horrible still, typically there is a near universal call for a prompt cessation of hostilities. It is entirely predictable that the usual suspects who like to speak for civilized values and for that notional, shadowy virtual entity known as the international community, will appeal for the fighting to stop. Generally the appeal is issued regardless of the rights and wrongs of the case in point. Probably uniquely in history, peace is widely treated as a value.[5] War is not viewed as a bracing, socially beneficial activity in most societies today. Unfortunately, this does not mean that the relevance of Clausewitz's theory of war has gone the way of the horse cavalry. Today and in the future, short of the farther shores of eccentric Islamic opinion of the al Qaeda ilk, war is regarded universally as a misfortune, even a disaster, albeit as an occasional regrettable necessity. This is indeed an historical sea change in attitude that has evolved over the past one hundred years. The three world wars of the twentieth century contributed mightily to the delegitimization of warfare. Both the two actual and bloody ones, and the one that remained virtual but could have put the others into the shade with respect to comparative casualty and damage assessments, produced a notable change of attitude towards war. At least such a change was characteristic of the Western world. However, the continuing prevalence of organized violence around the globe shows that the process of debellicization is distinctly uneven. The desire for peace is highly contextual. Those optimists who believe that war is becoming obsolescent, even obsolete, must recognize that attitudes to peace and war are shaped by people's perception of their interests. Values follow context, they do not make it. Culture drives ethics.[6] But, in its turn, culture reflects a society's response to its circumstances, past, present, and anticipated for the future.

From the topmost rank of strategic theorists, Edward N. Luttwak wrote in 1999 with characteristic iconoclasm to advance the provocative thesis, 'Give War a Chance'. He explained as follows:

> An unpleasant truth often overlooked is that although war is a great evil, it does have a great virtue; it can resolve political conflicts and lead to peace. This can happen when all belligerents become exhausted or when one wins decisively. Either way the key is that the fighting must continue until a resolution is reached. War brings peace only after passing a culminating phase of violence.[7]

Luttwak proceeds to lament that

> Since the establishment of the United Nations and the enshrinement of great-power polities in its Security Council, however, wars among lesser powers have rarely been allowed to run their natural course. Instead, they have typically been interrupted early on, before they could burn themselves out and establish the preconditions for a lasting settlement.[8]

Luttwak's argument echoed the popular ironic writings of humorist, P. J. O'Rourke, who had published a collection of essays with the title, *Give War a Chance,* in 1992.[9] The underlying thought is ancient, but the exact modern provenance of that wording is obscure. There is more than a germ of merit in Luttwak's argument, but it does not point unerringly to an all-cases panacea. Sometimes war will be the answer to a security problem. However, just as the conduct and outcome of wars must shape the peace that follows, for good or ill, so that peace often will carry the seeds of future conflict.[10] The relationship between war and peace is complex, highly variable, and to date has, strangely enough, scarcely been studied seriously by scholars. There is an obvious sense in which eras of peace are really inter-war periods, since history is both strategic and cyclical. The popular fallacy that 'war never solves anything', sadly invites the cynical corollary, 'nor does peace'. We have to be sceptical of all such grand generalizations, while seeking the trace of gold amidst the slurry. On occasions, it is wise to allow a political conflict to be settled on the battlefield. But whether or not the verdict of blood has lasting authority and legitimacy will depend upon the quality of the peace that follows. Bear in mind that all wars are preceded by periods of peace. Logically as well as historically, the problem, or condition, of war is the product of problems with peace.

War is not akin to a disease, but neither is it the product of the evil designs of diseased minds, at least not as a general rule. Instead, war is an act of policy; it is politics pursued by violent means. And it is about power. The liberal and humanitarian impulse to bring any and all instances of warfare to the speediest possible conclusion, is as understandable as it is often misguided. Warfare is not a natural catastrophe. It is purposeful behaviour, and that purpose is to solve a problem when other policy options have failed. Admittedly, this is a somewhat idealized view. There are many instances of wars waged for purposes that fall by the wayside as the strategic context evolves under fire: Iraq versus Iran, 1980–88, for example. Also, there are cases where the human and material costs are so enormous that they dwarf into insignificance the political stakes of the struggle.

Despite the caveats just offered, two unfashionable, some would probably say immoral if not shocking, arguments have some merit. First, as noted already, some wars should be allowed to run their course. They are the expression not so much of discretionary policy choice, but rather of deep-seated political and perhaps cultural antagonism. Sometimes, such wars were better settled by blood and iron, than suspended in time by the misguided efforts of an international community that rushes in to negotiate a ceasefire, and then to police the 'peace'. Even on humanitarian grounds alone, it is not always wise for the world's peacemakers to freeze-frame a war that is far from concluded militarily. Second, if war is sometimes useful, even necessary, a truly decisive outcome is especially valuable. Wars with inconclusive outcomes, at least in the authoritative opinion of one of the belligerents, are more likely than not to be renewed in the future. Today, nearly every military action is transmittable to a global audience by a media that is in the entertainment business. As a consequence, it is unprecedentedly difficult to achieve decisive military, which is to say strategic, success, because of the ugliness of the necessary behaviour. Moreover, there are occasions when warfare needs to be conducted with exceptional, albeit legally permissible, brutality, if a decisive outcome is to be secured. History advises that a condition of lasting peace is more likely to follow a decisive victory than it is an incomplete success. A classic example of this principle on the grandest of scales, was provided by the sharp contrast between the outcomes to the First and Second World Wars. Although Imperial Germany was decisively defeated in the field in 1918, the German people, and many German soldiers, did not believe it. Round Two had several leading causes, but one among them was a politically potent German desire for revenge.

Because most wars are waged for distinctly limited political purposes, it follows as a matter of strategic logic that the effort expended also should be limited. However, the nature and dynamics of war are not to be lightly mocked by undercommitment. To adapt from Clausewitz, the logic of policy is one thing, while the grammar of war may be something else, even something apparently contradictory to the spirit and aims of policy. To repeat a familiar thought, whether policy goals are great or small, warfare is warfare. Warfare is always ugly because invariably, and by definition, it entails the exercise of violence. Whatever the higher purposes might be, warfare, tactically, is about killing people and breaking things. That is the nature of the phenomenon. The tools of war have varied extensively over millennia, but not their functions, which are to threaten and inflict damage. War is not about death and destruction, but those are inherent in its nature.

The conclusion is inescapable that war remains, and will continue to be, a useful, indeed a necessary, instrument of policy. If that were not so, then war should cease to be a problem for humankind. It would simply fade away and disappear as an activity that had become irrelevant in the contemporary world. One might object that even if war were to become not merely obsolescent, but actually obsolete, there would be many strategically ill-educated political leaders who would either resist this new fact of history, or simply fail to recognize its authority.

Unfortunately, it is an entirely safe prediction that war is going to be with us for the indefinite future. The basic reason is that its political fuel shows no signs of exhaustion. War is not about war, though there are times in lengthy struggles when the proper relationships between policy and warfare can seem to be reversed. Policy may trail in the wake of the conduct of war, with the latter dominating the former. Certainly this appeared to be the case both in the First World War and in the arms competition that was so prominent a dimension of the Cold War. In both instances, however, the political struggle was only obscured, it was not overwhelmed, at least not quite. So long as security communities, be they states or some other kind of organization, compete for political power and influence, then for so long must war retain its utility as the court of final appeal. But is that too pessimistic a prognosis? We turn now to consider some bold approaches to war that, in the opinion of their advocates, carry the promise of abolishing permanently the scourge of organized violence for political ends.

GRAND SOLUTIONS, OR VENTURES IN FUTILITY

The problem with war is that it is not a problem. In principle, at least, problems can be solved. War is a condition of political life. We can even affirm that war is endemic to the human condition. But, one must ask, why is this so? More to the point, does it have to remain so? Here and in the next section we contrast approaches to the control of war that do not work, the grand solutions, with more modest approaches that sometimes do.

The title of this chapter specifies the control of wars, not of war. War is an abstraction; wars are historical phenomena. It is not useful to devote time and effort to an endeavour to control, perhaps eliminate, war. Clausewitz's general theory of war derived from, and is constantly revalidated by, the empirical evidence of actual historical conflicts. Each war has a great deal in common with every other one, past, present, and future. But each is the product of a more or less distinctive mix of the historically common ingredients. Politics is about power and its benefits; 'who gets what, when, how', as Harold Lasswell expressed the matter.[11] It has to follow that in a necessarily Clausewitzian world, war as an instrument of politics also must be about power. This is a touch too reductionist, in that it threatens to neglect the influence of honour or dignity, but still it captures most of what most wars are about. However, recognition of the centrality of the ever contestable concept of power, though historically well attested, is not especially helpful if we are searching for a single grand solution to war approached as a single grand problem.

Theorists who ask the wrong questions are all but condemned to come up with the wrong answers. One must say 'all but', because it would not do to discount entirely the possibility of a useful serendipity. While hunting for a wholly mythical beast that by repute is king of the war-causation jungle, intrepid scholars may yet stumble upon some real creatures who play significant roles. That is, however, a rather generous concession to a fundamentally foolish enterprise. Unsurprisingly, more than eighty years of modern scholarship on the causes of war has produced nothing of high value. Much as mediaeval alchemists sought in vain for the philosopher's stone that would transmute base metal into gold, so modern alchemists for peace have sought the magical solution that would rid the world of war. So-called peace theory and peace studies are wholly without merit if they postulate the possibility, even if distant, of a world without war. A commitment to rid the world of war is mission impossible. As we observed above, the concept of war is a great abstraction. In a devastating critique of theories on the causes of war, T. C. W. Blanning observes that 'war *per se* is only the aggregate of all wars, past and present'.[12] The complexity of warfare and the many dimensions of strategy defy those aspirations for victory that rest upon highly reductionist beliefs. Similarly, the actual historical complexity and multidimensional nature of particular wars ensure that simple solutions to war regarded as an undifferentiated problem must be futile.

It may seem churlish, at best misguided, to heap scorn upon those grand theories, and their authors and advocates who seek sincerely to rid the world of the scourge of war. Nonetheless, folly is folly, no matter how pure the motive. Since the next section is constructive in identifying practical approaches to the control of war and warfare, a prior destructive analysis of impractical suggestions is both justifiable and necessary.

Blanning makes an important contextual point when he asserts that 'it is violence which is universal, not war, which is just one very specialised form of violence'.[11] Recall that for violence to be labelled as warfare it has to be organized and its primary motivation must be political. Spontaneous rioting by the politically disaffected would not earn the war badge. However, it is useful to think of warfare, perhaps as opposed to war, in the terms just quoted from Blanning. The international, and even some of the customary, law of war, necessarily draws a sharp distinction between conditions of war and of peace. Moreover, our Western culture continues to regard war and peace as alternative states. Ours is a culture that favours the drawing of clear distinctions; intellectually it inclines us to see opposites, even to look for, and construct them. Truly ours is a conceptual world that favours sharp binary alternatives. There are cultures, though, which do not privilege such deconstruction, dissection, and exclusivity, but instead inhabit a mental universe that favours inclusion, even of apparent opposites. The relevance of this light philosophical argument to our subject could hardly be more profound. Those able to accept a strategic world of both/and, rather than either/or, are on track to understand that war and politics are not succeeding phases of behaviour, but actually are one. Also, they can grasp the historical reality of war in peace and peace in war. There will be future wars which, whether or not they are formally declared and legally concluded, will have definite start and end dates. But the protracted warfare waged by and against terrorists will have no clear beginning or unambiguous conclusion. Similarly, much of the world's warfare that is principally internal to states is likely to flare up, splutter and flare up again in a distinctly irregular fashion. Warfare of these kinds is best considered on a spectrum of violence, not in the restrictive neat binary terms of either war or peace. Because we in the West have difficulty with holistic, inclusive concepts, often we are inclined to evade the intellectual challenge of 'both / and' by referring to a condition that is neither peace nor war. We would be better advised to adopt the concepts of war in peace and peace in war.

Thus far the precise meaning of peace is a question that has not been permitted to muddy the waters of the argument. Far from being a typical example of scholastic indulgence in excessive analysis, the exact meaning of peace is of central practical importance to our story. To quote the excellent Blanning yet again, a satisfactory theory of war 'must be able to explain peace as well as war'.[14] But what is peace? A book on future warfare cannot ignore future peace. Peace may not come in quite as many varieties as war, but still it is not a single condition. When we explore the prospects for peace in the future it is helpful to distinguish four meanings of a peaceful context. I will present these in ascending order of intensity.

First, there is the kind of peace that is meant in the condition of neither peace nor war. Despite so-called peace agreements and the occasional armistice, conditions in Northern Ireland approximate this state. The province is not at war, but neither is it quite at peace. Politically motivated violence still occurs, and the extant peace is ever fragile. Second, peace can refer simply to a condition of non-war, but in a context where war is a distinct possibility. The virtual belligerency of the East–West Cold War of 1947–89 may be regarded as 'the long peace',[15] or as the no less long war that never quite exploded into violence directly between two superpowers. Those years certainly were technically ones of peace in East–West and Soviet–American relations, but so perilous was the strategic context and so intense the competition, that neither side regarded itself as being truly in a condition of peace.

Third, there is the peace not of balanced power, but rather of political agreement. In common with war, unsurprisingly peace is a political condition. During the Cold War some American defence analysts and officials were wont to forget that Clausewitzian point. They tended to talk and behave as if peace was a technological and military condition. While it is always prudent to be attentive to the actual and probable military capabilities of a rival, such a concern can become excessive. It can promote the dangerous fallacy that decisions for war could hang on fine-grained calculations of net military advantage or disadvantage. Fortunately, the world is not run by professional defence analysts, but rather by politicians who are apt to be sceptical of expert briefings on how the next war can be won. In this third variant of peace, military, or strategic, balance is of much reduced significance, indeed it may lose all significance because the states in question do not have a hostile political relationship. The transition in US–Soviet / Russian political relations over the past fifteen years is a good case in point. Looking further back, the sharp transition in Anglo-French and then Anglo-Russian relations in the 1900s, from a condition of fairly cold war to political entente (short of alliance), is no less plain an example.

Finally, the fourth condition of peace is that wherein war is not merely banished for a while by formal or informal political agreement, but rather becomes all but unthinkable. This happy condition may apply not only to states' relations with particular other states, but also to the entirety of their political world. It is often noted, by critics as well as by those who approve strongly, that 'old' EU-Europe comprises a set of variably post-military societies. Not only do those societies regard war among themselves as impossible and unthinkable, they appear to have become disdainful and intolerant of warfare conducted by anyone. It is an agreeable, flattering illusion to believe that you live in a post-modern society that has outgrown war; that has discovered better ways of resolving intersocietal disputes.[16] Admittedly, this description is something of a caricature. However, it makes the point that there is the kind of condition of peace, either in actuality or in perception, wherein war has been effectively banished. Some of the countries of EU-Europe, particularly those with NATO responsibilities, still go through the motions of maintaining a military establishment, but their defence preparations, so called, are fundamentally non-serious. To all intents and purposes, those societies, in their own estimation at least, now inhabit a post-military universe. They are, and expect to remain, firmly at peace in the fullest meaning that can be ascribed to the concept.

We have risked over-analysing what many people may regard as the obvious common-sense meaning and implications of peace, because common sense is not a reliable guide to the matter. Peace does not come in a single size that fits all conditions of the absence of active hostilities. Peace can be nearly as complex a matter as war, particularly when one grasps the fact that they are, in fact, the same subject. War is about the peace that is sought by violence, and as history reveals all too clearly, winning a war is not at all automatically synonymous with winning the peace that follows. Moreover, the fuel for future war is gathered during that period of peace. Future warfare can be treated in a relatively straightforward fashion, as does the US defence community today with its process of military transformation. But the political value of such warfare for a desirable peace, leveraged as always by strategy, is vastly more difficult a subject to handle.

This text has laid stress on complexity and has asserted that war and warfare have many dimensions. Perhaps that perspective reflects a scholar's hubris.[17] Might it be that a meaningful condition of peace could be promoted successfully by some simple, though grand, solution to the blight of war? Can we short-circuit the abundance of difficulties invariably specified by so called strategic experts, who tend naturally to be professional pessimists? Might we locate what would amount to a short-cut to a much more peaceful world? This is not to set an impossible standard. What follows is a brief review of some of the major ideas, and practices, that have been regarded quite widely as bearing outstanding promise for the creation, at least encouragement, of a less war-prone world. We are not implying, let alone claiming, that the more intelligent advocates of these approaches are convinced that they have found the philosopher's stone that will turn conditions of disorder, hostility, and violence into a context of peace. The ideas and behaviours discussed below are not universally ill conceived, though some of them certainly fit that label. The problem typically is that too much is expected of them. Seven would-be grand solutions have been chosen for comment from a list that could easily be double that length.

1. *Peace by disarmament and arms control.* The theory that competitive armaments are a primary cause of war was especially popular in the aftermath of the First World War. In fact some theorists in the inter-war decades took a comprehensively apolitical view of the chain of causation and identified the true villains as those who profited from the sale of arms. In the 1920s it was fashionable to attribute the dreadful events of 1914–18 to great impersonal forces, or at least to the malign influence of extra-political and astrategic motives. The problem of war frequently was reduced to a grand challenge. Pick your panacea solution. The leading options were: the 'merchants of death' whose interests were served by the consumption of their lethal products in war; the process of competitive arming, or arms racing; secret diplomacy; and competing alliance systems. The League of Nations spent more than twelve years preparing its great disarmament conference. Alas, when finally it did meet, in 1932, the political context had changed radically. The sorry enterprise effectively was the victim of a mercy killing in 1934, following the decision by the new Nazi government of Germany to decline to continue to participate.

Peace by negotiated disarmament is a complete non-starter. That thoroughgoing negative judgement is offered here with total confidence. There are occasions when negotiated measures of disarmament may be useful, but that utility derives from the political value of the measures. With only minor exceptions, disarmament is quite useless as a broad-gauged approach to the control of war. The disarmament that does work, at least for a while, is that of a one-sided kind imposed by the victor in war. Two fundamental reasons explain the irrelevance, or worse, of disarmament and even of much of what we have come to call arms control. Some readers may be sceptical of this view. Is it plausible to assert, as here, that the large, reasonably well-funded, multinational analytical and diplomatic industry devoted to arms limitation is largely a waste of effort?

What are the two reasons that, sadly, explain the basic futility of negotiated disarmament and arms control? First, states arm because they fear that they may have to fight, they do not fight because they are armed. Second, arms control agreements are negotiable only between states that do not need such measures; the feasibility of arms control treaties rises and falls with the tension level of the international political climate. This is known as the arms control paradox. Arms control is negotiable only among states that do not need it. These simple truths are examples of inductive, not deductive, logic. The historical evidence for both of them is literally overwhelming. But since when did true believers in a manifestly good cause, or officials locked into a seemingly permanent process of negotiation, pay attention to a historical record which demonstrates that their activities are a waste of effort?

In the interest of clarity, I have risked overstating the case against disarmament and arms control. Lest some people believe that my negative view of those approaches to the control of war is a little too summary, I can point to a book I wrote more than ten years ago which enjoyed the unsubtle title, *House of Cards: Why Arms Control Must Fail.*[18]

2. *Peace by universal institutions and community.* The more serious the problem facing the human race, the more one can be certain that elementary grand solutions will be recommended, sometimes even attempted. Much as a standard response to dire domestic conditions is to throw money at the problem, so there has long been an extensive body of theorists and diplomatic practitioners whose first, second, and third, reactions to the peril of war is to construct institutions. These people are known as liberal institutionalists and they have enjoyed a lengthy period of policy pre-eminence.

There is indeed a significant role for multinational institutions; that is not contested here. What is contested, though, is the belief that such institutions, the UN primarily, of course, can play a vitally important role in the control of war. My argument is that the control of war is not much helped by the diplomatic engineering represented by a collective security institution like the UN that has an all but universal membership. There are institutions that can contribute greatly to the control of war, NATO for example, but that is a political entity of quite a different character from the UN.

Michael Howard has provided the clearest explanation of why the creation of institutions cannot in and of itself be very useful for the control of war. He is worth quoting at some length.

> The establishment of a global peaceful order thus depends on the creation of a world community sharing the characteristics that make possible domestic order, and this will require the widest possible diffusion of those characteristics by the societies that already possess them. *World order cannot be created simply by building international institutions and organizations that do not arise naturally out of the cultural disposition and historical experience of their members.* Their creation and operation require at the very least the existence of a transnational elite that not only shares the same cultural norms but can render those norms acceptable within their own societies and can where necessary persuade their colleagues to agree to the modifications necessary to make them acceptable.[19]

There we have it! States bring their political and strategic culture to institutions. Their attitudes are not transformed either by the simple act of joining a multinational body or by the experience of behaving within it. In common with the first great panacea, disarmament, discussed already, this second one in effect ignores the nature both of war and of international politics. The quest for peace through institutionalization suffers from an all-too-familiar malady. It requires that the basic problem of war should be solved before the institutional solution might work. Needless to add, my judgement is that of a sceptic.

A recent variant upon the theme of peace by institutional engineering is the proposition that the effective solution to the problem of war is the creation of ever grander security communities.[20] If societies believe that they all belong to the same security community, then it should follow that war among them becomes unthinkable. The experience of the growth of the European Union following centuries of bloody intra-European rivalry, is often cited as proof positive that the creation of security communities, perhaps even a single universal one such, is the solution we need. But, what is it that creates the necessary communitarian culture? If states participating in global institutional arrangements do not already have the appropriate 'cultural disposition and historical experience', as Howard expressed the matter, there will be no magical transformation consequential simply upon institutional membership. Theorists have a tendency to assume away the difficult problem, the need for a sense of common security community, in favour of the easy task, the creation of institutions.

In Chapter One I cited the communitarian theory of the sociologist, Amitai Etzioni, as an attractive, but alas forlorn venture. His vision deals well enough with Michael Howard's argument, at least in theory. Etzioni believes that community and its values must and can precede some approximation to world government, global governance perhaps. He argues that the communitarian project is actually further advanced than most people appreciate. For example, he maintains that, effectively, there is already global governance to combat terrorism, while such other problem areas of global domain as trade, the environment, crime, and health, are plainly being addressed by rules and values developed and maintained by some global institutions. Etzioni recognizes the strength of cultural differences, but he discerns the gradual emergence of a 'global normative synthesis' that could and should be the cultural basis for a global civil society.[21] With no little persuasiveness he argues that in the face of the global problems of the twenty-first century, the 'old system' of national governments and intergovernmental organizations is unable to cope.[22]

It is a shame that Etzioni's moral vision is fatally flawed. Unfortunately, communitarianism suffers from some lethal weaknesses, four of which in particular are worth citing.[23] First, it offers global community as a grand panacea. In fact, the theory is in dire peril of being tautological, because it can answer criticism by claiming that the growth of community and its values must enable the maturing of community. In short, it is too large an idea, too grand a narrative, to look back to our discussion in Chapter Four. As a consequence of its excessive ambition, it seriously overreaches. The sense in the theory is drowned by the grandiloquence.

Second, communitarianism poses the wrong question and, as an inevitable consequence, comes up with the wrong answer. There is no single question of global security that can be met productively by a single grand answer. Of course, a true global community, a civil society with shared values on most matters of global significance, would be the solution to the problem of human organization to address supra-state challenges. But the panacea of global community is not a real answer. So many are the security questions that states must address, and so varied are their replies, that the communitarian vision is of only modest relevance. Bluntly stated, the absence of a global community worthy of the name is not really a problem at all, rather is it a lasting condition. So the communitarians' question, which amounts to an enquiry as to how we can forge the necessary global community, is one that cannot be answered productively: it is the wrong question.

Third, communitarian theory rests upon the fallacy that future history can register a grand benign transformation in security affairs. There is nothing in our history to suggest that such a lasting transformation is possible.

Finally, Etzioni's communitarianism makes the truly heroic and unsupported assumption that struggles for power and influence among the greater states will not occur in the future. Alas, communitarianism is one of those attractive grand solutions that is literally too good to be true. As a moral vision it is compelling. But as a would-be practical design for global security it is fatally flawed.

3. *Peace through democracy.* In Washington and London, though probably not in many other locales, the theory that the spread of democracy will prove to be a universal solution to the problem of war is today a fairly sincere assumption underpinning high policy. Note that all of the grand panaceas discussed in this section assume that war is a problem that can

be solved or hugely reduced, rather than a condition to be managed, endured, and hopefully survived.

There are two overall difficulties with democratic peace theory. The first is that it is not true, at least it is not convincingly true enough. The second is that it really does not matter whether the thesis of the democratic peace is true or false. To explain the meaning of the second difficulty, there is no, as in zero, prospect that major potential belligerents will grow rapidly into the character of liberal democracies. Even if we are somewhat relaxed over the domestic features necessary for a polity to be counted in the column of democracies, democratization must run into fatal inhibitions of culture, politics, and history.

Some years ago, this author was tasked to prepare a critique of democratic peace theory. That exercise was terminated, voluntarily, when the list of weaknesses in the theory hit fifteen. In case some readers are not completely familiar with the theory in question, I will state it as economically as possible. Democratic peace theory holds that although democracies are not inherently debellicized, they do not fight each other.[24] War and peace are complex conditions that tend to be overdetermined. The historical evidence for the theory is decidedly slim, highly arguable, and not especially persuasive.[25] The theory requires us to believe that it is democracy – defined how? – that makes the difference between the likelihood of war or peace. Presumably, democratically accountable governments find it difficult to justify the sacrifices and general horrors of war. Unfortunately, there is little if any historical evidence to suggest that the domestic political arrangements of potential belligerents figure significantly in decisions for peace or war. For an ancillary point, there is no evidence, let alone convincingly overwhelming evidence, to support the theory that authoritarian regimes are more bellicose than are democracies. However, the real killer of this attractive and popular theory is the persisting reality that a very extensive swathe of the world is not, and is not about to become, home to shining examples of Western-style liberal democracy. For leading examples, China, the entire Islamic world, and the Russian Federation, are not at all likely to qualify as card-carrying liberal democracies for generations yet to come, if ever. The reason is political culture. This, having developed over centuries, or even millennia, may be shaped by religious sanction; but it is not a candidate for near instant benign revolution.

4. **Peace by ethics.** One especially appealing notion is the theory that a revolution is underway in the public acceptability of warfare. This line of thought holds that the occurrence of war and the conduct of warfare may be controlled ever more effectively by norms of acceptable international behaviour that preclude organized violence. Whether or not this delegitimization of war is expressed in treaty form, in practice it would amount to a hopefully universal taboo that would have the force of law.[26]

This bold, even radical, proposition is not quite as absurd as it may appear at first sight. Attitudes to war do change. Erstwhile bellicose states have entered an all but post-military condition. Unfortunately perhaps, this transformation – of Sweden, Germany, France, Italy, for example – is no proof of enduring ethical advance. In fact, it is not an ethical advance at all. What has altered for the post-military states of EU-Europe are their political and strategic contexts. EU-Europe anticipates no danger of interstate warfare and judges war to be a policy option irrelevant to their situation. It is but a short logical, if gigantic actual, step to argue that as, or if, more and more of the rest of the world acquires attributes that are key to the current self-satisfaction of the EU, so a condition of happy postbelligerency must diffuse also.

One need hardly emphasize the facts that attitudes to war and peace are driven by culture, and culture is shaped by context. A post-military EU may feel itself morally superior to a somewhat belligerent, self-appointed American sheriff of world order. But that misplaced European pride is totally vulnerable to a change in its external security context. To repeat the simple logic chain: ethics follow culture, which follows strategic context. One must add an obvious, truly major, qualification. Even if large areas of the world do remain in a condition of such good order that they can abjure the conduct of war, assuredly there will be other regions nowhere near attainment of that blissful state.

5. *Peace through law.* Aspirations for world peace through world law have a lengthy history. This grand idea is, and has always been, a complete non-starter, but that fact has not deterred those who confuse desirability with feasibility. People who have discerned in law the solution to humankind's war-prone condition have been obliged to ignore the vital differences between the domestic and international contexts. With respect to matters of security, none of the reasons why the law generally functions well enough within states apply to relations between them. There is no international government, equipped with an independent judiciary and an overwhelming agency of physical coercion. Instead, we find elements of what has come to be known by the slippery concept of governance. Governance refers to a context wherein there are some rules and regulations, but they fall far short of what the concept of government requires. Also there is no policing agent responsible solely to the body that approximates the international 'government'. The only such body that enjoys some legal basis for assuming responsibility for world security is the Security Council of the United Nations. The Council was designed, wisely, to avoid some of the problems that had defeated the League of Nations. The fault, if such it be, is with the nature, some would say the character, of international relations.

States are not prepared to surrender judgement on matters vital to their national security to an external authority, should there be one. No international court of justice can substitute law for politics. Moreover, international law is entirely bereft of an enforcement agency. This is not to criticize international law. That law effectively regulates most of the affairs of states by mutual consent. International law with respect to commercial, health, criminal, and environmental, topics, for some examples, is both essential and generally obeyed, albeit not without frequent legal contention. But that benign and constructive condition does not extend to the realm of national security. States insist on being the judges of their own cause.

A century ago, legal-minded idealists, as well as others who should have known better, conceived the appealing idea that the problem of war could be solved, as it were at a stroke, by the creation of a system providing for international arbitration. This would be a grand solution indeed. Rather than fighting to resolve their quarrels, states would submit their cases to an independent body for fair decision. There are many instances where an arbitration commission of one sort or another can play, and has played, an important role. Over some boundary disputes or over rival claims for financial compensation, for example, arbitration has a most useful role to play.[27] However, no country will submit its vital national interests as it defines them to judgement by an outside body. The proposition is absurd, given the nature of international politics. It follows that world peace through world law is an idea whose time most probably will never come.

6. *Peace through the inutility of war.* For a century at least the idea that war does not 'work', does not perform its task, has attracted adherents. Of recent years, the thesis that war has become obsolescent, perhaps even obsolete, has acquired almost fashionable status, at least in Europe outside the ever bellicose Balkans. There are many reasons for the declining popularity of war as an instrument of policy. Most obviously there was the grim history of the two great hot wars of the twentieth century. After 1945, many people allowed hope to father the belief that the nuclear invention had rendered war impossible, or at least impractical. More recently, the processes that now are conflated into the term globalization are held to be rendering interstate warfare both impossible, or, again, impractical and pointless. In short, for the reasons just cited, among a long list that could be presented, world peace increasingly is believed to be all but guaranteed by its inutility. States will cease to fight because fighting can solve none of their problems. War will become an anachronism, if it has not reached that point already.

There is no denying the force of this logic. Alas, though, two difficulties intrude. First, is it true? Has war ceased to perform its traditional function of solving problems that elude resolution by other less expensive methods? Second, even if war has ceased to be a practical instrument of policy for many countries and groups, is it not the case that there are, and will be, other countries and groups that continue to find war useful? One size of peace theory is unlikely to fit all. If that is true, as seems certain to be the case, the whole theory must collapse.

It is a fallacy to hold that globalization is a force for peace. The world of 1914 was extensively globalized, indeed by some measures even more extensively than it is today. Similarly, the pervasively and perennially bellicose middle and late Middle Ages in Europe were globalized in ways of commerce, culture (most especially religion), and human traffic, to a degree beyond the aspirations even of today's more ardent globalizers.[28] In neither of the important examples just cited did globalization matter one whit for the prospects for war or peace.

The attractive idea persists that war does not solve anything. This is a fallacy. However, war does not always, perhaps not even usually, solve the problem that its instigator had in mind. Many wars may indeed warrant description as exercises in futility. That granted, history shows that war is uniquely capable of achieving political decision. The decision that a war provides might well be judged in retrospect not to have been worth the effort expended, but that is a different issue. War is a blunt instrument and will remain so, no matter how precise and surgical the application of violence. As we must keep insisting, following Clausewitz, war is never a reliable instrument of policy, notwithstanding its necessity. It is the realm of chance, risk, and uncertainty. But, it is not too uncertain a policy instrument to be useful. Moreover, there is no convincing evidence to suggest that that utility either has diminished, is diminishing, or is likely to diminish in the future. Indeed, in this author's reluctant opinion, war and the threat of war will be judged widely to have an increasing utility as the twenty-first century ages.

It is not true to claim that war will atrophy or has atrophied already because it has ceased to be useful. Many states and other belligerents, especially, though not only, the losers, have wished that they had not fought particular wars. In practice, war can threaten the integrity of policy and itself be in the driver's seat. The proper Clausewitzian relationship between war and policy, with the former plainly subservient, may be reversed. So all consuming may be war's voracious appetite, that the political purpose of it all becomes a matter of little relevance to a course of military events that takes on a life of its own. In such a situation war is fought for the end of victory for its own sake. Often it is claimed that the First World War was the exemplar of a war that escaped political control. It is argued that that war began principally because no one knew how to prevent it, and because the key players did not try very hard to do so. Similarly, allegedly it continued for four and a quarter years precisely because no one knew how to end it.[29] The only end that the bloody dynamics of warfare could provide in this instance was the end of a victory attributable mainly to the exhaustion of the weaker side.

As frequently is the case with popular liberal beliefs, the thesis that war is not useful as an instrument of policy is a fallacy, albeit one that many people find highly plausible. Even the abominable Great War of 1914–18 did what great wars are supposed to do. It solved a great problem. That problem was how to prevent the German Empire upsetting the balance of power in Europe, thereby creating a mighty disorder. The probable fact that Germany instigated war in 1914 more in fear than out of ambition is really beside the point. The verdict of the battlefield was that Imperial Germany would not rule Europe and, as a consequence, would be unlikely to rule much else in the world besides. The fact that 1914–18 had to be replayed yet more painfully twenty-one years later is a sad commentary on Allied statecraft; it is not evidence of war's futility.

War is probably the single most significant engine of historical change. I hedge the claim more as a bow to some readers' susceptibilities, than out of any genuine doubt as to the veracity of my belief. Wars do effect important decisions. They tend to accelerate processes of change. Also, it must be added, they are quite reliable in the unreliability of their consequences, even when their outcomes are predictable with confidence. Should war vanish from the annals of human history, on current evidence and reasonable expectation it will not be because it has ceased to be useful to policy.

IT MAY APPEAR STRANGE, even perverse, for the major part of the discussion in this chapter on 'the control of wars' to be devoted to approaches that do not work. Surely it would be more sensible to dismiss those failures peremptorily, and then move smartly up the hill to the bright sunlit uplands where more promising approaches are to be found grazing? There are two reasons for the apparent imbalance in my analysis. First, typically it is harder to expel a false but superficially attractive idea, than it is to persuade of the virtue in a correct but either unexciting or counter-intuitive one. So, in this case the devil has had to be accorded far more than his due. Second, because the control of wars is really a simple, albeit difficult, matter, it does not require a great measure of detailed explanation. The grand intended peace therapies, some of which we have bloodied above, are hugely popular. People, even some governments, want one or more of them to be true. For the past two centuries, peace has been a condition with a normative value as definite as its precise meaning and necessary preconditions have been uncertain.

I must admit that in the discussion above I deliberately omitted from treatment two of the grander of the grand theories of peace. The reason was nothing more sinister than my negative judgement as to their practicality. Also, I harbour doubts as to their validity, but that is a different issue. The two grand approaches that purposefully have been passed by in silence are those that insist that world peace will only be assured when justice prevails universally, or, perhaps and, when all of humankind are equally blessed, or cursed, with material prosperity. Heroic panaceas are impossible to kill. They can never be implemented, so they defy disproof.

Enough of the nonsense, troublesome though its popularity can be to those who must seek and apply practical therapies to warfare. Despite the pessimism that has pervaded the discussion above, the news on the control of wars is far from all bad.

HOW ARE WARS CONTROLLED? TREATMENTS THAT WORK (SOMETIMES)
Because both peace and the control of behaviour in war have normative value, it is not always easy to consider them in their full and proper contexts.

Neither peace nor the control of war have integrity as subjects. Although they are valued highly, they have to be considered in relation to their political and strategic contexts. If the false choice is posed with brutal reductionism between war and peace, the preference of course must be for peace. From time to time, though, there will be aberrant and abhorrent states or groups for whom peace holds no attractions (al Qaeda, for a contemporary example). Similarly, if the issue is reduced absurdly to the control or absence of control of war, the elementary choice makes itself. In the real world, however, the choice is never so simple. Security communities, states and others, do not select peace or the control of war as policy goals. The peace they seek will be one that is compatible at the minimum with their definition of the vital requirements of their security. Save when under extreme duress, polities do not sign on for peace at any price. As for the control of war, one needs to remember the basic point that wars are not waged, absurdly, for the purpose of their control. Wars are conducted to achieve political goals, and military behaviour is guided by strategy so that means and end are about the same enterprise. Given the difficulty of doing that successfully, at the highest level war is conducted by a process of dialogue between policy and military instrument.

A near fatal problem with much of the 'peace' and disarmament literature, is that it is founded on a wholly inadequate grasp of the subject of war. This is a classic case of asking the wrong questions and as a consequence, necessarily, deriving irrelevant, or worse, answers. To many people, peace is a value; it is a moral issue. I have no quarrel with that perspective, provided it is private and is not permitted to distort public discourse on public policy. The world politics of the twenty-first century, as in all centuries past, will not be conducted by leaders whose moral valuation of peace or the control of war's conduct will override all other values. Statecraft is not a morality tale. It never has been and there is no good reason to anticipate such a dramatic shift occurring in the near future.

Nearly everyone, everywhere, favours peace over war, and the control of warfare over its opposite. But to make that banal claim is to say nothing whatever of much value, because approval of peace and control invariably is conditional on the terms. There will be occasions in the future, as in the past, when peace, meaning simply the absence of war, is not available on acceptable terms. An aggressor will be eager to make peace once it has secured its prize. In every war there is a potential conflict between control and achievement. If a state attaches great value to the control of the violence, it may well discover that the price it pays is defeat. The enemy may wage its war in a less inhibited fashion. Because of fear of Chinese intervention, and the possible implications of that unwanted development for Soviet behaviour under the terms of their mutual security treaty with Beijing, the United States was extraordinarily circumspect in its approach to the military escalation of the war in Vietnam.[30] Belligerents, actual or would-be, have to ask themselves how the value of controlling warfare for its limitation compares with the values at stake in the conflict. Quite often the probable and possible price of war is just not worth the interests at issue. If a state cares more about limiting a conflict than winning, it follows that that is a conflict it should not be waging at all.

Every war is unique, even though each has the same essential nature. We have argued already that general theory on the causes of war and peace are entirely useless. All wars and periods of peace are distinctive, despite their common natures. We can explore the nature of war with Clausewitz as our competent guide. The nature of peace is more difficult and has yet to receive satisfactory theoretical attention. Plausibly, war and peace make sense only in relation to each other. Indeed, each has meaning only with reference to what it is not. War theory, if I may express it thus, explains the permanent structure of the subject, it does not, at least it should not, attempt to venture into the controversial zone of policy prescription. Because much of our peace literature is morally motivated by people strongly committed to peace as a value, virtually all of it requires an intellectual health warning sticker. The authors are sincere, but should not be trusted. Scholars morally energized to study peace find it next to impossible to give war its due. After all, they have already decided that war is the enemy: it is literally evil, ethically unacceptable save, possibly, in the most extreme circumstances of necessity.

359

Peace and the control of such warfare as does occur are indeed important values. However, they are values that cannot be promoted directly. By analogy, one cannot seek love, or security, as initial objectives. Both are the consequences of enabling conditions and behaviour. So it is with peace and the control of war. They can and should be valued highly and pursued, but only in the contexts from which they must derive. Time and again in this book we have risked readers' patience by insisting upon the critical significance of context. To the abstract mind, 'peace' and 'control' will appear as free-floating desiderata. But to responsible policy-makers and military professionals they always have a historical context that gives them specific contemporary meaning. In 1917, every belligerent in the Great War favoured peace. The trouble was that the particular terms of the notions of a tolerable peace held in the rival capitals were fundamentally incompatible. Whose peace would be adopted? In and of itself, a sincere wish for peace is likely to be valueless. This is not to deny that there are times when a leader's conviction that peace is contrary to his country's, or causes's best interests, does ensure a continuation of hostilities. For example, the Ayatollah Khomeini believed that prolongation of the war with Iraq (1980–88) was beneficial for the consolidation of his revolution. That conviction of the Supreme Leader foredoomed to futility any and all peace initiatives until he changed his mind in July 1988. Unfortunately, a sincere wish for war is more potent than is a sincere wish for peace. Alas, the former trumps the latter. In 1939, even in 1938, Hitler truly wanted war.[31] That was a desire which the international community of the late 1930s was not well equipped to deny him.

There is extant no grand theory of peace or for the control of war. However, for all the lack of powerful theory with an extensive reach, the historical record provides unambiguous evidence for the success of no fewer than six factors in achieving control, some control at least, over warfare. If that is good news, even better tidings lurk in the nature of those factors. What I cite and outline are not patent approaches to the occurrence and conduct of war that I favour personally. Readers are not invited to sign on for some bold alleged solutions to the admittedly major difficulties of war control. Instead, my argument is literally existential. The six factors simply are extant. They derive from the permanent nature, not the evolving character, of war, and also from its permanent generic contexts. Lest anyone is in danger of being over-persuaded by my positive prose, it is necessary to add the caveat that although these factors serve to control war, they do not do so to reliably agreeable conclusions. However, nor does anything else, not excluding the six grand designs presented earlier.

Because war is an instrument of policy, its control has always been treated as a vital necessity. After all, it is an expensive, albeit sometimes profitable and enjoyable, activity conducted purposefully to secure certain ends. War is controllable and, as a very general rule, it has always been controlled. Casual references to war escaping control tend to be either mere hyperbole, or imply a context that has ceased to be one of war. So, how is war controlled? More to the point for the focus of this enquiry, how will war be controlled in the future?

1. COST

First, paradoxically perhaps, war and warfare is self-controlling because of its cost. War may be a political instrument, but its nature requires the expenditure of scarce resources by both sides. Fred Charles Iklé chose *Every War Must End* as the title to his classic historical study of war termination.[32] War is an exhausting enterprise. Typically it lasts longer and costs more than the instigator anticipated. Political enthusiasm for hostilities certainly can be spurred on by the sunk costs of casualties and other forms of sacrifice, but generally speaking growing appreciation of the ever grimmer realities of the price of war dampen the commitment to more, and yet more, war. As a process of mutual multidimensional impoverishment, any war that does not yield a prompt and decisive victory is likely to be subject to control for reasons of the most obvious self-interest of the belligerents.

There is another, far more controversial, sense in which war can be a self-controlling phenomenon. Thinking cyclically, one may argue that war leads to peace. It is respectable to argue that decisive victories in wars great and small tend to promote long periods of subsequent, consequential, peace. Since war is about peace (in most cultures at least it is not a self-validating behaviour), it is scarcely shocking to advance the thesis that the road to a lasting peace tends to be driven via decisive, preferably very bloody, victory. Above all else, thinking of Germany in the aftermath of the First World War, the defeated side needs both to know that it has been defeated decisively and to accept that as a historical fact, however unwelcome. The thesis that war leads to peace is a contested one. It has some merit, but obviously it invites exploitation by the unscrupulous.

2. POLICY

Second, in their quest for wonder drugs to treat the malady of war, scholars can miss the glaringly obvious. By far the most effective agent controlling war and warfare is nothing more exotic than policy and the self-interest that it expresses and pursues. War is not only an eruption of primordial violence, an explosion of organized murderous behaviour. In addition, as the master wrote, and as we have quoted several times before, 'war is thus an act of force to compel our enemy to do our will'. Clausewitz tells us that 'the political object – the original motive for the war – will thus determine both the military objective to be reached and the amount of effort it requires'.[33] He argues further that 'generally speaking, a military objective that matches the political object in scale will, if the latter is reduced, be reduced in proportion; this will be all the more so as the political object increases its predominance'.[34] Policy is a content-neutral concept. The fact that it should control the outbreak and conduct of war tells us nothing whatsoever about its scope and character. A strategic bid for world hegemony, if not outright conquest, would need to be well controlled by policy lest pursuit of the immoderate goal should bankrupt the ambitious state or coalition long before decisive victory was anywhere in sight. If policy is moderate in its aims, has resort to force only in exceptional circumstances, and determines to use war as an instrument strictly on the smallest scale compatible with tolerable political success, then one could talk normatively of war being controlled. In practice, since war is a duel, the scope, scale, and character of violence cannot be determined unilaterally.

Furthermore, because war has a grammar of its own, aside from the political logic of policy,[15] its dynamics may drive military events rather more insistently than does the will or the goal of the policymaker. Nonetheless, war is an instrument of policy and by and large is controlled by it.

The question, 'who controls whom' in the conduct of war, does not admit of a simple answer, except as a matter of principle. There is no dispute over the theoretical primacy of policy and policymaker in relation to the military instrument. In practice, though, different cultures and changing historical contexts can ignite, or re-ignite, ancient difficulties in civil–military relations. To cite just one recent example, in the summer of 2002 Eliot Cohen argued in his major study of *Supreme Command* that war is much too important to be left to the generals.[16] Political leaders need to assert themselves over the military conduct of war if they are to be certain that war will be waged as vigorously as policy requires. But by 2005, two years on from the Anglo-American victory over Iraq's regular armed forces, it has become fashionable to claim that war is too important to be left to the politicians. In extreme form, this claim may be registered with a medical analogy. It is argued that just as a person with a brain tumour is obliged to trust his expert brain surgeon, so a society at war should be obliged to take the military advice of its military experts. The contemporary popularity of this view is very much a reflection of the historical political context. The opinion has grown that American strategic behaviour in Iraq has been driven unduly by the wishes of policymakers, and too little by those who are licensed as professionals in the management of violence. As with so much else about war and its conduct, the key to understanding lies mainly in the context. I should hasten to add that a major problem in Iraq has been the unreadiness of both American civilians and soldiers to cope with an insurgency. Neither grasped in advance the character of war upon which they were embarking, beyond, that is, the easy achievement of regime change.

3. STRATEGY

Third, braving changes of circularity of reasoning, war is controlled by strategy. There are those who believe that strategy does not rule in war.

Some go so far as to argue that war inherently is so chaotic and non-linear, that aspirations for its control by strategy, or anything else other than chance, are pure vanity.[37] I do not accept that war necessarily is chaotic, but I do grant that the battlespace, battlefield in 'old-speak', generally appears to be so. The ironic counter-intuitive bumper sticker, 'chaos rules', captures nicely the heart of the argument sceptical of the influence of strategy. As I have explained elsewhere, strategy is hard to do well.[38] Moreover, some countries seem hardly to 'do' strategy at all. The United States provides the leading example of a country that rarely 'does' strategy. The US defence community produces many books and studies, and holds many conferences, in praise of strategy. But in practice it is the American habit to fight tactically, and now operationally as well, not to fight strategically. That is to say, force is applied, but with scant political direction. Strategy is about threatening or applying force purposefully for the ends set by policy. In performing that duty when it is invited to the feast, strategy is the vital controller of military behaviour.[39] It should determine how much force to employ, as well as how to employ it. As with policy, strategy is value-neutral. In support of an expansive, ambitious policy, strategy too must be expansive and ambitious. Strategy should always control the course of warfare. Even states that either fail to comprehend strategy, or persist beyond remedial education in flouting strategic lore, will find that their military behaviour has strategic effect.

Strategy may be designed explicitly for the purpose of dissuasion and deterrence. In those cases undoubtedly it aims at the control of war. The degree to which strategy actually controls warfare must vary with local circumstance, principally of a cultural kind.

4. POWER

Fourth, war is controlled by power, just as it is always about relative power whatever the precise historical details may be. The control exercised by power can be achieved by a balance of the same, or by a gross imbalance. At the present time, viewed normatively, there is no global balance of power, unless one chooses to regard American military hegemony as just one state on the spectrum of possible power relationships. US activism in the role of global sheriff naturally attracts hostility that motivates self-defined enemies of the superstate to express themselves belligerently, if carefully. On the whole, a massive imbalance of power, especially one that favours a satisfied polity, operates as an effective control upon the outbreak and, if need be, the conduct of war. For so long as the United States is decisively superior militarily over all rivals, assessed singly or collectively, major inter-state war will be well controlled. No would-be rival will dare challenge the American superpower to trial by regular combat, because defeat must be their reward for such folly. Moreover, even in the wars that occur which do not engage the United States, at least initially, local recognition of the possibility of US intervention will likely have a dampening, controlling effect upon the course of strategic events. It may be unnecessary to mention that the value of unbalanced power for international order, justice, security, and peace depends non-trivially upon the identity of the society and the content of its culture that provides the unbalanced power of the period. A mature, even distinctly ageing, Nazi Germany might have survived and prospered so as to enter this new century as the contemporary realization of unbalanced power. I am not oblivious to the cultural fact that the American superpower is not entirely a satisfied, status quo polity. It is an ideological power, sometimes prone to attempt to spread its values forcibly.

5. FEAR

Fifth, it is worth mentioning the role of fear as a factor that can help control the occurrence and conduct of war. In a nuclear age, which means every age after 1945, the fear of escalation to nuclear use, or of intervention by a nuclear-armed associate, plays a positive role in the discouragement of expansive military behaviour. This discouragement is far from complete and reliable, however. Deterrence, even nuclear deterrence, is inherently unreliable. Leaders may decide that they are not deterred, whether or not they should be. Deterrence works on and through the mind of the policy-maker, not on his ability to act belligerently.[40]

Because war is always a roll of the dice, a leap in the dark, it is controlled to a highly uncertain and unpredictable degree by policymakers' fear of both the known and the unknown. As a prominent phenomenon in the world of chance, war will be unattractive to risk-averse politicians acting on behalf of a risk-averse culture. But not all politicians are risk-averse, and not all cultures take primary counsel of their fears when they confront perilous choices. There is no doubt, though, that the nuclear invention and its slow diffusion in weaponry and ideas among national military establishments, has raised the threshold of political antagonism that produces military hostilities. With respect to nuclear dangers, defence professionals in both superpowers worried perpetually about the details, extant and anticipated, of strategic advantage and disadvantage; such, after all, was their job. But, one can claim with high confidence that to the unknowable extent to which nuclear deterrence did function during the Cold War, policymakers were far more impressed by a simple generic bracket of the known and unknown. To explain: they knew that nuclear war must be a terrible event, one literally without historical precedent in degree of awfulness. But, they did not know what such a war would be like, beyond the fact that it would be catastrophic; neither did they know what their world would be like following such a conflict, if indeed that world survived in any meaningful sense. Fear is a potent agent of control. However, it is not at all reliable. Psychologically unstable leaders, desperate policymakers who choose to take counsel of their hopes rather than their fears, and the perennial malign influence of friction, may all, singly or ensemble, frustrate the benefits of fear for the control of war.

6. CULTURE

Sixth and finally, culture can have a dominant effect for good or ill upon the character of warfare, especially its intensity. For example, although there were potent practical reasons for European warfare in the eighteenth century to be waged with great restraint, it was also the case that such a style was in keeping with 'the spirit of the age'. The civilized Europe of the Enlightenment naturally conducted its wars in Europe in a civilized manner, insofar as that was possible. The social context of warfare includes an intellectual dimension. When European polities became more and more national in kind, and the people assumed importance both as combatants and as stakeholders in the outcome of war, a far more vigorous style in warfare was mandated.

Some scholars repose great hope in the cultural dimension of conflict, believing that warfare can be controlled and perhaps eventually even eliminated should public attitudes shift decisively against belligerency as a legitimate policy option. Recall the discussion of a possible nuclear taboo. Also consider the issue of whether the recent explosion of a global media, with its ability to reveal some of the horrors of war in real-time, is changing public perceptions of war as an acceptable way for societies to settle their differences.

As we have emphasized much earlier, culture is as important as it is difficult to employ as a reliable aid to understanding. There is no doubt that the attitudes, habits of minds, beliefs, and behavioural patterns that we mean by culture, are significant factors in war and warfare. However, culture is not an autonomous, extra-contextual factor. It is the product of historical experience, actual and legendary, and its influence on events is filtered through policy and strategic lenses that must be attentive to each element in the Thucydidean triptych. That triptych specifies not only culture, honour in the original, but also fear and interest. In practice, culture is shaped by the perception of events and their local implications, and is capable of encouraging a range of styles in national strategic behaviour, depending on the circumstances. That range will vary from society to society at any one time, but over a longer period culture has to be viewed as a variable. It can be a powerful force for restraint in warfare or it can encourage the utmost in ferocity. Whether or not culture will function notably to help debellicize societies in the future is a question that cannot be answered. But, given what we anticipate to be the general character of the relevant future, 'another bloody century' to coin a phrase, there is good reason to expect the cultural dimension to war and warfare to play a role that on balance is permissive of belligerency.

There is an endemic indeterminacy of cause and effect in the relationship between culture and war. Does a polity's decision to fight, and the subsequent military behaviour, stimulate a belligerent cultural response? Or does culture drive policy choice and style in warfare? The most that we can assert with some confidence is that public attitudes are not wholly malleable on short order by the influence of evolving events. Moreover, policymakers and citizens will share a common culture, with its assumptions, aspirations, and attitudes towards violence. The legitimacy of the resort to force, and the acceptability of certain kinds of violence (e.g., poison gas, nuclear weapons), will be cultural variables of importance. That granted, still we must insist that perceived necessity of reason of state is certain to override cultural misgivings or even hostility. Culture can function to limit or to expand the beastliness of war. It is an equal opportunity factor.

THERE IS NO DENYING the absence from this lengthy chapter of a dominant theory of peace and the control of war. This is not a case of failure of the imagination, of historical research, or of methodology. Rather is it just a reflection of historical experience. Whereas the main body of the analysis above was devoted to the essentially negative task of wreaking fatal damage upon some of the leading grand designs for a more peaceful world, the final act in this drama was distinctly constructive in tone and content. Alas, it was not able to offer even a highly contingent promise of the reliable control of war. The absence of such a promise was not evidence of a lack of intellectual and moral courage on the part of the author, but rather his understanding of the persistence of real-world constraints. In much the same way that I believe the scholars of strategic studies are also contributors to peace studies, so I find that the control of war is essential and necessary practical behaviour integral to the regular practice of statecraft and strategy. They may appear mundane and unimpressive, but the six factors advanced here as potent contributors to the control of war have a long history of success, albeit admittedly of failure also. Expressed tersely, we have argued that war is controlled, imperfectly and unreliably, by: the nature of war itself; policy and the self-interest it expresses; strategy; an imbalance of power in favour of a generally satisfied polity or coalition; fear; and, sometimes, culture. It would be agreeable to be able to reveal to a startled yet admiring public some novel approach to what many people misunderstand as the problem of war. That is not possible. War is a condition of humankind in somewhat rival societies, and will yield neither to scholarly ingenuity nor to moral outrage.

Conclusions

A Warlike Future:
The Long-running Story

COPING WITH IGNORANCE

Warfare is warfare, period. To write a book about future warfare is to risk implying that the subject has a distinctiveness, a unique integrity, that really it does not enjoy. Future warfare is distinctive only in the admittedly important sense that it has yet to happen. Aside from that non-trivial point, the subject is warfare, in this case warfare in the future. Because of its inescapably speculative nature, future warfare poses a severe challenge to the scholar. It cannot be researched, documented, illustrated with exciting maps, or indeed have its mysteries revealed conclusively. There is an obvious sense in which the standard scholarly impedimenta of extensive and discursive footnoting would be inappropriate and possibly even downright misleading. The future, of warfare or anything else, cannot be referenced directly. It has not happened. To give evidence of great scholarship, at least of mighty scholarly industry, might suggest to the unwary that such a worthy display of knowledge means a mastery of the topic of future warfare. Such mastery as we can obtain must derive from the study of history. After all, history is the only evidence available; but, evidence of what? Since history does not repeat itself in detail, and the character of warfare is ever liable to change, what value can there be in rooting around in the past? The best answer has been provided by the maritime historian Geoffrey Till, who advises that 'the chief utility of history for the analysis of present and future lies in its ability, not to point out lessons, but to isolate things that need thinking about ... History provides insights and questions, not answers'.[1] A good grasp of history will tell us what the future could bring, but there is no denying that history warns, rather unsportingly, that major surprises occur. Furthermore, because humans are active historical players, their beliefs about the future can function either as self-fulfilling or self-negating prophesies. The future is not 'out there', fixed, just waiting for the passage of time to see it unfold. Instead, the future remains to be made, to be constructed by people, including by people in conflict who will strive to make a future that they prefer.

The frustrations of the scholar who ventures upon the mission impossible of finding reliable knowledge about future warfare, are as nothing compared with the dilemmas that face the world's official defence planners and those who must provide them with policy guidance. The acute problems that an author confronts in attempting a book such as this are not by any means strictly an academic quandary. Those whom we entrust with our national security, who also, we hope, worry about the wider issues of international security, are in exactly the same position of essential ignorance as the scholar. There is a key difference between their situations, though. The scholar can avoid reaching a conclusion, and will move on to write his or her next book on a more researchable topic. In contrast, officials are required to pretend that they understand the future well enough to justify their claims for many billions from the public purse. Moreover, if officials guess wrongly about the future in the answers they provide to big questions, there could be dire practical consequences.

Readers who begin to read a book on future warfare are embarking on a speculative voyage. Fortunately, there are one or two useful maps to aid navigation, even though they can provide only general guidance. We happen to know a great deal about the nature of future warfare, because it will be unchanged, and unchanging, from past and present warfare. This is why

the general theory of war advanced by Carl von Clausewitz in his unfinished masterpiece, *On War*, retains its authority. Together with Thucydides
and Sun-tzu, Clausewitz tells us most of what we need to know about the
nature of war. Indeed, it is only a slight exaggeration to claim that what
those three theorists did not say about war and the statecraft bearing upon
it – in Thucydides and Sun-tzu for the latter – is not worth saying.

Studies of future warfare typically have a brief shelf-life. Since the
subject literally cannot be studied – after all, it does not exist! – the argument
is all but certain to reduce to an exposition of the concerns, beliefs, and
perspectives of the time of writing. How could it be otherwise? An answer,
a partial one at least, is to adopt the approach taken in this enquiry, and
strive to take a long, well longer, view than that which necessarily consumes
most of the efforts of policymakers. They are obliged to try to chart a
course as safely as they are able through the unknown country of the future,
bound they know not where. The scholar can sympathize, and should try
to help, but his or her mission is different. To be specific, in this study I
have sought to explain the structure of what we may regard collectively as
the problem or condition of future warfare. Wisely, Clausewitz offered
education rather than practical advice.[2] The latter can be deduced from
the former but unlike his distinguished and much longer living contemporary, the Baron Antoine Henri de Jomini, he did not provide a checklist,
or formula, for winning in future warfare.[3] What worked exceedingly well
for the great Prussian assuredly can serve adequately for this theorist. The
challenge is to present a study of future warfare that, first, is not instantly
dated by its discussion of the issues of the moment, albeit issues projected
some modest distance into the future. Second, the study has to avoid the
opposite sin of performing at such an Olympian level of detachment from
real-world detail as to amount to little more than pontifical, high-flown
banality. Readers must decide whether or not we have succeeded in navi-
gating successfully between the rock of inappropriate contemporaneity
and the hard place of vacuous generality.

Because the subject of future warfare is not only a long-running story,
but truly a story without end, there is a sense in which it is rather bizarre to

offer conclusions. On the historical evidence we must conclude that warfare, even strategic history writ large, is a story without a conclusion. That said, undaunted, we will bring this distinctly lengthy study to an end, if perhaps not strictly to a conclusion, by returning the analysis to the intellectual framework that was outlined as its starting point. The Introduction announced boldly that the discussion would be pervaded by the influence of five themes: continuity and discontinuity in strategic history; the roles of politics and technology in shaping the character of warfare; symmetrical versus asymmetrical styles in conflict; shifting relations among the expanding range of geographically specialized forms of military power; and the importance of the human dimension. Next the Introduction proceeded to itemize seven broad propositions, working assumptions perhaps, which collectively would comprise 'the argument' of the study as a whole. We will now bring this enquiry full circle. Those themes, and especially the seven items that make up the argument, will be considered in the light of the analysis pursued topic by topic and chapter by chapter. This explicit treatment of the book's working assumptions serves as the conclusion to this immodest enterprise.

THEMES

Before tackling head-on the seven-pointed collective argument that was proclaimed so fearlessly in the Introduction, it is important first to recognize the importance for the whole of this enquiry of the five major themes that were restated immediately above.

First, continuity and discontinuity is a compelling concern for the study of future warfare. What changes, and what does not? What can be learnt from the past, and, again, what cannot? Even if one can learn from history, is what is on offer very useful? For example, strategic history provides rich pickings for those who need to understand the terrorist mode of irregular warfare. But, there is no historical precedent for a religiously motivated terrorist organization with apocalyptic goals acquiring the technical means to inflict casualties in tens or hundreds of thousands; some would say millions. As Geoffrey Till quips, 'strategic thinking needs to keep up with technology in order to avoid being overwhelmed by it'.[4] The study of history cannot provide lessons or principles of the kind that would make up a manual for future action. As a consequence, much of the Anglo-American defence community is disinclined to regard it as anything other than an agreeable diversion from serious matters of policy and defence planning. This is unfortunate. In fact it is a grave error. It is, however, easily understandable, if not forgivable. Many of our public servants choose to face the future on what they regard as its own unique terms, and not in the context of previous experience; experience, that is, other than their own.

Second, the entirety of this enquiry has been about politics and technology. Since war, to be war, has to have political meaning, that theme is inescapable. As we emphasize below, the political context is by far the single most important factor in promoting or restraining the outbreak and conduct of war. Far too much of the literature produced by those who can fairly be labelled defence professionals, seeks to minimize the political dimension. For a prominent and timely example, a large fraction of the output of what elsewhere I have called, rather pejoratively, 'the (anti-)proliferation industry', is almost wholly technical and administrative in character.[5] Technical experts on the challenge of WMD proliferation are all too apt to focus contentedly and virtuously upon the technical issues. They treat proliferation as a supply side problem. How do we, in the West, discourage, inhibit, or prevent others from being supplied with weapons of mass destruction? This technical and rather apolitical focus is, of course, necessary. But, so also is an understanding of the demand side of WMD proliferation. Could it be that in some cases the diffusion of WMD are rational and reasonable responses to genuine national security concerns?

No study of future warfare can avoid adopting technology as a pervasive theme. Not only is ours a technological age, but the leading, indeed the hegemonic, power of this era has a long-standing love affair with technology. Time and again, with reference to topic after topic, we have argued that technology is only one dimension of warfare, and at that not the most important. The library of military history, especially the library of studies of future military history, is packed with works that all but treat the history of military, and military relevant, technology as synonymous with the history of warfare. This is a serious mistake. In Chapter Four, which outlined and discussed some alternative grand narratives of strategic history, we sought to discipline undue analytical enthusiasm for the 'toys' with which war is waged. That was probably a hopeless task.

Third, the very nature of the subject of war, the fact that it is a duel, compels respect for the pervasive influence of contrasting styles in warfare. No pair of belligerents are ever identical, while many will differ markedly in political purposes, capabilities, and culture. Every dimension of future warfare considered in these chapters has to be approached from the perspective of possible combatants who must strive to exploit the ways in which they are different – the common-sense meaning of asymmetry – in order to offset their weaknesses. WMD and terrorism, for only the most obvious of examples, today are the weapons of the materially weak. The strength of the superpower sheriff of world order in all forms of regular conventional warfare, leaves its adversaries with little practical choice other than to seek compensation at one or both of the two extremes of the combat spectrum: terrorism or WMD.

Fourth, the relative significance of the different kinds of military power has been a theme in this discussion, albeit one that generally we have chosen to treat more as a background than as a driving matter. The reason for this apparent reticence is the conviction that warfare is a joint, even an integrated, enterprise. It is our conviction that its past, present, and future is not usefully to be understood from the perspective of the rise and fall of a succession of allegedly 'dominant weapons'.[6] Nonetheless, the last century has witnessed the historically extraordinary expansion of geographically distinctive forms of military power. We now can have warfare in no fewer than five dimensions; land, sea, air, space, and cyberspace. The twentieth century did see the rise, and further rise, in the potency of air power. Victory in future warfare, in the guesstimate of many technical enthusiasts, belongs to the powers that will 'command the nets'.[7] Information has always been a crucial asset in warfare. But does the transformation of armed forces by the full exploitation of state of the art IT carry the credible promise of all but guaranteeing military, strategic, and political success? I think not. However, the dominant view in Washington today does not agree with me.

Fifth, the last theme is the overwhelming significance of the human element: people matter most. This seemingly unremarkable proposition is universally acknowledged to be true, but in practice is denied pervasively. Defence analysts are drawn to metrics that compute, and human behaviour is notoriously difficult to subject to accurate computation. One of the many glories of Clausewitz's theory of war is its insistence upon the primacy of moral factors. Many analysts and officials do not want to be told that military prowess and strategic effectiveness is more a matter of will and skill, than it is of machines and numbers.[8] Every topic treated in this book has a vital human dimension. If the discussion sometimes failed to convey that fact, if it appeared to reduce to mere technicalities, then it was much at fault. To risk stating a truth that is as blindingly obvious as it is of the utmost significance, the human element is the greatest of continuities in the long bloody history of warfare.

THE ARGUMENT

For all the diversity of topics treated above, a master argument, expressing a definite attitude, has provided an essential unity to the story. The narrative trajectory began with a warning about the perils of prediction, and discussion of the nature of war and the much contested question of the continuities and discontinuities of history (Chapter One). Next, we insisted upon the vital importance of war's several contexts, primarily the political, social, and cultural (Chapter Two). Chapter Three tackled war's ever-dynamic technological dimension, striving to dampen undue enthusiasm for the military, strategic, and political rewards of new machines. In Chapter Four we sought to convey a broad, nuanced, and complex view of the course of strategic history. We suggested that there are many different ways in which that history can be organized and deployed to help explain what happened and why. Overall, though, we were sceptical of the merit in very grand narratives. Chapters Five and Six, the core of this work, addressed nearly all forms of future warfare under the decidedly inclusive banners of regular and irregular warfare respectively. Relatively recent, new, and in some cases especially troublesome weaponry and modes of warfare were described and analysed in Chapters Seven and Eight. We considered the diverse character of WMD and the problems that they pose to both user and victim. Next we discussed the future of warfare in and from space, which is to say in and from Earth, and just possibly Lunar, orbit. That chapter, number eight, also ventured into the unexplored jungle that is the strategic value of cyberwarfare.

Admittedly, it went somewhat against the grain of this study to isolate particular weapons and forms of war for separate analysis, as we did with WMD, space warfare and cyberwarfare. But, we sank our principles for those special cases. They are special cases, however, only in the sense that they are not yet well integrated in policy and strategy, or, of course, in public understanding of security matters. We argued vigorously that WMD, space, and cyber forces, are all subject to what is best described as the lore of strategy and the theory of war. Clausewitz rules! – no matter what the mode of warfare or the character of weapons employed. Finally, in Chapter Nine we adopted a rather unusual approach to the question of the control of warfare. We suggested that such control is effected all the time by policy, strategy, and resource limitations. Also, we ventured the politically incorrect view that some of the world's armed conflicts should be allowed to proceed to a military conclusion, rather than being frozen in stalemate by order of some international body and its so-called peacekeepers. Naturally, there will be exceptions to that rule, but still there is some merit in the ironic call to 'give war a chance'.

Despite the range of topics in this enquiry, and notwithstanding our unavoidable ignorance about the details of future warfare, the tale told here does have coherence and unity. Furthermore, this study can offer definite conclusions in which the author has confidence. This seeming miracle is achieved by the framework provided by the master argument outlined baldly in the Introduction. Presented and developed here as conclusions, the seven items that collectively comprise the book's argument have important meaning for everything discussed in the text.

1. *War and warfare will always be with us: war is a permanent feature of the human condition.* War is a social institution and warfare is a social activity. Recall that war is defined as *organized* violence for political ends. Human beings may be the agents of war as well as behind every one of its possible origins, causes, and precipitating events, but individuals, as individuals, do not wage war. To repeat, war is social behaviour conducted for political purposes. Peace-loving, gentle people can be trained to be killers, for the public good, of course. Analyses of human nature are largely beside the point when it comes to speculation about the future of war. States, societies, tribes, groups, and other collectivities, not individuals, wage war. I did not devote extensive attention to the huge, sad literature which offers theories on the causes of war. Those writings are interesting, sometimes insightful, but with only rare exceptions, thoroughly unconvincing to the point of being useless. Chapter Nine handled roughly some popular panaceas for the condition of war, misunderstood as a solvable problem. Somewhat unhelpfully, one can note that individual and even group violence of a distinctly unorganized kind is universal. But organized violence for political goals, war, is not.[9] Most states and societies do not live in a constant state of war. For the other side of the coin, just as a frequency of domestic violence need not, and usually does not, correlate with a state of war, so that state has no known connection with domestic violence. The only exception to this judgement would be when a government finds foreign war attractive as a means to provide distraction from an impending domestic insurrection. It has been claimed, for example, that one reason why Britain's decidedly pacific liberal cabinet chose to intervene in the continental war in August 1914, was in order to head off the civil war in Ireland that was about to be launched by the 100,000 members of the Ulster Volunteer Force in opposition to home rule. This claim has little, if any, merit; in no way does it suffice to explain why Britain entered the Great War.[10] British participation

transformed a European war into a global conflict and guaranteed that the struggle would be protracted.

War may not be an institution with which we humans will be cursed forever. Although there must always be a human agency in decisions for war, it would be a serious error to confuse states or other groups with individuals. From time to time the personality and beliefs of particular political leaders will be the principal element driving events, while that element must always be a relevant dimension to the subject of war. But people, even powerful political leaders, behave in a political context and define their options and make their choices for reasons that cannot totally be explained by a psychologist or an anthropologist. States are not moral persons. Policymakers acting on behalf of their polity prefer to behave in ways that domestic and foreign publics are likely to judge legitimate and just. Ultimately, though, statecraft and strategy is not an exercise in applied morality, at least not in applied personal morality. Because we are often violent as individuals, it does not follow that we must be violent collectively for political reasons. Indeed, some would argue that the former might help reduce public pressure for the latter. This author is entirely unimpressed with arguments of that kind, or indeed of any kind which attempt to explain war, as contrasted with particular wars. War is a part of the human condition, it is not a problem that can be solved. However, it is a condition some of the worst features of which can be alleviated by law, custom, norms, and plain self-interest. What is a problem, usually a tangled mix of problems, is any individual potential or actual war. Particular wars have distinctive origins, unique causes, and specific precipitating, or triggering, events. Those can be studied and, in theory, addressed.

War is about power in its several forms. It is about the power to influence others, to improve the security context of the polity, and to enhance or restore the reputation for success that yields the political capital of prestige. The details vary from case to case, but relative power invariably is the dominant and common issue. When one accepts that fact, and considers it in the context of Thucydides famous triptych of 'fear, honor, and interest', there is little left of a general character about war that is worth explaining. It is always possible that we humans will find some magical political or ethical elixir which buries war forever as an instrument of policy. One should never say never. However, sceptics such as this theorist advise that we should not hold our breath waiting for that happy, and exceedingly improbable, event. In the meantime, we should keep our powder dry.

2. *War, and warfare, has an enduring, unchanging nature, but a highly variable character. It follows that history is our best, albeit incomplete, guide to the future.* Warfare, and the use of warfare to pursue political goals, which we call strategy, is eternal in nature yet everchanging in character. Strangely, appreciation of this simple distinction continues to elude many people. As we have cited several times in this work, Clausewitz explained in terms that should be clear enough to all that war has two natures, objective and subjective, following the philosophical fashion of his day.[11] We conclude, as we must, that in all essential respects future warfare will be the same as all of past warfare. Since we have access to a vast storehouse of historical experience with warfare, the nature of our subject is anything but mysterious. Lest the point needs further emphasis, we affirm that war is war and strategy is strategy. In its structure and fundamental ideas, Clausewitz's theory of war is literally timeless. Not only is it eternally valid, it is beyond falsification by developments of any kind. For so long as humankind engages in warfare, Clausewitz must rule. Contrary to appearances, perhaps, this is not to deify the Prussian master. There is always room for improvement, correction, and further explanation. But his theory of war is pitched at such a high level that it transcends the need for constant amendment to accommodate shifts in political, economic, social, cultural, and technological, conditions. Intellectual taste in strategic matters can shift rapidly. The American defence community is especially prone to capture by the latest catchphrase, the new-sounding spin on an ancient idea which as jargon separates those who are truly expert from the lesser breeds without the jargon. 'Competitive strategies', 'military transformation', 'network-centricity', 'effects based operations', 'Fourth Generation

Warfare', and the rest, no matter how novel and exciting they may seem, are all of them mere pimples of varying merit upon the body of war's essential and enduring nature.

Changes in the grammar of warfare are, of course, of great importance. But whether those changes happen as by 'evolutionary slither', as Till suggests engagingly,[12] or after the manner of an explosion, they cannot transform war, warfare, and strategy. No one was more alert to the significance of changes in warfare than was Clausewitz himself. His professional career encompassed the whole of the transformation of war that was effected by the dramatic alteration in the social and political contexts for French military power. It was the sharpness of the contrast between the moderate style of warfare that was most characteristic of eighteenth-century Europe, and the state-smashing, and initially ideological, style of operations attempted by the new France, that fuelled Clausewitz's theoretical endeavour. Unlike most of today's theorists of war, the Prussian (from the ripe age of 12!) had witnessed and participated extensively in the subject of his treatise.

It follows that future warfare must be approached as it were bifocally. At the higher level, all possibilities of future combat, in every environment, with every potential weapon, among all possible belligerents, conducted in every mode or style, will be covered by Clausewitz's theory. That theory applies to war in space and cyberspace as it does to combat in swamps, mountains, and cities. The theory is impervious to attrition by shifts in technology, political ideologies, or geopolitical focus. But at the lower level, that of war's 'subjective' nature, what we term its character, the changes sometimes can be profound, surprising, and unwelcome. Clausewitz's theory of war educates the receptive mind so that it should be able to cope well enough with those changes, be they surprising or otherwise. It is precisely because the changing character of warfare is so significant that this book is not a pale replay of Clausewitzian truths. Rather have we offered a fairly detailed examination of some very different modes of warfare and some hugely dissimilar weapons.

Our past is our future, at least in the strategic essentials. Regular and irregular warfare have scarred all of human history. The struggle for power and influence among the great and would-be greater polities is a narrative of ancient lineage. Only history is available to help educate us about the future. It is imperfect as a guide, but what else is there? If we reject the past, or simply choose to be ignorant of it, we are at the mercy of prophets of sundry new revelations. Those who are blissfully unaware of the past, will be acutely short of the prudent scepticism that should greet the advocates of schemes for radical benign transformation in security affairs. The transnational defence debate is awash with purveyors of glossy designs which, on close inspection, transpire to be rediscovery of well-aged fallacies, dressed up in novel and exciting language. A respect for history should encourage understanding of the unity of our past, present, and future. Similarly, that respect should help protect us from overvaluing the influence of discontinuities, real or apparent. The next item in my argument provides vivid illustration of a major unwelcome continuity in strategic history, one that currently is scarcely acknowledged by the strategic cognoscenti – the inevitable return of great power struggle.

3. *Irregular warfare may well be the dominant mode in belligerency for some years to come, but interstate war, including great power conflict, will enjoy a healthy future.* It is the argument of this book that the strategic future does not belong to irregular conflict. Of course, terrorism and insurgency will be rife, and of course al Qaeda and its shadowy associates will be a plague for decades to come. Would that all our strategic troubles were confined to their kind. Unfortunately, the twenty-first century is going to witness a new cycle, or two, of the historically familiar struggle for power and influence between great power rivals and their allies and fellow travellers. To venture a perilous bold prediction, what we can discern today appears to be the early stage of what has the potential to develop into a new Cold War. Specifically, a Sino-Russian continental axis already may be forming and carefully gathering some crucial allies, for the purpose of constructing a bloc of states and assemblage of assets (oil in particular), capable of challenging the current American hegemony. While most Western

defence experts are focusing laser-like on the problems of terrorism and insurgency, it looks very much as if a new great struggle is taking shape under-recognized. This grim, though probably unavoidable development, can be dated from 2003, when Russia had to decide whether to continue its de facto quasi-alliance, certainly entente, with the United States, or instead to go with France in mounting strong opposition to US policy towards Iraq. Russia chose the path of non-cooperation. More recently, the Russian decision to ignore American concerns about Iran's nuclear programme by providing the vital assistance needed by Teheran for the completion of its first nuclear power station, assistance which includes the provision of nuclear fuel, simply underlined the change in Russia's foreign policy.

Although at present I believe that a Sino-Russian axis is emerging to oppose the United States globally, the detail in that prediction is not of primary importance for this study. What does matter is to recognize that the pattern of great power struggles for primacy is far from over. What matters also is the need to avoid being over-impressed by the more active conflicts of the moment, conflicts which, admittedly, are overwhelmingly of an irregular character. There will be much terrorism and insurgency to blight the future, especially the near-term future. But the mischief promoted by irregular conflict pales into near insignificance when compared with the potential for harm that resides in great power antagonism.

4. *The political context is the principal, though far from sole, driver of war's incidence and character. Above all else, warfare is political behaviour.* War is political behaviour and political behaviour is about power. That elementary and elemental addition to the Clausewitzian principle has bred much misunderstanding. John Keegan for example, insists that war is a cultural phenomenon, rather than a political one.[13] He is right to emphasize the importance of culture, a thesis that we endorse strongly. But he is far from right in identifying culture as the somewhat diffuse and elusive element that gives meaning to organized violence. One could as well claim with Colin McInnes that war today is a global spectator sport, which, to expand

on his thesis, the electronic media would need to stage were political actors not so obliging as to do it for them.[14] War has become a spectator sport for publics who are not personally engaged in warfare. Combat is conducted on their behalf by military professionals. But, war is not sport, even though it shares some of sport's characteristics: an adversary with an independent will; the nature of a duel; the possibility of surprise; the salience of planning, leadership, physical and moral strength, and much else besides. Similarly, the necessary fact that war is a cultural activity does not mean that war, at root, is conducted for cultural reasons. That would be the case if one were to define culture so inclusively that it embraced what usually is meant by politics. For yet another crime against logic, one might try to claim that because there are people who enjoy participating in war, we humans fight because we find it pleasurable. It is true that a great deal of domestic, even civic, violence is motivated by nothing more purposeful than the instant excitement of combat and the satisfaction that some derive from inflicting pain. From football hooliganism to alcohol-fuelled loutish brawls in city centres, violence can be an end in itself. But, because there are people who enjoy acting violently, and indeed because we train elite soldiers to be warriors who can take pride in their skill in administering death and injury, it does not follow that war is somehow about satisfying a human lust for violence. We do not deny that there are soldiers who enjoy their work, on those typically rare occasions when they are required to kill people and break things for Queen and country. Similarly, we do not deny that the world is heavily populated by armchair warriors who enjoy a daily dose of real-time warfare provided via satellite by video feed from some preferably distant battlespace. Overall, there is no denying the pervasive influence of culture, however defined, over military and strategic behaviour.

Despite the many issues that propel communities to fight, and notwithstanding the personal and social features inseparable from warfare, war is *about* politics, which is to say, to repeat, it is about relative power. From time to time some scholars notice that the principal subjects of contention among security communities appear to be less and less of a traditional geopolitical and geostrategic kind. For example, those subjects may be questions of: ethnic identity; economics – especially trade; the movement of people; disease; and environmental change. These so-called 'new agenda' topics are held to demote items of a strategic kind and possibly even to transcend the political.

The agenda of concerns and the priorities among its items will vary over time and in its assessment by different polities. However, history shows that war not only alters its character as conditions change, but also can be promoted and precipitated by an extremely wide range of policy concerns. We need to be alert to the emergence of new, or old but refurbished, issues that have the potential to trigger wars. But we must not allow ourselves to be so confused by 'new agenda' items of a plainly extra-strategic kind, as to believe that war is no longer a political matter. War is about politics and is an instrument of policy, regardless of the character of the particular issues that fed the conflict and lit the flames. Of course war is about a great deal more than politics, as we have noted. It is about culture, economic interests, particular personalities, and so forth. Principally, though, war is about politics and it continues, correctly, to be defined as such. Nothing considered here leads us to wish to revise our long-standing Clausewitz-ian view that war is an instrument of policy, or politics.

5. *Warfare is social and cultural, as well as political and strategic, behaviour. As such it must reflect the characteristics of the communities that wage it.* The cultural analysis of warfare is both important and frequently contro-versial.[15] The discussion in these pages of the several categories of future warfare has not provided powerful reasons to argue that war's local social and cultural contexts are in the process of losing their significance. Not unreasonably, perhaps, many people believe that globalization is eroding the potency of local culture, even of erstwhile distinctions among civi-lizations. Notwithstanding its popularity, globalization remains somewhat elusive as a process and context. As an associated phenomenon, many are convinced that the global diffusion of new technologies is trimming, if not cancelling, the influence of local and regional preferences, including those bearing on military matters.

This fifth element in the master argument is of extraordinary importance. It expresses a thesis to which seemingly all defence professionals pay lip-service, but few take seriously. In war after war, the social and cultural contexts are neglected, often with lethal effect upon strategic performance. Moreover, following Sun-tzu, the social and cultural contexts of interest include our own as well as those of the adversary.[16] Some of the theorists of an allegedly new American way of war, one keyed to dominance in C⁴ISTAR (Command, Control, Communications, Computers, Intelligence, Surveillance, Targeting, and Reconnaissance), in short to the leveraging of information technologies, claim that information-led warfare is the way of the future. 'Dominant battlespace knowledge' is prominent in the creed of the true believer.[17] Historical precedents for technology-led optimism are not hard to find. In modern times, at least, whenever there has been a major technical innovation, or set of such, many theorists have argued that they can see the future for all significant strategic players. They are usually correct. But where they err is in the assumption that a major military innovation must be developed and employed in just one particular manner. This error is evidenced abundantly in the modern history of warfare. Up to a point, the theorists of air power and of armoured and mechanized warfare were correct. To be competitive in battle every great power had to invest heavily in those capabilities. But, would one size fit all in key ideas for the development and employment of aircraft and tanks? Given the differences among societies and cultures, their distinctive histories, geopolitics, and military institutions, was it even probable that there could be a single 'best buy', a transnational doctrine for air power and armoured warfare? The answer revealed eventually by historical experience was that each country 'did it my way', and not only for reasons of strict economic or military necessity.

It would be difficult to exaggerate the relevance of this element of our argument to the general thrust of the book. We are not at all convinced that the process of globalization is effecting a homogenization of the cultural and associated social contexts that increasingly are critically important for the occurrence and conduct of war. Democratization, and access to a global media even more, closely engage societies and their values in the issues of war. Globalization does indeed promote the diffusion of technological innovation and of ideas. But history tells us that each security community approaches military–technical opportunities through the filter both of its own social and cultural contexts, and of its unique geopolitical and geostrategic circumstances.

Consider the major subjects treated here in the light of this element of the argument. We have considered regular and irregular warfare, including terrorism; WMD of all kinds; and attitudes towards international order and peace with security. Is it likely that the domestic and external contexts of highly diverse polities and groups could coalesce upon a single body of axioms, a common lore, for the control of future strategic history? For a leading example of our scepticism, while the Western world holds further nuclear proliferation to be an abomination, a small but important fraction of states, societies, and cultures, does not agree. Moreover, they are entirely rational, and even reasonable, in their disagreement. The current nuclear weapon states are not alone in judging that eponymous status to be useful for national security.

Each community prepares for, and if need be wages, war after its own social and cultural fashion. This can only be a limited truth. Because war is a duel, the enemy imposes some discipline upon local cultural preference. If one fights solely as culture prefers, paying no regard to the culture and character of the foe, then defeat is probable, if not certain. As noted already, witness the disasters that befell the Aztec and Inca ways of war, when they met the way of war of Spanish mercenaries early in the sixteenth century. The issue of each society expressing its own character and value in its way of war is pertinent to one of the more prominent topics running through our analysis; American performance in future warfare. As the sole remaining superpower, world order, which is to say peace with security and some justice, needs the United States to be effective as international sheriff.[18]

Some problems of a cultural kind in particular currently are under-appreciated by American policymakers. The United States performs magnificently at those tasks that suit its character and values. Admittedly, this is a rather circular claim, that Americans do well what they do well. Technology-led war, preferably conducted on a large scale, is the American forte. Historically, American interest in understanding their enemies has not been a marked national characteristic. As an ideologically confident superpower, the United States has not been much interested in the military and strategic choices that its enemies might make. When you are confident of victory, you are inclined to believe that almost any path will take you there, no matter what the enemy throws your way.

Americans today talk about, and are planning, to develop more agile and adaptable armed forces, ones that should be able to meet the changing demands of future warfare. They are sincere, the idea is sound, and to some degree they should succeed. But the United States is what it is.[19] It is almost certainly a canard to hold that American society is inappropriately casualty-averse. But it is certainly not an error to believe that Americans are unlikely to be able to transform their armed forces into culturally empathetic and subtle practitioners of the waging of cunning ways of war against asymmetrical enemies. The US Army appears to recognize the need to excel in those ways, but I suspect strongly that American political, strategic, and military culture will prove prohibitively obstructive. The arrogance, or self-confidence, of military hegemony, leaves the United States vulnerable to enemies whose cultures facilitate their exploiting the weaknesses of American strengths.

6. *War and warfare do not always change in an evolutionary, linear fashion. Surprise is not merely possible, or even probable, it is certain.* Future wars must occur in a historical context largely shaped by trends and developments of some longevity. One must add the qualifier, largely, because of the important factor of surprise, which is treated below. Early on in this enquiry we explained that trend analysis was highly unreliable. While the identity and character of future wars by and large will be signalled more or less clearly well in advance, the signals will be unmistakable only to future historians. Those of a teleological bent are wont to regard history as a series of marches to some unavoidable temporary climax. Hence the

bookshelves groan under the scholarly studies of 'the coming of war in', say, 1914 or 1939, 'the path of', or to, 'empire', and 'the hard road to victory'. The recent flurry of works of 'virtual history' are useful in that they remind us of the power of contingency, and they probably have some merit as a stimulus to the imagination.[20] On balance, however, they are a menace to historical understanding. To play God in a highly selective manner is inherently near certain to produce hugely misleading results. If we approach war holistically, as we should, we need to recognize that everything can influence everything else. To invent an exciting scenario say, for July–August 1914, or for November 1989 when the Berlin wall came down, is to do so with no realistic possibility of taking due account of all of the knock-on consequences of the fictitious events. 'What if' is fun, but it is not history and it has the potential to mislead the unwary into believing that they understand how events otherwise might have developed. Such a belief would not be well founded.

There are times when the pace of strategic history appears to quicken, and what amounts to a revolutionary change in warfare occurs. Such occurrences have been discussed for several decades, initially by Soviet strategic thinkers, more recently by American. They have come to be known as RMAs, revolutions in military affairs. There are conceptual and acronymic variants on RMA, but for the purpose of this concluding section of the enquiry, citation of RMA alone will suffice. A trend or trends in the grammar of war meets permissive, if not compelling, political, social, and cultural contexts, and the result is a radical change in warfare's character. On the basis of powerful seeming military–technical evidence, and some recent historical experience in Kosovo, Afghanistan, and Iraq, the United States today believes that it is in the process of implementing just such an RMA. The American conduct of future war, so the story goes, will be led by a dominance in all aspects of information acquisition, processing, dissemination, and by exploitation at the sharp end of ever more precise firepower and a greater capability to effect decisive manoeuvre. Whether or not the transformed forces will be transformed into a tool suitable to contain and possibly defeat irregular enemies is, of course, another matter entirely. The concept of a transformation of war is a very old term of art that has been recently rediscovered and adopted officially in Washington.[21] The popularity of the idea of transformation is probably attributable largely to the potent strategic imagination of a brilliant Israeli military historian, Martin van Creveld. It is ironic that van Creveld's transformation is a light year distant from the aspirations for information-led military wizardry which dominate the dreams of the more technologically optimistic among contemporary Pentagon 'transformers'. His transformation is principally political, social, and cultural.[22]

What does this mean for future warfare? Must it be conducted with ever greater military effectiveness, broadly according to the information-led vision of the American defence community? Perhaps rather more to the point, how well will the historical market leader fare in action with its transforming military instrument? The balance of the evidence of history suggests strongly that RMA leadership proffers no reliable guarantee of strategic success. The reasons why this should be so are hardly obscure. As we have insisted before, there is more to war than warfare. One of the many dimensions of war and strategy is the inescapable element of an adversarial relationship. Past, present, and future warfare is a duel. If they are able and moderately competent, enemies can be trusted not to permit each other a free ride in exploiting military advantage, virtually no matter how apparently radical that advantage may seem to be. The historians Williamson Murray and MacGregor Knox conclude their outstanding edited study of historical RMAs with a thought-provoking judgement. They find that 'every RMA summons up, whether soon or late, a panoply of direct countermeasures and "asymmetrical responses"'.[23] American transformers of war, be warned. There is no last move in strategic and military competition.

A good part of the problem facing those who labour diligently, imaginatively and patriotically to develop a more swiftly lethal, yet precise, and casualty-minimizing new way for future warfare, is that that warfare will come in many shapes and sizes. An American way of future war may well be all but certain to defeat any enemy in open combat between regular forces. But that excellence in a regular style of combat is unlikely to win many Oscars when the enemy is decidedly irregular and hides among civilians in third-world towns and cities. Future warfare will have many variants, and a single way of war will not suffice to produce optimal results in them all. Furthermore, some of the enemies of the West in future warfare may prove to be politically and diplomatically gifted. Also, there are precedents for those enemies to be led by people who are strategically competent and imaginative. In that predictable circumstance, the practical limitations of Western IT-led military–technical proficiency will swiftly become apparent. Historically speaking, we have been there before. Remember Indo-China! Recall Vietnam! And do not forget Algeria, where the French colonial army won the warfare, but lost the war and the subsequent peace. It is less than self-evident that the Algerians really won much of the subsequent peace, but that is another story.

As a final thought on possible non-linearity in future war and warfare, it is essential not to forget the apparent, or real, wild card of the major surprise event or process. History is full of great surprises, which is to say of occurrences that no reputable defence planner or analyst would have dared predict. We can be certain that the warfare which future history will surely bring, will be notably influenced, in some cases even triggered, by genuine surprises of huge magnitude. Such surprises would be huge in their consequences, not necessarily in the events or processes themselves. When we consider future warfare, it is only prudent to keep our minds open to education by strategic experience from history. What other strategic experience is there?

Every one of the four great wars of the past two centuries was, in one or another, or several, respects a major surprise. The Great War against Revolutionary and Napoleonic France, which dominated the years 1792–1815, almost literally erupted upon an unsuspecting and wholly unprepared Europe. The First Great War against Germany, from 1914–18, was not overmuch of a surprise in its occurrence. But it was a surprise in the consequences of the character of its warfare. The principal belligerents required three years to learn how to conduct it successfully. They required a similar lead time to arm and train themselves to wage the new way in artillery-led combined arms warfare effectively. The Second Great War against Germany came as a great surprise to those millions of decent people and their hopeful governments who chose to believe that the First such Great War had been the 'war that will end war'. The Great Depression, with its dire economic, and hence social and political consequences in Germany, produced a 1930s that was not predictable on the basis of trend analysis conducted in the 1920s. The Fourth Great War, the cold one between the superpowers, came as a surprise to countless millions, and even to many policymakers who should have known better. People have understandable difficulty effecting a leap of the political and strategic imagination from the context of the day, to a very different one which could characterize the day after tomorrow. For a final example, one of more recent vintage, what else was 9/11 if not a great political and strategic surprise? The newly elected Bush Jr. Administration initially was consumed strategically by a determination to move out smartly on the iconic Republican issue of active missile defence to frustrate roguish foes, as well as on the high-tech transformation of the armed forces. The need to wage a global war against religiously motivated catastrophe terrorists was not at the top of the national security agenda.

A trouble with history's great non-linearities is that their occurrence is well heralded only to the futurist looking backwards. We do not and cannot know what great surprises the twenty-first century will produce for our discomfiture. I am tempted to observe that we are limited only by our imagination and by the laws of physics. However, the latter have a way of changing, so that much that currently is impossible is unlikely always to remain so. Our imagination should be a useful guide, were it not for the amply attested historical fact that the record of political and strategic prediction is anything but impressive. Furthermore, as we have noted previously, there is no way of knowing who among our seers is broadly correct.

To illustrate what we mean by a great surprise that would have strategic consequences of the first magnitude, we will cite and quote from a study by

American analysts Peter Schwartz and Doug Randall. The title alone implies the storyline: 'An Abrupt Climate Change Scenario and its Implications for United States National Security'. Climate change is not surprising, but if it were to occur in a truly *abrupt* manner, assuredly it would be. Schwartz and Randall speculate as follows:

> The report explores how such an abrupt climate change scenario [average annual temperatures drop by 5 degrees far. over Asia and N. America, and 6 degrees far. over Asia; temperatures rise by 4 degrees far. over Australia, S. America, and southern Africa; drought persists; winter storms and winds intensify] could potentially de-stabilize the geo-political environment, leading to skirmishes, battles, and even war due to resource constraints such as:
>
> 1. Food shortages due to decreases in net global agriculture production.
> 2. Decreased availability and quantity of fresh water in key regions due to shifted precipitation patterns, causing more frequent floods and droughts.
> 3. Disrupted access to energy supplies due to extensive sea ice and storminess.
>
> As global and local carrying capacities are reduced, tensions could mount around the world, leading to two fundamental strategies: defensive and offensive. Nations with the resources to do so may build virtual fortresses around their countries, preserving resources for themselves. Less fortunate nations especially those with ancient enmities with their neighbuors, may initiate struggles for access to food, clean water, or energy. Unlikely alliances could be formed as defense priorities shift and the goal is resources for survival rather than religion, ideology, or national honor.[24]

I do not offer this extensive quotation as a prediction. Rather is it a perfect example of a great surprise that would have the potential to transform war's political, economic, social, cultural, and strategic contexts. What it could not effect, however, would be an alteration, radical or otherwise, in the nature of war and strategy. Readers are invited to invent their own possible, if improbable, scenarios of great surprises in the future that must have profound implications for war and warfare. No matter how diligent the response to my challenge, I will venture the prediction that our venture in 'great surprise spotting' assuredly will miss the mark. And, to repeat a familiar caveat, there is no way we can know which among our predictions are well founded, let alone which have the potential to be self-negating prophecies. As a general rule, in the words of one of the epigraphs to this book, 'we judge the unknown to be unlikely'.[25]

7. *Efforts to control, limit, and regulate war, and therefore warfare, by international political, legal, and normative–ethical measures and attitudes are well worth pursuing. However, the benefits from such endeavours will always be fragile, vulnerable to overturn by the commands of perceived belligerent necessity.* Chapter Nine was devoted to a detailed examination of this element of the master argument. Unfortunately, historical experience, political and strategic logic, and even just common sense, all support it convincingly. Moreover, it cannot be denied that there is some tension between the judgement in the first sentence and that in the second. The underlying reality is that politics rules. Efforts to alleviate the problems of war, let alone abolish them entirely, are foredoomed to fail if they rely upon means calculated to evade political difficulties. War and warfare cannot be controlled by diplomatic skill, law, administration, or ethics, considered as alternatives to political reasoning. In practice, those extra-political approaches to the control of war are all either the product of political assessment, or are vulnerable to interdiction by political judgement. The problem lies not with diplomacy, law, or ethics. Rather is the stumbling block the semi-anarchic character of international politics. For a parallel thought, it is largely inappropriate to condemn the United Nations for its all too obvious incapacity to serve as the effective defender of international order, peace, security, and justice. The UN can behave no more effectively than its leading members permit.

In the Thucydidean trinity of 'fear, honor, and interest', we have the bare but most essential bones of a convincing theory of the principal motives for war. I will update Thucydides by suggesting that his trinity should be amended to 'fear, culture, and interest'. Culture includes what we mean by honour. The extent to which war and warfare can be controlled in practice literally depends upon the intensity with which Thucydides' motives are held in a particular case. Moreover, that uncertainty will pertain to all the belligerents. Even when combatants obviously strive to abide by diplomatic agreements, law, and normative injunctions, that behaviour will reflect the political judgement that it is prudent so to do. As usual, Clausewitz was correct. War is an instrument of policy, and its conduct, which is to say warfare, should reflect the scope and scale of the political stakes. Strategy being an eminently practical matter, the conduct of war also must reflect the contemporary grammar and dynamics of combat, as well as the character and intensity of hostilities that enemy action allows.

We must conclude that politics rule – over diplomacy, law, and ethics. Even when the agenda for action appears extra-political, as with religiously motivated terrorism, for example, closer inspection reveals a political logic informing the strategy. Martyrdom and the death of many apostates and unbelievers may have virtue in and of themselves, but they are not the object of the Islamic terrorist and insurgent enterprise. That object ultimately is politically millenarian, and *both* adjectives are significant.

We conclude also that the politics which rule over diplomacy, law, and ethics are capable of directing warfare according to any rules, including none, that bear a credible promise of producing strategic success. It is only with a merciful rarity that warfare approaches its absolute or total form. Only in exceptional cases is it directed to achieve the utter destruction of the enemy. Genocide is historically uncommon, while even regime change is far from constituting a standard war aim. Nonetheless, history requires us to believe that humankind's political behaviour is capable of anything. No atrocity is reliably beyond the pale of possibility. In a strategic context perceived to be so desperate as to warrant description as the last resort, there is nothing that belligerents will not do. If fear, honour, and interest are engaged with sufficient intensity, no prior diplomatic agreements, laws, or ethical precepts, will serve to regulate the character of warfare. When survival is at stake, the end will always be held to justify whatever means are believed likely to be effective. This is not to deny the relevance of the political option to surrender, or at least seek an armistice. But it is to maintain that such a decision will be motivated by political calculations of interest, filtered by culture. It will not be shaped by independent political, diplomatic, legal, or ethical arguments. The study from which we have quoted already offers a frightening yet plausible view of the strategic context should the world's climate be abruptly transformed.

> All of that progressive behaviour could collapse if carrying capacities everywhere were suddenly lowered drastically by abrupt climate change. Humanity would revert to its norm of constant battles for diminishing resources, which the battles themselves would further reduce even beyond the climatic effects. Once again warfare would define human life.[26]

We must conclude that the control of war and warfare is fragile. No other judgement is possible, given the danger, exertion, uncertainty, and chance that comprise the climate of war, to which one must add the unpredictable effects of friction. Nonetheless, control is feasible, and in practice is surprisingly resilient in face of the sources of harassment just cited. Self-interest is a potent regulator of strategic behaviour. Different cultures may define their interests in ways that seem strange to outsiders. But war is an instrument of policy and strategy is about the purposeful linkage of means with ends. Policy and strategy are the true, tolerably reliable sources of control over the occurrence and conduct of war.

BY WAY OF CONCLUSION to the conclusions, the more one worries about future warfare, the more one is drawn to the view that history is by far the best guide available. To be yet more direct, history is the *only* guide available. Many people do not, certainly do not want, to accept this claim. They harbour the noble hope that somehow we will be able to order our security affairs in a much more peaceable manner in the future than we have in the past or the present. I share that yearning, but must resist it as a belief. For the final words, I turn to the wisdom of historian MacGregor Knox. He expresses almost exactly the attitude and some of the argument of this enquiry.

> In this bewildering world, the search for predictive theories to guide strategy has been no more successful than the search for such theories in other areas of

human existence. Patterns do emerge from the past, and their study permits educated guesses about the range of potential outcomes. But the future is not an object of knowledge; no increase in processing power will make the owl of history a daytime bird. Similar causes do not always produce similar effects, and causes interact in ways unforeseeable even by the historically sophisticated. Worse still, individuals – with their ambitions, vanities, and quirks – make strategy.[27]

We may not like it, assuredly we wish to do better as strategic futurists, but Knox describes the way things are and the way they will remain.

References

Publication details are provided in the 'Biblio-graphy of Works Cited', p. 450

INTRODUCTION **The Plot**
1. Freedman (2001)
2. Huntington (1996)
3. Goldman and Eliason
4. Echevarria (2000)
5. Strachan, pp. 1005–14
6. Howard (2004)

CHAPTER ONE **Back to the Future**
1. Strassler, p. 43
2. Blanning, ch. 1
3. Clausewitz, p. 75 (emphasis in the original)
4. Ibid., p. 85
5. Ibid., p. 104
6. Ibid., p. 89
7. Ibid., p. 606
8. Howard (1984), pp. 214–15
9. Clausewitz, p. 593
10. Singer and Wildavsky
11. Corum
12. Hughes, p. 22
13. Howard (2002), p. 1
14. Ibid.

15. Kaldor (1999); van Creveld (1991); Lind (1989); Hammes
16. Etzioni; Gray (2005b)
17. Browning, p. 2
18. US Department of Defense (2001), p. iii
19. Clausewitz, p. 605
20. Pitt, p. 16
21. Payne (1986), pp. 64–5
22. Hirst, p. 9
23. Clausewitz, pp. 566–73
24. Weigley, p. xiii
25. The Economist, 3 April 2004, p. 94
26. Luttwak (1986), ch. 5
27. Peters (2004)
28. Gray (2004a)
29. US Army (2004a)
30. Brodie (1973), p. 452
31. Echevarria (2004)
32. Posen
33. US Army (2004b)
34. Millen, p. 2

CHAPTER TWO **Context, Context, Context**
1. Clausewitz, p. 88 (emphasis in the original)
2. Black (2001), p. vii
3. Hanson (2003), p. 11
4. Gray (1999a), ch. 5
5. Keegan, p. 12

6. Ibid., p. 385
7. Ibid.
8. Clausewitz, p. 87
9. D. Kagan, p. 8
10. Buzan; Terriff et al.
11. Betts (1997), p. 9
12. Peters (1999), p. 172
13. McInnes
14. Hanson (1989; 1999; 2001; 2003)
15. Lynn
16. Strassler, pp. 350–51 (emphasis added)
17. Ibid., p. 352
18. Ibid., p. 354
19. Bacevich; Ferguson (2004)
20. Strassler, p. 353
21. Hirst, p. 105
22. Bush (2002a), p. 29
23. Fukuyama
24. Bush (2002a), p. 30
25. Ibid., p. 26
26. Weigert, p. 4
27. Spykman, ch. 4; Mackinder, ch. 4
28. Baylis and Smith, p. 7
29. Hassig, ch. 16; Hanson (2001), ch. 6
30. Standage; Kennedy (1979), ch. 3
31. Van Creveld (1999)
32. Schwartz and Randall
33. Black (2001), p. 114 (emphasis added)
34. English
35. McInnes, ch. 4; Duyvesteyn and Angstrom
36. Desch; Glenn, Howlett and Poore.
37. Waltz; Mearsheimer
38. Gray (1971; 1976)
39. Hines, Mishulovich, and Shull
40. Callwell, p. 70
41. Johnston, ch. 1; Gray (1999a), ch. 5
42. Howard (1972), p. 57
43. Hiro, p. 259
44. Burleigh
45. Huntington (1996)
46. Freedman (2004), ch. 8
47. Black (2002), pp. vii–viii
48. Kurth; Black (2001)
49. Feaver and Kohn; Cohen (2002a)
50. Goldman and Eliason, p. 397
51. Ibid., p. 390

CHAPTER THREE **Technology and War**
1. Fuller, p. 31
2. Clausewitz, p. 77
3. Mahan, p. 102
4. Cohen (2002b), p. 236
5. Owens, p. 14
6. 'Barfleur' (pseud. Custance)
7. Milne, pp. 44–51
8. Kaldor (1999), p. 13
9. Clausewitz, p. 608
10. Black (2004), p. 1
11. Murray and Millett (1996); Winton and Mets
12. Alexander
13. Triandafillov; Harrison
14. Keaney and Cohen, p. 188
15. Cohen (1996), p. 39
16. Gray (2002a)
17. Murray and Knox, p. 192 (emphasis in the original)
18. US Army (2004c), p. 8
19. Ibid., Foreword
20. US Department of Defense (2003)
21. Posen
22. Gray (2005c)
23. Krepinevich, p. 30
24. Fadok, p. 375; Warden
25. Murray and Knox, p. 192
26. Ferguson (1998), p. 294; Murray and Millett (2000), p. 558
27. Friedman (2000a), chs. 36–8
28. Tilford, p. 151
29. I. Hamilton
30. Alger
31. Bailey (1996), p. 32
32. Bailey (2004), p. 535
33. (emphasis added), ch. 7
34. Rumsfeld, p. 11; Barnett; Lambakis (2004)
35. Murray; Freedman (1998); Gray (2002a)
36. Freedman (1998)
37. Buzan, Waever, and de Wilde
38. Colin
39. US Army (2004b), p. 4
40. Hamilton and Herwig; Strachan, ch. 1
41. R. Kagan
42. Bailey (1996)

43. Gray (1999a, ch. 1; 2001)
44. Millett, p. 345
45. Zamoyski
46. Terraine, p. xii
47. Emery, p. 130
48. Peters (1999), p. 171

CHAPTER FOUR **Grand Narratives of War, 1800–2100**

1. Keegan, p. 6
2. Lind et al.
3. Knox (2001); Gray (2002a), ch. 6
4. Peters (2002), pp. 22–65
5. Gray (1999b)
6. Chickering, p. 14
7. Ibid., p. 16
8. Ibid.
9. Metz and Millen, p. 7
10. Honig; Kaldor (1999; 2005)
11. Collins, p. 186
12. Metz and Millen, p. 14
13. Van Creveld (1977; 1982; 1985; 1989; 1991)
14. Lind (1989); K. F. McKenzie
15. Lind (2004), p. 1
16. Gudmundsson
17. Lind (2004), p. 3
18. Ibid., p. 7
19. US Army (2004b), p. 4
20. Hammes, p. 2
21. Clausewitz, p. 75
22. Goldsworthy, p. 103
23. Hirst, p. 104
24. Ibid., p. 105
25. Mackinder, pp. 241–64
26. Blouet, p. 11
27. Mackinder, p. 249
28. Ibid., p. 277
29. Ibid., p. 260
30. Weigert; Herwig
31. Gray (2005a)
32. Fettweis, p. 119 (emphasis in the original)
33. Knox and Murray; Gray (2002a)
34. Murray
35. Berkowitz, p. 18
36. Dupuy; van Creveld (1989)
37. Berkowitz, p. 150

38. Cox and Gray
39. Warden, ch. 9
40. Clausewitz, p. 140
41. Cohen (2001; 2004); Biddle (2002); Murray and Scales
42. Peters (2004)
43. Watts, p. 122 (emphasis in the original)
44. Sellar and Yeatman
45. Quinlan, p. 19
46. Bush (2002b)
47. Green
48. Roberts and Guelff, p. 138
49. Walzer, pp. 44–7
50. Peters (2004)
51. Clausewitz, p. 593
52. Luttwak (1995)
53. Black (1998; 2000; 2004)
54. Liang and Xiangsui
55. Liddell Hart, p. 366
56. Black (2004), p. 1
57. Kaplan (2002)

CHAPTER FIVE **Regular Warfare**

1. Mao Tse-tung (1963), pp. 210–19
2. Gray (1990; 1999a; 2002a)
3. US Army (2004a), p. 4
4. Baylis and Smith; Hopkins; Lechner and Boli
5. Green, pp. 320–35
6. Mueller; Mandelbaum
7. Avant
8. Millett and Maslowski, p. 238
9. Hobkirk, p. x
10. Cohen (2002b), p. 244
11. Cochran et al., p. 25; Brodie, ch. 9
12. Lavoy, Sagan, and Wirtz
13. Gray (2004)
14. Bush (2002a), pp. 14–15
15. R. Kagan; Gray (2002b)
16. F. W. Kagan, p. 10 (emphasis in the original)
17. Ibid.
18. Haldon, pp. 112–27
19. Bush (2002b), p. 1
20. US Army (2004a; 2004b; 2004c; 2004d)
21. Callwell; US Marine Corps

22. Roberts and Guelff
23. Lind (1985); US Marine Corps (1994)
24. Utley (1972; 1988)
25. Peters (2002), p. 323
26. Echevarria (2004)
27. Huntington (1964), p. 11; Cohen (2002a)
28. Clausewitz, p. 610 (emphasis added)
29. Ibid., p. 608
30. Rosen; Murray and Millett (1996)
31. Liddell Hart
32. Boot (2002)
33. Boyd; Hammond; Coram
34. Biddle (2002; 2004)
35. Bailey (2004), p. 527
36. US Army (2004b), p. 10
37. Crile
38. Biddle (2002)
39. De Gaulle; Holden Reid, ch. 3
40. Murray and Scales, p. 249
41. Boot (2003), p. 42
42. Boot (2002)
43. Krepinevich (1986)
44. Clausewitz, p. 88
45. Wylie, p. 66 (emphasis in the original)
46. Hirst, p. 9
47. Posen
48. Brennan; Panofsky
49. Odom, pp. 66–71
50. Breemer
51. Corbett, pp. 15–16
52. Hallion, p. 267
53. Lambeth (2001)
54. Ullman and Wade
55. Cohen (1994); Lambeth (2000)
56. Towle
57. Marquis
58. Goldman and Eliason
59. Warden, pp. 34–50; Clausewitz, pp. 595–7

CHAPTER SIX Irregular Warfare and Terrorism

1. Hamilton, ch. 1; Beckett
2. Roberts and Guelff, pp. 22–5
3. Kiras (2002), p. 211 (emphasis in the original)
4. Hoffman, p. 43
5. Kiras (2002), p. 211
6. Ibid.
7. Laqueur (1996)
8. Gray (1999c)
9. Bell
10. Van Creveld (1991), p. 212
11. Ibid.
12. Ibid., p. 189
13. Peters (1999; 2002; 2003); Kaplan (2000), ch. 1
14. Asprey
15. Gunaratna, pp. 222–3
16. Gray (1993), pp. 95–9
17. Sun-tzu, p. 179
18. National Commission, p. 311
19. Shubik; Betts (1998)
20. Goldman and Ross, p. 398
21. Wawro, p. 309
22. Callwell, p. 125
23. Utley (1988), ch. 9
24. Callwell; Mao Tse-tung; Lawrence, ch. 33
25. Peters (2002), pp. 22–65
26. Akbar
27. Moran; Beckett; Black (2002), ch. 8
28. Clausewitz, p. 75
29. Mao Tse-tung (1961), p. 52
30. Callwell, p. 21
31. Hanson (1991); Mitchell
32. Mahnken (2003a), p. 265
33. Callwell, p. 23
34. National Commission, chs. 2–4; Gunaratna, pp. 21–22; Laqueur (2003), p. 53
35. Crile
36. Crocker and Hampson
37. Kaplan (2000), ch. 1
38. Marshall, Martin, and Rowen, chs. 9, 15
39. Hoffman, p. 121
40. Lewis (2002; 2003)
41. Burke
42. Schiff, Boston Globe, 5 April 2004
43. Jenkins, p. 144
44. Bartov
45. Brodie (1973), p. 332
46. Jenkins, pp. 132–3
47. Hedges
48. Arquilla

49. Gray (1992a); De B. Taillon
50. Paret and Shy
51. Echevarria (2004)
52. Lummis, p. 17
53. Ibid., p. 19
54. Tugwell and Charters, p. 35
55. Gray (1996a, chs. 7–8; 1999c); Kiras (2004)

CHAPTER SEVEN Old Rules for New Challenges, I: Weapons of Mass Destruction

1. Cirincione
2. International Institute for Strategic Studies (IISS), p. 251
3. Clausewitz, p. 605; Aron
4. Barnaby, p. 100
5. Green, pp. 135–7
6. Iklé (1961)
7. Price
8. US Congress
9. Barnaby
10. Mackenzie; Rip and Hasik
11. Barnaby, p. 113
12. Ibid., p. 36
13. US Congress, p. 71
14. Koblentz; Lederberg
15. Barnaby, p. 42
16. Davis and Gray, p. 277
17. Barnaby, p. 56
18. Spiers, ch. 2
19. Hiro, p. 201
20. Cordesman and Wagner
21. Barnaby, p. 63
22. Ibid.
23. DeGroot; Freedman (2003); Gray (1982)
24. Gray, (1999b); Payne (2001); Freedman (2004)
25. Rumsfeld, ch. 7; Payne (2004)
26. Blair (1985; 1993); Pry
27. Stern
28. Payne (2001)
29. Walzer, p. 240
30. Sagan; Gray (1999b), ch. 3
31. Hines, Mishulovich, and Shull
32. Sheffield, p. 1018
33. Harris, p. 53
34. Roberts and Guelff, pp. 155–67
35. Brodie (1946), p. 76
36. Price
37. Navias and Hooton; El-Shazly
38. Clausewitz, p. 104
39. Wylie, p. 72
40. Freedman (2000), pp. 201–2
41. Gilinsky
42. Allison
43. Gray (1999b), pp. 103–8

CHAPTER EIGHT Old Rules for New Challenges, II: Warfare in Space and Cyberspace

1. Clausewitz, p. 85
2. McDougall
3. Clausewitz, p. 75 (emphasis in the original)
4. Neufeld
5. Oberg, p. 39
6. Dolman, p. 73 (emphasis in the original)
7. Lambeth (2003)
8. Tangredi; Klein
9. Friedman (2000b)
10. Marder, p. 41
11. Parry, p. xi
12. Wegener
13. Gray (1996b), p. 307
14. Cohen (2002b), p. 250
15. Preston et al.
16. Lambakis (2001)
17. Showalter, chs. 1–3
18. Bialer, pp. 35–7
19. Rumsfeld, p. 73
20. Ibid.
21. Anson and Cummings
22. Wylie, p. 72
23. Heuser, p. 10
24. Berkowitz, p. 30
25. Lonsdale (2004)
26. Arquilla and Ronfeldt (1993; 1997, ch. 2)
27. Arquilla and Ronfeldt (1997), p. 30
28. Cebrowski, pp. 31–2
29. Ibid., pp. 34, 37
30. Ibid., p. 31
31 Echevarria (2004), p. 16
32. Arquilla and Ronfeldt, p. 32
33. Berkowitz, p. ix
34. Black (2004), pp. 9–10

35. Berkowitz, ibid.
36. Gray (1999a), ch. 1
37. MacIsaac, p. 624
38. Ibid., p. 635
39. Ellis (2003, pp. 8–9; 2004, pp. 6–7)
40. Clausewitz, p. 75
41. Mack; Arreguin-Toft; Mahnken (2003b)
42. Lonsdale (2004)
43. Lukasic, Goodman and Longhurst, p. 8
44. Rattray
45. Lukasic, Goodman and Longhurst, p. 26
46. Wylie, p. 72 (emphasis in the original)
47. Berkowitz, p. 179
48. Lonsdale (1999), p. 143
49. Ibid., p. 145 (emphasis in the original)
50. Fontenot, p. 159

CHAPTER NINE **The Control of Wars**
1. Gray (1999b), ch. 5
2. Stevenson (1988; 2004, ch. 5)
3. Philpott
4. Montefiore, p. 346
5. Howard (2002)
6. Gray (1999a), pp. 68–74
7. Luttwak, p. 36
8. Ibid.
9. O'Rourke
10. Hughes and Seligman
11. Lasswell
12. Blanning, p. 4
13. Ibid.
14. Ibid., p. 23
15. Gaddis
16. R. Kagan
17. Gray (2002b)
18. Gray (1992b)
19. Howard (2002), p. 105 (emphasis added)
20. Adler and Barnett
21. Etzioni, p. 211
22. Ibid., p. 143
23. Gray (2005b)
24. Doyle; Weart
25. Brown, Lynn-Jones, and Miller; Brown et al.
26. Schell

27. Howard (1978), p. 53
28. Hopkins
29. Stevenson (1988)
30. Walton
31. Kershaw, pp. 228–30
32. Iklé (2005)
33. Clausewitz, p. 81
34. Ibid.
35. Ibid., p. 605
36. Cohen (2002a)
37. Beyerchen; Betts (2002)
38. Gray (1999d)
39. Betts (2001–2002)
40. Payne (2001); Morgan; Freedman (2004).

CONCLUSIONS **A Warlike Future:**
The Long-running Story
1. Till (1982), pp. 224, 225
2. Clausewitz, pp. 141, 578
3. Jomini, p. 70
4. Till (2004), p. 378
5. Gray (1999b), ch. 3
6. Fuller, pp. 21–2
7. Berkowitz, ch. 16
8. Biddle (2004)
9. Blanning, p. 4
10. Strachan, p. 131
11. Clausewitz, p. 85; Echevarria (2003)
12. Till (2004), p. 138
13. Keegan
14. McInnes
15. Hanson (2001); Lynn
16. Sun-tzu, p. 179
17. Johnson and Libicki
18. Gray (2004)
19. Huntington (1986)
20. Ferguson (1997); Cowley; Roberts
21. Rumsfeld, ch. 6; Binnendijk
22. Van Creveld (1991)
23. Murray and Knox, p. 193
24. Schwartz and Randall, p. 2
25. Smith, p. 147
26. Schwartz and Randall, pp. 16–17
27. Knox, p. 645.

Bibliography of works cited

Adler, Emanuel, and Michael Barnett, eds., *Security Communities* (Cambridge, 1998).

Akbar, M. J., *The Shade of Swords: Jihad and the conflict between Islam and Christianity* (London, 2002).

Alexander, John B., *Future War: Non-Lethal Weapons in Twenty-First-Century Warfare* (New York, 1999).

Alger, John I., *The Quest for Victory: The History of the Principles of War* (Westport, CT, 1982).

Allison, Graham, *Nuclear Terrorism: The Ultimate Preventable Catastrophe* (New York, 2004).

Anson, Peter, and Dennis Cummings, 'The First Space War: The Contribution of Satellites to the Gulf War', *RUSI Journal* 136 (1991).

Aron, Raymond, *Clausewitz: Philosopher of War* (London, 1983).

Arquilla, John, ed., *From Troy to Entebbe: Special Operations in Ancient and Modern Times* (Lanham, MD, 1996).

Arquilla, John, and David Ronfeldt, 'Cyberwar is Coming!', *Comparative Strategy* 12 (1993).

—— eds., *In Athena's Camp: Preparing for Conflict in the Information Age,* MR-880-OSD (Santa Monica, CA, 1997).

Arreguin-Toft, Ivan, 'How the Weak Win Wars: A Theory of Asymmetric Conflict', *International Security* 26 (2001).

Asprey, Robert B., *War in the Shadows: The Classic History of Guerrilla Warfare from Ancient Persia to the Present* (new edn, Boston, 1994).

Avant, Deborah D., *Political Institutions and Military Change: Lessons from Peripheral Wars* (Ithaca, NY, 1994).

Bacevich, Andrew J., *American Empire: The Realities and Consequences of U.S. Diplomacy* (Cambridge, MA, 2002).

Bailey, Jonathan, *The First World War and the Birth of the Modern Style of Warfare,* The Occasional 22 (Camberley, UK, 1996).

—— *Field Artillery and Firepower* (Annapolis, MD, 2004).

'Barfleur' (pseud. R. Custance), *Naval Policy: A Plea for the Study of War* (Edinburgh, 1907).

Barnaby, Frank, *How to Build a Nuclear Bomb and other weapons of mass destruction* (London, 2003).

Barnett, Roger W., *Asymmetrical Warfare: Today's Challenge to U.S. Military Power* (Washington, DC, 2003).

Bartov, Omer, *Hitler's Army: Soldiers, Nazis, and War in the Third Reich* (New York, 1991).

Baylis, John, and Steve Smith, eds., *The Globalization of World Politics: An Introduction to International Relations* (Oxford, 1997).

Beckett, Ian F. W., *Modern Insurgencies and Counter-Insurgencies: Guerrillas and their Opponents since 1750* (London, 2001).

Bell, J. Bowyer, *The Myth of the Guerrilla: Revolutionary Theory and Malpractice* (New York, 1971).

Berkowitz, Bruce, *The New Face of War: How War Will Be Fought in the 21st Century* (New York, 2003).

Betts, Richard K., 'Should Strategic Studies Survive?', *World Politics* 50 (1997).

—— 'The New Threat of Mass Destruction', *Foreign Affairs* 77 (1998).

—— 'Is Strategy an Illusion?', *International Security* 25 (2000).

—— 'The Trouble with Strategy: Bridging Policy and Operations', *Joint Force Quarterly* 29 (2001–2002).

Beyerchen, Alan, 'Clausewitz, Nonlinearity, and the Unpredictability of War', *International Security* 17 (1992/93).

Bialer, Uri, *The Shadow of the Bomber: The Fear of Air Attack and British Politics, 1932–1939* (London, 1980).

Biddle, Stephen, *Afghanistan and the Future of Warfare: Implications for Army and Defense* (Carlisle, PA, Nov. 2002).

—— *Military Power: Explaining Victory and Defeat in Modern Battle* (Princeton, NJ, 2004).

Binnendijk, Hans, ed., *Transforming America's Military* (Washington, DC, Aug. 2002).

Black, Jeremy, *War and the World: Military Power and the Fate of Continents, 1450–2000* (New Haven, CT, 1998).

—— *War: Past, Present and Future* (Stroud, UK, 2000).

—— *War in the New Century* (London, 2001).

—— *Warfare in the Western World, 1882–1975* (Chesham, UK, 2002).

—— *Rethinking Military History* (London, 2004).

Blair, Bruce G., *Strategic Command and Control: Redefining the Nuclear Threat* (Washington, DC, 1985).

——— *The Logic of Accidental Nuclear War* (Washington, DC, 1993).

Blanning, T. C. W., *The Origins of the French Revolutionary Wars* (London, 1986).

Blouet, Brian, *Geopolitics and Globalization in the Twentieth Century* (London, 2001).

Boot, Max, *The Savage Wars of Peace: Small Wars and the Rise of American Power* (New York, 2002).

——— 'The New American Way of War', *Foreign Affairs* 82 (2003).

Boyd, John R., 'A Discourse on Winning and Losing', briefing (Aug. 1987).

Breemer, Jan S., 'Naval Strategy Is Dead', U.S. Naval Institute *Proceedings* 120 (1994).

Brennan, Donald G., 'The Case for Missile Defense', *Foreign Affairs* 43 (1969).

Brodie, Bernard, ed., *The Absolute Weapon: Atomic Power and World Order* (New York, 1946).

——— *War and Politics* (New York, 1973).

Brown, Michael E., Sean M. Lynn-Jones, and Steven E. Miller, eds., *Debating the Democratic Peace* (Cambridge, MA, 1996).

——— et al., eds. *Theories of War and Peace* (Cambridge, MA, 1998).

Browning, Peter, *The Changing Nature of Warfare: The Development of Land Warfare from 1792 to 1945* (Cambridge, 2002).

Burke, Jason, 'Al Qaeda', Foreign Policy 142 (2004).

Burleigh, Michael, *The Third Reich: A New History* (London, 2000).

Bush, George W., *The National Security Strategy of the United States of America* (Washington, DC, Sept. 2002a).

——— *National Strategy to Combat Weapons of Mass Destruction* (Washington, DC, Dec. 2002b).

Buzan, Barry, *People, States and Fear: An Agenda for International Security Studies in the Post-Cold War Era* (2nd edn, Boulder, CO, 1991).

——— Ole Waever, and Jaap de Wilde, *Security: A New Framework for Analysis* (Boulder, CO, 1998).

Callwell, Charles E., *Small Wars: A Tactical Textbook for Imperial Soldiers* (repr. of 1906 edn, London, 1990).

Cebrowski, A. K., *Military Transformation: A Strategic Approach* (Washington, DC, Fall 2003).

Chickering, Roger, 'Total War: The Use and Abuse of a Concept', in Manfred F. Boemeke, Chickering, and Stig Forster, eds., *Anticipating Total War: The German and American Experiences, 1871–1914* (Cambridge, 1999).

Cirincione, Joseph, *Deadly Arsenals: Tracking Weapons of Mass Destruction* (Washington, DC, 2002).

Clarke, Arthur C., *Profiles of the Future: An Enquiry into the Limits of the Possible* (London, 1962).

Clausewitz, Carl von, *On War,* Michael Howard and Peter Paret trans., and ed. (Princeton, NJ, 1976).

Cochran, Thomas B., et al., *Nuclear Weapons Databook: Vol. IV, Soviet Nuclear Weapons* (New York, 1989).

Cohen, Eliot A., 'The Mystique of U.S. Air Power', *Foreign Affairs* 73 (1994).

—— 'A Revolution in Warfare', *Foreign Affairs* 75 (1996).

—— 'Kosovo and the New American Way of War', in Andrew J. Bacevich and Cohen, eds., *War Over Kosovo: Politics and Strategy in a Global Age* (New York, 2001).

—— *Supreme Command: Soldiers, Statesmen, and Leadership in Wartime* (New York, 2002a).

—— 'Technology and Warfare', in John Baylis et al., eds., *Strategy in the Contemporary World: An Introduction to Strategic Studies* (Oxford, 2002b).

—— 'Change and Transformation in Military Affairs', *The Journal of Strategic Studies* 27 (2004).

Colin, Jean, *The Transformations of War*, L. H. R. Pope-Hennessy trans. (London, 1912).

Collins, *The Collins Atlas of Military History* (London, 2004).

Coram, Robert, *Boyd: The Fighter Pilot Who Changed the Art of War* (Boston, 2002).

Corbett, Julian S., *Some Principles of Maritime Strategy* (Annapolis, MD, 1988).

Cordesman, Anthony H., and Abraham R. Wagner, *The Lessons of Modern War: Vol. II, The Iran–Iraq War* (Boulder, CO, 1990).

Corum, James S., *The Roots of Blitzkrieg: Hans von Seeckt and German Military Reform* (Lawrence, KS, 1992).

Cowley, Robert, ed., *What If? Military Historians Imagine What Might Have Been* (London, 2000).

Cox, Sebastian, and Peter Gray, eds., *Air Power History: Turning Points from Kitty Hawk to Kosovo* (London, 2002).

Crile, George, *My Enemy's Enemy: The Story of the Largest Covert Operation in History: The Arming of the Majahideen in Afghanistan by the CIA* (London, 2003).

Crocker, Chester A., and Fen Osler Hampson, eds., *Managing Global Chaos: Sources of and Responses to International Conflict* (Washington, DC, 1996).

Davis, Malcolm R., and Colin S. Gray, 'Weapons of Mass Destruction', in John Baylis et al., eds., *Strategy in the Contemporary World: An Introduction to Strategic Studies* (Oxford, 2002).

De Gaulle, General, *The Army of the Future* (London, 1940).

DeGroot, Gerard J., *The Bomb: A Life* (London, 2004).

Desch, Michael C., 'Culture Clash: Assessing the Importance of Ideas in Security Studies', *International Security* 23 (1998).

Dodds, Klaus, and James D. Sidaway, eds., 'Halford Mackinder and the "Geographical Pivot of History"', *The Geographical Journal* 170, Special Issue (2004).

Dolman, Everett C., *Astropolitik: Classical Geopolitics in the Space Age* (2002).

Doyle, Michael W., *Ways of War and Peace: Realism, Liberalism, and Socialism* (New York, 1997).

Dupuy, Trevor N., *The Evolution of Weapons and Warfare* (Indianapolis, IN, 1980).

Duyvesteyn, Isabelle, and Jan Angstrom, eds., *Rethinking the Nature of War* (London, 2005).

Echevarria, Antulio J., II, *After Clausewitz: German Military Thinkers Before the Great War* (Lawrence, KS, 2000).

—— *Globalization and the Nature of War* (Carlisle, PA, Mar. 2003).

—— *Toward an American Way of War* (Carlisle, PA, Mar. 2004).

Ellis, Admiral James O., Commander U.S. Strategic Command, *AFA National Symposia* (13–14 Feb. 2003). http://www.aef.org/pubellis203.asp

—— Statement before the Strategic Forces Subcommittee, Senate Armed Services Committee on Strategic Deterrence and Strategic Capabilities (24 Mar. 2004).

El-Shazly, Nadia El-Sayed, *The Gulf Tanker War: Iran and Iraq's Maritime Swordplay* (London, 1998).

Emery, Frank, *The Red Soldier: The Zulu War, 1879* (Johannesburg, 1983).

English, Allan D., *Understanding Military Culture: A Canadian Perspective* (Montreal, 2004).

Etzioni, Amitai, *From Empire to Community: A New Approach to International Relations* (Basingstoke, UK, 2004).

Fadok, David S., 'John Boyd and John Warden: Airpower's Quest for Strategic Paralysis', in Phillip S. Meilinger, ed., *The Paths of Heaven: The Evolution of Airpower Theory* (Maxwell AFB, AL, 1997).

Feaver, Peter D., and Richard H. Kohn, eds., *Soldiers and Civilians: The Civil–Military Gap and American National Security* (Cambridge, MA, 2001).

Ferguson, Niall, ed., *Virtual History: Alternatives and Counterfactuals* (London, 1997).

—— *The Pity of War* (London, 1998).

—— *Colossus: The Rise and Fall of the American Empire* (London, 2004).

Fettweis, Christopher J., 'Revisiting Mackinder and Angell: The Obsolescence of Great Power Geopolitics', *Comparative Strategy* 22 (2003).

Fontenot, Gregory, Book review, *Parameters* 32 (2002–03).

Freedman, Lawrence, *The Revolution in Strategic Affairs,* Adelphi Paper 318 (London, Apr. 1998).

—— *Kennedy's Wars: Berlin, Cuba, Laos, and Vietnam* (Oxford, 2000).

—— 'The Third World War?', *Survival* 43 (2001).

—— *The Evolution of Nuclear Strategy* (3rd edn, Basingstoke, UK, 2003).

—— *Deterrence* (Cambridge, 2004).

Friedman, Norman, *The Fifty-Year War: Conflict and Strategy in the Cold War* (Annapolis, MD, 2000a).

—— *Seapower and Space: From the Dawn of the Missile Age to Net-Centric Warfare* (London, 2000b).

Fukuyama, Francis, *The End of History and the Last Man* (New York, 1992).

Fuller, J. F. C., *Armament and History* (London, 1946).

Gaddis, John Lewis, *The Long Peace: Inquiries into the History of the Cold War* (New York, 1987).

Gilinsky, Victor, 'Iran's "Legal" Paths to the Bomb', in Henry Sokolski and Patrick Clauson, eds., *Checking Iran's Nuclear Ambitions* (Carlisle, PA, Jan. 2004).

Glenn, John, Darryl Howlett and Stuart Poore, eds., *Neorealism Versus Strategic Culture* (Aldershot, UK, 2004).

Goldman, Emily O., and Leslie C. Eliason, eds., *The Diffusion of Military Technology and Ideas* (Stanford, CA, 2003).

—— and Andrew L. Ross, 'Conclusion: The Diffusion of Military Technology, and Ideas – Theory and Practice', in Goldman and Leslie C. Eliason, eds., *The Diffusion of Military Technology and Ideas* (Stanford, CA, 2003).

Goldsworthy, Adrian Keith, *The Roman Army at War, 100BC–AD200* (Oxford, 1996).

Gray, Colin S. 'The Arms Race Phenomenon'. *World Politics* 24 (1971).

—— *The Soviet–American Arms Race* (Lexington, MA, 1976).

—— *Strategic Studies and Public Policy: The American Experience* (Lexington, KY, 1982).

—— *War, Peace, and Victory: Strategy and Statecraft for the Next Century* (New York, 1990).

—— ed., 'Special Operations: What Succeeds and Why? Lessons of Experience, Phase I', unpub. report by National Institute for Public Policy (Washington, DC, 1992a).

—— *House of Cards: Why Arms Control Must Fail* (Ithaca, NY, 1992b).

—— *Weapons Don't Make War: Policy, Strategy, and Military Technology* (Lawrence, KS, 1993).

—— *Explorations in Strategy* (Westport, CT, 1996a).

—— 'The Influence of Space Power upon History', *Comparative Strategy* 15 (1996b).

—— *Modern Strategy* (Oxford, 1999a).

—— *The Second Nuclear Age* (Boulder, CO, 1999b).

—— 'Handfuls of Heroes on Desperate Ventures: When Do Special Operations Succeed?', *Parameters* 29 (1999c)

—— 'Why Strategy Is Difficult', *Joint Force Quarterly* 22 (1999d).

—— *Weapons for Strategic Effect: How Important is Technology?*, Occasional Paper 21 (Maxwell AFB, AL, Jan. 2001).

—— *Strategy for Chaos: Revolutions in Military Affairs and the Evidence of History* (London, 2002a).

—— 'European Perspectives on U.S. Ballistic Missile Defense', *Comparative Strategy* 21 (2002b).

—— *Defining and Achieving Decisive Victory* (Carlisle, PA, 2002c).

—— *The Sheriff: America's Defense of the New World Order* (Lexington, KY, 2004).

—— 'In Defence of the Heartland: Sir Halford Mackinder and His Critics a Hundred Years On', in Brian Blouet, ed., *Global Geostrategy: Mackinder and the Defense of the West* (London, 2005a).

—— 'Sandcastle of Theory: A Critique of Amitai Etzioni's Communitarianism', *American Behavioral Scientist,* forthcoming (2005b).

—— *Transformation and Strategic Surprise* (Carlisle, PA, forthcoming, 2005c).

Gray, John, *Al Qaeda and What it Means to be Modern* (London, 2003).

Green, Leslie C., *The Contemporary Law of Armed Conflict* (2nd edn, Manchester, UK, 2000).

Gudmundsson, Bruce I., *Stormtroop Tactics: Innovation in the German Army 1914–1918* (New York, 1989).

Gunaratna, Rohan, *Inside Al Qaeda: Global Network of Terror* (New York, 2002).

Haldon, John, *The Byzantine Wars: Battles and Campaigns of the Byzantine Era* (Stroud, UK, 2001).

Hallion, Richard P., *Storm over Iraq: Air Power and the Gulf War* (Washington, DC, 1992).

Hamilton, Donald W., *The Art of Insurgency: American Military Policy and the Failure of Strategy in Southeast Asia* (Westport, CT, 1998).

Hamilton, Ian, *The Soul and Body of an Army* (London, 1921).

Hamilton, Richard F., and Holger H. Herwig, *Decisions for War, 1914–1917* (Cambridge, 2004).

Hammes, Thomas X., *The Sling and the Stone: On War in the 21st Century* (St Paul, MN, 2004).

Hammond, Grant T., *The Mind of War: John Boyd and American Security* (Washington, DC, 2001).

Hanson, Victor Davis, *The Western Way of War: Infantry Battle in Classical Greece* (London, 1989).

—— *The Soul of Battle: From Ancient Times to the Present Day, How Three Great Liberators Vanquished Tyranny* (New York, 1999).

—— *Why the West Has Won: Carnage and Culture from Salamis to Vietnam* (London, 2001).

—— *Ripples of Battle: How Wars of the Past Still Determine How We Fight, How We Live, and How We Think* (New York, 2003).

—— ed., *Hoplites: The Ancient Greek Battle Experience* (London, 1991).

Harris, J. P., *Amiens to the Armistice: The BEF in the Hundred Days' Campaign, 8 August – 11 November 1918* (London, 1998).

Harrison, Richard W., *The Russian Way of War: Operational Art, 1904–1940* (Lawrence, KS, 2001).

Hassig, Ross, *Aztec Warfare: Imperial Expansion and Political Control* (Norman, OK, 1988).

Hedges, Chris, *War Is a Force That Gives Us Meaning* (New York, 2002).

Herwig, Holger H., '*Geopolitik:* Haushofer, Hitler and Lebensraum', in Colin S. Gray and Geoffrey Sloan, eds., *Geopolitics, Geography and Strategy* (London, 1999).

Heuser, Beatrice, *Reading Clausewitz* (London, 2002).

Hines, John G., Ellis M. Mishulovich, and John F. Shull, *Soviet Intentions, 1965–1985*, 2 vols (Mclean, VA, 22 Sept., 1995).

Hiro, Dilip, *The Longest War: The Iran–Iraq Military Conflict* (New York, 1991).

Hirst, Paul, *War and Power in the 21st Century* (Cambridge, 2001).

Hobkirk, Michael D., *Land, Sea or Air? Military Priorities, Historical Choices* (London, 1992).

Hoffman, Bruce, *Inside Terrorism* (London, 1998).

Holden Reid, Brian, *J. F. C. Fuller: Military Thinker* (New York, 1987).

Honig, Jan Willem, 'Strategy in a Post-Clausewitzian Setting', in Gert de Nooy, ed., *The Clausewitzian Dictum and the Future of Western Military Strategy* (The Hague, 1997).

Hopkins, A. G., ed., *Globalization in World History* (London, 2002).

Howard, Michael, *The Continental Commitment: The Dilemma of British Defence Policy in the Era of the Two World Wars* (London, 1972).

—— *War and the Liberal Conscience* (New Brunswick, NJ, 1978).

—— *The Causes of Wars and Other Essays* (London, 1984).

—— *The Invention of Peace and the Reinvention of War* (London, 2002).

—— 'Military History and the History of War', in Strategic and Combat Studies Institute, *Contemporary Essays,* The Occasional 47 (Shrivenham, UK, 2004).

Hughes, Daniel J., ed., *Moltke on the Art of War: Selected Writings,* Hughes and Daniel J. Bell trans. (Novato, CA, 1995).

Hughes, Matthew, and Matthew S. Seligman, *Does Peace Lead to War? Peace Settlements and Conflict in the Modern Age* (Stroud, UK, 2002).

Huntington, Samuel P., *American Military Strategy,* Policy Papers in International Affairs 28 (Berkeley, CA, 1986).

—— *The Clash of Civilizations and the Remaking of World Order* (New York, 1996).

Iklé, Fred Charles, 'After Detection – What?', *Foreign Affairs* 39 (1961).

—— *Every War Must End* (2nd rev. edn, New York, 2005).

International Institute for Strategic Studies (IISS), *The Military Balance, 2004–2005* (London, 2004).

Jenkins, Brian Michael, 'Countering Al Qaeda', in Russell D. Howard and Reid L. Sawyer, eds., *Defeating Terrorism: Shaping the New Security Environment* (Guilford, CT, 2004).

Johnson, Stuart E., and Martin C. Libicki, eds., *Dominant Battlespace Knowledge* (rev. edn, Washington, DC, Apr. 1996).

Johnston, Alastair Iain, *Cultural Realism: Strategic Culture and Grand Strategy in Chinese History* (Princeton, NJ, 1995).

Jomini, Antoine Henri de, *The Art of War* (reprint of 1862 edn, London, 1992).

Kagan, Donald, *On the Origins of War and the Preservation of Peace* (New York, 1995).

Kagan, Frederick W., 'War and Aftermath', *Policy Review* 120 (2003).

Kagan, Robert, *Paradise and Power: America and Europe in the New World Order* (London, 2003).

Kaldor, Mary, *New and Old Wars: Organized Violence in a Global Era* (Cambridge, 1999).

—— 'Elaborating the "New War" Thesis', in Isabelle Duyvesteyn and Jan Angstrom, eds., *Rethinking the Nature of War* (London, 2005).

Kaplan, Robert D., *The Coming Anarchy* (New York, 2000).

—— *Warrior Politics: Why Leadership Demands a Pagan Ethos* (New York, 2002).

Keaney, Thomas A., and Eliot A. Cohen, *Revolution in Warfare? Air Power in the Persian Gulf* (Annapolis, MD, 1995).

Keegan, John, *A History of Warfare* (London, 1993).

Kennedy, P. M., 'Imperial Cable Communications and Strategy, 1870–1914', in Kennedy, ed., *The War Plans of the Great Powers, 1880–1914* (London, 1979).

Kershaw, Ian, *Hitler, 1936–45: Nemesis* (London, 2000).

Kiras, James, 'Terrorism and Irregular Warfare', in Baylis et al., eds., *Strategy in the Contemporary World: An Introduction to Strategic Studies* (Oxford, 2002).

—— 'Rendering the Mortal Blow Easier: Special Operations and the Nature of Strategy', unpublished PhD dissertation (Reading, UK, 2004).

Klein, John J. 'Corbett in Orbit: A Maritime Model for Strategic Space Theory', *Naval War College Review* 57 (2004).

Knox, MacGregor, 'Conclusion: Continuity and revolution in the making of strategy', in Williamson Murray, Knox, and Alvin Bernstein, eds., *The Making of Strategy: Rulers, States, and War* (Cambridge, 1994).

—— 'Mass Politics and Nationalism as Military Revolution: The French Revolution and After', in Knox and Williamson Murray, eds., *The Dynamics of Military Revolution, 1300–2050* (Cambridge, 2001).

Koblentz, Gregory, 'Pathogens as Weapons: The International Security Implications of Biological Warfare', *International Security* 28 (2003).

Krepinevich, Andrew F., Jr., *The Army in Vietnam* (Baltimore, 1986).

—— 'Cavalry to Computer: The Pattern of Military Revolution', *The National Interest* 37 (1994).

Kurth, James C., 'Clausewitz and the Two Contemporary Revolutions: RMA and RAM', in Bradford A. Lee and Karl F. Walling, eds., *Strategic Logic and Political Rationality: Essays in Honor of Michael Handel* (London, 2003).

Lambakis, Steven, *On the Edge of Earth: The Future of American Space Power* (Lexington, KY, 2001).

—— 'Reconsidering Asymmetric Warfare', *Joint Force Quarterly* 36 (2004).

Lambeth, Benjamin S., *The Transformation of American Air Power* (Ithaca, NY, 2000).

—— *NATO's Air War for Kosovo: A Strategic and Operational Assessment* (Santa Monica, CA, 2001).

—— *Mastering the Ultimate High Ground: Next Steps in the Military Uses of Space*, MR-1649-AF (Santa Monica, CA, 2003).

Laqueur, Walter, 'Postmodern Terrorism', *Foreign Affairs* 75 (1996).

—— *No End to War: Terrorism in the Twenty-First Century* (New York, 2003).

Lasswell, Harold D., *Politics: Who Gets What, When, How* (New York, 1950).

Lavoy, Peter R., Scott D. Sagan, and James J. Wirtz, eds., *Planning the Unthinkable: How New Powers Will Use Nuclear, Biological, and Chemical Weapons* (Ithaca, NY, 2000).

Lawrence, T. E., *Seven Pillars of Wisdom: A Triumph* (New York, 1991).

Lechner, Frank J., and John Boli, eds., *The Globalization Reader* (2nd edn, Oxford, 2004).

Lederberg, Joshua, ed., *Biological Weapons: Limiting the Threat* (Cambridge, MA, 1999).

Lewis, Bernard, *What Went Wrong? Western Impact and Middle Eastern Response* (London, 2002).

—— *The Crisis of Islam: Holy War and Unholy Terror* (London, 2003).

Liang, Qiao, and Wang Xiangsui, *Unrestricted Warfare: Assumptions on War and Tactics in the Age of Globalization*, FBIS trans. (Beijing, Feb. 1999).

Liddell Hart, B. H., *Strategy: The Indirect Approach* (London, 1967).

Lind, William S., *Maneuver Warfare Handbook* (Boulder, CO, 1985).

—— et al., 'The Changing Face of War: Into the Fourth Generation', *Military Review* 69 (1989).

—— 'Understanding Fourth Generation War', 6 January, 2004. Available at http://www.lewrockwell.com/lind/lind3b.html

Lonsdale, David J., 'Information Power: Strategy, Geopolitics, and the Fifth Dimension', in Colin S. Gray and Geoffrey Sloan, eds., *Geopolitics, Geography and Strategy* (London, 1999).

—— *The Nature of War in the Information Age: Clausewitzian Future* (London, 2004).

Lukasic, Stephen J., Seymour E. Goodman, and David W. Longhurst, *Protecting Critical Infrastructures Against Cyber-Attack,* Adelphi Paper 359 (London, 2003).

Lummis, Charles R., *General Crook and the Apache Wars* (Flagstaff, AZ, 1966).

Luttwak, Edward N., *On the Meaning of Victory: Essays on Strategy* (New York, 1986).

—— 'Toward Post-Heroic Warfare', *Foreign Affairs* 74 (1995).

—— 'Give War a Chance', *Foreign Affairs* 78 (1999).

Lynn, John A., *Battle: A History of Combat and Culture* (Boulder, CO, 2003).

MacIsaac, David, 'Voices from the Central Blue: The Air Power Theorists', in Peter Paret, ed., *Makers of Modern Strategy: from Machiavelli to the Nuclear Age* (Princeton, NJ, 1986).

Mack, Andrew J., 'Why Big Nations Lose Small Wars: The Politics of Asymmetric Conflict', *World Politics* 27 (1975).

MacKenzie, Donald, *Inventing Missile Accuracy: A Historical Sociology of Nuclear Missile Guidance* (Cambridge, MA, 1993).

Mackinder, Halford J., *Democratic Ideals and Reality* (New York, 1962).

Mahan, A. T., *The Influence of Sea Power upon the French Revolution and Empire, 1793–1812*, Vol. I (Boston, 1898).

Mahnken, Thomas G., 'Beyond Blitzkrieg: Allied Responses to Combined-Arms Armored Warfare during World War II', in Emily O. Goldman and Leslie C. Eliason, eds., *The Diffusion of Military Technology and Ideas* (Stanford, CA, 2003a).

—— 'Why the Weak Win: Strong Powers, Weak Powers, and the Logic of Strategy', in Bradford A. Lee and Karl F. Walling, eds., *Strategic Logic and Political Rationality: Essays in Honor of Michael Handel* (London, 2003b).

Mandelbaum, Michael, 'Is Major War Obsolete?', *Survival* 40 (1998–99).

Mao Tse-tung (attrib), *On Guerrilla Warfare,* Samuel B. Griffith trans. (New York, 1961).

—— *Selected Military Writings* (Peking, 1963).

Marder, Arthur J., *From the Dreadnought to Scapa Flow, The Royal Navy in the Fisher Era, 1904–1919: Vol. I, The Road to War, 1904–1914* (London, 1961).

Marquis, Susan L., *Unconventional Warfare: Rebuilding U.S. Special Operations Forces* (Washington, DC, 1997).

Marshall, Andrew W., J. J. Martin, and Henry S. Rowen, eds., *On Not Confusing Ourselves: Essays on National Security in Honor of Albert and Roberta Wohlstetter* (Boulder, CO, 1991).

McDougall, Walter A., *The Heavens and the Earth: A Political History of the Space Age* (New York, 1985).

McInnes, Colin, *Spectator-Sport War: The West and Contemporary Conflict* (Boulder, CO, 2002).

McKenzie, Kenneth F., Jr., 'Elegant Irrelevance: Fourth Generation Warfare', *Parameters* 23 (1993).

Mearsheimer, John J., *The Tragedy of Great Power Politics* (New York, 2001).

Metz, Steven, and Raymond Millen, *Future War/Future Battlespace: The Strategic Future of American Landpower* (Carlisle, PA, Mar. 2003).

Millen, Raymond A., 'The "New" American Way of War', US Army War College and Strategic Studies Institute, XIV Annual Strategy Conference, Carlisle, PA, April 8–10, 2003, *Conference Brief.*

Millett, Allan R., 'Patterns of Military Innovation in the Interwar Period', in Williamson Murray and Millett, eds., *Military Innovation in the Interwar Period* (Cambridge, 1996).

—— and Peter Maslowski, *For the Common Defense: A Military History of the United States of America,* (rev. edn, New York, 1994).

Milne, A. A., *The Complete Winnie-the-Pooh* (London, 1989).

Mitchell, Stephen, 'Hoplite Warfare in Ancient Greece', in Alan B. Lloyd, ed., *Battle in Antiquity* (London, 1996).

Montefiore, Simon Sebag, *Stalin: The Court of the Red Tsar* (London, 2003).

Moran, Daniel, *Wars of National Liberation* (London, 2001).

Morgan, Patrick M., *Deterrence Now* (Cambridge, 2003).

Mueller, John, *Retreat from Doomsday: The Obsolescence of Major War* (New York, 1989).

Murray, Williamson, 'Thinking About Revolutions in Military Affairs', *Joint Force Quarterly* 16 (1997).

—— and Allan R. Millett, eds., *Military Innovation in the Interwar Period* (Cambridge, 1996).

—— and Allan R. Millett, *A War To Be Won: Fighting the Second World War* (Cambridge, MA, 2000).

—— and MacGregor Knox, 'Conclusion: The future behind us', in Knox and Murray, eds., *The Dynamics of Military Revolution, 1300–2050* (Cambridge, 2001).

—— and Robert H. Scales, Jr., *The Iraq War: A Military History* (Cambridge, MA, 2003).

National Commission on Terrorist Attacks Upon the United States, *The 9/11 Commission Report* (Washington, DC, 2004).

Navias, Martin S., and E. R. Hooton, *Tanker Wars: The Assault on Merchant Shipping During the Iran–Iraq Conflict, 1980–1988* (London, 1996).

Neufeld, Michael J., *The Rocket and the Reich: Peenemünde and the Coming of the Ballistic Missile Era* (Cambridge, MA, 1995).

Oberg, Jim, *Space Power Theory* (US Air Force Academy, CO, Mar. 1999).

Odom, William E., *The Collapse of the Soviet Military* (New Haven, CT, 1998).

O'Rourke, P. J., *Give War a Chance: Eyewitness Accounts of Mankind's Struggle Against Tyranny, Injustice and Alcohol-free Beer* (New York, 1992).

Owens, Bill, *Lifting the Fog of War* (New York, 2000).

Panofsky, W. K. H., 'The Mutual Hostage Relationship between America and Russia'. *Foreign Affairs* 52 (1973).

Paret, Peter, and John W. Shy, *Guerrillas in the 1960s* (rev. edn, New York, 1962).

Parry, J. H., *The Discovery of the Sea* (Berkeley, CA, 1981).

Payne, Keith B., *Strategic Defense: 'Star Wars' in Perspective* (Lanham, MD, 1986).

—— *The Fallacies of Cold War Deterrence and a New Direction* (Lexington, KY, 2001).

—— 'The Nuclear Posture Review and Deterrence for a New Age', *Comparative Strategy* 23 (2004).

Peters, Ralph, *Fighting for the Future: Will America Triumph?* (Mechanicsburg, PA, 1999).

—— *Beyond Terror: Strategy in a Changing World* (Mechanicsburg, PA, 2002).

—— *Beyond Baghdad: Postmodern War and Peace* (Mechanicsburg, PA, 2003).

—— 'In Praise of Attrition', *Parameters* 34 (2004).

Philpott, William James, *Anglo-French Relations and Strategy on the Western Front, 1914–18* (Basingstoke, UK, 1996).

Pitt, William, *The War Speeches of William Pitt the Younger* (Oxford, 1915).

Posen, Barry R., 'Command of the Commons: The Military Foundation of U.S. Hegemony', *International Security* 28 (2003).

Preston, Bob, et al., *Space Weapons, Earth Wars*, MR-1209-AF (Santa Monica, CA, 2002).

Price, Richard M., *The Chemical Weapons Taboo* (Ithaca, NY, 1997).

Pry, Peter Vincent, *War Scare: Russia and America on the Nuclear Brink* (Westport, CT, 1999).

Quinlan, Michael, *Thinking About Nuclear Weapons* (London, 1997).

Rattray, Gregory J., *Strategic Warfare in Cyberspace* (Cambridge, MA, 2001).

Rip, Michael Russell, and James M. Hasik, *The Precision Revolution: GPS and the Future of Aerial Warfare* (Annapolis, MD, 2002).

Roberts, Adam, and Richard Guelff, eds., *Documents on the Laws of War* (3rd edn, Oxford, 2004).

Roberts, Andrew, ed., *What Might Have Been: Leading Historians on Twelve 'What Ifs' of History* (London, 2004).

Rosen, Stephen Peter, *Winning the Next War: Innovation and the Modern Military* (Ithaca, NY, 1991).

Rumsfeld, Donald H., *Annual Report to the President and the Congress* (Washington, DC, 2002).

Sagan, Scott D., 'Why Do States Build Nuclear Weapons? Three Models in Search of a Bomb', *International Security* 21 (1996/97).

Schell, Jonathan, *The Unconquerable World: Power, Nonviolence and the Will of the People* (London, 2003).

Schwartz, Peter, and Doug Randall, 'An Abrupt Climate Change Scenario and Its Implications for United States National Security' (Alexandria, VA, Oct. 2003).

Sellar, W. C., and R. J. Yeatman, *1066 and All That* (London, 1960).

Sheffield, Gary, *Forgotten Victory: The First World War, Myths and Realities* (London, 2001).

Showalter, Dennis E., *Railroads and Rifles: Soldiers, Technology, and the Unification of Germany* (Hamden, CT, 1986).

Shubik, Martin, 'Terrorism, Technology, and the Socioeconomics of Death', *Comparative Strategy* 16 (1997).

Singer, Max, and Aaron Wildavsky, *The Real World Order: Zones of Peace/Zones of Turmoil* (Chatham, NJ, 1993).

Smith, S. Douglas, Book review, *Naval War College Review* 57 (2004).

Spiers, Edward M., *Chemical Warfare* (London, 1986).

Spykman, Nicholas J., *The Geography of the Peace* (Hamden, CT, 1969).

Standage, Tom, *The Victorian Internet: The Remarkable Story of the Telegraph and the Nineteenth Century's Online Pioneers* (London, 1998).

Stern, Jessica, *The Ultimate Terrorists* (Cambridge, MA, 1999).

Stevenson, David, *The First World War and International Politics* (Oxford, 1988).

—— *Cataclysm: The First World War as Political Tragedy* (New York, 2004).

Strachan, Hew, *The First World War: Vol. I, To Arms* (Oxford, 2001).

Strassler, Robert B., ed., *The Landmark Thucydides: A Comprehensive Guide to 'The Peloponnesian War'*, Richard Crawley trans. (rev. edn, New York, 1996).

Sun-tzu, *The Art of War,* Ralph D. Sawyer trans. (Boulder, CO, 1994).

Taillon, J. Paul de B., *The Evolution of Special Forces in Counter-Terrorism: The British and American Experiences* (Westport, CT, 2001).

Tangredi, Sam J., 'Space Is an Ocean', U.S. Naval Institute, *Proceedings* 125 (1999).

Terraine, John, *The First World War, 1914–18* (London, 1983).

Terriff, Terry, et al., *Security Studies Today* (Cambridge, 1999).

Tilford, Earl H., Jr., 'Reviewing the Future', *Parameters* 30 (2000).

Till, Geoffrey, *Maritime Strategy and the Nuclear Age* (London, 1982).

—— *Seapower: A Guide for the Twenty-First Century* (London, 2004).

Towle, Philip A., *Pilots and Rebels: The Use of Aircraft in Unconventional Warfare* (London, 1988).

Triandafillov, V. K., *The Nature of the Operations of Modern Armies* (London, 1994).

Tugwell, Maurice, and David Charters, 'Special Operations and the Threats to United States Interests in the 1980s', in Frank R. Barnett, B. Hugh Tovar, and Richard H. Shultz, eds., *Special Operations in US Strategy* (Washington, DC, 1984).

Ullman, Harlan, and James Wade Jr., *Shock and Awe: Achieving Rapid Dominance* (Washington, DC, 1996).

U.S. Army, *The Way Ahead* (Washington, DC, 2004a).

—— *Army Campaign Plan* (Washington, DC, 2004b).

—— *Serving a Nation at War* (Washington, DC, 2004c).

—— *Army Transformation Roadmap* (Washington, DC, 2004d).

U.S. Congress, Office of Technology Assessment (OTA), *Technologies Underlying Weapons of Mass Destruction, Background Paper,* OTA-BP-1SC-H5 (Washington, DC, Dec. 1993).

U.S. Department of Defense, *Quadrennial Defense Review Report* (Washington, DC, 30 Sept. 2001).

—— *Transformation Planning Guidance* (Washington, DC, April 2003).

U.S. Marine Corps, *Small Wars Manual, United States Marine Corps, 1940* (Manhattan, KS, no date).

—— *Warfighting* (New York, 1994).

Utley, Robert M., *Frontier Regulars: The United States Army and the Indian, 1866–1891* (New York, 1973).

—— *Cavalier in Buckskin: George Armstrong Custer and the Western Military Frontier* (Norman, OK, 1988).

Van Creveld, Martin, *Supplying War: Logistics from Wallenstein to Patton* (Cambridge, 1977).

—— *Fighting Power: German and U.S. Army Performance, 1939–1945* (Westport, CT, 1982).

—— *Command in War* (Cambridge, MA, 1985).

—— *Technology and War: From 2000 B.C. to the Present* (New York, 1989).

—— *The Transformation of War* (New York, 1991).

—— *The Rise and Decline of the State* (Cambridge, 1999).

Walton, C. Dale, *The Myth of Inevitable U.S. Defeat in Vietnam* (London, 2002).

Waltz, Kenneth N., *Theory of International Politics* (Reading, MA, 1979).

Walzer, Michael, *Just and Unjust Wars: A Moral Argument with Historical Illustrations* (3rd edn, New York, 2000).

Warden, John A., III, *The Air Campaign: Planning for Combat* (Washington, DC, 1989).

Watts, Barry D., *Clausewitzian Friction and Future War,* McNair Paper 52 (Washington, DC, Oct. 1996).

Wawro, Geoffrey, *The Franco-Prussian War: The German Conquest of France in 1870–1871* (Cambridge, 2003).

Weart, Spencer R., *Never at War: Why Democracies Will Not Fight One Another* (New Haven, CT, 1998).

Wegener, Wolfgang, *The Naval Strategy of the World War* (Annapolis, MD, 1989).

Weigert, Hans W., *Generals and Geographers: The Twilight of Geopolitics* (New York, 1942).

Weigley, Russell F., *The Age of Battles: The Quest for Decisive Warfare from Breitenfeld to Waterloo* (Bloomington, IN, 1991).

Winton, Harold R., and David R. Mets, eds., *The Challenge of Change: Military Institutions and New Realities, 1918–1941* (Lincoln, NE, 2000).

Wylie, J. C., *Military Strategy: A General Theory of Power Control* (Anapolis, MD, 1989).

Zamoyski, Adam, *1812: Napoleon's Fatal March on Moscow* (London, 2004).

Index